*Sunday
Visaya*

TEACHING
THE
LANGUAGE
ARTS

Willard F. Tidyman

Professor of Education, Emeritus
State College, Fresno, California

Charlene Weddle Smith

Associate Professor of Education
State College, Fresno, California

Marguerite Butterfield

Professor of Education, Emeritus
State University Teachers College
Potsdam, New York

TEACHING THE LANGUAGE ARTS

THIRD EDITION

McGraw-Hill Book Company
NEW YORK
ST. LOUIS
SAN FRANCISCO
TORONTO
LONDON
SYDNEY

TEACHING
THE
LANGUAGE
ARTS

Library of Congress Catalog Card Number 68-9560

64603

1 2 3 4 5 6 7 8 9 0 M A M M 7 6 5 4 3 2 1 0 6 9

PREFACE

The recognition of the importance of language as a vital experience of childhood, as a factor in the development of a wholesome personality, and as a means of securing stability in a world made up of increasingly complex racial, social, linguistic, and economic elements, continues to grow. Language is a valuable resource to a child-adult in assimilating experiences, in carrying on activities in groups of peers and adults, in developing a sense of personal worth, and in finding a place in social and economic life adapted to his capacity and personal preference.

Fortunately the study of language as an art and as a school discipline has kept pace to some extent with the growing recognition of its importance. Continued interest in the study adds considerably to a body of knowledge about language teaching that has been accumulating over a number of years. Although continued research is necessary, it is safe to say that a sound program of instruction can be set up on the basis of present knowledge. The problem is to collect, interpret, organize, and present this knowledge so that teachers can acquire it with a minimum of effort and can readily apply it in the classroom. This book is designed to help serve that end.

The revision of our earlier editions permits us to clarify the overall organizational pattern; to give greater emphasis to such important topics as listening, linguistics, and evaluation; and to add reading and children's literature to the categories of the communicative arts. The functional point of view continues to prevail. On the last point, it is maintained that there is no basic conflict between a functional and a completely integrated program; that the difference is mainly one of organization and scheduling; that both require definite teaching; and that the same processes of teaching and learning are applicable in the two programs.

As in the earlier books, the main emphasis is on work at the elementary level—preschool through grade 8; but it is felt that the principles and processes are equally applicable at the secondary level because growth is continuous, because the same kinds of language experiences face children at both levels, and because the same abilities and skills operate in language activities in elementary and secondary schools.

Indebtedness to writers and teachers is apparent throughout the book, and it is specifically acknowledged in many instances. The authors have drawn freely on the knowledge and experience of colleagues and friends in the profession. Special recognition for contributing samples of children's work should go to the following teachers of the Campus School, State University College, Potsdam, New York: Beatrice LaVigne, Erma Randall, Ella Mae Stiles, and Ronhild Stillman. Special contributions have been made by Alla Laflin, Director of Public Relations, and Professor Olive Fite, Western Illinois University, Macomb, Illinois; and by Dr. Hazel Lambert, Fresno State College, Fresno, California.

Willard F. Tidyman
Charlene Weddle Smith
Marguerite Butterfield

CONTENTS

Part 4. Planning a Language Arts Program

TEACHING
THE
LANGUAGE
ARTS

PART I

NATURE
AND
SCOPE

I.

A

PERSPECTIVE

The language teacher of today has inherited from preceding generations of teachers some patterns of instruction that are as strange and as obsolete as a Model T Ford or a high celluloid collar. Traditional practices were not questioned fifty years ago, although even then many of them were poorly adapted to the needs of children and society. Unfortunately some faulty traditional patterns, not consciously learned but painfully acquired through years of tuition under the zealous efforts of misguided teachers, are still to be found in schools. To break the shackles of tradition requires fortitude and determined effort. Changes in life and in school continue, whether or not we like what is happening. Helping to formulate a program of instruction in language, patterned to meet the needs of children and of society today, is the challenge to teachers. This book is designed to help teachers meet that challenge.

Definition and scope of the book The language arts, as treated in this book, include the commonly recognized curriculum areas of speaking, listening, reading, and writing. The arts of oral communication are those of speaking and listening, involving first-hand transmission of thought between speaker and listener. The arts of written communication are those of writing and reading, involving a secondary transmission of thought from the writer to the reader. When ideas are transmitted in oral communication, the listener becomes the speaker as he questions and further explores a topic with the original speaker. As the reader learns, assimilates, and personally interprets a written passage, he then adapts his behavior, perhaps by doing further reading on the topic, perhaps by jotting down his findings for further use, or perhaps by engaging in a discussion with another person.

Learning may be regarded as a change in behavior, and the language arts are gateways to learning. If learning is to take place, teachers need to understand the components of an ordered program in the language arts so that they can help children understand and participate in the various school and life roles that are expected of them in a literate society. Children must learn to be competent listeners, speakers, readers, and writers.

Most of the discussion and a majority of the examples in this book are pointed toward work at the elementary level, kindergarten through grade 8. However, a long-range view of language arts instruction from preschool educational experiences through the secondary school level will be noted. Most of the principles and procedures suggested are adaptable to the secondary as well as to the elementary school level.

Plan of the book   The book is organized around the main areas of the language arts. Part 1, the first three chapters, is general, dealing with basic points of view, types of content, and a preview of the general principles and procedures of learning. This part obviously includes an overview of the field as a whole, and a listing of the components of a language arts program with enough detail to serve the purpose of identification. But it includes, also, mainly in Chapter 3, an introductory statement of principles and procedures applicable to work throughout the remainder of the book. Part 2, Chapters 4–10, deals with the major emphasis of instruction in the communication areas of speaking, reading, and writing, in the functional as well as in the creative aspects of these arts. The language arts activities—experiences—are taken up early in the book because they constitute the main components and deserve the first consideration of the student and teacher. It will be observed that the philosophical and psychological elements—skills and abilities, including attitudes, knowledge, and understandings— that condition the handling of language activities are treated in the experience phases as necessary ingredients of language activities, but they are treated as incidental factors in these connections.

Part 3, Chapters 11–17, is concerned explicitly and directly with the attitudes, understandings, and skills needed to implement and perfect communication. Presumably, it will be necessary in most school situations to give some special and separate attention to some or all of the psychological factors—elements—and therefore each group of psychological factors is taken up separately. The final section, Part 4, deals with the practical problems of setting up a curriculum as a whole and with planning work for a particular class. The concluding chapter is presented as an idealized program of integrated work, a challenge to the teacher who aspires to a very high level of mastery. In it also are reviewed by implication, but not specifically named, principles and procedures relating to many phases of a total language program.

Flexibility in the use of the book　The arrangement of the material in the text provides a sequence that the authors regard as adaptable to many situations, but it is too much to expect that it will be adaptable to all. The approach to the treatment of the language arts is generally a deductive one, going from the general to the particular, from the abstract to the concrete. Conceivably some people may prefer an inductive approach; and if so, they may desire to treat the third, generalizing chapter later in the course, possibly in the final section. As organized, Chapters 4–20 largely embody concrete applications of general principles and procedures developed in the first part, especially in Chapter 3.

Some teachers, of course, following the general order of chapters as laid out in the book, will find occasion to refer back to the general principles and processes of Chapter 3 from time to time throughout the book in order to illuminate certain points.

The challenge of today　In language, as in other areas of the curriculum, a clue to a modern program is found in current need. Occasions for communication appeared early in the life of man— in conveying immediate needs, in planning a defense against a common enemy, in transmitting the traditions of the tribe, and in controlling social action.

The same needs appear today with increasing clarity and urgency. Furthermore, the performance of complex processes and the use of tools require new vocabularies and more exactness of explanation. As work becomes more specialized and the vocabulary of technology rapidly grows, there is increasing need for a populace that is equipped with the knowledge-obtaining and the knowledge-transmitting resources of the language arts.

In our democracy, mutual cooperation through communication is a truism; yet there is accumulating evidence that class and status barriers exist in our society that affect the school orientation and success of a vast number of children and their future functioning in the adult world. If children of limited experiential backgrounds tend to score lower on standardized tests of reading, vocabulary, and language skills than children of the more economically favored middle class, and if the language arts are the basic means by which human beings function socially and economically, then the challenge of schools today is that of meeting the demand for a style and approach in the teaching of the communicative arts adaptable to the needs of these children.[1]

Language in the development of the child   Language is as important in the development of the child as in the development of society. The order of development of language is in part vague, but it is obvious that the first experience to appear is oral communication, as the infant attempts to make known his needs through cries, gestures, grimaces, and words. The first language efforts are practical and utilitarian in purpose, relating to food, comfort, and pain.

When immediate physical needs have been met and a degree of maturity reached, the child becomes absorbed with the intriguing task of making the acquaintance of a great variety of things. *What's that?* is asked frequently. Inquiries concern animals, cars, people, houses, trains—all sorts of novel objects and experiences. Asking questions is the characteristic type of language activity at this stage. A three-year-old asked 376 questions and a four-year-old 397 questions during one day. In inquiry, the emphasis shifts from the use of language for communication to the use of language for thinking. The child is struggling to identify the various objects in his environment, to bring order into a confusing world of sight, sound, smell, and feeling. In this exploratory-naming stage, which continues for some years, the child's vocabulary is composed largely of nouns. At two years there is a high proportion of nouns (50 to 60 percent). Gradually, with increasing maturity and wider experiences, the child's concepts become more clearly defined and ideas of relationship take shape.

Thus, as the dog, horse, and cow are distinguished and identified, the *bow-wow* ceases to be any four-legged animal; the train says *too-too;* the dog *runs;* flowers are *pretty.* Correspondingly,

[1] Patricia C. Sexton, *Education and Income*, The Viking Press, Inc., New York, 1961, pp. 256–266.

language changes. Other parts of speech appear: descriptive words (adjectives and adverbs), action words (verbs), connectives, and pronouns. Growth in the uses of these various parts of speech goes on simultaneously. All phases of language development proceed at a fairly uniform rate. This indicates that language is learned by wholes, rather than by isolated and individual responses, and that the relative proportion of various parts of speech is fixed by one general pattern. Words in phrases soon follow the use of single words, as in *Tommy cold*. The verb is finally added and the sentence form takes shape: *Tommy is cold*. At first, sentences are predominantly simple: declarative, interrogative, and finally imperative; but the complex and compound sentences are used early.

It would seem that another kind of language experience that begins to take shape early is dramatic play. The first manipulation of objects is probably purely mechanical in nature; but soon the use of materials with a purpose seems to appear, as in loading a truck, moving blocks, or constructing an airport. Words accompany actions. Dramatic play becomes more complex and social when several children play together. Children express in action and words ideas about phases of life that interest them: preparing food, taking care of a baby, storekeeping. Further differentiation in kinds of experiences performed appears with increasing maturity and the response to the demands of life in and outside the school.

It is apparent also that growth in performing an increasing variety of language experiences is paralleled by growth in the component abilities and skills, as was discussed above in the development of vocabulary and in the use of sentences. This growth is likewise true of the mechanics of speaking: articulation, voice management, and pronunciation; the general abilities of having something to say and speaking to the point; and later the mechanics of writing.

Factors in growth are maturation and stimulation by environment. Maturation concerns the natural development of speech functions and processes of thinking. For example, the utterance of sounds follows a natural order, beginning with vowels and the consonant "m." But maturation is also directly affected by language patterns set by other people and by the stimulation to thought and action of rich, varied experiences.

From this brief sketch of growth in language there appear certain basic principles significant for teaching. It has been observed in the first place that language is a vital part of the growth process. It is a vital part of the process of adjusting to life, physical and social, a means of gaining control of people and thought; and a means of bringing order into a bewildering world. Training children in language is training in living, in understanding, and in getting along with people. In the second place, it has been observed that, although natural equipment provides potentialities of growth, actual growth is conditioned very largely by the stimulation and direction provided by parents and teachers. A rich environment of varied experiences is essential to good language development. A third implication is that language is purposeful, not a perfunctory act. The purpose is largely utilitarian—communicating and extending experience—but not exclusively so, because there is a place for the development of creative, artistic impulses. A fourth significant principle is that language develops as a whole—a whole made up of many complex, interrelated elements.

The nature of language   Language is made up of arbitrary verbal symbols, basically oral, that have become associated with ideas and objects through use.[2] Patterns for putting words into sentences are systematic and peculiar to a particular language. This suggests that language is learned primarily by imitation, and that to be clear and acceptable one must use words and patterns of expression that people of the group understand and accept, and that have the same meaning for the hearer as for the speaker. For the child who is a native speaker of English and who has had actual experience with the concrete objects that are symbolized by the words *dog, chair, book,* there is little difficulty. There may be confusion, however, when adults use words such as *truth, loyalty, justice, democracy,* and *communism.* In the use of the highly abstract qualities inherent in many of the concepts that we express in words, each person brings his own experience and background into the formulation of his personal interpretation of the words. As the mechanics of speech are learned by imitation, the connotations of the word, phrase, or slogan are often learned by the information attached to them by the members of the immediate environment.[3]

The complexity of language is revealed in the many purposes it serves and in the situations in which it is used. Language takes different forms in all the common uses. Moreover, standards of acceptability vary in different social situations, such as taking part

[2] Mildred A. Dawson and others, *Guiding Language Learning,* Harcourt, Brace & World, Inc., New York, 1963, pp. 3–17.

[3] S. I. Hayakawa, *Status, Symbol, and Personality,* Harcourt, Brace & World, Inc., New York, 1963, pp. 18–28.

in an informal conversation, making an important address, participating in a discussion for community improvement—giving rise to the idea that one must learn several forms of language, or dialects, if you please, suitable to different occasions. The various social uses of language have something in common, but they also have some important differences.

When one turns from the social uses of language to consider what actually makes language effective, one discovers such elements as vocabulary, sentences, speech, writing mechanics, content, willing participation on the part of the speaker, and the ability to stick to the point. These elements appear in many social uses, but not in equal importance in all of them. Sticking to the point, for example, is not so important in conversation as it is in discussion and reporting. The change of focus in the purpose of the listener when he is taking part in a conversation and when he is taking part in a discussion is as distinct as when the individual reads the latest novel in one evening and when he researches books to substantiate an hypothesis. The teacher's job is to deal with whole language experiences, such as reporting, discussing, and letter writing, that are closely interrelated but to some extent distinct; and to provide for development in the various language elements that also are interrelated and somewhat distinct. The complexity of setting up an effective program of language arts instruction is largely caused by the nature of language itself.

Interrelationships among the language arts   The language arts—oral and written composition, listening, and reading—naturally have much in common. All have a common purpose, the exchange of ideas; and they are concerned with the use of words as symbols, and with the use of sentences for the expression of larger thoughts. One art contributes to another, as reading develops vocabulary, sentence forms, and types of literary expression; and as written composition contributes to reading and the appreciation of literature. The relation between oral and written composition is particularly close because they require the same general abilities and skills in such matters as choosing topics, handling content, sticking to the point, varying sentence structure, and using appropriate words. Much punctuation simply indicates in writing the pauses and emphases in speaking.

Certain differences, however, are apparent among the language arts. Speaking and writing involve giving expression to ideas, thus calling into play quite different, though related, abilities. Spelling and handwriting are clearly tools of written expression.

The mechanics of speech production are tools of oral expression. Vocabulary, sentences, and usage understandings are needed in both oral and written expression.

Customary practice continues to treat the assimilative art of reading and the expressive arts of oral and written language as distinguishable areas in the curriculum. Training in oral and written expression is merging in response to the practical demands of communication as presented by natural language situations. The close, practical relationship between spelling and handwriting and written language is recognized in current programs; but the mastery of distinct, complex skills in handwriting and spelling seems to require separate, systematic treatment at various levels of work.[4]

Factors conditioning language development   A teacher must set up a program of language work with a full understanding of the child and the environmental factors that affect the development of language. The child comes to school with well-established habits of expression, especially habits of listening and speaking, determined by the home and community environment from which he springs. These environmental forces continue to operate during the school life of the child, aiding or hindering the teacher in his efforts to bring about improvement. Primarily important, of course, is the home. The mother is the first teacher of language. Patterns of sentence construction, vocabulary, voice quality, pitch of voice, and rhythm of expression are molded by the language the child hears during the first five years. The child from a more endowed home has much to say on many topics which are foreign to the experience of the less favored child. A friendly, sympathetic, informal home atmosphere invites child participation in conversation and discussion. Overprotective or domineering parents cause types of withdrawal behavior and may contribute to speech defects such as stuttering.

The school influences are no less significant. The teacher can provide at least one situation in which the child hears clear, vigorous, idiomatic English; children, particularly younger children, tend to pattern their speech on the example set by the teacher. Also important is making reasonably good language acceptable to the group so that social pressure favors good language.[5]

---

[4] A. Sterl Artley and others, *Interrelationships among the Language Arts*, National Council of Teachers of English, Champaign, Ill., 1954, pp. 3, 34. See also R. B. Ruddell, "Oral Language and the Development of Other Language Skills," *Elementary English*, vol. 43, May, 1966, pp. 489–498.

[5] Dorothea McCarthy, *Factors That Influence Language Growth*, National

TV and radio are among the community influences with which parents and teachers must reckon. Some programs stimulate interest in nature, history, and literature, providing a wholesome type of entertainment. Many programs, however, are not suitable for children either as entertainment or as purveyors of moral and social ideals. Improbable adventure, crime, and unreal sentimentality are not a healthy diet for children. Parents possibly can bring some influence to bear on children to have them choose the substantial types of programs; and teachers, instead of ignoring how children spend their leisure time, can talk about and direct children's attention to the better kinds of programs. Teachers and parents may cooperate with advertisers and with broadcasting companies in their efforts to present programs acceptable for children. Estimates of the extent of the medium of television indicate that 91 percent of the total households in the continental United States are equipped with one or more television sets. While it has been argued that television viewing has made children word conscious, aware of language, and more avid readers, the average hours per day of televiewing by children make the daily one-hour average of reading run a poor second in the bid for the children's out-of-school time.[6]

Especially significant for the teacher of today is the consideration of the work that has been undertaken to point out the vast differences between the standard school English of the middle-class teacher and the vocabulary and usage of the children who come to the public schools. To further remove teaching practices from the celluloid-collar stage of development, it is necessary to remember that many children, who formerly were thought to be essentially nonverbal, simply speak another form of American English and function with difficulty in a traditional classroom.[7]

Studying a second language in the grades   Two world wars, with the resulting international entanglements—political, economic, and linguistic—have served to show us how pitifully inadequate we in the United States are with regard to foreign languages. In govern-

Council of Teachers of English, National Conference on Research in English, Champaign, Ill., 1953. See also National Council of Teachers of English, *Language Programs for the Disadvantaged*, Champaign, Ill., 1965, pp. 74–98; and F. B. May, "The Effects of Environment on Oral English," *Elementary English*, vol. 43, October, 1966, pp. 587–595; November, 1966, pp. 720–729.

[6] Paul A. Witty, "Studies of the Mass Media: 1949–1965," *Science Education*, vol. 50, March, 1966, pp. 119–126.

[7] Martin A. Deutsch, "The Disadvantaged Child and the Learning Process," in A. Martin Passow, *Education in Depressed Areas*, Teachers College Press, Columbia University, New York, 1963, pp. 172–177.

ment and in business there is a desperate need for workers trained in a second language, and our ever-increasing tourist exchange is fast making this need a general one. Should we not begin to do something about this in the elementary school? [8]

In the post-Sputnik era in the United States, there has been a mushrooming of programs designed to teach a second language in the elementary schools. There seems to be some agreement that the speaking-listening approach to the learning of a second language is the one most suited to the elementary school child. However, there are many unresolved questions relating to the teaching of a second language, which pose problems in curriculum construction and implementation. The issues regarding which language should be taught in an elementary school, the objectives for teaching the language, the materials to augment the learning objectives, and the sequence of learnings from the elementary school through the junior and senior high schools are unresolved. The Modern Language Association of America is a private organization that has assisted in effecting changes in the total picture of the teaching of second languages, through its foreign language program. The periodical of the Association, *PMLA*, reports studies of the teaching of a second language. The Foreign Language in the Elementary School (FLES) program studies are significant for those teachers who are undertaking or planning to undertake the teaching of a second language in the elementary schools.[9]

Language teaching then and now   In considering a modern program of teaching the language arts, it is necessary to give some attention to how language was taught in the past. Some vestiges of past practices are still found in the classroom.

Doubtless, isolated examples of vital, vigorous, functional teaching can be found in the past practices, but the prevailing kind of instruction was characterized by artificiality, formality, and drill. Composition centered around the formal types of narration, description, and argumentation. The essay was highly favored in the later grades. Little attention was given to the actual uses of language in school and in life, and instruction was predominantly in

[8] J. Vernon Jensen, "Effects of Childhood Bilingualism," *Elementary English*, vol. 39, February and April, 1962, pp. 132–143, 358–366. See also Charlotte K. Brooks, "Some Approaches to Teaching English as a Second Language," *Elementary English*, vol. 41, November, 1964, pp. 728–733.

[9] The address of the Modern Language Association of America is 70 Fifth Avenue, New York, N.Y., 10003. See W. R. Parker, *The National Interest and Foreign Language*, U.S. National Commission for UNESCO, Department of State, Washington, D.C., 1961, pp. 17–24.

the written forms. Children were urged to write about impersonal topics, such as clouds, trees, spring, birds—topics that carried little personal appeal. Great emphasis was placed on formal grammar, including the memorizing of definitions and rules, parsing, analyzing, and diagraming. Formal exercises were chiefly relied on in dealing with sentence study, usage, punctuation, and capitalization. Children were expected to listen attentively, without instruction in the skills and abilities necessary for listening. The fundamentals of learning to read were taught to the first-grade children without reference to the supporting elements of speaking, writing, and literature. In sum, language teaching was isolated from the real purposes and experiences of listening, speaking, writing, and reading; and learning proceeded in small, isolated drill segments.

It should be observed that prevailing practices in the past were not inconsistent with conceptions of the learning processes then current. The psychology of habit formation underlying most of the instruction in language justified the analysis of learning tasks into specific elements and isolated drill. It was assumed that elements learned singly could be combined as needed in performing certain language functions. Thus, handwriting, spelling, usage, punctuation, the forming of sentences, and the organization of ideas into paragraphs could be learned separately and then effectively put together in writing a story or letter. An older mental disciplinary theory had come into disrepute, but a new mental disciplinary theory had been substituted based on unwarranted assumptions regarding the possibilities of transfer in learning.

Now we have a better understanding of the learning processes. The best learning situation is real, lifelike experience, providing meaning and adequate motivation and demanding the exercise of essential language abilities and skills. Learning involves a significant, meaningful *whole* rather than practice on isolated, disconnected habits and skills.

Continued research provides information that requires constant revision of the language program. As a result of this research a clearer picture of the nature and extent of individual differences emerges. Experimentation under carefully controlled classroom conditions reveals the ineffectiveness of some of our traditional procedures, such as red-inking and the correcting of children's compositions by the teacher, class drills on usage, and the study of formal grammar. On the positive side, we have proof of the effectiveness of new procedures; for example, the elimination of errors by individual diagnosis and the beneficial results of individual or group remedial instruction have been conclusively demonstrated.

A broad basis for projecting a modern program of language instruction is provided in the concept of language as an essential part of the growth process and as a means of securing unity of purpose and social action. "We can no longer think of communication, therefore, as a narrow set of linguistic skills. It is a process which involves ways of living—ways of thinking, of looking at oneself, of adjusting to social situations, of dealing with reality. The communication program of the school should be conceived imaginatively in terms of this new conception." [10] Primary emphasis is placed on real, current language experiences, such as conversation, discussion, reporting, dramatization, reading, letter writing, arising in dynamic classroom situations. Current work in all subjects provides topics to talk, read, and write about and motivation for, as well as practice in, using effective language. Children are encouraged to write about things they know and in which they are interested. Oral language experiences are stressed because oral language is a basis for writing and precedes reading. Practice is introduced only as it relates to immediate needs. It is not expected that all children have the same capabilities and needs; individual differences are recognized in oral and written communication, in readiness to read, in creative work, and especially in practice phases—correct usage, spelling, handwriting, punctuation.

It should be noticed that what we refer to as a modern program of language instruction is not something entirely new. Trends toward the modern program may be observed over a period of years. The modern program is the culmination of a long period of thinking and classroom practices, not a current revolution. Gradual changes can be found in courses of study and textbooks.

To teach or not to teach language   The dissatisfaction of teachers with the traditional program of instruction in language—caused by the antipathy of children to the program and the mediocre results achieved—and the necessity of forming some kind of new program raises the issue, Shall we or shall we not teach language? A natural reaction to the bald formality and unimpressive results of the traditional program is to do away entirely with systematic instruction. It is observed that language training is provided in language experiences growing out of work in other subjects and in out-of-school activities. Children discuss, outline, summarize, and report in the social studies; dramatize in health and safety activities; extend vocabulary in science; and give directions in

[10] J. J. DeBoer, "The Teaching of Communication," *Progressive Education*, October, 1951, pp. 24–25.

connection with the playing of games. Language unquestionably is used constantly in all phases of school work. The question is, Does this constant use of language in itself provide for growth and mastery of the basic language abilities and skills? Use in itself is no guarantee of mastery. Also it may be observed that while children are using language constantly outside the school the language experiences of all children are not equal. Bloom has stated:

> The absolute scale of vocabulary development and the longitudinal studies of educational achievement indicate that approximately 50 per cent of general achievement at grade 12 (age 18) has been reached by the end of grade 3 (age 9). This suggests the great importance of the first few years of school as well as of the preschool period in the development of language patterns and general achievement. These are the years in which general language patterns develop most rapidly, and failure to develop appropriate achievement and learning in these years is likely to lead to continued failure throughout the remainder of the individual's school career.[11]

If the school does nothing more than set up situations for using language, it achieves nothing more—and probably much less —than life outside the school. The conclusion seems inescapable that a positive program of the crucial language arts must be provided.

The question, then, is *how* it should be provided: as opportunities arise in the course of schoolwork in various areas of the curriculum (incidental, integrated instruction), or in a planned series of experiences set up for the specific purpose of training (systematic instruction), or in some combination of both. The authors believe that the difference is primarily a matter of organization and scheduling; that some instruction is necessary, and that it should be planned even when incidental—a closely related or integral part of work in other areas. The authors believe also that the principles and processes for bringing about improvement of learning are basically the same whether applied incidentally in connection with other subjects or systematically in a separate period.

Language in the total program Emphasis on the importance of planned instruction in language, whether integrated or systematic, should not blind us to the fact that language is a necessary part of the work in all areas of the curriculum. It must be recognized as a

---

[11] Benjamin Bloom, *Stability and Change in Human Characteristics*, John Wiley & Sons, Inc., New York, 1964, p. 27. Quoted with special permission of author and publisher.

part of the total curriculum as it is part of the life of the child outside the school. The implication is that all subjects provide material for listening, reading, speaking, and writing; that in all subjects real situations arise that give point and purpose to language activities; and that in all subjects opportunities arise to sharpen language abilities and skills. For language training the values of work in other subjects are potential values only; they become real as the teacher deliberately uses them for training in language.

Research in the language arts Currently there is an upsurge of interest in the language arts, probably reflecting a new recognition of the importance of language in modern life and in the development of children, a better understanding of the learning processes, and a growing concern about the inadequacy of traditional methods. Much important research has been done. Complete publishing data for the material following may be found both in the footnotes throughout the book and in the bibliographical lists at the ends of chapters. The student will be rewarded by going into these sources as far as time permits for confirmation of points of view and for more detailed treatments of topics discussed in the book. Consulting primary sources can be laborious and time-consuming; the student and the teacher may prefer to use authoritative summaries, several of which are noted.

For some years leadership in the language arts has been taken unquestionably by the National Council of Teachers of English. In 1945 the Council appointed a commission to reexamine the place language holds in modern life and to review and stimulate research in the field. A five-year program was projected, covering basic principles and work at the several grade levels, elementary through college. The foundation book of principles, *The English Language Arts*, came out in 1952, and offers a comprehensive and authoritative statement of principles underlying the curriculum. This was followed by *Language Arts for Today's Children*, 1954, and *The English Language Arts in the Secondary Schools*, 1956. These books dealt more specifically than the earlier volume with the work at the elementary and secondary levels. Concurrently, committees of the National Council of Teachers of English compiled research material in several specialized areas and issued several important bulletins: Nila B. Smith and others, *Areas of Research Interest in the Language Arts*, 1952; Dorothy McCarthy and others, *Factors That Influence Language Growth*, 1952; David H. Russell and others, *Child Development and the Language*

Arts, 1953; A. Sterl Artley and others, *Interrelationships Among the Language Arts,* 1954.

The National Council of Teachers of English continues to stimulate and direct interest in the language arts through its various committees and commissions. Published reports make available their findings from time to time, such as the following: Commission on the English Curriculum, *Ends and Issues,* 1966; *Language Programs for the Disadvantaged,* 1965. Committee on the Teaching of English in Grades 7, 8, and 9, *Ideas for Teaching English, Grades 7–9,* 1966. Conference on Research Design and the Teaching of English, *Research Design and the Teaching of English,* 1964; *Research on Handwriting and Spelling,* 1966. Committee to Report Promising Practices in the Teaching of English, *Classroom Practices in Teaching English,* 1965–1966; *On Teaching English to Speakers of Other Languages,* 1964.

The research of the fifties was an intensification of effort going back much further. In the twenties there was considerable interest in what were regarded as minimum essentials of content in arithmetic, language, social studies, and other subjects. In language, research was concerned with such topics as the frequency of usage errors, grammar relating to errors of usage in speaking and writing, the derivation of objective measuring instruments, grouping of pupils for instruction, and standards for evaluating pupils' work. The results of investigations in the early years were synopsized by R. L. Lyman, *Summary of Investigations relating to Grammar, Language, and Composition,* 1929. Much of the information noted has not been superseded in more recent investigations, but the conclusions should be reappraised.

Initial impetus toward a modern curriculum of language work was given by the National Council of Teachers of English as early as 1935 in a pilot study of a functional program: W. W. Hatfield, *An Experience Curriculum in English.* A "pattern" curriculum was developed with a basic organization around language experiences and their related "enabling" objectives, abilities, and skills. The basic plan of dividing language work into experience units (social objectives) is still sound in theory and has been followed generally in recent language textbooks. This volume was followed by a second dealing with the language curriculum as an experience curriculum: Angela M. Broening and others, *Conducting Experiences in English,* 1939. An attempt was made to include reports of efforts of teachers throughout the country to put into effect the principles of an experience curriculum. The volume includes many examples of classroom work. A bulletin similar in purpose, reporting the practices of outstanding teachers throughout the country, was written by Jess S. Hudson and others, *Language Arts in the Elementary School*, 1941.

Attention was given to working out the details of a functional program by the National Society for the Study of Education: M. R. Trabue and others, *Teaching Language in the Elementary School*, Forty-third Yearbook, part 2, 1944. It brought together the thinking of ten specialists about various phases of the language program and the place language occupies in the growth and development of children.

In 1921 the National Society for the Study of Education published its Twentieth Yearbook, part 2, *Report of the Society's Committee on Silent Reading*, which focused educators' attention on silent reading procedures rather than on the oral methods that for generations had been the means by which reading was taught. The Twenty-fourth Yearbook, part 1, *Report of the National Committee on Reading*, 1925, was a further investigation into the processes of teaching reading and presented a broader picture, recognizing several avenues of reading instruction. Subsequent yearbooks—The Forty-eighth Yearbook, part 2, *Reading in the Elementary School*, 1949; and the Sixtieth Yearbook, part 1, *Development in and through Reading*, 1961—have indicated the continued interest in the processes of reading instruction. Since reading and reading instruction occur not only in the elementary school, the Forty-seventh Yearbook, part 2, *Reading in the High School and College*, 1948, and the Fifty-fifth Yearbook, part 2, *Adult Reading*, have focused attention on reading instruction as a sequential process.

Month-by-month reports of research studies on language arts teaching can be found in several professional magazines: *Elementary English* (National Council of Teachers of English), *Childhood Education* (Association for Childhood Education), and *The Reading Teacher* (International Reading Association). These periodicals are the official journals of their associations and contain many articles of value.[12]

Several recent professional books dealing with the language arts, current courses of study locally available, and recent textbooks for children are all worth examining.

---

[12] Walter T. Petty and P. C. Burns, "A Summary of Investigations Relating to the English Language Arts in Elementary Education," *Elementary English*, vol. 42, March, 1965, pp. 252–277. See also R. C. Staiger, "Language Arts Research: 1966," vol. 44, *Elementary English*, October, 1967, pp. 617–638.

For your consideration

1 Are you able to recall any specific practice or task that you performed repeatedly as a child in English, reading, or poetry? Why do you suppose you remember this particular practice? Was the task one that should be incorporated into a modern program of teaching the language arts?

2 Observe children in and out of school and report language patterns. Are there apparent differences between the in-school and out-of-school patterns? What might be some of the reasons for the differences you note?

3 As you observe children and note their language patterns, do you detect individual differences in language abilities? What kinds of environmental factors might cause language differences among children of the same chronological age?

4 Report observed changes in the language development of children from age to age. If possible, listen to children of preschool age and compare their language development with that of older children. What differences do you note in word choice, usage, sentence structure, and continuity of thought?

5 Review the weekly television schedule in your Sunday newspaper. What particular programs might relate to aspects of science, social studies, mathematics, and other school subjects?

6 What are the requirements of a language program geared to the needs of life today? Can you project your thinking into the future by attempting to envision the language needs of the present first-grade children as they become adults?

References

ANDERSON, VERNA D., AND OTHERS: *Readings in the Language Arts,* The Macmillan Company, New York, 1964, chaps. 1 and 9.

APPLEGATE, MAUREE: *Helping Children Write,* Harper & Row, Publishers, Inc., New York, 1954, chap. 1.

BEREITER, CARL, AND SIEGFRIED ENGELMANN: *Teaching Disadvantaged Children in the Preschool,* Prentice-Hall, Inc., Englewood Cliffs, N.J., 1966, pp. 33–40.

CORBIN, RICHARD, AND MURIEL CROSBY: *Language Programs for the Disadvantaged,* National Council of Teachers of English, Champaign, Ill., 1965, pp. 3–16.

DALLMAN, MARTHA: *Teaching the Language Arts in the Elementary School,* W. C. Brown Company, Publishers, Dubuque, Iowa, 1966, chaps. 1–2, pp. 297–301.

DAWSON, MILDRED A., AND FRIEDA H. DINGEE: *Children Learn the Language Arts*, Burgess Publishing Company, Minneapolis, Minn., 1966, chap. 1.

—— AND G. C. NEWMAN: *Language Teaching in Kindergarten and the Early Primary Grades*, Harcourt, Brace & World, Inc., New York, 1966, chap. 1.

ERICKSON, MARGUERITE, AND OTHERS: *Foreign Languages in the Elementary School*, Prentice-Hall, Inc., Englewood Cliffs, N.J., 1964.

FROST, J. L., AND OTHERS: *The Disadvantaged Child*, Houghton Mifflin Company, Boston, 1966, pp. xi–12.

GREENE, H. A., AND W. T. PETTY: *Developing Language Skills in the Elementary Schools*, Allyn and Bacon, Inc., Boston, 1967, chaps. 1–2.

HERRICK, VIRGIL E., AND LELAND B. JACOBS: *Children and the Language Arts*, Prentice-Hall, Inc., Englewood Cliffs, N.J., 1955, chap. 1, pp. 435–438.

JEWETT, ARNO, AND OTHERS: *Improving English Skills of Culturally Different Youth in Large Cities*, U.S. Office of Education, Washington, D.C., 1964, pp. 1–31.

LEE, J. MURRAY, AND DORRIS M. LEE: *The Child and His Curriculum*, Appleton-Century-Crofts, Inc., New York, 1960, pp. 279–288.

LYMAN, R. L.: *Summary of Investigations Relating to Grammar, Language, and Composition*, University of Chicago Press, Chicago, 1929, chap. 2.

MAC CAMPBELL, J. C., AND OTHERS: *Readings in the Language Arts in the Elementary School*, D. C. Heath and Company, Boston, 1964, chap. 1–2.

MAY, FRANK B.: *Teaching Languages as Communication to Children*, Charles E. Merrill Books, Inc., Columbus, Ohio, 1967, part 1.

MC KEE, PAUL: *Language in the Elementary School*, Houghton Mifflin Company, Boston, 1939, chap. 1.

NATIONAL COUNCIL OF TEACHERS OF ENGLISH, COMMISSION ON THE ENGLISH CURRICULUM: *The English Language Arts*, Appleton-Century-Crofts, Inc., New York, 1952, chap. 1, pp. 179, 186, 326–327.

——: *Language Arts for Today's Children*, Appleton-Century-Crofts, Inc., New York, 1954, chap. 1, pp. 324, 345–353.

RUSSELL, DAVID H., AND OTHERS: *Child Development and the Language Arts*, National Council of Teachers of English, Champaign, Ill., 1953, pp. 6–9, 22–25, 27–34, 41–52.

SHANE, HAROLD G., AND OTHERS: *Improving Language Arts Instruction in the Elementary School*, Charles E. Merrill Books, Inc., Columbus, Ohio, 1964, chap. 1.

SMITH, NILA B., AND OTHERS: *Areas of Research Interest in the Language Arts*, National Council of Teachers of English, Champaign, Ill., 1952, pp. 3–7.

STRICKLAND, RUTH G.: *Guide for Teaching Language in Grades 1 and 2*, D. C. Heath and Company, Boston, 1962, chaps. 1–2.

TRABUE, M. R., AND OTHERS: *Teaching Language in the Elementary School*, Forty-third Yearbook, National Society for the Study of Education, University of Chicago Press, Chicago, 1944, part 2, pp. 6–11, 77, 222.

2.

THE COMPONENTS OF A LANGUAGE ARTS PROGRAM

An effective program of instruction in the language arts must be planned; it cannot be left to chance. The school must utilize or contrive situations in which language is needed for specific immediate purposes and must plan to manage the situations in such a way that real growth in language power takes place.

A first step in planning is identifying the important lines of language growth and analyzing the lines of growth into specific elements that can be dealt with effectively. The task is a difficult one because language serves a variety of purposes in many social situations such as entertaining guests, introducing friends, enjoying a TV program, persuading others to accept policies or programs; because language takes many different forms appropriate to different situations such as reporting, outlining, discussing, dramatizing; and because language is a complex of many interrelated abilities and skills such as capitalizing proper nouns, using commas in a series, selecting topics for reporting, planning an organization of ideas in reporting. Any attempt at analysis and classification of the various components of a language program is likely to be somewhat arbitrary, and may tend to distort the true picture of language as a closely knit body of experiences, abilities, and skills, operating as a whole in achieving social purposes. Nevertheless an analysis and a classification must be attempted.

In this chapter we shall seek to identify the chief components of a language program and to combine them into significant related groups for further study. We shall be concerned with such matters as the identification of important experiences, the place of each experience in the total program and in the development of children, and the identification of the classes of elements in experiences. The chapter provides an overview of the total language program.

Kinds of goals in modern education   It may help in the analysis of language goals to note similar types of goals in other areas of the curriculum. Modern education has adopted a functional point of view, as opposed to an earlier disciplinary concept. The modern view is the substitution of real, lifelike learning experiences for much drill on isolated elements or skills. In vocal music, for example, emphasis is placed on rote singing and on listening, rather than on training in sight reading. In instrumental music, children from the beginning participate in a complete musical experience— the playing of a selection—rather than in practice of scales. In industrial arts, pupils early begin on projects and the making of real objects. Skills of sawing, hammering, sanding, and finishing are learned largely through use. In the social studies, work centers on problems, rather than on events, dates, and places. In the area of health education, physiology is giving way to a study of practices of healthful living. In all these areas it should be noted that facts, skills, and abilities are needed and that provision is made for learning them. Skills and abilities are learned incidentally through use, but specific instruction and practice are provided as needed.

The functional point of view is consistent with the natural learning of children—learning by doing. Children's lives are made up of many varied activities, each of which is purposeful and complete in itself. There is often little use for practice or drill as such. One of the writers had an opportunity to observe a boy whose instrumental music education began in a class at the fourth-grade level, using a melody approach. In the fifth and sixth grades he had learned enough to play in the elementary orchestra. He continued to play his instrument in the junior high school, senior high school, and college orchestras, finally achieving first position in his group in the college symphony. The boy never practiced at home, as far as the parents observed, and he never had private lessons. Apparently he never felt the need for instruction or for practice until well along in college. Then, for the first time, he asked for private lessons.

Experiences as goals in language   It may be inferred from the natural activities of children and from practices in other areas of the curriculum that real language experiences—conversation, storytelling, dramatization, letter writing, reports—should receive primary emphasis in language instruction. This is true. The basic importance of real language experiences is recognized in courses of study, in textbooks, and in current books dealing with educational theory. In expressing educational purpose from a modern social point of view, Greene and Petty say, "Education has as its essential purpose the preparation of the individual to do in a better way all the desirable things he will do anyway." [1] The modern school program recognizes the social uses of language not only as ultimate goals but also as immediate goals. For example, the school equips the child for adult participation by giving him real experiences in conversation. This is a modern functional point of view in language corresponding to the functional point of view in social studies, in music, in health education, in industrial arts— in fact in all other areas of schoolwork.[2]

Skills, knowledge, and attitudes as goals in language   Proficiency in using language is gained in part through real language experiences; but learning is facilitated also by giving special attention to the factors or elements that condition the way the child talks, reports, dramatizes, and writes letters. It is now necessary to identify the kinds of elements more explicitly.

Perhaps the identity of the language elements can be made clear by noting similar elements in another familiar activity, such as playing a game. In football, for example, the real experience is actually playing the game. Athletes have occasion to pass and catch the ball, punt, tackle, evade the opponents by dodging or straight-arming, run interference, call plays, and the like. Skills are recognized at once as important elements or factors affecting the way boys play the game. But there are also judgment factors, such as calling plays and deciding whether to pass or run. Other factors, more intangible, concern the attitude of the players such as the will to win, good sportsmanship, and team morale. In developing teams coaches take steps to develop the basic skills—"fundamentals"; to develop understanding of the principles of the game, as strategy in playing various positions; and to build the desire

[1] H. A. Greene and W. T. Petty, *Developing Language Skills in the Elementary Schools*, Allyn and Bacon, Inc., Boston, 1967, p. 5.

[2] J. C. MacCampbell and others, *Readings in the Language Arts in the Elementary School*, D. C. Heath and Company, Boston, 1964, pp. 16–30.

to win and to pay fairly. A very large part of the training time is devoted to work on skills and on principles of playing the game. Good football teams are made not by scrimmage only, nor by instruction on how to play the game and by drill on mere fundamentals, but by a judicious combination of the experiences of playing a game and of practice on elements or factors.

As in football, the analysis of language work reveals various elements that affect performance. In writing a story, the child selects an appropriate topic, plans a sequence of incidents, uses appropriate words and phrases, spells and writes, and forms sentences that express ideas clearly and emphasize important ideas. In planning and carrying through an informal dramatization, a child or group of children selects a suitable topic such as a story; reads the story to get the main sequence of events; lists characters and parts; outlines the scenes; puts the ideas for each scene into appropriate words; plans the costuming and stage business; performs; and with the help of classmates evaluates the performance. Similar analyses of elements can be made for any language experience.

Skill elements   The skill elements in language are apparent. In speaking we find pronunciation, enunciation, voice projection, phrasing, sentence structure, and usage. In written work we find capitalization, punctuation, paragraphing, usage, sentences, handwriting, and spelling. Many skill elements are determined by rule or by convention. Proficiency requires repetition or practice. There is a minimum of freedom of choice or thinking. The skill elements of language correspond roughly to the skill elements of football.

Knowledge elements   There is a clear difference between such factors as pronouncing or spelling a word—skill elements—and selecting an appropriate topic for a story or sticking to a point in discussion. The last two elements depend on knowledge, understanding, and judgment. There are appropriate principles that apply, but no rules. Practice is required for mastery, but it is practice in evaluative thinking. These are similar to such elements of football as knowing whether to pass or run, what play to call, and how to defend against a particular formation of opponents. The knowledge-understanding-judgment factors operate in phases where no fixed rules of procedure apply, where choice can be made, where principles are invoked. Other examples where understanding operates are in selecting the most appropriate reference book, determining *loaded* words in a speech, and preparing an outline. Understanding also is called into play in some of the mechanical phases of the work, as in the use of punctuation in the materials we read and in our own writings. Learning why certain mechanics are used and the purposes they serve in speaking and in writing adds interest to often dull phases of work and facilitates control and retention.

Attitude elements A third set of factors or elements in language experiences can be distinguished—the factors that relate to attitudes, desires, values, and standards of quality. An eight-year-old boy not noted for his serious attention to schoolwork was observed at home writing a letter. It was the spring of the year, and interest in baseball was mounting. He was struggling with a letter to a mail-order house requesting a ball, a bat, and a glove. He was concerned about the form of the letter, the spelling, the legibility of the handwriting; about stating clearly what he wanted, determining the exact amount of money to enclose, and giving the return address. Apparent was the desire to write a letter, growing out of a real social situation. Obviously, attitudes were important in this as they are in many phases of language work; they are key factors in development, providing motivation that triggers study and practice. This motivation grows out of various situations in and out of school. Successful learning through language experiences requires the acceptance of appropriate standards in skill and ability elements.

In sum, real experiences and the elements of attitudes, knowledge, and skills are the chief components of language that must be considered in planning a total program of instruction.

What language experiences?

Having established the point that language experiences constitute an important part of the total language arts program, it is now necessary to list the language experiences that should be included in the program. In general, they should be those most useful to the child and to the adult outside school; and to the child in school, incident to various phases of school life and curricular work. Within the framework of maturational factors and school-life needs, language arts experiences should be planned to help each child develop an ever-widening and deepening sequence of significant language capabilities. The different language experiences that the child meets in life and encounters in school are numerous, complex, and overlapping. To treat each experience separately, for even the young child, would involve duplication, since many are similar in nature and in purpose. The proposal in this chapter is to group the various experiences into related groups for further study.

Speaking and listening Speaking and listening are the first language experiences of the child. They provide basic patterns of expression and they lay a foundation in abilities and skills for later language development. Oral communication continues throughout school life to be the most commonly used form of expression.

An obvious characteristic of the group of oral communication experiences is the exchange of thoughts and feelings, primarily for pleasure. There is a characteristic informality in conversation and in telephoning. Discussion and meetings, on the other hand, are experiences designed to reach common understanding and agreement.

Listening is an essential component of oral communication. One talks to say something to someone, and unless one is heard and understood there is no exchange of ideas. Communication may be difficult because words may not carry the exact meanings intended and because the hearer interprets what he hears in terms of his own experience. Listening and auding involve more than giving passive attention to what is said; they are active processes requiring concentration, understanding, and interpretation. Listening plays an important role in the home and in the play groups of young children. It grows in importance in school, where most of the instruction is oral. Listening and auding continue to be important in adult life. (See p. 81.)

Giving information orally Giving information orally places a special emphasis on accuracy, clarity, completeness, and conciseness of expression. Specific experiences vary considerably in frequency of use and in importance, depending in part on the school program, curricular and extracurricular. The most common types are expository talks, oral reports, explanations, and directions; of less frequent use are announcements, introductions, and interviews. While information can be given in oral or written form, depending on the situation and the maturity of the children, the desired qualities are the same in both forms.

Reading Of all the experiences of the child, one of the most important is that of learning how to read. Success in school and in life is very greatly determined by one's ability to grasp meaning from the printed page. Reading throughout life is used to obtain information, to keep up to date with daily national and international happenings, and to provide variety and entertainment. The attitudes developed by the children toward the processes of reading are dependent on the understanding and skill of their teachers. The instructional program of teaching children to read is generally based on the sequential phases of (1) the experiences of a prereading program, (2) a period of initiation of the reading book, and (3) the provision for growing independence and versatility.

Writing   Written communication, which is similar to oral communication in purpose, appears as one of the early, natural experiences of children and continues in importance throughout the grades. The first written communications are dictated to the teacher by the pupils. Later, as the pupils acquire the skills of handwriting and spelling, they write letters, invitations, acceptances, and thank-you notes. Friendly letters predominate, but in modern programs occasions also arise in which the business letter has a place. Letter writing requires the learning of various conventions and the observance of courtesies, as well as the clear expression of ideas and the exercise of various other abilities and skills.

Study, research, and reporting   Included in this group are experiences commonly occurring in various phases of the school program. The chief types of study, research, and reporting are: records, charts, problems, questions, lists, outlines, summaries, indexes, bibliographies, and dictionary work. The experience chart is commonly used in the earlier grades as a means of summarizing observations on field trips and on discussions of topics in the social studies, health, and science. The completed chart provides interesting reading material as well as a summary and record of important facts. Children contribute ideas, formulate key sentences, and consider the orderly sequence of sentences in the paragraph. The pupils face the problem of clear, orderly expression, and they gain familiarity with some of the simple elements of composition. Early in the grades, also, opportunities appear for using charts and records of a different type—the tabulation of selected facts in concise, orderly form. Thus children prepare lists of materials needed to carry on an activity; a list of individual duties in working on an activity or in performing classroom chores; or a chart record of observations of the weather, of birds, or of flowers.

In the later grades, as study becomes more independent, some of the more mature study-research activities appear. In connection with the handling of a topic in the social studies, children are encouraged to formulate large problems and key questions, to prepare a logical study guide or list of questions, to outline and summarize material on a given topic from a variety of sources. A written report—class, group, or individual—may require a table of contents or an index for the convenient locating of material and for the identification of sources of information by the use of proper bibliographical references.

It should be observed that study and research experiences call into play certain general language abilities, such as clearness, conciseness, and orderliness of expression; and also that specific skills are needed.

Children's literature   Children need to meet the world of children's literature. To become acquainted with traditional literature, modern books, and poetry early in life is to begin the development of the habit of reading for pleasure, for recreation, for insight. In our highly technological age, the need for the humanizing elements of literature grows increasingly greater. Children's literature, skillfully interwoven into the school day, the school year, and the total school program, can provide balance in the ever-expanding world of information represented by the basic school curriculum. Literature can add new dimensions to learning about the world and to one's own place in the scheme of things. For children, the natural outgrowth of meeting the various types of literature is the sharing of fun, joy, and excitement. In this way the teacher can lead the children into various activities appropriate to their ages and interests. Various forms of dramatization—finger play, pantomime, improvisation, and informal dramatization—are means of interpreting literature and sharing mutual enjoyments. Verse choir, properly handled by an enthusiastic teacher, is another medium by which the joys of literature may be shared.

Storytelling and creative writing   Some authorities and teachers regard creative work as the basis of the language arts program; others regard it as a valuable supplement—another kind of activity. If by creative work is meant expressing one's own thought and feeling, then certainly all work should be creative. If, on the other hand, creative work refers to a kind of expression that is highly imaginative, emphasizing feelings and emotions, employing many figures of speech, and striving for especially vivid words and phrases, then creative work seems to take its place as a distinct activity. Creative work in the latter sense provides an emotional outlet, stimulates the imagination, broadens the vocabulary, and through efforts at reproduction lays a basis for enjoyment of imaginative literature. It has value for all children in individual and group stories, verse, and plays.

What attitudes, skills, and abilities?

Attitudes We turn now to the categories of attitudes, abilities, and skills, noting some of the specific goals in each category and considering the relation of these goals to the total language program, particularly to experiences. Authorities agree that willingness to participate in language experiences is a basic condition of learning. Participation should not be forced; situations and conditions must be created that will catch the children's interests. The desire and willingness to speak, listen, write, and learn to read constitute the dynamics of all language work.

Closely related to interest is the desire to improve in the quality of performance. Desire to improve leads to self-evaluation and responsiveness to criticisms and suggestions, and to the discipline of training exercises on abilities and skills that are essential to success in school and later to effective functioning as an adult.

Courtesies Language is essentially a social activity and due regard for the thoughts and feelings of others is a consideration in many types of communication. Courtesy is not confined to the use of polite forms; it represents and expresses a feeling of sincere friendliness and respect for others. Two aspects of courtesy are primarily apparent—feeling and form. Rudeness may be due to a lack of sensitivity to the feelings of others or to thoughtlessness or ignorance of correct behavior. It may be due on occasion to self-consciousness.

Key courtesies that contribute to pleasant and effective discourse are attentive listening, the giving and taking of criticisms objectively, and amiability of manner. It should be recalled that attentive listening is more than giving passive attention to the speaker and even more than avoiding inconsiderate interruptions; it involves active thought about what the speaker is saying and an attempt to follow, understand, interpret and evaluate. Continuing the line of thought by comment or question is evidence of good listening. Other courtesies can be distinguished and possibly set up with profit as goals for socially mature pupils: avoiding rude re-marks, exhibiting tactful disagreement, knowing when and where to talk, avoiding unpleasant topics and personalities, appreciating good humor, respecting authority, and expressing approval of good work.

Content   There is general agreement that, after attitudes, content is most important in any consideration of language teaching. The change from the mechanical to the functional concept of language teaching places primary emphasis on saying something. Real com-munication is weighed in terms of ideas, and the school to be realistic must give a similar emphasis to the meat of the composi-tion. The necessity of making a worthy contribution provides the leverage for dealing with the *means* for making a worthy contribu-tion—the abilities and skills that contribute to clarity, force, and beauty of expression.

Important factors that contribute to good content are a suitable topic, interesting details, complete treatment, originality in express-ing thoughts and feelings, and ability to distinguish between the real and the make-believe. A topic is good when it lies within the child's experience and interest, is limited to a specific phase of a subject, and provides opportunity for expressing original thoughts and feelings. The other factors vary in significance with the language experience and the maturity of the children.

Organization   Organization, closely related to content, contributes clarity and force to expression. It concerns ordering sentences in a paragraph and planning a sequence among paragraphs in larger compositions. Among the important specific abilities in organization are unity in sticking to the point, logical sequence, good beginning and ending sentences, and proper paragraphing.

Speech   Attention to speech derives its importance from the dominance of oral communication. Speech training is a means of improving oral communication and, more profoundly, a means of giving the child a feeling of confidence in establishing social rela-tions. Good speech habits are factors in personality development. It hardly needs to be reiterated that speech work is subordinate to the expression of content ideas and that it is best handled in relation to purposeful expressional situations.

The teacher is concerned with the 90 percent of his pupils who need some training in speech as a means of effectively ex-pressing ideas and emotions, as well as with those pupils having serious speech defects. Desirable goals are audibility; distinctness of enunciation; accurate pronunciation; voice control in volume, pitch, quality, and melody; a delivery that is easy, natural, and free from distracting mannerisms; and audience contact.

The needs of children are largely local and individual in character, and the teacher should set up standards and goals in terms of the needs of his pupils. There is a wide range of articulation, enunciation, and pronunciation in English as it is spoken in the United States. The teacher recognizes varieties of American English pronunciation and seeks to determine those elements that will help children learn the dominant patterns of the geographical area. Children will continue to speak the familiar variety of American English in order to communicate in the home and in the neighborhood; however, they should come to recognize the importance of acquiring the conventional dialect as a step in achieving success in school and possibly in later employment.[3]

There remains to be considered the children who have marked speech deficiencies, conspicuously serious, such as stammering and stuttering. The handling of these problems requires special knowledge and training; but the general teacher can acquire some understanding of the basic causes of difficulty and at least avoid contributing to these children's difficulties.

Vocabulary Language development is characterized by growth in range, variety, and selectivity in the use of words. Children and adults find pleasure in hearing apt, well-chosen, and expressively vivid words. But ideas and feelings precede words. The basis for word study is found in expanding experience and in a growing desire for clear, vivid expression. Words are the tools for the clarification of thinking and for the satisfying expression of ideas. When this principle of function is violated, word study becomes mechanical and may result in words being used without understanding. Further, single words unduly analyzed out of context and spoken as a unit lose their normal sound and this may result in "word calling," hampering the reading progress of a child.[4]

Sentences Traditionally, the definition of a sentence has been that of *a complete thought*. In actuality, the concept of a *complete* or of an *incomplete sentence* is difficult to defend. In the language development of a child, words serve to express thoughts for the

[3] Ruth L. Golden, "Ways to Improve Oral Communication of Culturally Different Youth," in Arno Jewett and others, *Improving English Skills of Culturally Different Youth in Large Cities*, U.S. Office of Education, Washington, D.C., 1964, pp. 100–109.

[4] Carl A. Lefevre, *Linguistics and the Teaching of Reading*, McGraw-Hill Book Company, New York, 1964, pp. 5–6.

first two or three years; later, groups of words and finally sentences serve the purpose of precise communication. It is significant to note, also, that there are occasions in the adult's life when, as in informal conversation, phrases and single words adequately convey meaning to the listener.

The significance of the close relation between sentences and the need for expression should not be lost to the teacher. The study of sentences is not an end in itself and it should not be mechanical. The emphasis should *not* be on the sentence form, use, and errors, but on the clarification of the ideas that the pupil is trying to express. The common errors of *run-ons, ands,* and the use of meaningless phrases for sentences should be approached from the point of view of expression of ideas. Sometimes the expression of ideas requires the *and* construction; often it does not. The phrase without a verb is used by good speakers and writers, but it represents a maturity of expression beyond most children. Also, it should be noted that if the teacher takes the time to observe the child's patterns of oral language by encouraging free oral communication, the discovery may be made that sentences in varying forms may be in use long before the child has learned to read or write highly developed patterns.

Usage   In the traditional program, drill on usage occupied a large part of the children's time and took precedence over other, more important phases of the language program. In spite of excessive drill, crudities persisted throughout the grades and even into the high school and college. What place does usage have in the modern program?

In the first place it is recognized that standards of acceptable English are changing. Language is a living, growing instrument, flexible and adaptable to the demands of modern life for a direct, vigorous, idiomatic form of expression. The standards of formal, pedantic correctness persist, if at all, in the classroom. Usage by good speakers and writers is the criterion of acceptability; but some conservatives continue to set up rules, and teachers continue to set up exercises, which are consistently violated by good speakers and writers and by the teachers themselves. Acceptability rests on usage, not on rules; and oral language is the language that provides patterns of acceptability.[5] Through usage it is acceptable to say: *I've absolutely got to go; I don't know if I can; It is me.*

[5] National Council of Teachers of English, Commission on the English Curriculum, *The English Language Arts*, Appleton-Century-Crofts, Inc., New York, 1952, pp. 275–277.

In the second place it is recognized that usage is relative to the situation. The same expression may be appropriate on one occasion, but inappropriate on another. In greeting, one may say: *Hi; Howdy; Hello, there; Give me five; How do you do?* The choice of expression should fit the occasion. There are many levels of acceptability, not one level.[6] Colloquial speech is appropriate in natural and informal situations, in conversation, and in letter writing. Formal speech is appropriate in talks and reports.

It should be pointed out in the third place that patterns of usage vary in communities and that efforts to raise children far above the standards of the social group may be futile and even harmful.[7] There are, it is recognized, certain usages that will penalize children in their present educational lives. Certain systematic patterns of verb form usage on the "vulgar" level are common throughout regional United States: *ax* (ask), past—*axt*, past participle—*axt; bring, brung, brung; teach, teached, teached.* It may be concluded that the verb usage of regional speech is not chaotic but has a structure, even though the structure varies from the usage most frequently heard in schools.[8]

In conclusion it may be said that the usage program should concentrate on a relatively few serious crudities, determined in part by the standards prevailing in the community and by the needs of individual children, and that these few crudities should be attacked vigorously and persistently through the grades.

Grammar The place that English grammar has in the language curriculum is determined by the demonstrable contribution that it can make to the power of expression. The value of grammar is determined by what grammar is taught and by how it is taught. Several approaches to the handling of grammar are recognizable in past and in present practice, treated here under the labels of formal, functional, and linguistic.

Formal grammar consists of the learning of rules and principles dealing with parts of speech and with the various elements of the sentence. The child frequently begins with memorized definitions and rules, and it is hoped that he will apply them to his composition. Unfortunately the complacency with which formalists lead children through the complexities of grammar is

[6] *Ibid.*, pp. 277–279. See also Robert C. Pooley, . . . "What Is Correct English Usage?" *National Education Association Journal*, vol. 49, December, 1960, pp. 17–20.

[7] Donald Lloyd, "Subcultural Patterns Which Affect Language and Reading Development," in Arno Jewett and others, *op. cit.*, p. 113.

[8] Eddie Ponder, "Understanding the Language of the Culturally Disadvantaged Child," *Elementary English*, vol. 42, November, 1965, p. 771.

violently challenged by repeated investigations showing that knowledge of grammar has little relationship to the practical use of language.

The failure of formal grammar to materially change children's habits of expression is due—in part, at least—to the content of formal grammar. Grammar as most of us know it is the result of an attempt to adapt to the English language the terminology and principles of Latin grammar. The attempt to force English into a Latin mold results in confusion. An example is offered in the matter of tense. Though the six tenses of formal grammar—present, past, future, present perfect, past perfect, and future perfect—tally exactly with the Latin, English can be thought of as having only two true tenses, simple present and simple past. Unlike Latin, which expresses time by variations in the form of the root word (*amo, amabo, amavero*), English, to express time in all but the simple present and simple past, uses phrases with generally no change in the root words (*love, will love, will have loved*).

Modern formal grammarians are engaged in an attempt to develop a new English grammar based on the structure of the English language as it is actually used. While recognized and acclaimed in academic circles, their work has had little effect on classroom teaching. Latin grammar still tends to prevail in the schools.[9]

A second approach to grammar is narrowly functional. The content of functional grammar from the narrow, older point of view is determined by a study of the crudities, or "errors," made by children and adults in speaking and writing. The purpose is not the understanding of language, as in the formal approach, but the correction of crudities. There is a difference in methodology as well as in content.

A third approach to grammar is found under the head, linguistics. Linguistics is designed to offer the pupil an understanding of the structure of language, and through understanding of concepts and principles to provide both appreciation and control. Control implies the elimination of errors, as does the functional-instrumental approach, but goes much further in helping the child to improve the power of expressing himself with clarity, variety, force, exactness, and interest. Grammar is learned not as formal study but incidentally as a means of resolving problems of expression in particular situations. Thus a child learns about

[9] National Council of Teachers of English, *op. cit.*, pp. 279–284. See also R. C. Pooley, *Teaching English Grammar*, Appleton-Century-Crofts, Inc., New York, 1957, chap. 6.

dependent clauses by tying together several ideas loosely connected with *ands*, attempting to express his ideas more clearly and forcefully. In writing a report on the westward movement, a child wrote: "Farmers in Kansas, Oklahoma, and Texas were driven out of their homes by dust, and they moved west to find better living conditions." After careful consideration he changed the statement to: "Because farmers in Kansas, Oklahoma, and Texas were driven from their homes by dust, they moved west to find better living conditions." The revised statement shows more clearly the relations of the facts and expresses them more vividly.

Concepts of linguistic grammar *may* be useful in detecting and correcting "errors." Thus a child who had fallen out of a swing said, "I didn't hurt myself very bad, but it was bad enough." The teacher led the child to see that when he spoke of himself he should use the word *badly*, an adverb, and suggested a revision of the statement: "I didn't hurt myself very badly, but badly enough."

In acquiring grammatical concepts and principles in these ways, the child improves his expression and at the same time builds up a vocabulary of terms and a body of principles that are useful in writing and in reading. There is no formal learning of definitions and no formal memorization of principles. Grammar is learned as needed in use. In a very real sense, this is functional grammar.[10]

Form and mechanics in written work   The basic language habits of construction and use are established in oral work. If oral work is well handled, difficulties in written work will be reduced to a minimum; if not, deficiencies in oral training will appear in glaring form in written work. In addition, in written language there are problems relating to the mechanics of capitalization, punctuation, paragraphing, and form; and the problems of poor spelling and handwriting.

For your consideration

1   Keep a record of your speaking, listening, reading, and writing activities for one day. What types of activities do you find in

[10] George H. Owen, "Linguistics: An Overview," in Verna D. Anderson and others, *Readings in the Language Arts*, The Macmillan Company, New York, 1964, pp. 19–25. Paul McKee, "Linguistics and the Elementary Language Arts," *The Instructor*, vol. 75, March, 1966, pp. 19 and 136. W. K. Trauger, *Language Arts in Elementary Schools*, McGraw-Hill Book Company, New York, 1963, chap. 7.

each category? For what purposes was each activity undertaken?

2 Prepare a list of statements that reflect your understanding of the interrelationships between (*a*) listening and reading and (*b*) speaking and writing.

3 Discuss: The forms that language takes are determined by social purposes.

4 Examine a course of study or a language arts textbook and report the different kinds of language goals found there.

5 What colloquial expressions are found in your community? Are they generally acceptable?

6 Make a list of (*a*) experiences and (*b*) attitudes, abilities, and skills for several grades, using as your authority the observation of children, a course of study, or a language arts textbook.

References

ANDERSON, PAUL S.: *Language Skills in Elementary Education*, The Macmillan Company, New York, 1966, chap. 1.

APPLEGATE, MAUREE: *Easy in English*, Harper & Row, Publishers, Inc., New York, 1963, chap. 1.

BEAUCHAMP, GEORGE A.: *The Curriculum of the Elementary School*, Allyn and Bacon, Inc., Boston, 1964, chap. 5, pp. 86–120.

EVERTTS, ELDONNA, AND OTHERS: "A Minimal Professional Reference Library on the Language Arts for Elementary School Teachers," *Elementary English*, vol. 44, May, 1967, pp. 536–539.

FOWLER, MARY E.: *Teaching Language, Composition, and Literature*, McGraw-Hill Book Company, New York, 1965, chap. 3.

HUDSON, JESS S., AND OTHERS: *Language Arts in the Elementary School*, Twentieth Yearbook, National Education Association, Department of Elementary School Principals, Washington, D.C., 1941, pp. 243–252.

LAMB, POSE: *Linguistics in Proper Perspective*, Charles E. Merrill Publishing Company, Columbus, Ohio, 1967, chap. 1.

LEE, J. M., AND DORRIS M. LEE: *The Child and His Curriculum*, Appleton-Century-Crofts, Inc., New York, 1960, pp. 356–366, 417–420.

LYMAN, R. L.: *Summary of Investigations Relating to Grammar, Language, and Composition*, University of Chicago Press, Chicago, 1929, pp. 5–49, 71–133.

MC KEE, PAUL: *Language in the Elementary School*, Houghton Mifflin Company, Boston, 1939, chaps. 1 and 5.

NATIONAL COUNCIL OF TEACHERS OF ENGLISH: *Language Arts for Today's Children*, Appleton-Century-Crofts, Inc., New York, 1954, pp. 103–107, 113–133, 209–249.

———: *Language, Linguistics, and School Programs*, Champaign, Ill., 1963.

———: *Language Programs for the Disadvantaged*, Champaign, Ill., 1965, pp. 3–16.

NUNNELLY, J. C.: *Educational Measurements and Evaluation,* McGraw-Hill Book Company, New York, 1964, parts 1–3.

OGILVIE, MARDEL: *Speech in the Elementary School,* McGraw-Hill Book Company, New York, 1954, chap. 1.

POOLEY, R. C.: "Dare Schools Set a Standard in English Usage?" *English Journal,* vol. 49, March, 1960, pp. 176–181.

———: "What about English Grammar?" in Iris M. Tiedt and S. W. Tiedt: *Readings on Contemporary English in the Elementary School,* Prentice-Hall, Inc., Englewood Cliffs, N.J., 1967, pp. 79–84.

RAGAN, W. B., AND CELIA B. STENDLER: *Modern Elementary Curriculum,* Holt, Rinehart and Winston, Inc., New York, 1966, chap. 9.

SHANE, HAROLD G., AND OTHERS: *Improving Language Arts Instruction in the Elementary School,* Charles E. Merrill Books, Inc., Columbus, Ohio, 1964, chaps. 3–4.

STAUFFER, RUSSELL G.: *Language and the Higher Thought Processes,* National Council of Teachers of English, Champagin, Ill., 1965.

STRICKLAND, RUTH G.: *Guide for Teaching Language in Grades 1 and 2,* D. C. Heath and Company, Boston, 1962, chap. 5.

TIEDT, IRIS M., AND S. W. TIEDT: *Contemporary English in the Elementary School,* Prentice-Hall, Inc., Englewood Cliffs, N.J., 1967, chap. 2.

3.

PRINCIPLES
AND
PROCESSES

The language arts teacher needs to arrive at an understanding of the basic principles underlying his practice. Basic principles concern the place that language occupies in the life of the child and of the adult, the nature of language, the growth and development of the child, the significant factors that contribute to language development, the nature and identification of goals, the general curricular program of work, the differentiation of work to meet individual differences, and the techniques and procedures essential to the implementation of the program. Basic principles relating to some of these topics have been stated in the two preceding chapters. This chapter will be concerned briefly with the last item in the category, principles and procedures relating to the learning processes. Because philosophy and psychology inherently relate to every practical problem of curriculum and teaching, the basic principles and procedures will reappear from time to time in the remaining chapters of the book, as appropriate to the treatment of the various phases of the language program.

The study and practice of teaching are threatened at two extremes. At one extreme the beginning teacher is occupied with abstract generalizations, which, because of inexperience, he conceives vaguely and applies indifferently. Knowledge of this kind may have little effect on what the teacher actually does. At the other extreme, the beginning teacher is primarily occupied with acquiring a set of fixed patterns and with using them more or less mechanically. If the patterns are adaptable to particular situations, he may do a good job for a time; but inflexibility may result in inefficiency, helplessness, and stagnation. If a teacher must make a choice, perhaps the second evil is to be preferred. But choice may not be necessary; it may be entirely possible for the beginning teacher to gain a command of practical techniques and, at the same time, gain an understanding of the basic principles upon which the techniques are based. This double grasp results in teaching on a high level.

It is impossible to equip a student with a full complement of understandings and skills to meet specifically all the multiple situations that teaching presents. Each principle and example given in the book may be regarded as applicable to many other specific situations not cited. Initiative and resourcefulness are required. Also, continuous reappraisal and readjustment are necessary as research continues to add to our store of professional knowledge.

Individual differences   In Chapter 1 an attempt was made to trace the general order of development of language in children. The teacher is no less concerned with individual differences than with the general course of language development. Individual differences are marked in oral and written work. Some children participate freely in conversation and discussion and show marked ability in thinking and expression; others do not. In written work—letter writing, reporting, story writing—individual differences are apparent in both quantity and quality. Variations are no less wide and no less significant in the specific skills and abilities of writing and speaking. These differences appear as the teacher makes a checklist analysis of speaking skills—pronunciation, sentence structure, usage habits; and of writing skills—capitalization, punctuation, spelling, form. The results of standardized tests of written skills and abilities indicate progress in average achievement from grade to grade, but with great overlapping among grades. Goodlad reports a range in grade norm scores of 2.7 to 11.2 in a fifth-grade reading class, supposedly homogeneously grouped.[1]

The class average on a standardized test and the range of individual differences do not give a clear, detailed picture

[1] John I. Goodlad, "Classroom Organization," *The Encyclopedia of Educational Research,* The Macmillan Company, New York, 1960, p. 224.

of the individual children with whom the teacher must deal. General facts of variability are interpreted in terms of concrete realities as the teacher works with individual children from day to day in the varied intimate situations that arise in the classroom. Gradually each child emerges as a person, a complex of specific attitudes, abilities, and skills, and of general powers. Each element appears as a clearly identifiable entity, but its significance is revealed only when it is considered in relation to other factors that combine to form an organic whole. The teacher must deal with each child as a person, as well as make general adjustments by providing different levels of work and by organizing general programs of instruction for children with varying levels of ability. The child is an individual, not a statistic.

Participation as a factor in growth Language has been found upon examination to consist of a variety of experiences through which the child carries on the business of living and learning and by which he exercises and gains control of specific attitudes, abilities, and skills. Normal growth in language takes place through participation and the simultaneous exercise of a number of component elements. It follows that the school, to be realistic and lifelike, must base its program on actual participation. The school must recognize the common language experiences of children and adults, and it must train children in carrying on these experiences. Situations in which language experiences serve an immediate purpose must be provided by the school. Emphasis must be placed on the whole learning situation; interest must be secured; insight and understanding achieved; and specifics—attitudes, skills, and abilities—learned as related, integrated components of the whole.

Attitudes as factors in learning The whole, organic theory of learning is not inconsistent with concentration on specific elements as factors in the learning process. The teacher must recognize that it may be necessary *at times* to separate from the total learning situation specific elements for emphasis in order to bring about improvement in total performance. However, practice and training exercises should be handled so that their usefulness is clearly evident. The purpose of practice and its relation to a whole language experience must be recognized by the learner; and practice must be motivated by desire for improvement.

Of all the basic factors, attitudes are at once the most fundamental and the most elusive. Attitudes constitute the dynamics of learning, the drives to participate in experiences and to improve

abilities and skills. Although real life provides adequate stimulation
for certain kinds of experiences, the teacher may find that children
in school are verbally inactive and unresponsive. The solution is
to make schoolwork challenging and interesting and to set up
conditions that encourage free participation.

Even more difficult is creating a desire for improvement in the
quality of performance; children may be satisfied with low-level
performance. Some leverage for improving quality may be found
in purposeful experiences, but good form is to some extent a
matter of convention. The teacher may show the social value of
maintaining certain standards and may cite examples and authorities. The mutual teacher-pupil responsibility in setting up specific
goals and discussing and recording accomplishments creates a
group consciousness in which individual attitudes can develop.

Practice as a factor in learning   There is, in the new psychology,
no magic that eliminates the need for practice. But that practice
alone may fail to assure competency in language is amply proved
by the results of traditional teaching. Making practice effective
involves certain basic considerations.

In the first place, it is recognized that practice must be purposeful to the learner. Purpose derives from the recognition by the
individual of his shortcoming and from the situation—an immediate one—in which the need for the skill or ability is felt.
Implied is some form or standard with which a pupil can compare his work and some means of diagnosis. Need is often revealed
by failure to make meaning clear or to convey a message adequately. Thus, a child who mumbles is not heard, and the class
protests; and a child who combines his sentences interminably
with *ands* is a bore. Going from obvious effect to cause is the most
convincing evidence of need for improvement that the teacher can
present. However, at times the teacher must resort to the appeal
of convention, such as: "*January* is spelled with a capital J."
Diagnosis is achieved by having a child compare his performance
and products with a given standard and by testing; but often it
is necessary for the teacher to call attention to a specific difficulty
of which the child is not aware. Thus, a pupil through long use
becomes accustomed to certain inadequate language patterns and
to the common mispronunciation of various words, and the teacher
must take positive steps to have the pupil hear and get a feeling
for the correct forms. Implied in the consideration of purpose is
the basic principle that a pupil should be required to practice only
forms needed by him individually and that practice should be ap-

plied at the point of error. The frequent assignment of class exercises, except for testing purposes, results in a waste of time and lowered class morale.

A second basic principle states that practice should approximate as closely as possible the situation in which the form is normally used. According to this principle, the teacher creates opportunities during the total school day for practice and maintenance. A point of error is the reliance on written blank exercises in correct usage. The guide should be the sound of the spoken language.

A third basic principle emphasizes that repetition should follow clear ideas of correct form. Live examples should be set by the teacher and the textbook; incorrect forms should be analyzed as to the nature of difficulty and the cause of error; and incorrect forms should be compared with correct forms in the remedial phases of the work. More than passive attention to explanations is here required. The pupil should show recognition of correct form by choosing correct forms, by reproducing them, and by using them in original examples. The repetition following recognition is at first deliberate, attentive, and consciously directed; later it is used in connection with larger units; and finally it is practiced in total language situations with marginal attention given to the specific skill or ability. The situations in which a given form is practiced should be varied. Multiple use in a variety of situations increases the range of applicability and tends to maintain a high level of interest.

The checking of progress toward the mastery of a specific skill or ability may be recognized as a fourth basic principle. Lists and record sheets used in the diagnostic phase of the work are useful for recording progress. If possible, the evaluation should be the pupil's own, and he should keep his own record of progress. The teacher should check and confirm the pupil's judgments. Repeated checking in tests and actual use, as well as restudy and practice, is constantly required until mastery is confidently achieved.

Adequate repetition, carried to the point of mastery, requires time, but effort should be concentrated on a short list of basic skills and abilities determined by cruciality and by the needs of particular pupils. Extensive treatment is necessarily sacrificed to concentration on a relatively few key language elements.

Understanding as a factor in learning   Traditionally, primary emphasis in learning has been placed on seeing, doing, hearing, and saying. Language is still largely learned by imitation, and adequate language is largely judged by its sound. However, understanding is recognized as an important factor in learning situations in which generalizations, rules, and principles can be formulated and applied. The traditional skill subjects are now being approached in part from the point of view of meanings. It is too early to say how far we may go in making the mechanics of language meaningful to elementary school pupils, but some interesting guidelines are being cited in current literature. For example, Ruth Strickland points out that children in the middle grades frequently use many "run-on" sentences; and she suggests that the study of the sentence, from its minimum core or kernel to its possible expansions, should be undertaken. Experiences in building sentences and in manipulating patterns of transformation would assist children in seeing "how some parts of what they want to say can be put into subordination so that all necessary elements are incorporated in a closely knit sentence of fewer words." [2] As an auxiliary outcome of such experiences, perhaps the writing mechanics of punctuation and capitalization might be better understood and used.

Differentiation of instruction   A differentiation of work suited to the needs of individuals in the class is necessary. This differentiation concerns all phases of work. In handling the experience phases, the teacher assists pupils in identifying and setting up general standards but allows each pupil to select a specific standard as he gives his talk and engages in conversation or dramatization. Moreover, the teacher judges each pupil in terms of his ability, not in terms of what other children do. For example, in handling a lesson on reporting at the fifth-grade level, the teacher may develop with the class the following standards:

1   Give facts that relate to the topic.
2   Tell the facts in order.
3   Use words that tell exactly what you want to say.
4   Speak clearly.
5   Show interest in your topic.

All the pupils are engaging in a common experience—reporting; the reports may be on the same or different topics. The standards set up are those which the teacher and pupils feel have some significance for the class as a whole at its current stage of language development, but it is not assumed that all the pupils have the same

[2] Ruth G. Strickland, "The Contribution of Structural Linguistics to the Teaching of Reading, Writing, and Grammar in the Elementary School," *Bulletin of the School of Education*, Indiana University, Bloomington, Ind., vol. 40, no. 1, 1964, p. 19.

specific needs. Each child is encouraged to discover his weaknesses and to pick a specific language goal on which he needs to work and to concentrate on that goal during the preparation and delivering of the report. The pupil is judged by how well he does what he sets out to do, not in terms of the total list of standards. Thus, differentiation and specific, individualized training are provided within an experience that superficially has the appearance of traditional whole-class work.

In the practice or corrective phases, differentiation is of the essence. The teacher makes an inventory of specific individual needs, groups children with the same needs, and provides the necessary instruction and practice. Concerning certain elements of language usage, Loban says,

> Because many English verbs form their principal parts irregularly, those occurring most frequently in English speech will always require high instructional priority for individual pupils who have not mastered them. The irregular verbs frequently used in nonstandard form are *lie, see, break, come, go, run, do, give, write, ring, sit, drink,* and *begin.* Other irregular verbs, less frequent in use but critical when they do occur, are such verbs as *sneak, drown, sing, know, throw.* Individual pupils, but not whole classes of pupils, will need help if they are to use the standard forms of such verbs.[3]

It is desirable for children, as well as the teacher, to know what their specific needs are; and therefore each child should have an inventory of his own skills and abilities. The inventory serves as a goal sheet, and the child refers to it in preparation, in evaluation, and in recording progress. Provision is made for extreme variants in the form of individualized self-help materials.

Significance of unit organization   The organization of learning experiences around lifelike situations contrasts sharply with the traditional emphasis on small, isolated language elements, chiefly skills. Through unit organization children are trained not only *for* practical experiences but *in* them; the ultimate goals become the immediate goals. Also, the larger unit of learning preserves the integrity of the learning experience; the varied and complex elements of language are combined and to a large extent learned as they function in purposeful expression; the learning experience is an organic whole. Practice on specific, component abilities and skills is related to some experience and has an obvious, immediate purpose.

The significance of unit organization is apparent whether

[3] Walter Loban, *Problems in Oral English,* National Council of Teachers of English, Champaign, Ill., 1966, p. 56. Quoted with special permission of author and publisher.

the language program is developed independently or as a part of larger curriculum units based on the social studies and science. The trend toward large unit organization in language gains additional respect when it is observed that the same trend prevails in other areas of the curriculum.

Processes

It must now be obvious that not one but a battery of procedures is required to handle the various phases of the language program. Three, or possibly four, basic procedures will be used at various times, according to the nature of the learning situation and the learning outcome.

Handling an experience unit. The first step in handling an experience unit is to set up or utilize a situation that creates a definite reason for carrying on the work. The situation may be one that requires the writing of a thank-you note after the appearance of a guest speaker, writing a letter to a sick friend, keeping the minutes for a school council meeting, writing a play as a culmination of a unit in the social studies, or summarizing information gained in a nature-study field trip. The situation presents a real motive and imposes requirements for worthy performances. Alert teachers readily find occasions calling for the various experiences in both the school and the out-of-school experiences of children.

A second step is to develop ideas of good performance. From past work or from trial performances in the experience, initiated for that purpose, the class and teacher presumably discover the need for further training. What is good letter writing, reporting, storytelling, outlining, and the like? Good models may be secured and studied. It is relatively simple to secure good models of written work. Textbooks provide them; the teacher may accumulate a file from children's previous work; or children may supply examples in the form of letters from home (with the help and permission of parents). It is less easy to provide study examples of oral work. Live examples of good performance in the class provide the best material; recordings are invaluable. The material should approximate the level of work normally expected of the grade. Having pupils study examples of varying degrees of merit and choose the best is a procedure of considerable value. Study should be directed first to content and general effect and then to the specific literary devices employed by the author to produce the effect. Some attention must be given to mechanics, oral or written.

Analysis of models reveals key points that should be listed as goals or standards to aim at, to imitate, and to use in evaluation. Goals should be set with due regard to the normal expectancies for the class and should be varied enough to give every child something to work for. Generally, a few key goals are better than many; the list may be extended as the class grows in ability. Too many goals lead to scattering of attention and effort. Thus, for a second-grade class giving talks, it may be sufficient to set as immediate goals willing participation, having something to say, and sticking to the point. As these goals are reached or approximated by a considerable number of the pupils, the teacher may add to the list others such as the use of complete sentences and apt, vivid words and phrases, a clear, pleasing, well-modulated voice, good pronunciation and enunciation, and interest-catching opening sentences.

3. A third basic phase of the work is one commonly neglected or poorly handled—the setting up of individual goals. Too often this is postponed until after the child has completed his recitation or written exercise, and setting individual goals then assumes the form of a postmortem. This method violates the sound psychological principle that the learner should fix his attention on the skill to be performed before practice, not after, except as a check on performance. Individual goals, therefore, should be set up early, before recitation and even before preparation for recitation.

4. The fourth phase, following the setting up of individual goals, is preparation. The child prepares his assignment with both the overall purpose and his specific, individual goal in mind.

5. The fifth phase is participation, such as giving a talk, writing a letter, or taking part in a dramatization. There should be evidence in the child's work that he has kept in mind his individual goal as well as the general purpose of the assignment.

6. Evaluation by the pupil, class, or teacher follows as the sixth phase. This should be in terms of the pupil's individual goals and should always be friendly and constructive, with full recognition of differences in individual capacity. Self-criticism is usually worth more than class and teacher criticism, although a pupil is also often stimulated by the approval of the class and teacher.

The initial lesson or series of lessons is followed by other similar lessons or series in which gains are preserved and further improvement is sought. Records of accomplishments in specific skills and abilities may be kept on the pupil's individual goal sheet and on the teacher's class record sheet. Opportunities will arise for the individual correction of mistakes without the pupil's losing sight of the major purpose of the experience.

Handling a general-ability lesson.—A general-ability lesson is a definite practice exercise designed to bring about improvement in some specific ability, such as selecting an appropriate subject, choosing pertinent content, dealing with a sufficiently small and manipulable aspect of a topic, organizing effectively, or composing a good beginning and ending. The emphasis is on knowledge, understanding, and judgment rather than on specific skills. An understanding of what constitutes a good subject, for example, evolves from a study and comparison of specific examples, such as "The Fish I Didn't Catch," "Hired, Tired, and Fired," and "Taking Home My Report Card," and from an analysis of key qualities, such as personal approach, definiteness, and brevity. The procedure is that which is characteristic of all knowledge getting—the solution of problems; it is never that of drill, as in the pronunciation of *get*.

The need for the lesson appears, of course, in an experience phase of the work, and it results from an analytical evaluation of the experience in terms of the specific factors that condition performance. The training lesson presumes inadequate performance and need for improvement. The need may appear as a result of pupil, class, or teacher evaluation; but it is important that the learner recognize the need.

The second step, logically, is to gain some understanding of what constitutes good performance. In the selection of subjects, for instance, the teacher may present to the class examples, good and bad, taken from current or previous work, from textbooks, or from reading. The examples are studied and the pupils are led to feel the difference between good and poor subjects. The teacher may present such subjects as the following and have the pupils discuss them:

POOR	GOOD
Where I Went	Catching a Rat
What I Heard	False Alarm
What I Did	Too Sure
Sunday	A Bad Shot
An Adventure	An Unexpected Ducking
My Trip	A Hasty Reply
Work	A Wet Seat
My Friend	The Battle of Chicken Run
What My Aunt Has	No Pie

Titles in the first list are found to be vague and weak. Titles in the second list arouse curiosity and a desire to hear more; they tap sources of personal experience and feeling; and they set specific limits on a composition.

From the study of examples the children proceed to a consideration of their own experiences, searching for phases that are interesting to others and worth writing or talking about, avoiding overworked topics. Then they formulate good subject titles. Tentative lists of these titles are profitably presented to the class for evaluation and discussion. Approved subjects are then chosen, and compositions are prepared and delivered. The value of the subject is proved in the composition. When some assurance as to competency has been gained, the children use their improved ability in selecting subjects for all oral and written work.

Handling specific-skill lessons The third type of lesson or exercise with which the teacher is necessarily concerned involves the development of a specific language skill, such as the pronunciation of words (*often, going, athletic*), use of the comma in a series, and capitalization of *I*. Standards of usage are set by convention. The primary emphasis in learning is on hearing or seeing and doing; understanding enters into the learning process to the extent that it is possible to show reasons for certain conventions and to develop rules or principles. Understanding naturally adds to ease of learning in this as in other phases of language work.

The point of departure for a training lesson on a specific skill is an immediate need, revealed usually by performance in an experience. For example, in giving a talk a child may say *I seen* for *I saw;* or in written work he may fail to indicate clearly the persons attending a party by the omission of commas in a series of names, as in *Jo Ann Caryl and Tommy came to the party.* The pupil may be led to discover his difficulty by skillful questioning. The next step is to show the correct form to the child by explanation and demonstration or by directing the study of examples, correct and incorrect. Recognition of the correct form and, if possible, the reason for it is followed by deliberate practice in selected examples. Finally, consistent use in exercises and in related speaking or writing is provided. Work of this type is largely remedial, and involves breaking old habits as well as forming new ones. The work should be individualized, concentrated on a few of the most important skills, and followed up consistently and persistently until definite progress is made. The use of individual record sheets is helpful in making a diagnosis and later in recording progress.

There are many ways of handling directed training lessons on specific skills and at the same time employing good principles of learning. Specific procedures vary somewhat in oral and in written work, although the basic principles are the same. One approach to practice is to have the children give original sentences in which difficult forms are correctly used. For example, sentences containing the words *saw* and *seen* are put on the chalkboard; the children are directed to make their own sentences, using each word correctly. The results may be something like the following: *I saw a cat; I saw a dog; I saw a horse; I saw a bird.* This kind of practice can be oral or written, but the temptation will be to have the children write the sentences because (from the teacher's point of view) this makes good busywork.

To improve an exercise of this sort and to make it mean more to the children, the procedure can be changed somewhat. The teacher, to begin with, asks the children to tell, in their sentences, about something that they really did see. John gives the first sentence, *I saw a cat.* The teacher remarks that this sentence is correct but that it would be more interesting to the class if he could tell a little more so that everyone could see the cat that he saw.

With a suggestion or two, John changes his sentence to something like the following, *I saw a big black cat with green eyes.*

The class likes this sentence much better than the first one; others may try to imitate it. Then the teacher will suggest that there are many, many kinds of sentences using *saw* and *seen*. She will give an example or two: *When the boys went to the circus, they saw an elephant doing tricks,* or *If Mary had not seen the funny little puppy, she would have gone right home.* This will encourage the children to think out original sentences also. It is remarkable how much a few suggestions add to the vitality of practice. The children, instead of being bored by meaningless repetition, will be stimulated by the opportunity for creative expression.

Place of evaluation   It must be apparent to the student in the field of language instruction, and even to the casual reader, that evaluation is an essential part of a modern language arts program, and that such evaluation is continuous and cumulative, serving various purposes and taking various forms throughout the year. These purposes and forms, briefly noted here, will appear in detail as integral phases of the language program in succeeding chapters.[4]

The teacher's first task is an evaluation survey (1) to determine early in the school year levels of achievement of the class

[4] J. R. Gerberich, H. H. Greene, and A. N. Jorgensen, *Measurements and Evaluation in the Modern School*, David McKay Company, Inc., New York, 1962, chaps. 15–16.

and of individuals, in terms of performance in language experiences and in related abilities and skills; and (2) provide a means of diagnosing individual and class needs. The teacher should always be alert to the fact that he is dealing with several different kinds of language experiences and a multiplicity of skills, oral and written. Evaluation forms and procedures therefore will be adapted to the experiences and to the nature of the learning elements. The teacher's subjective judgment must be the chief evaluation factor in most phases of oral experiences, abilities, and skills. Checklists, made up of desirable goals or standards, add validity to the teacher's judgment. Recordings of children's work are helpful in showing desirable goals and revealing individual and class weaknesses. In evaluating written phases and reading abilities, the teacher uses a variety of techniques: observation, anecdotal records, informal tests, tests provided in textbooks and workbooks, and standardized tests. Availability and reliability will determine the choice.

In addition to determining preliminary status or levels of achievement and diagnosing class and individual needs for purposes of organizing and directing instruction, a third evaluative purpose may be identified—to measure the achievement of children during short periods of time, from unit to unit or from difficulty to difficulty. Here again the teacher must rely on his judgment of achievement in most phases of the language program. Records of progress on specific items should be kept on goal sheets. The objective phases of the work—usage, capitalization, punctuation, spelling, and handwriting—can be measured in large part by informal objective tests prepared by the teacher or selected from the textbook to cover the specific items involved. In reading, progress can be noted in word identification skills—use of content and use of the beginning letter of a word to figure out the meaning of a new word, and the use of the dictionary. These types of informal objective tests are similar to those used in diagnosis.

The final purpose of evaluation is to measure progress at the end of the year. The forms and procedures are similar to those used in the preliminary evaluation at the beginning of the year, such as the examples that follow. (1) Judgments of general abilities and improvement in oral and written experiences are made by the teacher, using checklists of specific items for increased validity. (2) Samples of written work, as in handwriting and composition, are compared with the samples taken early in the year. (3) Improvement in handwriting can be determined in part by scores on a standard scale. (4) A final, teacher-made test in spelling, covering the year's work, shows the progress of individuals and of a class; a standardized spelling test can also be given, but the results should not be taken too seriously. (5) Informal objective tests covering essentials of usage, capitalization, and punctuation can be given and compared with scores on similar tests given early in the year; or standard tests can be repeated. Scores on tests of mechanics should be supplemented by observation of what children can do. Mechanics are mastered only when they are used habitually in purposeful expression—in writing, speaking, listening, and reading.

For your consideration

1 Analyze one language experience, such as conversation, to show the relation to other kinds of language experiences and their abilities and skills.
2 If possible, observe two or more children of the same age and report differences in language abilities.
3 Plan to visit a classroom to observe the teaching of any of the components of the language arts. Attempt to identify the "average" achievement.
4 Investigate informal techniques that teachers can use to evaluate children's progress, such as: observation, checklists, anecdotal records, collection of samples of work, teacher-made tests.
5 Relate appropriate means of evaluation to particular phases of language learning.

References

ANDERSON, PAUL S.: *Language Skills in Elementary Education,* The Macmillan Company, New York, 1966, chap. 10.

BEREITER, CARL, AND SIEGFRIED ENGELMANN: *Teaching Disadvantaged Children in the Preschool,* Prentice-Hall, Inc., Englewood Cliffs, N.J., 1966, chap. 5.

Bruner, Jerome: *Toward a Theory of Instruction,* The Belknap Press, Harvard University, Cambridge, Mass., 1966, chap. 1, pp. 1–21.

DALLMAN, MARTHA: *Teaching the Language Arts in the Elementary School,* W. C. Brown Company, Publishers, Dubuque, Iowa, 1966, chaps. 13 and 15.

DAWSON, MILDRED A., M. ZOLLINGER, AND A. ELWELL: *Guiding Language Learning,* Harcourt, Brace & World, Inc., New York, 1963, chaps. 3 and 21.

GREENE, H. A., AND W. T. PETTY: *Developing Language Skills in the Elementary Schools,* Allyn and Bacon, Inc., Boston, 1963, chaps. 17–18.

HILDRETH, GERTRUDE: *Learning the Three R's*, Educational Publishers, Inc., Minneapolis, Minn., 1947, chaps. 1–2.

LAMB, POSE: *Guiding Children's Language Learning*, W. C. Brown Company, Publishers, Dubuque, Iowa, 1967, chap. 11.

MAC CAMPBELL, J. C.: *Readings in the Language Arts in the Elementary School*, D. C. Heath and Company, Boston, 1964, chap. 11.

MC KEE, PAUL: *Language in the Elementary School*, Houghton Mifflin Company, Boston, 1939, chap. 1.

NATIONAL COUNCIL OF TEACHERS OF ENGLISH, *Language Arts for Today's Children*, Appleton-Century-Crofts, Inc., New York, 1954, chaps. 2 and 13.

PETTY, WALTER T.: *The Language Arts in Elementary Schools*, The Center for Applied Research in Education, Inc., Washington, D.C., 1962, chap. 6.

RUSSELL, DAVID H., AND OTHERS: *Child Development and the Language Arts*, National Council of Teachers of English, Champaign, Ill., 1953.

SHANE, H. G., AND OTHERS: *Improving Language Arts Instruction in the Elementary School*, Charles E. Merrill Books, Inc., Columbus, Ohio, 1962, appendix 3, pp. 495–513.

——, MARY E. REDDIN, AND MARGARET C. GILLESPIE: *Beginning Language Arts Instruction with Children*, Charles E. Merrill Books, Inc., Columbus, Ohio, 1961, chaps. 10 and 15.

STANLEY, J. C.: *Measurements in Today's Schools*, Prentice-Hall, Inc., Englewood Cliffs, N.J., 1964, chaps. 1, 7, and 10.

STRICKLAND, RUTH G.: *The Language Arts in the Elementary School*, D. C. Heath and Company, Boston, 1957, chaps. 1–3, 18.

TRAUGER, W. K.: *Language Arts in Elementary Schools*, McGraw-Hill Book Company, New York, 1963, pp. 18–20, chap. 15.

PART 2

THE
ARTS

4.

SPEAKING
AND
LISTENING

Man is a social being. With his mouth, tongue, larynx, and chest cavity he emits sounds to others that bear meaning and significance. Through the medium of his ears, he receives the coded messages of others. Where do we begin in the creation of a program designed to help children develop the lively arts of speaking and listening?

Preliminary considerations Before making detailed plans for handling the instructional phases of the language program, it is assumed that the teacher has taken certain steps. First, he has selected the language experiences to be stressed in the grade according to the apparent needs of the pupils and the course of study and textbook provisions, and he has considered their relative importance. Second, he has made a working list of abilities and skills needed by the pupils in carrying on the experiences. Third, he has made at least a beginning in the diagnosis of the needs of his pupils in experiences as well as in abilities and skills. Fourth, he has blocked out the semester's work, mainly in terms of major experiences. And fifth, he has set up tentative on-going evaluative procedures to assist him in assessing the progress of the children and his own teaching effectiveness.

At this point the teacher is ready to develop plans for handling the various instructional phases. The program includes experience phases and ability and skill phases; both require consideration in planning. The primary basis for planning is, of course, experiences; abilities and skills are treated as integral parts of the experiences, and as separate phases to the extent that organized instruction and practice are required for mastering them.

The first experiences to be considered are those included in the group "oral communication," consisting of conversation, discussion, telephoning, and taking part in meetings. Oral communication experiences are taken up first because fundamental oral abilities are in use by the time the child enters school, because oral work is the basic medium of instruction in the early years, and because (and this is a point that may not receive the attention it deserves) habits of oral communication lay the basis for all later language development. Listening is treated as a phase of oral communication.

The oral communication experiences are characterized by informality and spontaneity. The objectives are the social purposes of enjoyment, exchanging ideas, giving information, and, to some extent, reaching a conclusion or deciding on a course for group action. Informality and spontaneity are encouraged in the spirit and manner of carrying on the experiences and in the setting of standards appropriate to them. It is not required, for example, that children use complete sentences in conversation at all times; and the teacher accepts slang and nonschool usage in this initial stage of communication.

The several experiences have much in common and also have important differences the teacher will do well to note. Thus, conversation is very general in purpose; the entertainment feature dominates. Discussion, on the other hand, has a more definite goal and follows more rigid requirements in setting up and carrying out problems. Telephoning is sometimes handled as a specialized phase of conversation, but it has its own language requirements. Meetings involve several kinds of language experience, such as talks, reports, discussion, and written minutes, as well as those especially relating to parliamentary procedures and courtesy; meetings are treated here with emphasis on the discussion phase, while the other component language phases will be treated in later chapters.

Conversation

Objectives   The first language experience in school is the informal type that we call conversation. The child learns how to talk with other people and begins the improvement of basic language habits. It follows, therefore, that through early school-life conversation the child may be favorably conditioned toward language, and that he should begin to acquire the attitudes, abilities, and skills that will be useful later in all forms of expression, oral and written.

Attitudes Primarily important is the desire, the willingness, to participate. Shyness, fear of expressing himself orally before others, must give way to confidence and poise before the pupil can accomplish much in improving abilities and skills that lead to easy and comfortable expression. The teacher of any age group needs to be aware of the language backgrounds of the children he teaches. In the middle-class home, there tends to be corrective language feedback, opportunities for listening to varied verbal usage, and a range of objects that are verbally related. On the other hand, there are children who come to school from homes in the community where the spoken language lacks syntactical organization and subject continuity. These language deficiencies, coupled with limited experiential background, need to be recognized by the teacher. There may be children who do not *understand* the teacher simply because of the wide communication gap between them and the middle-class teacher.[1]

Somewhat later in development is the desire to improve in the quality of expression and in the willingness to admit need and to seek help in correcting mistakes. This development comes gradually under favorable classroom conditions, when teachers accept individuals and acquire skill in creating an atmosphere of exploration into the world of the symbolism of language.

Courtesy is closely related to willingness to participate; the attentive, friendly class and teacher stimulate the speaker. The courteous speaker does not offend or alienate his audience. The courteous critic offers suggestions in a constructive, friendly manner. The courteous listener not only keeps quiet but also follows the thought of the speaker and shows his attention and interest by asking stimulating questions and making pertinent comments.

Content Primary emphasis in the early years is properly placed on what is said—on content. The teacher can aid the pupil in forming a habit of saying something worthwhile by helping him select a topic within his interest, knowledge, and experience. Children need training in choosing topics, such as those that provide

---

[1] Martin Deutsch, "The Disadvantaged Child and the Learning Process," in A. Harry Passow, *Education in Depressed Areas*, Teachers College Press, Columbia University, New York, 1963, pp. 174–175.

opportunities for expressing personal feelings. Another consideration in choosing topics is limiting them in scope to a single phase —a single experience, incident, idea, or feeling. A suitable topic is personal, definite, and brief. At times conversation will be improved by inclusion of details, so that the whole story is told. In the primary grades children tend to follow patterns in their comments and talks, and sometimes confuse fiction and reality; therefore, teachers wisely advise children to express their own thoughts and to distinguish between the real and the make-believe.

Organization Emphasis on sticking to the point may well begin early in the grades, although gradual growth is recognized as a necessity. Primary children can give attention to simple sequence by telling things in the order in which they occurred. Later, some attention can be given to improving beginning and ending sentences.

The idea that communication involves the expression of organized thoughts is one of the basic language concepts, and the development of sentence sense is properly stressed. Although many sentence fragments are used in informal conversation, sentences are conventional in more formal situations, such as talks and reports. Children should early recognize and use sentences; they should be taught to avoid meaningless phrases and sentences loosely joined by *ands*. The more mature pupils in the primary grades can learn to use a variety of sentence constructions. They can also make a beginning in learning to choose words that express meaning exactly and to avoid trite, overworked words.

Skills The basic elements of audibility, distinctness, standard pronunciation, voice control, and possibly phases of audience contact can be emphasized in the primary grades. Baby talk is a not uncommon phenomenon that should be corrected by removing the cause.

Usage should not be emphasized to the detriment of content, but work on gross crudities may well begin early, particularly on the use of common verbs. The child should have many opportunities to hear the correct form, and occasionally incidental correction can be used.

The teachers of later grades will naturally locate children in their various stages of development and will begin instruction at the proper level. Individual differences will be noted at all grade levels and the necessary adjustments made. Specific techniques for later development may include talking about topics of mutual interest; avoiding long, tedious accounts; avoiding personalities; avoiding a change of topics too abruptly; avoiding debates; and talking in terms of other people's interests.

Emphasis on specific objectives Although any language experience involves the exercise of many abilities and skills, not all of them can be stressed at one time. It is necessary to set up specific points of emphasis. Instead of specific language aims, such general aims as the following are often given:

1. Ability to converse easily, agreeably, and effectively.
2. Ability to present facts clearly.
3. Habit of expressing ideas in clear, ready speech.
4. Ability to express one's thoughts orally to an audience.
5. Ability to respond effectively to an inquiry.

Any such general aims may, of course, be factored into a number of specific aims. If the primary teacher makes no further analysis of the language teaching situation than that she wants the children to improve in conversation, or that she hopes they may learn to express their thoughts orally to an audience, there will probably be little improvement. Without greater focusing of attention she is not able to plan definite procedures which will make for progress. Her plan is vague, and her efforts are spread over too broad a field.

In order to ensure progress in such a complex subject as language, the teacher should single out for attention one or more specific aims and plan each lesson with a definite aim in mind.

If he has not already done so, the teacher may well make a checklist of general and specific language goals and an analysis of the status and specific needs of his class and of individual pupils in relation to the broad language experience. The individual-class record sheet is helpful in this task. Diagnosis takes the form of observations and informal judgments of pupils' performances. The teacher must make a selection of specific goals from the analysis, using his best judgment as to needs and order of treatment. In the statement of objectives above, an attempt was made to suggest an order of emphasis. The wide variability in pupil capacity and performance requires that individual goals, as well as class goals, be defined. Children should recognize their own needs, possibly making individual checklists. Recognition of specific, individual needs will be apparent in the way the teacher directs the work and in the concentration of the pupils on specific goals.

Finding purposeful occasions   Children have so many experiences in and out of school and they enjoy so much the sharing of real experiences that the teacher should never be at a loss for stimulating topics of conversation. Many of these will arise in connection with various curricular activities, such as the care of the teeth, a study of how pioneers made clothes, the reading of items in current newspapers and magazines, field trips, flowers and birds, books, pictures, and music. Others will arise from children's out-of-school interests, such as hobbies, movies, pets, sports, and occurrences in the community. In addition to real experiences, interesting possibilities for later grades are found in imaginary conversations among historical and fictional characters, such as between tourist and guide in Holland, among representatives of various colonies attending the Constitutional Convention, and among representatives of countries in a United Nations assembly.

Materials   In certain situations, such as working with children beginning to learn English, objects and pictures will provide a basis for vocabulary work and will stimulate conversation; but even these will be chosen for their value as sources of information in important curricular areas, particularly the social studies and science. The modern language textbooks, especially those for the primary grades, contain pictures for conversation. Pictures are used not only to provide topics but also to direct children in developing certain language abilities. For example, in McKee and Harrison's second-grade book, *Let's Talk*, a series of pictures represents narrative episodes in logical sequence, designed to develop the idea of organization.[2]

Procedures in conversation   A suitable procedure for handling conversation experiences, either in a single lesson or a series of lessons, is the following:

1. Set up a suitable occasion.
2. Encourage free and informal participation.
3. Call atttention to satisfactory contributions and make a list of important standards.
4. Have each child select an important goal.
5. Prepare for further participation.
6. Proceed, evaluating each child's performance in terms of progress toward his own goals.

[2] Paul McKee and M. Lucile Harrison, *Let's Talk*, Houghton Mifflin Company., Boston, 1968, pp. 20–21. See also Marion Monroe and others, *Learn to Listen, Speak, and Write*, Scott, Foresman and Company, Chicago, 1961, pp. 34–35.

The present, worthy occasion is one naturally arising in some phase of the work, as suggested under the headings, Finding Purposeful Occasions, or Materials, or one specially set up by the teacher for the purpose of inducing conversation. The teacher may relate a personal experience; for example, he may tell about the unusual behavior of a squirrel he saw that morning and ask, "Have any of you had similar experiences in observing the interesting and unusual behavior of animals?" Another topic might be a recent assembly program: "Did you," asks the teacher, "enjoy the program? What did you like about it?" The show-and-tell period in the primary grades is productive of spontaneous talk. "Plans for Our Trip to the Zoo" is a pertinent topic as a class trip is planned.

Young children should be allowed to participate in the language experience at once, without preliminary admonitions regarding goals, ways, and means. As classroom conversation opportunities increase, the time arrives when attention may be diverted from the content of the conversation to the processes involved. Gradually the children can be led to observe that each person should have an opportunity to participate and that problems occur when several children want to talk at the same time. Points appropriate to the age and grades of the children are listed on the chalkboard or preserved on a chart. The teacher guides the children in choosing a few key points of major importance. Enjoyment of a conversation should not be lost in overconcern with technicalities; and, properly handled, the development of process guidelines can add to the satisfaction of a good conversation.[3]

It may be assumed that work on conversation will continue for some time, in either consecutive or discrete periods. The listing of general goals in the early phases of the work will be followed by analyzing individual contributions and by noting individual goals for improvement. In preparation for participation and in the experience itself children will profit from concentrating on their individual goals. The caution regarding the limitation of the number of goals for any one child is worth repeating. Efforts and evidence of improvement should be looked for and rewarded with favorable comment. Improvement in total performance, not simply in a single ability or skill, should be observed; participation should not become merely a practice exercise for the development of skills and abilities.

The teacher will exercise judgment in the nature and amount of running comments and suggestions for improvement. Occasionally a timely suggestion, when an immediate need is felt, is very

[3] Jayne A. DeLawter and M. J. Eash, "Focus on Oral Communication," *Elementary English*, vol. 43, December, 1966, pp. 880–891.

helpful. Generally, children should not be interrupted; at the conclusion of a contribution, specific suggestions for improvement may
be in order, such as the pronunciation of a common word or the
consideration of an item of usage. The nature and amount of incidental practice will be determined in considerable part by the relationship of the individual child, the class, and the teacher.

   In the report of the lesson that follows, some good points are
illustrated: selecting a topic of interest to the children, sticking to
the point, and allowing only one person to talk at a time. The
lesson is reported by Vera L. White, third grade, Del Paso Heights,
California.

   A flood at Yuba City provided an opportunity to begin a unit
on water transportation by means of an informal conversation
lesson. One little boy during a sharing period told the class that his
father had been at Yuba City to help rescue people. The conversation started from this story.

   JOHN: My dad offered to go up and help save some of those people. A
man called him on the phone and told him to get someone else to go with
him, so he did.
   DAVID: Was he a life saver in the coast guard?
   JOHN: Well, he used to be, but he isn't now. He just wanted to help.
   KAREN: Did he go right up to the houses and get the people out?
   JOHN: Yes, because many people were on top of their tables and even on
top of their houses trying to get saved.
   TEACHER: Were any other kinds of boats used in the flood?
   JOHN: My dad said they used some kind of rubber boat that was used in
the last war.
   FRANK: What kind of boat did your dad have?
   JOHN: He had a motor boat. It has a motor on the back that is run by
gas. It has a thing that goes round and round and it makes the boat go.
   JUDIE: Did your dad get wet?
   JOHN: Sure, but he didn't care.
   TEACHER: Did anyone else go to see the flood? Was anything else used
to save those people?
   PATRICIA: The helicopters worked all day and night. My mother said
some people fell out of the baskets when they were being rescued.
   TEACHER: That is right. Some of the helicopters did not have good
baskets to pull the people up in. Connie just came from Hawaii a few days
ago. Would you like to tell us how you came across the ocean?
   CONNIE: I didn't come on a boat. I came on an airplane.
   CHILDREN: Was it fun? Were you scared? How long did it take you? I
would like to do that, etc.
   TEACHER: We are all talking at once, and we decided that it was better
for only one person to talk at a time. (Connie was very new to the class and did
not want to answer all their questions.)
   TEACHER: Let's listen to some other pupils who have been in boats.
   FREDDIE: I came from England in a big ship. I was quite little but it was
a great big ship.

HOWARD: I rode along the Sacramento River in a boat they called—I can't remember the name of it.

FRANK: Was it a yacht?

HOWARD: Yes, that's what they called it. It had a cabin in it. It drug another boat behind it.

TEACHER: We are going to have a good time in learning about the many kinds of boats that are used in transporting people and goods across the water.

TEACHER: I liked the way you boys and girls talked today. I am sure that everyone heard you. Should we make a list of the things you would like to learn about boats? Let's use complete sentences that say only one thing, so that we can make our meaning clear.

Other problems   Other problems confront the teacher in handling conversation. It is desirable, in the first place, to work for an informal type of situation. In order to get free expression, it is necessary to reduce self-consciousness. This condition is achieved largely by the attitude assumed by the teacher and his handling of the work, and includes such matters as freedom in pupil choice of topics and in participation, friendly and helpful criticisms, and expressions of appreciation. The seating of the pupils in a compact, social group is a factor also; the children should face one another, and the teacher should participate as a member of the group. Contributing from a sitting position adds to the informality.

Stimulating the shy child and tactfully restraining the garrulous one present problems. Timid children appreciate and respond to attention and approval. The teacher will encourage the shy child by inviting participation but not by forcing it. The garrulous child may be restrained by suggesting that everyone should have his turn, by neglecting to notice imperious hand waving, and by advising the child to be brief and to the point.

In one primary grade it was the practice several times a week to invite any child who wanted to take part in conversation to bring his chair and join the group at the front of the room. The teacher gave the signal by arranging several chairs in the morning. As the children came in and observed the chair arrangement, they knew it meant a conversation period, and anyone who wanted to tell something joined the group. Others took books or busied themselves otherwise. It was an adult situation. No hands were raised, but each child strove to be courteous, to be a good listener, and to speak plainly, concisely, and interestingly.

In the general sharing and pooling of ideas during an informal conversation period, shy children who will not talk from the isolation of their seats will usually contribute; voices do not have to be raised, and the pupils feel a sense of protection from the physical nearness of the other children. The loquacious child has to learn that he must listen or he cannot join the group. In this situation the teacher may get very close to the children and learn much about the interests of the group; recurring crudities of usage may be easily noted, and sometimes gross bits of misinformation are brought to light and explained.

The judicious use of criticism by the teacher is effective. Approval of worthy effort is also always in order; such approval does not necessarily have to be for superior levels only, but for any work that is good for a particular pupil. The heartiness of the approval should be adapted to the particular child. At times, ignoring obvious faults is necessary to avoid hurting and discouraging an extremely shy child. The value of class criticism is open to question. Group approval is a vital force in classroom behavior, but the offering of discriminating criticism is something that challenges even the mature and wise teacher. Some teachers feel that children, particularly in the primary grades, are not ready for that responsibility. When such critical comment is permitted, children should be inducted gradually into its use; it should be definitely limited in scope. Other teachers report favorable results from the use of some class criticisms. Observing the effects of class criticism on a particular class should give the teacher the answer.

For various reasons, the class is sometimes divided into several small groups for conversation. These groups provide opportunities for general participation, which, however, cannot be closely guided; and they simplify the social situation for the shy child. Teacher direction may be given to group work by preliminary discussions and by reports in a checkup period following group work. Sometimes selected groups demonstrate for the whole class.

Discussion

Definition   Discussion unquestionably occupies a key position in the total school program, as well as a prominent place in adult activities. It is a means for learning in much of the work in social studies, science, health, mathematics, and art, and in school and life activities. Discussion in essence is problem solving, the effort to reach an important understanding by cooperative class thinking. Discussion differs from conversation in that it has a definite purpose or goal. The goal in much of the work is apparent to the pupils as well as to the teacher. In the so-called "informal discussion" of the primary grades, the goal is apparent to the teacher but possibly not so apparent to the pupils. The procedure is a combination of conversation and the more rigid procedure of discussion. This type of discussion is transitional or hybrid. Children need guidance in the processes of reasoning, and they need direct, positive help in setting up problems and in working out logical solutions. Appropriate situations and problems arise in many activities of the school day.

Discussion should be distinguished from argument. In discussion the goal is the honest attainment of knowledge; in arguing, the purpose is to defend a position or conclusion already reached by the participant. Discussion should lead to new and better understanding; arguing merely strengthens the convictions of the participants in the soundness of their own original positions. In discussion there is an open-minded search for all the facts; in argument facts not supporting a favored position are carefully ignored.

Key objectives The general language objectives apply in discussion as in conversation and other language activities. These objectives are basic and important, and provide the teacher with possible points of attack and emphasis. They are reviewed above under Procedures in Conversation, but omitted here to save space. It will suffice here to consider the key objectives that distinguish discussion from conversation, in emphasis if not in kind. The clue to distinguishing the key objectives in discussion is found in its purpose, i.e., arriving at a sound understanding or conclusion.

In the first place, there must be a definite problem before the class, often arising during a science or social science unit. The children must be guided in recognizing the problem, and in planning steps to help solve it, commensurate with their age, their past experience in the development of problems, and their maturity in group functioning.[4] A second matter for emphasis is sticking to the point. A certain amount of freedom to change the topic in conversation is permissible, and even desirable, because it adds variety and novelty. In discussion, however, diverging from the point is a waste of time; sticking to the point has purpose and value because it provides opportunity for acquiring an important ability in thinking and speaking. The third point concerns tactful disagreement. Differences of opinion are bound to occur—concerning facts, the interpretation of facts, and the drawing of conclusions. An attitude of trying to see the other person's point

[4] John Jarolimek, *Social Studies in Elementary Education*, The Macmillan Company, New York, 1967, pp. 81–85. See also Edward Victor, *Science for the Elementary School*, The Macmillan Company, New York, 1965, pp. 86–88.

of view and of toleration for a different point of view should be cultivated in all situations involving disagreements. The form as well as the spirit of expressing disagreements is important. In discussion, in the fourth place, there should be respect for authority. Pupils need to discriminate between sources and to respect the statements and conclusions of competent persons. A fifth point for emphasis involves forming independent judgments based on the facts and stating one's own convictions. The pupil should learn to resist the temptation to let other people do his thinking and the temptation to follow merely plausible leaders or even majority opinion if he sincerely holds contrary convictions. Other possible goals for the improvement of discussion techniques in later grades include the abilities to distinguish between important and unimportant issues, to raise questions and ask for explanations freely, to avoid repeating what others have already said, to suppress anger when one's opinions are attacked, to give accurate and complete information, to obey the chairman, to wait for recognition before speaking, and to participate but not to monopolize.

Situations   Many natural situations for discussing real problems arise in various phases of schoolwork, such as planning a party; deciding how to construct the front of a cardboard store or how to make a panorama; organizing the playground for play; determining how to keep the playground clean; emphasizing the importance of care in crossing the street; and investigating why the rabbit lives in a hole in the ground, what makes an airplane fly, or what the fireman does for us. The many fertile suggestions for discussion that appear in language textbooks are most helpful in supplementing the more immediate problems of school and community life.

Procedures   The procedure for handling discussions is practically the same as that for conversations. First, the pupils must become conscious of a present, worthy occasion, a problem stated by the teacher or by the pupils. The problem, of course, is not bluntly announced as the work for the period but is allowed to grow out of a consideration of facts and issues in which the reality and significance of the problem are sensed. The problem is defined, if necessary. Second, the pupils begin the discussion of the problem. If the discussion proceeds satisfactorily, it is allowed to continue; but if not, the teacher calls the attention of the pupils to the cause of the difficulty and leads in considering means for improvement.

Possible rules or standards are set up. The textbook, of course, provides ready-made lists of standards; but such standards will be more clearly understood and accepted if they are first proposed and formulated by the pupils. The textbook is useful as a check, however. Third, the pupils consider their own performances, past or present, in terms of the standards; they select one or two for emphasis; and they prepare for further participation, using the standards as guides. Fourth, the pupils again engage in discussion, now attending to specific goals as well as to furthering the discussion. Fifth, reevaluation is made in terms of progress toward the solution of the problem and in terms of individual performances. Sixth, the work is continued in somewhat the same fashion in immediately following or in later periods, and individual progress in specific abilities and skills is noted and possibly recorded. During all the work, incidental attention is given to, and some practice provided on, specific abilities and skills as needed by individuals.

Problems   Careful planning on the teacher's part is necessary for directing the lesson in conversation if substantial results are to be achieved; even more is this procedure obligatory in discussion. Planning in discussion takes the form of listing key questions to stimulate and guide the thinking of the class. Planned questions are also useful to aid the teacher in recognizing profitable leads of pupils and to throw before the class when profitable spontaneous questions fail to appear. It is highly desirable, of course, for the pupils to see issues and supply the questions whenever possible. Not many key questions are required, possibly only three to five for a lesson.

Sticking to the point is as difficult for children as it is for adults. Having a definite problem helps. The pupil speaker or the class audience may be asked whether a contribution is on the point. Key questions, with a concise statement of the problem, may be written on the board for reference. Irrelevancies may be ignored or critically considered, depending on the seriousness of the interruption, economy of time, and the personality of the pupil.

Worthy contributions are sometimes lost by the failure of the class to recognize their value or relevancy to the discussion. A good procedure is to make a progressive evaluation of the contributions and an oral summary of points or to keep a running log on the board. A summary may be made at the end of the period; but it is better to keep a cumulative running log, noting and summarizing points as made, while the material is fresh in mind.

Pupil leaders for class or groups are sometimes used. Pupil

leadership is stimulating, gives a feeling of class responsibility, and provides training in group action. To secure smooth working conditions, it is necessary to give some attention to the discussion of the duties and responsibilities of the members of the group, including the chairman, and to learn certain rules of procedure. This training is even more pertinent to the handling of meetings. The class under pupil leadership, no less than under teacher leadership, should be held responsible for substantial accomplishments.

Problems of behavior and discipline may arise in the discussion activity when problems vital to the pupils are considered and when feelings are aroused. Heedless interruptions, personality clashes, and wrangling may defeat the dual purposes of learning something and of developing the techniques and habits of orderly, democratic group behavior. Setting up an organization after the pattern of adult organizations and using adult procedures tend to lend dignity and preserve order. But the teacher at times may have to perform the functions of a firm but friendly moderator.

Implied in this discussion is the idea that the class will work as a unit. However, discussion groups and other subdivisions such as round tables, panels, and forums may be used to advantage. These variations will appeal to pupils and teachers in the upper grades because they add variety and training in adult procedures.

EXAMPLE OF DISCUSSION, GRADE 5 OR 6

Situation   *Time has been lost by pupils wandering from the point in the discussion of problems in the social studies. The class is a superior class, accustomed to participate freely in discussions and to take responsibility for leadership. The teacher previously has developed the idea of sticking to the point and has directed class practice lessons. The lesson is a follow-up.*

Objective   *To improve ability to stick to the point in class discussions.*

Preparation   *The teacher wrote on the board three problems growing out of the study of Mexico:*
1. Why are the Mexicans poor now when they once had many rich mines?
2. How has the United States helped Mexico?
3. What is Mexico doing for her people today?
   The teacher appointed a capable child to act as a discussion leader on each of the three problems. A research period was given, during which each child learned something about each problem.

Procedure
1. If possible, a circle is formed, so that everyone can see and hear each member of the group.
2. The teacher announces the discussion lesson and has the pupils recall the need for sticking to the point.

3. The discussion leader of problem 1 announces his problem and be-
    gins the discussion by commenting on it or by telling a few of the
    facts about it. He asks whether there is something that can be
    added or whether there is a question. He has been instructed
    previously to try to bring everyone into the discussion and to pick
    up the discussion when it drags. The leader must not interrupt un-
    less members are getting away from the topic. The leader can use
    various procedures to bring the class back to the problem, such as:
    a. Ask the speaker or the class whether the discussion is on the topic.
    b. Reread the topic under discussion.
    c. Ask any member of the group to rise to a point of order when a
    speaker wanders from the topic.
    d. Encourage any member of the group when in doubt to ask whether
    the speaker is sticking to the point.
    e. Enter the discussion at the first opportunity and by comments or
    questions bring the speaker or the class back to the topic.
    f. Keep a running memorandum on the board of the points made.
4. When the discussion of the first problem has been concluded, the
    problem is restated by the leader and a conclusion as to whether it
    was properly solved is drawn by the class.
5. Through the guidance of the leader, there is a group evaluation of
    the class improvement in sticking to the point.
6. The two remaining problems are handled in the same way, improve-
    ment in sticking to the point being noted at the conclusion of the
    discussion of each problem.

Follow-up   *The class is divided into four or five groups, and each group
prepares and engages in a group discussion of a topic, giving special
attention to sticking to the point. The teacher moves from group to
group, advising and guiding as need arises.*

Telephoning

Telephoning, of course, is not an experience common to school
life. We generally train pupils for the use of the telephone in
the home rather than in the school.

Specific objectives Training pupils in the use of the telephone
provides opportunities for the cultivation of certain desirable social
attitudes and understandings and for the development of important abilities and skills. They include the following:

1. Formulate the message or inquiry concisely before making the
    call.
2. Give your name and state the purpose when making a call.
3. Identify your home telephone number in answering a call.
4. Speak clearly and distinctly when using the telephone.

The use of a party line poses problems of courtesy. A person makes
sure that the line is clear before making a call, and he hangs up

promptly when he finds the line in use. Understanding that one answers a telephone courteously when it rings at home is a necessity. Children should be taught how to take messages from an unknown or unidentified caller without relaying unnecessary family information.

Speech and language objectives include brevity, pointedness, speaking distinctly and slowly, and using a well-modulated tone of voice. In addition, certain other specific techniques must be learned: using the directory to find numbers, getting central or dialing, care of the instrument and its hygienic use, and making out-of-town calls.

Situations   Since situations in telephoning are generally situations outside the school, the situation that is set up for learning in the school is usually a recalled or imaginary situation, adapted to the level of maturity of the pupils. The situations represent social uses and include:

1   Calling mother to see whether one can visit a friend
2   Receiving a message for some other member of the family
3   Making an emergency call to a doctor
4   Reporting a fire
5   Extending an invitation
6   Expressing thanks for a favor

Processes   The processes are similar to those for other types of oral communication but require certain modifications. First, the occasion for using the telephone may be created by recalling the uses of the telephone in the home or possibly by setting up a situation where a pupil must make a particular call for himself or for the class. Second, opportunity for discussion is provided, adapted to the particular purpose and to the grade level. In the discussion, a telephone is useful for study and demonstration. Listing steps of procedure may help. Third, pupils can carry on typical, imaginary telephone conversations before the class, using situations such as receiving a "wrong-number" call, taking a message about a Scout meeting for an older brother, and calling a parent at his work in an emergency. Fourth, there should be evaluation of specific points by the class. As demonstration and practice work continue the tape recorder, which allows the participants to hear their own conversation, is a valuable tool. As a follow-up, the pupils can make calls at home and report experiences to the class, noting good and questionable practices. Especially discourteous practices can be highlighted by dramatization or monologue. A representative of the telephone company may explain and demonstrate, or the class may take a trip to the telephone exchange. Thus, discussion, demonstration, dramatization, and reporting are the basic procedures of instruction.[5]

Meetings

Meetings have a place, even if not a prominent one, in the school life of children and, of course, in adult life as well. Training in organized group behavior not only contributes to the effectiveness of the children's voluntary, cooperative enterprises but also sets up situations in which there is a definite and immediate need for certain types of social behavior and language abilities. The training received in meeting techniques should carry over into other types of group situations involving discussion.

Specific objectives Pupil participation in meetings gives point and emphasis to many of the language abilities and skills, particularly those of discussion, and in addition involves certain parliamentary procedures. Specific social objectives in the latter area include gaining the attention of and addressing the chairman, making a motion, discussing a motion, seconding a motion, amending a motion, calling for a vote to end unduly prolonged debate, voting, choosing officers, presiding, acting as secretary or treasurer, presenting reports, observing order of business, delaying action for further consideration, and adjourning.

Specific language and speech techniques concern such matters as having a point and sticking to it, speaking at the proper time, giving convincing reasons for a proposal, organizing ideas and presenting them with clarity and directness, proposing tactful disagreement, avoiding personalities, and speaking clearly and forcefully.

Situations Situations should be natural ones growing out of the organized activities of the children, including class, student council, and club meetings. Need and desire for improved handling of the activities provide the motives for the language lesson.

Procedures The general procedure for directing oral communication experiences applies very well to the handling of meetings.

[5] Consult the local Bell Telephone Company for sources, both people and materials, including the Teletrainer, a device for two-way communication.

The occasion, of course, is provided by some school activity. Participation follows immediately; or if the teacher feels that it is necessary, he leads in a preliminary consideration of organization and procedure. If the meeting proceeds in an effective, orderly manner, the pupils are allowed to continue without interruption. Otherwise, time is taken out for providing the needed instruction and guidance. Children should be thoroughly conscious of the immediate purpose—which is to secure well-planned, reasoned action—and of the value of learning useful parliamentary procedures. They should experience the satisfaction of, and gain confidence from, noting and checking progress in both areas. They should bear responsibility in proportion to their maturity and capabilities.

A third grade organized a book club and then nominated and elected the following officers: president, vice-president, and secretary. The pupils decided that the duty of the secretary was to write down the title of each book reported, its author, and the name of the child reporting it. This information was later printed on a large chart which hung on the wall and was used by the group as a reference when the pupils wanted to draw books from the library. The club met every Tuesday for a half hour. The following is a stenographic report of a part of the fourth meeting:

PRESIDENT (*After taking her place at the front of the room*):   The Book Club will now open. How many have books to report? Neil, do you want to report first?

NEIL (*Coming to front of room*):   I read a book, *Cinder the Cat*. The author is Miriam Blanton Huber. There are seven chapters. The story's quite good, I think. It's about a cat.

PRESIDENT: Are there any questions?

CHILD: Is it real interesting?

NEIL: I thought so.

CHILD: Are the pictures colored?

NEIL: Yes, black and yellow. They're quite good.

CHILD: Is it a true story?

NEIL: No.

CHILD: Is it easy to read?

NEIL: Yes.

PRESIDENT: How many would like this book on our list?

(*The majority votes for it and the secretary records it.*)

PRESIDENT: Who else has a book to report? Jack!

JACK (*Coming to front of room*):   I read a story about Teeny Weeny Town. I can't remember the name of the author, but I'll bring it tomorrow. It's about what they make their stuff out of.

CHILD: What stuff?

JACK: Well, the top of the ketchup bottle was used for a washtub. The characters are a dunce, a policeman, a Chinaman—

CHILD (*Interrupting*):   Aw, that comes in the paper. It's a comic.

PRESIDENT: Any questions?
CHILD: Did you get it at the public library?
JACK: Yes. It's not a comic.
CHILD: Are the pictures colored?
JACK: Some of them.
CHILD: Is it hard to read?
JACK: Yes, for me. Maybe some of you could read it better.
(*Class votes this book on the list.*)
PRESIDENT: Grant, do you want to report?
GRANT: I read two books. One was *Old Mother West Wind*. It's about Old Mother West Wind and all her people—Reddy Fox, Johnny Chuck, Jimmy Skunk, Billy Mink, and all of them. They all get into mischief. They're all the little people of the forest. Jimmy Skunk steals eggs (*chuckles*) and that's funny. The author is Thornton W. Burgess. It's very exciting at the end.
PRESIDENT: Are there any questions?
CHILD: Is it hard to read?
GRANT: No.
CHILD: Did you get it from the shelf?
GRANT: Yes.
CHILD: Are there pictures?
GRANT: Yes, black and white, and they're on slippery paper.
PRESIDENT: How many want that book on the list?
(*Majority votes for it.*)
GRANT: My other book was *Our Farm Babies* by a man named Hamer. It tells all about farm animals and their babies. Tells how they're first born and all about them. The boy's name is Johnny. He lives at the farm too.
PRESIDENT: Questions?
CHILD: Is it true?
GRANT: It could be.
CHILD: Are there pictures?
GRANT: Yes.
CHILD: Is it hard to read?
GRANT: No, not very.
PRESIDENT: Do you want that book on the list?
(*Majority wants it.*)

These reports were, of course, very immature, but the children were struggling with the problem of telling something about the story without telling the story itself, which is something of a problem even for adults. Their experience with chapter books had been very limited. They had only a few stock questions, and replies in some cases were given without much thought. There were few inquiries about content. It was, however, the children's own club, and they were very serious about it. They ran it themselves, and even the slowest readers were interested and reported easy books from time to time. Usually the question "Is it hard to read?" came from some slow reader, and the reply was given in terms of the reporting child's capacity. The teacher felt that she could see progress from week to week in interest, in the number of children who wanted to report, and in the quality of the reports. She saw definite improvement and interest in reading. The day before the weekly book club meeting children were so anxious to finish a book to report that it was not unusual for some pupils to prefer to read during the art or game period. It was felt for this reason alone that the project was worthwhile. Other goals and accomplishments of pupils included greater ease and poise before the class when reporting; speaking distinctly; speaking in sentences; vocabulary growth; ability to answer questions and take criticism; and, of course, greater discrimination in the choice of books and increased enjoyment of good books. In addition to all these points, the project afforded excellent training in sticking to the point, being a good listener, not repeating a question, not wasting time, and participating in simple parliamentary procedures.

Evaluation   In reviewing the preliminary considerations necessary for handling any phase of the instructional program in the language arts, we need to reconsider the planning that must be done by the teacher. Evaluative measures and devices must be considered in conjunction with the framing of objectives. Standardized tests are not available to measure the progress of children in their willingness to contribute actively and to listen actively during conversations, dramatizations, discussions, and meetings. The teacher is advised to develop informal checklists and record sheets to help him assess the growth of attitudes and skills of individuals and of the group. Pupil-teacher evaluation can take place directly after an activity. A major pitfall is to evaluate oral participation in terms of the mechanics of pronunciation, vocabulary, and sentence sense. Although it is necessary to assess these elements, the teacher is responsible for evaluating the more important areas of attitude and content. Listening ability, as an integral part of communication, can be assessed by the teacher largely through the pupils' questions, comments, and reactions. There are several standardized tests of listening ability that have some interest and value.[6] Tests such as these might be incorporated into a school or a school district's overall testing program.

[6] James I. Brown and C. R. Carlsen, *Brown-Carlsen Listening Comprehension Test*, Harcourt, Brace & World, Inc., New York, 1955 (grades 9–13); and the *Sequential Tests of Educational Progress: Listening*, Educational Testing Service, Princeton, N.J., 1957 (grades 4–14).

Listening

Listening as an art is not new in the history of man's cultural development. Long before he learned written forms, man communicated his thoughts orally to someone who listened and who handed them on to someone else. Throughout history masses of people have been swayed by listening.

The importance of listening as a language ability, however, is a very recent discovery; so recent, in fact, that it has not yet materially affected classroom practices. The ability has been taken for granted, apparently under an assumption that as the child matures mentally he acquires without conscious effort facility in listening, or that listening facility is acquired as a by-product of other language experiences. It is now apparent that the child does not learn to listen well either by growing up or through casual experiences. The child does not necessarily learn how to listen by listening.[7]

Listening in life A strong case can be made for the changed emphasis on listening by observing the place it has in the development of the child and in life today. The child's first language is a listening experience. He gains his first ordered knowledge of the world through the spoken word, and the spoken word provides channels for his thinking and patterns of expression. Learning by hearing continues to be the chief means of learning in the preschool and early school years. Parents use oral communication to give children information about food, dress, manners, and playmates. Inspirational talks on moral values constitute a large part of religious education. Play activities in peer groups are carried on largely by means of conversation and discussion. Thousands of words a day are poured into children's ears by radio and television. In sum, the dominance of oral communication is paralleled by the companion activity of listening.

Listening in school Now, bombarded by radio and television, which have shifted interest and emphasis away from reading to a considerable extent, we suddenly realize that a large percentage of our children do not listen with comprehension, or discrimination, nor are they able to appreciate or evaluate what they hear. Listen-

---

[7] National Council of Teachers of English, *Ends and Issues: 1965–1966; Points of Decision in the Development of the English Curriculum*, Champaign, Ill., 1966, pp. 29–30. See also Paul C. Burns and Alberta Lowe, *The Language Arts in Childhood Education*, Rand McNally & Company, Chicago, 1966, chap. 3, pp. 48–69.

ing habits are important. Listening is as much an intake skill as reading. Both require active participation. Listening comprehension is very closely related to reading comprehension, usage, and other language abilities.

The teacher as a listener   In discussing the need for the development of the art of listening in the adult world, Hildebrandt [8] notes that listening is to be considered as an active engagement, not as an automatic response. In listing problems that interfere with efficient listening, this author discusses the factors of attention, understanding, and environment. These factors might well be interpreted in the light of pupil-teacher communication in the classroom; indeed, the teacher himself should consider these factors in analyzing his own attitudes toward the children's oral contributions. Due to the pressures frequently felt in subject-matter objectives, schedules, and attainment goals for the class, teachers are not always good listeners.

Since the teacher is involved in the total process of observing the child, he tends to note the overall appearance, manners, and attributes of the child as he speaks. The teacher may be concerned with the fact that the child looks sleepy or ill and listening for the moment is neglected. Perhaps attention to the content of the child's remarks might aid in the interpretation of his physical appearance. Also, classes composed of large numbers of children may divert the beginning teacher to the extent that listening to individual children in any situation other than a highly structured one seems an impossible task. The mature teacher, feeling secure in his role, experiments with varied approaches so that individual children will have a chance to be heard.

Problems concerning understanding children arise for the teacher. In working with young children, the teacher may find baby talk or a peculiar family terminology that requires some pointed investigation. Children grope for the means by which they can express their thoughts; and the adult listener, thinking at a far greater rate of speed than the child talks, may miss some of the expressed ideas as he predetermines the child's message. Listening effectively to children precludes jumping to conclusions about the nature and intent of ideas that may be haltingly expressed.

While environmental factors of physical setting require con-

[8] Herbert W. Hildebrandt, "Now Hear This—Some Points on the Neglected Art of Listening," in Sam Duker, *Listening: Readings*, The Scarecrow Press, Inc., New York, 1966, pp. 389–393.

sideration in providing the best possible listening situation, the teacher must remember that he himself is part and product of a set of factors, an environment. Seeking to listen objectively to children, the teacher recognizes his own prejudices, attitudes, beliefs, and moods. Ideas that are brought to school by the children, language usage, and vocabulary may all be factors that cause the teacher to miss the import of the children's comments (similar to the situations when the children *tune out* the teacher) because a topic is not understandable or because there is a deficiency of vocabulary background. A teacher with sensitive receptive abilities is one who encourages oral language and who listens when the children talk.

Kinds of listening   Several kinds of listening can be identified: (1) simple listening—telephone conversation, chatting with friends; (2) discriminative listening—animal and traffic sounds, identifying birds by songs, changes in the teacher's voice to express mood; (3) listening for relaxation—poetry, stories, records; (4) listening for information—announcements, answers to questions, listing of ideas; (5) listening to organize ideas—putting together material from several sources, discussing findings, summarizing, distinguishing points made in a speech, illustrating a point; (6) critical listening—analyzing the purpose of a speaker in discussion, controversy, talk or sermon, and recognizing bias, emotion, exaggeration, propaganda, perplexity, irritation, etc; (7) creative listening in the enjoyment of music, pictures, drama—listening to and dramatizing stories, expressing thoughts or feeling in own words, getting from a movie an idea for creative writing.

Russell has analyzed listening activities, and also listening levels, that range from the inexact to the detailed and from the passive to the creative. He has suggested that teachers provide sequential experiences in which children may engage in purposeful listening, termed *auding*, that is, listening with comprehension and appreciation. To fully describe the term *auding*, he has related the process of the necessary involvement in listening to the involvement which is necessary in reading—Seeing: observing: reading = hearing: listening: auding.[9]

Teaching listening   The question arises, How can young children be taught to listen intelligently? Four main principles regarding

[9] David H. and Elizabeth F. Russell, *Listening Aids through the Grades,* Teachers College Press, Columbia University, New York, 1959, pp. 1–4.

listening activities in the classroom are noted by Duker.[10] First, listening should be motivated, rather than demanded of children. Second, within the school day, teachers should adjust the often unreasonable amounts of time that children are required to give to the teacher's oral explanations, directions, and reminders. Third, children should be guided in learning to listen not only to the teacher but to other children in the classroom. Fourth, listening activities should be planned so that children are aware of the purposes to which their attention is directed—obtaining needed facts, detecting a general mood, following a sequence of events, or predicting an outcome. Specific applications of these principles follow.

Without realizing it, many teachers have a habit of repeating every directive as often as the children ask for it. This may be due to nervousness on the part of the teacher, lack of concentration, poor preparation, lack of material—just putting in time; but whatever the reason, it is a careless habit and it leads to inattention on the part of the children. Why listen the first time if the teacher is going to repeat? Many teachers also are careless about enunciation and tone quality. This puts a strain on listening, and under the strain young children soon become tired and inattentive. Why listen if you can't understand anyway?

A pleasant atmosphere for listening and adequate motivation can be noted in the report of the third-grade reading club given earlier in the chapter. Rereading the discussion, one can note the give-and-take of the children and the degree of motivation that was evident in this discussion. By the prior setting of standards by both the children and teacher, this discussion was held without teacher participation, and the children listened carefully to the contributions of their classmates.

For younger children a teacher can tell a story and then, without repeating any part of it, ask the children to recall the important events in the order of their occurrence. The important events can be listed on the board or depicted in a series of pictures drawn by the children, or the principal characters can be listed or drawn in the order of their appearance.

Games can be used to develop the skill of auding and listening. In the riddle game the teacher takes a pair of scissors from a box, some coins from his pocket, and an eraser from the chalkboard; cuts paper, lets water run into a jar, etc.; and the children, who have buried their heads in their hands, tell what he did.

[10] Sam Duker, "Goals of Teaching Listening Skills in the Elementary Classroom," *Elementary English,* vol. 38, March, 1961, p. 170.

Children love sound riddles. Lists of certain kinds of sounds can be made up to help children identify and become conscious of certain sounds. The following list was given by a third grade:

Sounds we hear in the Spring
1   Birds singing
2   Rain on the roof
3   Children roller skating
4   A skip rope hitting the sidewalk
5   Water roaring over the dam
6   The grating sound of sand on bare sidewalks
7   The laughing of the brook
8   Flies buzzing
9   Frogs peeping in a pond
10   Baby chicks cheeping

In the directions game, the teacher gives the children three simple directions to follow, such as: "Go to the cupboard; take a piece of yellow chalk; and hop to your seat." The fun of the game is the realization by the children that the directions will be given slowly but will not be repeated. Or, the teacher can give a simple message to the child and see whether he can deliver it correctly to someone in the class. In playing the directions game and in practicing relaying messages to someone else, the teacher and the children are able to evaluate immediately how well listening is taking place. Handling a simple message in this fashion is similar to taking a message over the telephone at home.

In the music period, the teacher asks the class to listen carefully to a record and to hold up one, two, or three fingers to show the number of instruments or voices they hear. Or, the children can be asked to listen for the different kinds of instruments that they hear on the record. In music also children can be taught to hear the rhythm of working machinery—steam shovel, bulldozer, vacuum cleaner, motor idling, washing machine. They can make up tunes for the sounds they hear.

Routine preparedness for certain listening activities can be established by the teacher and the children early in the year. A simple signal, such as flicking off the lights, or a chord on the piano, can indicate the end of the time devoted to committee work—the time when children put away their work materials, return to their seats, and prepare for the next activity. By assisting in planning the day's schedule of activities, children can learn to appreciate the value of blocks of time. Understanding that when the time comes to take the spelling test, the teacher will pronounce the word, use it in a sentence, and then pronounce it for the final time, eliminates the need for the teacher to repeat any part of the procedure.

Helping children learn to formulate their own questions promotes learning. Why should the teacher have all the practice in asking questions? As children themselves have more opportunity to ask questions and as the teacher demonstrates that he feels that each contribution is worthwhile, the class will feel more compulsion to listen.

Although the teacher systematically builds up the skills, attitudes, and abilities of skillful listening and auding, it is equally essential that children be taught that not all oral information is given systematically. The very nature of oral language in life usage presents a less structured form of thought reception than does the process of reading, where one can reread, outline, or summarize, proceeding at one's own determined rate. Hence, it is necessary to provide children with techniques for securing the maximum information and insight possible from the spoken word. The ability to listen and aud effectively in a world where oral language predominates may assist the child in his day-by-day human relationships by teaching him to accept the opinions of others, to learn to evaluate varying opinions and points of view, and to develop his own power to draw conclusions.[11]

Remembering   Good remembering goes hand in hand with good listening and it is equally important. Ability to remember is largely a matter of organizing thought and associating ideas. Association of ideas, recall, recognition, and retention are important in the development of a good memory. These abilities should be taught, not as separate undertakings, but as a part of daily work. Several means of helping children remember are noted below.

The teacher can discuss with the children vivid word pictures or sensory impressions. A list of colorful and dramatic descriptive words can be developed in class. Vocabulary building is important here because one must have words with which to describe what one remembers. In a talk about a wind storm, third-grade children listed words that described: (1) the kinds of winds they heard—breeze, hurricane, cyclone, tornado; (2) sounds the winds made—howling, whistling, roaring, humming, singing, moaning, screeching; and (3) what the wind did—broke trees, made static

[11] Clarence Wachner, " 'Listening' in an Integrated Language Arts Program," in J. C. MacCampbell and others, *Readings in the Language Arts in the Elementary School*, D. C. Heath and Company, Boston, 1964, pp. 141–147.

on the radio, blew hats off, blew clouds, made windows chatter, made waves in the river, rattled shutters, made dust storms, shook the house, piled snow in drifts.

There is also the familiar exercise of having children enumerate all the articles on a table. Several articles relate to clothing —pins, caps, etc.; several represent food; and several show building materials. The children are shown how to organize the articles into groups.

Organizing powers are further facilitated by the teaching of science and social studies. For example, in studying animals, children can be led to the determination of the various categories by classifying them according to similarities and differences. By determining that cows, pigs, and dogs have certain characteristics in common, children are on the way to classification of mammals. Association of known facts leads to better learning than does the memorization of rules and statements.

For your consideration

1 Observe a conversation or discussion period in a classroom. Note the following: (a) the amount of participation of various members of the class; (b) the individual differences represented by the contributions of the children; (c) the involvement of the teacher during the period.
2 Listen to children's spontaneous conversations outside school and evaluate them. Do the same for adults. Compare your findings. What are the similarities—differences?
3 Make a list of goals and standards for discussion at a particular grade level. Use as your guide a language textbook or a curriculum guide for the language arts.
4 Determine by inquiry and observation children's experiences in using a telephone in and out of school.
5 Develop a lesson plan for the initial teaching of one of the oral communication experiences suggested in this chapter.
6 Discuss: No language arts textbook can ever adequately instruct children in the art of listening.

References

ANDERSON, PAUL S.: *Language Skills in Elementary Education*, The Macmillan Company, New York, 1966, pp. 81–91.

ARTLEY, A. STERL: *Interrelationships among the Language Arts,* National Council of Teachers of English, Champaign, Ill., 1954, pp. 34–40.

BEREITER, CARL, AND SIEGFRIED ENGELMANN: *Teaching Disadvantaged Children in the Preschool,* Prentice-Hall, Inc., Englewood Cliffs, N.J., 1966, chap. 6.

BROENING, ANGELA M., AND OTHERS: *Conducting Experiences in English,* Appleton-Century-Crofts, Inc., New York, 1939, pp. 121–132.

BRUNER, JEROME: *Toward a Theory of Instruction,* The Belknap Press, Harvard University, Cambridge, Mass, 1966, chap. 5, pp. 102–112.

DALLMAN, MARTHA: *Teaching the Language Arts in the Elementary School,* W. C. Brown Company, Publishers, Dubuque, Iowa, 1966, chap. 4.

DAWSON, MILDRED A., AND FRIEDA H. DINGEE: *Children Learn the Language Arts,* Burgess Publishing Company, Minneapolis, Minn., 1966, chap. 5.

——— AND G. C. NEWMAN: *Language Teaching in Kindergarten and the Early Primary Grades,* Harcourt, Brace & World, Inc., New York, 1966, chaps. 3–5.

GREENE, H. A., AND W. T. PETTY: *Developing Language Skills in Elementary Schools,* Allyn and Bacon, Inc., Boston, 1967, chaps. 6 and 7.

HATFIELD, W. W.: *An Experience Curriculum in English,* Appleton-Century-Crofts, Inc., New York, 1935, pp. 138–147, 159–166, 170–173, 176–181.

HERRICK, VIRGIL E., AND LELAND B. JACOBS: *Children and the Language Arts,* Prentice-Hall, Inc., Englewood Cliffs, N.J., 1955, chap. 7.

LAMB, POSE: *Guiding Children's Language Learning,* W. C. Brown Company, Publishers, Dubuque, Iowa, 1967, chap. 4, pp. 343–358.

LEE, J. M., AND DORRIS M. LEE: *The Child and His Curriculum,* Appleton-Century-Crofts, Inc., New York, 1960, pp. 288–304.

LEWIS, T. R., AND R. G. NICHOLS: *Speaking and Listening,* W. C. Brown Company, Publishers, Dubuque, Iowa, 1965.

LOBAN, W.: *Problems in Oral English,* National Council of Teachers of English, Champaign, Ill., 1966.

MACKINTOSH, HELEN K.: *Children and Oral Language,* National Council of Teachers of English, Champaign, Ill., 1964.

MC CARTHY, DOROTHEA, AND OTHERS: *Factors That Influence Language Growth,* National Council of Teachers of English, Champaign, Ill., 1953, pp. 29–32.

NATIONAL COUNCIL OF TEACHERS OF ENGLISH: *The English Language Arts,* Appleton-Century-Crofts, Inc., New York, 1952, pp. 305–313.

———: *Language Arts for Today's Children,* Appleton-Century-Crofts, Inc. New York, 1954, chap. 4, pp. 106–133.

NICHOLS, R. G., AND LEONARD STEVENS: *Are You Listening?* McGraw-Hill Book Company, New York, 1954.

OGILVIE, MARDEL: *Speech in the Elementary School,* McGraw-Hill Book Company, New York, 1954, chap. 9.

PETTY, WALTER T.: *The Language Arts in Elementary Schools,* The Center for Applied Research in Education, Inc., Washington, D.C., 1967, chaps. 6–7.

RUSSELL, D. H., AND E. RUSSELL: "Listening and Speaking," in Verna D. Anderson and others, *Readings in the Language Arts,* The Macmillan Company, New York, 1964, chap. 2.

SHANE, HAROLD G., AND OTHERS: *Improving Language Arts Instruction in the*

Elementary School, Charles E. Merrill Books, Inc., Columbus, Ohio, 1964, chap. 12.

SMITH, NILA B.: *Areas of Research Interest in the Language Arts*, National Council of Teachers of English, Champaign, Ill., 1952, pp. 27–34.

STRICKLAND, RUTH G.: *The Language of Elementary School Children: Its Relationship to the Language of Reading Textbooks, and the Quality of Reading of Selected Children*, Indiana University School of Education, Bloomington, Ind., 1962.

TIEDT, IRIS M., AND S. W. TIEDT: *Contemporary English in the Elementary School*, Prentice-Hall, Inc., Englewood Cliffs, N.J., 1967, chap. 5.

5.

GIVING

INFORMATION

ORALLY

In this chapter we take up a group of language experiences which have the common purpose of giving information but which vary considerably in importance in school and in outside life. The group consists of talks and reports, explanations and directions, announcements and advertisements, introductions, and interviews. Although presenting talks, making introductions, and engaging in interviews are oral experiences, it should be recognized that making reports, giving explanations and directions, making announcements, and creating advertisements may be written experiences also. The study and research aspects of accurate writing and reporting will be expanded further in Chapter 8. Since oral communication is more frequent in terms of life usage, this chapter will be directed toward the oral phases of giving information.

As in the preceding chapter, the most important experiences are taken up first, and basic principles and procedures characteristic of the group are developed in some detail; then the remaining experiences are treated in terms of significant differences.

Talks and reports

The key purpose in talks and reports is to give information; a secondary purpose is to persuade. The information-giving talk is to be distinguished from storytelling, in which the emphasis is on entertainment and in which the specific purposes, materials, and language techniques are appropriate to the entertainment function.

Informational talks and reports, oral and written, have an important place in the modern school program in which children gather material from a variety of sources and pool it for class consideration in the solution of problems. Occasions for talks and reports in adult life are usually less frequent, but they are equally important. As language experiences, talks and reports provide useful training in clear thinking, sound reasoning, logical organization, accurate reporting, and the drawing of valid conclusions.

Some key points in the information-giving experience of reporting may be found in one child's third-grade report. The child brought to school a small glass jar containing a dried leaf and a white cabbage butterfly. She reported to the class: "Last fall I found a caterpillar. I put it in this jar, and Mommy put it in the cupboard. We forgot all about it until last night, when we looked at it and found this butterfly." The children looked at the butterfly and immediately asked questions: What is the difference between a butterfly and a moth? Is this a butterfly or a moth? Does it lay eggs? Does it eat? Three children were delegated to go to the library to find answers to the questions. In the afternoon they reported:

FIRST CHILD: We went to the library, and I found this book that tells all about butterflies and moths. These paper markers are where there are pictures I want to show you. (Opens book and displays pictures.) These pictures at the top show the different parts of a butterfly and tell what they're called—see, these are the feelers. This picture over here is a moth. This is a tiger swallowtail. That's the male and here's the female. I think this is a Polyphemus. Isn't it beautiful? This is like Leona's butterfly. It just says, "common white."

SECOND CHILD: The book that I looked at says that moth eggs are very small, but we knew that. It said some butterflies and some moths dig holes in the ground for protection until their hard shell forms. When a moth starts to fly around it's all grown up. It just took ours a day and a half to grow up.

THIRD CHILD: I found that butterflies fly by day and most moths fly at night. Butterflies and moths all have six legs and four wings. Butterflies live longer than moths, and they each have a pair of feelers and smellers. Then the book told about the knobs on the ends of the butterflies' feelers, but we knew that.

A fourth child, not on the committee, had found a sentence which he read: "No moth or butterfly eats, but some drink nectar from flowers."

Specific objectives   In mature reporting in the later grades, the primary phase of a report is a clear, definite statement of a problem. The initial statement delimits the scope of the talk or report and outlines subdivisions of the problem. The selection of pertinent, valid, authoritative material is another phase of reporting. Materials should be factual, illustrative, and concrete; diagrams and objects are often helpful. In the presentation of the report, the main requirement is clarity, which is obtained by precise and concise language and by an organization or sequence that distinguishes points clearly and shows their relations to the main problem. Outlining is helpful in such an organization. A summary of essential information (conclusions, inferences or implications, and recommendations) frequently comes at the end of the talk or report and provides a comprehensive answer or solution to the main problem. In informational talks and reports pupils should clearly distinguish between authority and personal opinion, and should avoid alienating the group by offensive language or dogmatism. There is often room for honest differences of opinion on important issues; a speaker may hope to convince his audience, but he cannot rightly demand agreement.

In talks and spoken reports, the basic oral language abilities naturally operate, particularly those that contribute to clarity and force: clear, deliberate speaking; looking directly at the audience; emphasizing important points by inflection and pauses; and an easy, natural manner. In written reports all the general objectives and most of the mechanics of writing are to be observed; particularly to be emphasized is the use of the topic sentence, of quotation marks, of bibliographies, and of the outline.

In the first grade, information-giving activities are handled largely by use of the informal conversation and discussion techniques. Sometimes the children like to report what they did the night before. In the first-grade news period reported below, one child sat in the front of the room. Acting as chairman, he called upon anyone who indicated that he wished to report. All reports were given from the front of the room, and the class handled itself.

FIRST CHILD: My daddy gave me some money and I didn't want to spend it, so I hidded it and then I put it in the big bank. I've got $50 now.

SECOND CHILD: Susan and I, before we came to school, Susan and I were playing with kites. Then we decided to do something else, so we went around in back and I found this (*shows old radio tube*). I told Susan it might explode.

THIRD CHILD: Last night I went to a concert with Mother and Daddy.

FOURTH CHILD: I went to a concert too. I had a popcorn ball and I shot a BB gun and hit a thing and won a prize. It was a squirt gun.

In the second grade, especially in the latter half, the children are mature enough to begin to give individual and simple committee reports. For example, a child may have noticed the arrival of a new bird in the spring and wishes to describe it in sufficient detail to make it recognizable to others; or a pupil may have observed the construction of a new house and wishes to report some of the things the builders were doing; or a boy whose father is a fireman may want to tell about how a fireman dresses and what he does at a fire. The organization in these little talks or reports is based on a simple incident sequence or time sequence.

Much use of reports is made in science. In reporting on a bird seen in the early spring, the child should recognize the need for including pertinent facts, such as color, size, song or call, where seen, actions, and nest-building habits. In developing the children's powers of observation and training them in the ability to put essential facts into words, the teacher may begin by bringing specimens or pets into the classroom. The children have a common basis of experience and can compare statements. It may be necessary to direct observation by stimulating questions, such as, What is the color of the bird? What is it doing? How big is it? What is its shape? What kind of song does it have? [1]

A child gave the following report on her trip to Florida: [2]

On the train I slept in an upper berth. I watched the porter make it up.

First he pulled down a shelf that was set up against the ceiling of the coach. It had pillows and blankets on it. He used some of these to make Mother's bed in the lower berth. The others he used to make my bed.

When the bed was ready, the porter brought a little ladder and I climbed up. It was fun to sleep so high up.

Reporting, individual and committee, continues to be a common form of language experience throughout the grades; and standards in terms of content, organization, sentence structure, vocabulary, etc., naturally rise from grade to grade. Increasing maturity of expression may be observed in the study of typical reports at the several grade levels.

Sometimes more detailed lists of objectives are set up for talks and reports. In the authors' judgment it is better to concentrate

[1] Mildred A. Dawson and Georgianna C. Newman, *Language Teaching in Kindergarten and the Early Primary Grades*, Harcourt, Brace & World, Inc., New York, 1966, pp. 104–105.

[2] *Ibid.*, p. 107.

on a few key objectives than to scatter attention over many. It must be recognized, however, that classes vary in ability and that within any class there are individual pupils who are ready for work on higher levels.

Occasions The occasions for giving talks and reports in school appear in those situations where problems and issues arise and where information is available for individual, supplementary handling. The informational type of subject—social studies, science, or health—is an especially fertile source for reports of excursions, observations, interviews, reference reading, and experiments. Such subjects as art, music, and literature supply opportunities for talks or reports on particular artists, programs, and selections. Book reports are valuable as means of extending acquaintance with and interest in a variety of literary works. The business of schoolkeeping, school-life activities such as clubs, committees, and pupil councils, provide many occasions for talks and reports. Other occasions are supplied by magazine articles, radio programs, community problems and projects, hobbies, and home-life activities.

The following oral reports are given here exactly as spoken by fourth-grade children, all members of the same group, during the first month of the school year:

Sunday, my mother and I took our little dog, Bambi, to the vet. She had a piece of twine in her throat.

This vet gave Bambi a needle in the back of the neck, and my little toy terrier is better.

On a TV show I saw "Dennis the Menace," and it was about a boy who got into trouble.

One day Dennis went into Mr. Wilson's yard and took Mr. Wilson's plant and put it in his own yard. Then Dennis took a sweet potato and put it into Mr. Wilson's yard.

After this, Dennis won a prize for Mr. Wilson's plant, and Mr. Wilson won a prize for the sweet potato.

My father, my brother, and me went to visit Fort Ticonderoga. First, we went into a room that had many wax figures of great men. Next, we went into the sun gallery where there were muskets and cannons. In the next room, there were lots of uniforms. Then we went to see where Lake Champlain starts; and we saw many more interesting things; and we had a great time.

I have been reading about famous people in the United States, and one of my favorites was Clara Barton.

Clara Barton was a shy little girl. After a while, she grew out of it. In the year 1832, Clara's brother, David, fell off a barn roof, and she helped care for him.

In the year 1860, the Northern and Southern states began to quarrel, which started the Civil War. Now Clara hated to see men die. So Clara asked permission to go to the front and help the men. Clara needed passes from the War Department to get to the men.

The first personal experience, spontaneously and tersely presented, was spoken by a boy who felt very deeply about his pet's recent experience. Not having sufficient information about the process of the actual aiding of the dog, the class sympathetically asked questions to round out the story; and the boy responded with phrases and simple "yes-no" answers.

The smiling girl who reported on the television program had apparently found fun in her televiewing. Some of the others, who also had watched the program, mentioned other aspects of the plot and the characterization of the principal figures. This report opened the door to the teacher's subsequent work in exploring the world of television with her class.

The third personal experience report was given by a boy who was very much excited about his trip over the weekend. The teacher did not worry about the use of the pronoun *me*, rather than *I*. This was the first time the boy had contributed to the loosely structured "report time" given over to the children in the morning; and the nature of this report to the class gave the boys especially an opportunity for questioning and participation.

The report about Clara Barton was made by a girl who was an avid reader. During the summer, she had read several books about heroines in the history of the United States. The questions that followed from the class were: Did you read about Clara Barton in a book? Was Clara Barton a nurse? Do you know the titles of any other books about her? From the resulting questioning by the class, the groundwork was laid for future pupil-teacher planning in the presentation of oral book talks and book reports. Further, the girl had made notes on a small slip of paper to help her remember the dates that she felt were important and key ideas (War Department and "passes"). This fourth-grade child seemed to be ready for instruction in the techniques of making book reports and in the skills of notetaking.

Key steps   A first step in reporting is to select a worthy occasion. The occasion often arises in connection with a problem or issue under general consideration by the class, or a special committee assignment. The individual who is to report must first select and define an appropriate topic and then set the limits of his treatment.

The topic should be one about which the reporter is interested and has some basic information. It may be a personal experience that he has had or a subject that requires gathering information by interview or research. Often topics chosen are too general and vague for good reporting; the child may not realize that it cannot be treated in a short period. Instead of "Safety" as a topic, the child should choose "Safety in Crossing Streets" or "Safety in Using Bicycles near the School." A study of the use of mathematics in a business office is a better project than a general survey of business practices. The study of weather may be made specific by listing and explaining the variabilities of the weather in a particular area.[3]

Some practice may be given in defining and limiting the scope of topics by having the class consider specific examples. For example, lists of paired topics may be presented to help children judge which of two topics would be the more suitable for a talk-report. Consideration and evaluation of the scope of various topics help fourth, fifth, and sixth graders analyze the manageability of topics. A discussion list of paired topics might include:

1. The Modern Newspaper—The Difference between an Editorial and a News Article
2. Festivals of Mexico—The Celebration of Las Posadas
3. Pets—What I Feed My Dog
4. The History of Boats—The Equipment on Whaling Vessels
5. Benjamin Franklin—Twenty Proverbs Found in *Poor Richard's Almanack*
6. The Astronauts—Special Clothing Worn by John Glenn
7. The Persuasion of Mass Media—What Is a Television Commercial?
8. Superstitions of the World—What I Think When I See a Black Cat
9. Food Production on the Great Plains—The Planting of Wheat in Kansas
10. The Western Expansion—Tracing the Route of the Oregon Trail

In a discussion of Topics and Titles, Martha Dallman says: "Many of the topics and titles on which pupils will talk can be determined by the activities significant in the on-going school program involving the social studies, science, health, literature, and even modern mathematics." However, guidance in selecting suit-

[3] L. Millsap, "Oral Reporting," *Elementary English*, vol. 42, February, 1965, pp. 197–200.

able topics in these fields is necessary. Examples of suitable topics are largely personal: "Tricks I have taught my dog," "An exciting moment on our trip," "It happened to me." [4]

The next step in developing the talk-reporting technique is to give the children some idea of what constitutes a good talk or report. Two procedures have been used by teachers with good results: the experience or the discovery method, or presenting to the class examples of reporting, good and bad, and allowing the children to decide which is better. In the first procedure, the children are allowed to begin giving talks and reports without much preliminary guidance. The children soon discover by listening to each other that some reports are good and others are inadequate. Attention is then given to the good reports, and analyses are made to reveal what makes them good, to discover the qualities of an effective report.

The second procedure begins directly with the study of models. The textbook often provides illustrative reports, and original examples of written reports may be presented by the teacher. Reports of both children and adults are usable, but children's reports are more realistic and suggestive. This second procedure comes more directly to the point of setting up standards, but it fails to provide the desirable orientation to the issues involved that is provided by the procedure which begins with the children's own work. Both methods have the same purpose, and both culminate in a clear definition of what constitutes a talk or report and in a list of specific standards.

As a third step in developing the talk-reporting technique, the teacher may summarize or outline an appropriate procedure for making a report, such as: (1) Choose a suitable topic; (2) limit the scope of the topic to a single incident or phase; (3) outline the main points; (4) add vividness and interest by using illustrative material, examples, details, apt words and phrases, figures of speech, comparisons, and variety in sentences; (5) plan a good beginning and ending; (6) select an appropriate title; and (7) give some attention to delivery.

The last step logically is for the children to collect material and plan their reports. Material may be gathered in a number of ways, varying with the topic. In reporting on a personal experience, it is necessary to recall exactly what happened and how one felt about it and to select the parts that are significant and interesting. If the report is on a topic in the social studies, it is necessary to

[4] Martha Dallman, *Teaching the Language Arts in the Elementary School,* W. C. Brown Company, Publishers, Dubuque, Iowa, 1966, pp. 42–45.

select, evaluate, and put together verbal material. Other reports require interviewing and observing.

Planning a report   Planning the report requires keeping the main topic or problem in mind and organizing the material into significant subtopics or heads. Making an outline, as the gathering of material progresses, will be helpful. This requires judgment in the selection of crucial subtopics and in the placement of related material under the same topics.

For example, in a social studies unit on the Pueblo Indians, third-grade level, the following main problems were established:

1 Who were the Pueblo Indians and where did they live?
2 What kinds of homes did they originally have?
3 What kinds of food did they eat?
4 What kinds of clothing did they wear?
5 What was their family and community life like?
6 What kinds of travel, trade, and communication did they use?
7 What have the Pueblo Indians given to America, and how do they live today?

These problems, naturally, were set up by the teacher and class working together; it would be a mature group of pupils indeed who could compose such a list independently. The problems provided a working outline, a basis for gathering and organizing material. The entire class may take up the problems singly or may be divided into groups, each group working on a separate problem. In either case, a detailed list of subtopics is worked out for each main problem. In the Pueblo Indian unit, under (1), the following subtopics were listed:

a. Where they came from
b. Where they settled; cliff dwellers
c. Where they next moved and why
d. The new country and its climate
e. The geographical features of the country; tree and plant life
f. Neighboring tribes and enemies

An outline such as this is a useful guide to purposeful study. The main problems provide a logical breakdown of the topic of Pueblo Indian life, each main problem sets up a distinct area of study, and the detailed topics under each main problem point clearly to the information desired.

The extent to which children can participate in preparing such a study outline depends on the abilities of the children and more particularly on the training the children have received in doing this kind of work. At first the teacher will have to do much guiding. A good plan is to take a topic or problem on which source material is available to the whole class and to develop together a common outline. Following class development of a study outline, each child may be assigned the task of working out another outline independently, possibly using a common source of material. Language books may provide useful exercises for training in outlining.

After they have prepared their reports, the children may give them to the class or group. During the training phases of the work, the reports are evaluated by the children and the teacher in terms of key goals. Worthy accomplishments are approved, and weak points requiring further training and improvement are noted.

Rapid maturation of ability cannot be expected or achieved; development is gradual. From handling material from one source in the elementary grades the children advance to handling material from several sources at the junior high school level; and the process of reporting becomes vastly more complex and difficult. Inevitably the problem of dealing with conflicting statements and authorities arises, and children learn how to weigh sources, how to reconcile or explain differences, and how to draw sound conclusions and make inferences. The ability to gather and report information is so important in the later stages of schooling and in adult life that the teacher can afford to be patient and to be satisfied with a slow and steady improvement in ability.

EXAMPLE OF PROCEDURE: A GIVING-REPORTS LESSON, GRADE 6 [5]

Situation   *The social studies center of interest was "Living in Greece Long Ago." The current theme about which reports centered was "What Greece Has Contributed to the World." Some information had been gathered on various topics, and previous reports had shown need for improvement.*

Objectives
  1. To improve ability to select the most significant ideas to present to the class, narrowing the subject
  2. To improve ability to organize ideas
  3. To improve ability to present well-selected and well-prepared material in an interesting manner

Procedure

  1. Need for the improvement in reports was discussed.
  2. The teacher read a sample report to the class:

[5] Provided by Miss Marjorie Brewster, former demonstration teacher of the College Laboratory School, Fresno State College.

I never knew until I studied the story of Greece that our form of government began in that country. The Greeks started the idea of allowing all people to help rule themselves. This kind of government is called a democracy. People in Greece were allowed to vote, to choose their officers, to have trials, and to help make laws. I think this was the greatest contribution Greece made.

3. The sample report was discussed as follows:
   a. The beginning sentence.
   b. The narrowness and organization of the material.
   c. The information given.
4. As an outgrowth of the discussion, standards for the reports were established.
5. The children gave good beginning sentences for their respective topics for practice.
6. The pupils planned brief, pointed oral reports, using about ten minutes.
7. Following the planning period, the class discussed the necessity of the audience situation and established standards for listening.
8. Plans were made for taking notes on essential points.
9. Reports were given, organized around the major points of the problem:
   a. Government.
   b. Art.
   c. Literature.
   d. Architecture.
   e. Education.
10. Each child evaluated each report, using a check sheet on which were recorded the standards set up in 3 above.

Problems   Dealing adequately with information requires a thorough understanding of subject matter and the ability to think logically. Problems arise in connection with both requirements; a child's knowledge of the subject may be vague or confused, and he may lack the ability to make a logical breakdown of the subject into key points and to combine related materials. One problem that arises very early and persists steadily involves sticking to the point. A clear, definite, specific assignment, in which the topic is exactly defined by the teacher or class, will help pupils achieve unity in their reports; but if the assignment is vague, the report usually will be vague and confused. Procedures suggested earlier in the chapter should help in achieving unity. Given a specific goal, the reporter may still have difficulty, however, in sticking to it. It is well for the teacher to require, as a fundamental habit in reporting, that the child state early in his report just what he is trying to show or prove. In the evaluation period following the report—or possibly during the report if the irrelevancy is too obvious or wasteful of time—questions of pertinency may be raised. The reporter should have the first chance to judge his own report, but the class and teacher should add their critical comments. In a discussion of relevancy and unity, it may be helpful to write the main topic or problem on the board and to list under it the key points made.

2. A second problem concerns the difficulty of teaching the child to give the report in his own words when the material is taken from books. Often the whole report is lifted verbatim from the book; and frequently words, phrases, and sentences which clearly the reporter does not understand are quoted without source credit. Plagiarism of this sort may be due to unfamiliarity with the material or to laziness and indifferent preparation. It is well to insist on thorough preparation, even if the reports are limited in number or scope, and to have the child put the substance of the report in his own words. Questioning and discussion will reveal shortcomings and will generally tend to secure more careful preparation.

3. A third difficulty arises in connection with bringing together material from several sources and relating it to a particular topic or problem. This is a mature ability which appears late in the grades and the mastery of which continues to give difficulty through high school and college. A clean-cut breakdown of a topic or problem into specific subtopics will help. Mechanical aids, such as the use of sheets of paper or cards for separate topics, may be suggested for extensive reports. Having gathered the material and classified it by topics, the pupil is still faced with the problem of organizing the report. He must decide what the best order of topics is and how to join them in logical sequence so that his report will develop smoothly step by step.

4. A fourth difficulty arises from a fault of the teacher rather than of the pupil; that is, the material of the report is not used by the class in the solution of the problem under study. Presumably the information sought is needed in the consideration of a particular problem; therefore, the teacher should have the content of every report discussed and evaluated and its contribution to the solution of the problem noted. The pupil should definitely know whether he has or has not made a significant contribution.

Explanations and directions

Here we are concerned with information-giving kinds of language experiences second in importance only to talks and oral reports. Outside the school, all people, at some time, give explanations to one another. In the school, much of the teacher's time is devoted to information-giving language experiences, and the pupils also find many occasions for such experiences among themselves, as telling how to make a costume, how to play a game, how to reach the principal's office, how to behave at assembly, how to perform an experiment, and how to perform an operation or solve a problem in arithmetic. A realistic, vitalized kind of language program organized around the actual experiences of children and adults will find an important place for giving explanations and directions.

Explanations and directions should be clear, complete, brief—omitting unessential details—accurate, and well organized. The language should be simple and direct. The organization should be logical, indicating steps to be taken in a proper order. (Diagrams, charts, and outlines may be helpful.) For example, in directing a person to a place, the pupil should tell in what direction to go, how far to go, what left or right turns to take, and how to recognize the destination. And in describing how to play a game, he should tell how many can play, where they are to be, what they are to do and in what order, how to score, and how to know who wins. Explanations and directions, of course, can be oral or written, but they are usually oral. The same general qualities of conciseness, completeness, and clarity apply to both. The written form will make use of lists, colons, semicolons, and dashes.

As to procedure, the teacher will naturally take advantage of real situations to introduce and provide training in the experiences. Good examples may be studied and good points noted. Then follow preparation and practice; through class discussion weaknesses are noted, and suggestions for improvement are made; and eventually the experiences are used in appropriate phases of the curricular and school-life program.

An illustrative procedure is provided by Viola Moseley, fifth-grade demonstration teacher of the Fresno State College Elementary School, showing a well-defined purpose, a clear formulation of goals by means of class discussion, and provision for practice:

EXAMPLE OF PROCEDURE: GIVING DIRECTIONS TO PLACES

Situation   *Education Week was close at hand. The children were to act as guides for visitors.*

Objectives
1. To develop the ability to give clear directions.
2. To develop a set of guidelines by which directional questions can be answered effectively.
3. To develop the understanding that one needs to anticipate and courteously answer questions about directions.

Procedure
1. How are we planning for next week? What is the meaning of Education Week?
2. How many of our parents are coming? How many have never visited school?
3. How will our parents be able to find us? How will other parents find the places they want to visit? (Discussion brings out the need for guides.)
4. All the teachers will be busy, and the principal suggests that our older pupils may wish to act as guides.
5. Have you ever asked a stranger to direct you to a certain place? Could you find it? Why?
6. What rules can we follow in giving directions? Discussion leads to items such as the following:
   a. Understand clearly what is asked for.
   b. Be exact.
   c. Arrange the steps in the proper order.
   d. Be careful of left and right turns.
   e. Leave out details that are not helpful and are possibly confusing.
   f. Draw a diagram on paper, if it will help.
7. Suppose someone came to this room and asked for the principal's office; how would you direct him? Look at the guidelines again. Close your eyes and plan the directions. Open your eyes and check with the guidelines on the board.
8. Individual children give directions to the class; the class evaluates according to the guidelines.
9. In dramatizations the pupils practice giving other directions:
   a. To the school library.
   b. To the lunchroom.
   c. To the several grades.
   d. To the playground.
10. Pupils are chosen by the class to act as guides during Education Week.

Means of evaluation
1. By discussion and dramatization, the teacher and the pupils can determine group needs for future practice in giving directions.
2. Through reevaluation of the developed guidelines, discussions after Education Week may reveal any omissions.
3. In later dramatizations, pupils may reveal the appreciation expressed by persons who received help.

Announcements and advertisements

School announcements and advertisements include news items of interest to the class (dictated by the pupils and written on the board by the teacher in primary grades); memoranda of room duties or other tasks to be performed by individuals or committees;

bulletin-board notices of coming events; notices of lost and found articles; written and oral announcements of school events to parents and friends; poster advertisements of shows and sales; notices of club activities; and information on the decisions of pupil councils regarding school policies and rules of behavior.

The key qualities of such announcements are those that also characterize explanations and directions: brevity, clarity, completeness, exactness, and logical organization. Speech should be straightforward, clear, and emphatic. Written techniques requiring special attention include the use of commas in dates, underlining of titles, listing of items, and use of abbreviations.

The procedure for teaching is practically identical with that used in handling explanations and directions.

Introductions

The inclusion of introductions in the information-giving group may seem to place a strain on logic because introductions are commonly limited to giving name and title. However, proper introductions do more than that; they tell something about the persons introduced, providing points of common interest, so that conversation may proceed easily and promptly.

Situations arise in school in which introductions are appropriate, such as the arrival of a new pupil, a child guest, a mother coming to meet the teacher, guests of interschool play days, and chance visitors. Sometimes class hosts and hostesses are selected to handle the amenities, but every child should be trained in the proper procedures. Outside the school many situations arise in which introductions are required, and acquaintance with the proper etiquette gives the child confidence in social situations.

In making and responding to introductions there are rather rigid conventions to be observed. The child should become familiar with using the proper forms in such common situations as being introduced to an older person or to another child, introducing one child to another, or introducing one older person to another. Of course, meeting people involves not only mere use of the proper words and actions, but also genuine politeness and courtesy growing out of friendliness and interest in other people.

Natural occasions should be used, as far as possible, for teaching the proper procedures; but the teacher cannot always await the actual occasion to begin instruction. Imminent occasions should be anticipated and preparations made for meeting them. There should be a discussion of the occasions that may arise, and definite instruction should be given in proper forms and attitudes. Discussion is not enough, however, to give ease and assurance. Imaginary situations should be set up, dramatized, and practiced.

When an appropriate occasion occurs, such as a school visiting day, the teacher should have the children list the specific situations that may arise. Then follows naturally a discussion of how to make the necessary introductions: Who is introduced to whom? What titles are used? What should one say in addition to giving names? Some children will know the proper forms, but others will have only vague ideas. It is also profitable in the discussion phase of the work to stress the *why* as well as the *how* of making introductions. It may be pointed out that introductions serve to put people at ease, to make them feel a part of the group, and to overcome the awkwardness that often arises when people meet for the first time and have nothing to talk about. It should be stressed that such courtesy gives to the person being introduced a feeling of welcome and that it adds to the pleasure of the host. Children may report experiences at home, and they may refer to the textbook for models of procedure. When all the situations that can possibly arise have been thoroughly considered, it will be well to dramatize typical situations. Children may be chosen to represent various persons and practice the necessary introductions before the class. Each dramatization should be followed by a discussion of key points, noting the use of approved procedures and difficulties. Difficulties should be discussed and possibly redramatized. Practice may be required to give assurance, and the teacher may suggest that the children use the situations arising at home for practice in the proper forms.

Interviews

The interview is important in adult life, chiefly in securing jobs or employees. To some extent, children as well must use the interview for securing positions. In school, there is also an increasing use of the interview as a means of gathering material by word of mouth for use in working out problems in various phases of the school program, particularly in the social studies and health programs. Much of the interviewing is done with parents and friends; but it extends also to strangers—business people, officials, and heads of various community agencies. Specific situations in which children make use of the interview are the following:

1 Soliciting news or advertisements for a school newspaper
2 Asking parents for information on a topic of current interest to the class
3 Interviewing a fireman about his duties
4 Making an application for summer employment
5 Asking the support of a citizen for a school bond issue

Specific objectives concern the attitudes and techniques peculiar to or especially important in carrying on the experience. Because the person interviewed is frequently a busy person and the service is voluntary, it is necessary for the interviewer to make an appointment in advance. The interviewer should be prompt, state directly what information is wanted, avoid wasting time on nonessentials, and leave promptly. The importance of the person being interviewed suggests courtesy in address, tact in formulating questions, and an expression of appreciation for a favor. Language techniques include listing the key points on which information is desired; formulating questions in clear, concise manner; listening attentively to avoid the necessity of repetition; and taking brief notes on key points of fact.

Discussion and possibly dramatization provide the means of preparing children for interviewing. Discussion should bring out the key points noted above. The interview may be planned by the class, key points listed, etc. The dramatization of imaginary situations will help to clarify ideas and provide practice. The results of interviews, of course, should be reported to the class and assimilated. The class may also profitably consider reports of a child's experiences in conducting an interview, noting suggestions for future use.

Evaluation

The evaluation of children's abilities in giving information orally is dependent on the goals set by the teacher, and by his attitudes and expectations for the class. As with conversation and discussion, the teacher's objectives and the situations in which children have opportunities to learn specific techniques and skills determine the outcomes. Provisions for actual participation in these activities create a proving ground where behavior becomes observable and teacher-pupil evaluation can take place. Throughout the school day, opportunities are present that can help the child realize his own growth in the use of oral language, which is, and will continue to be, his main avenue of communication with the world.

For your consideration

1   Discuss: When parents ask their children, "What did you do at school today?" they are in fact asking the childen for oral reports. Determine ways by which you as a teacher can assist the children in this phase of reporting.
2   Make a tentative list of the kinds of information-giving experiences appropriate to a selected grade. Consult the teacher's guide for a language arts textbook or a course of study.
3   Make a checklist of important abilities and skills used in oral reporting. If possible, observe a class giving oral reports and utilize your checklist to evaluate needs and accomplishments.
4   Plan a discussion-developmental procedure for one oral information-giving experience for a selected class.
5   Plan a dramatization procedure for one information-giving experience in which dramatization is appropriate.
6   List the characteristics of successful listening in an information-giving situation.

References

ANDERSON, PAUL S.: *Language Skills in Elementary Education,* The Macmillan Company, New York, 1966, pp. 356–370.

BROWN, KENNETH L.: "Speech and Listening in Language Arts Textbooks," parts 1 and 2, *Elementary English,* vol. 44, April and May, 1967, pp. 336–341 and 461–465, 467.

BURROWS, ALVINA, AND OTHERS: *They All Want to Write,* Holt, Rinehart and Winston, Inc., New York, 1964, chap. 3.

DAWSON, MILDRED A., AND GEORGIANNA C. NEWMAN: *Language Teaching in Kindergarten and the Early Primary Grades,* Harcourt, Brace & World, Inc., New York, 1966, chap. 5.

DELAWTER, JAYNE ANNE, AND MAURICE J. EASH: "Focus on Oral Communication," *Elementary English,* vol. 43, December, 1966, pp. 880–891, 901.

HATFIELD, W. W.: *An Experience Curriculum in English,* Appleton-Century-Crofts, Inc., New York, 1935, pp. 153–158, 166–170, 174–176, 191–205.

HERRICK, VIRGIL E., AND LELAND B. JACOBS: *Children and the Language Arts,* Prentice-Hall, Inc., Englewood Cliffs, N.J., 1955, pp. 137–144.

MC KEE, PAUL: *Language in the Elementary School,* Houghton Mifflin Company, Boston, 1939, pp. 143–160, 195–203.

OGILVIE, MARDEL: *Speech in the Elementary School*, McGraw-Hill Book Company, New York, 1954, chap. 7.

OLSEN, JAMES: "When Children Are Silent," *Elementary English*, vol. 43, December, 1966, pp. 877–879.

PRONOVOST, W. L.: *The Teaching of Speaking and Listening in the Elementary School*, Longmans, Green and Company, New York, 1959, chap. 2.

STRICKLAND, RUTH G.: *Guide for Teaching Language in Grades 1 and 2*, D. C. Heath and Company, Boston, 1962, chap. 4.

TRAUGER, W. K.: *Language Arts in Elementary Schools*, McGraw-Hill Book Company, New York, 1963, chap. 3.

6.

READING

Man has been endowed with the ability to develop graphic symbols that serve as a code for a secondary transmission of thought when person-to-person communication is not feasible. His eyes observe the graphic symbols; he interprets the meanings from his past experience; he reacts in his unique way to the significance he reaps from the written passages. The ability to read provides an individual with the opportunity to transcend time and space. When does this process of learning to read begin? Of what parts is this art composed?

Preliminary considerations

Reading implies wresting meaning from the printed page, and the processes of reading involve the utilization and organization of many essential skills.[1] Reading instruction is composed of three phases: a program of learning to read and the directed extension and maintenance of needed attitudes, abilities, and skills; a pro-

[1] See, for example, Miles A. Tinker and Constance M. McCullough, *Teaching Elementary Reading*, Appleton-Century-Crofts, Inc., New York, 1962, pp. 23–24.

gram of instruction in the reading study skills (reading-research skills); and a program in children's literature.

In this chapter, we discuss the basic experiences of learning to read and the extension and maintenance of the requisite attitudes, abilities, and skills. These experiences include prereading instruction, the beginning reading program, and instruction to develop independence and versatility in reading.

The prereading program

The prebook phase of reading instruction is concerned with teacher awareness of and provision for extending various operational factors of readiness. Four kinds of readiness are recognizable:

1   *Mental readiness*, based on awareness of differences in children's abilities affecting the varying lengths of readiness instruction, the nature of the instructional materials, and instructional procedures
2   *Physical readiness*, involving visual and auditory discrimination; experiences in the development of accurate speech patterns; and visual, auditory, speech, and general health deficits
3   *Social and emotional readiness*, providing a common background of classroom experiences
4   *Educational readiness* through the use of field trips, audiovisual material, records, participation in conversation and discussion, and experiencing basic middle-class English vocabulary and constructions.[2]

Typical situations   The description of typical classroom situations shows the need for versatility and understanding on the part of the teacher. The reader is asked to interpret these situations in the light of the development of readiness for reading and for use in grouping procedures. Activities such as these might be found in classrooms, where the reader might observe:

1   Children are talking with the teacher about the content of a large picture that depicts a playground scene with children, very similar to the discussants, playing in groups, jumping rope, and swinging. Most of the remainder of the children are working independently at work papers, matching letters of the alphabet that have been arranged in rows on the papers. Several children have completed their papers and are seated

[2] Guy L. Bond and Eva Bond Wagner, *Teaching the Child to Read*, The Macmillan Company, New York, 1966, pp. 25–48.

at the library table, browsing through the book selections and picture files.

2 The class is seated on the floor in front of the teacher. The teacher first asks the children to listen carefully and then to put up their hands when they hear a word that begins with the same sound as *boy*. The teacher then repeats the words *cat, box, mother*. The teacher continues with several examples for five minutes and then requests that the children return to their chairs. She asks the children who are wearing red shoes to return first; these then are followed in turn by the children wearing brown, white, and any other color shoes.

3 The children and the teacher have developed a Helpers pocket chart for various daily room duties. As a child volunteers his services, the teacher writes his name on a piece of tagboard after the prescribed duty, which has an accompanying picture clue for identification. In finally reviewing the duties and the children responsible for each one, the teacher moves his hand across each duty-name line in a left-to-right-hand sweep.

4 Using an overhead projector and especially prepared transparencies, the teacher asks the children to repeat sentences that are relevant to the pictures and objects being projected. The sentences include certain speech sounds that are potential trouble spots. The children repeat the sentences and then phrase questions about the pictures and objects; the questions are answered by other children. Sometimes she presents a new poem in this manner, with picture clue and the appropriate portion of the poem being shown and said simultaneously.

5 In a free activity reading time, some children are working in groups and others by themselves. It is six children's turn to hear a story that has been tape-recorded by the teacher; they are seated at a round table with their earphones in place. Several girls have a flannel board and are retelling the story of *The Three Bears* by using cut-out figures that have been placed in a box labeled "Stories We Can Tell." Some individual children are looking at library books especially selected for the science unit dealing with animals and their homes. One child at the chart rack is turning the pages, on which have been pasted pictures painted by the children showing their pets. Several boys, working independently, are on the floor, each matching his own set of large blocks with numbers on them with other blocks that have a corresponding number of dots. Some children are looking at the new bulletin-board display of children's paintings and torn-paper artwork, which have dictated captions on them. During this interval, the teacher assists individuals and groups, when needed; helps in reminding all pupils that each set of materials needs to be

returned to its proper location after use; and provides suggestions for children who "don't have anything to do."

Whether the teacher is using as a guide basal reading materials for readiness, the school district's outline for prereading experiences, or a multifaceted approach in the preformal reading period, the objectives must be clearly defined. A basic requisite to the development of readiness for beginning reading is the check sheet or inventory, in which each child's progress in the acquisition of needed skills, abilities, and attitudes is noted.[3] Informal inventories, kept by the teacher, can assist in determining the progress of individuals and can serve as guidelines for grouping children to meet individual needs. Standard tests, used to assess the degrees of readiness for beginning reading, are available to reinforce teacher judgments obtained through observation and sequential recording activities.

Individual differences   For the beginning teacher, one of the most surprising elements of teaching young children is the range of differences found among them. Although educational psychology, sociology, and methodology textbooks repeat this truism and cite the relevant studies, the differences continue to present an element of surprise. They pose problems in the organization of the classroom and in the selection of appropriate materials. Differences in language facility and readiness to learn to read are apparent in children who are entering the first grade. The teacher will find some children who are already reading at varying degrees of proficiency.[4] Within the same classroom may be found children who have not had preschool or kindergarten experiences, or who have been limited in home opportunities from developing an orientation for the school. As a result there has been wide discussion of the role of the kindergarten in the development of readiness for reading.[5] In the author's opinion, preschool and kindergarten should provide children with the backgrounds essential for beginning instruction in reading. Regarding prereading instruction at the kindergarten

    [3] Lawrence W. Carillo, *Informal Reading Readiness Experiences*, Chandler Publishing Company, San Francisco, Calif., 1964, pp. 21–24. See also Emmett A. Betts, *Foundations of Instruction*, American Book Company, New York, 1957, pp. 229–233.

    [4] Dolores Durkin, *Children Who Read Early: Two Longitudinal Studies*, Teachers College Press, Teachers College, Columbia University, New York, 1966.

    [5] Anne Nugent, "The Role of the Kindergarten in the Reading Program," in A. J. Mazurkiewicz, *New Perspectives in Reading Instruction: A Book of Readings*, Pitman Publishing Corporation, New York, 1964, pp. 129–135.

age, the issues that emerge are those of the kinds of activities to be utilized, the children who will be participating in the varied experiences, the provisions for individual differences, and the continuity of the experiences from kindergarten through the primary grades. To attempt to keep all kindergarten children at the same instructional level of readiness would be as ineffective as the attempt to put all five-year-olds in preprimers by January of the kindergarten year.

The nature of readiness   Another problem that hampers the thinking of teachers is that of the term *readiness* itself. As used in this section, readiness signifies the presence of skills, abilities, and attitudes needed by the children to learn to read; and we have used the terms *prereading experiences, prebook activities,* and *readiness for beginning reading* to describe this aspect of readiness. Throughout the instructional program in the language arts, however, readiness experiences for most tasks must precede the task itself. For example, the first-grade teacher writes on the chalkboard long before most of the children can form the letters. On the chalkboard, the third-grade teacher summarizes a discussion undertaken by the class in outline form before the children have had any instruction in the technique of outlining. In the reading program, experiences that promote reading to follow a sequence of activities, experiences leading to the selection of the appropriate sourcebooks, and experiences preceding the reading of a selection to evaluate and assess critically are equally readiness activities. In short, readiness as a concept permeates the entire instructional program in the language arts and should not be confined in its interpretation to that period of instruction that precedes beginning reading.

Reading in the primary grades

There is no sharp differentiation in the instructional program of beginning reading and that of the preceding readiness program. Children in a first-grade class continue to participate in experiences in which visual and auditory discrimination are refined. Library books, hopefully, are plentiful in the classroom; activities and games that are reading-oriented remain in evidence. Continuing experiences offer children the opportunity to utilize oral communication in conversation and discussion and to extend their auding powers. The teacher remains a model for speech patterns and the agent for the adaptation of children's techniques in speech. Labels on work materials and charts of information that should not be forgotten are in the classroom. Pictures and displays for discussion are also to be found.

With the utilization of a basal reading system, the main evidence of the initiation of a program in beginning reading is the appearance of the preprimers. In the prereading phase, the basal system has sought to initiate concepts and common speaking vocabulary to the children, either in the form of the introduction of characters who will appear in the preprimers and primers or in situations that will appear in their first reading books. Because of the variance in children's abilities, it is doubtful that an entire class should ever embark on the first page of the first preprimer at the same time.

Chief components   In a program of beginning reading the teacher proceeds in the four components of the reading process: (1) word perception, (2) comprehension of ideas, (3) reaction to these ideas, and (4) combining new ideas with old.[6]

In considering the development of word perception and recognition, the techniques that are most effective for associating the the printed symbol with meaning are (a) meaning clues to words, (b) visual perception techniques, and (c) analytical techniques.[7] Briefly stated, (a) meaning clues to words are those techniques of using accompanying pictures to aid in the determination of an unknown or forgotten word; context clues, use of other words in the sentence or in the passage to help figure out a word; and expectancy clues, awareness of specialized vocabulary that will appear in the selection; (b) visual perception techniques include those of the shape or configuration of words and the distinguishing of the personal pronoun, *I;* (c) analytical techniques for associating the printed symbol with meaning are those of phonics understandings. The analytical techniques are understandings of associations of letters and letter combinations with sounds; and structural analysis, understandings dealing with root words and their inflected and derived forms.

Reading implies grasping meaning from the printed symbols on the page. Far from being a passive activity, reading involves comprehending, judging, and reacting to the ideas presented. The child in the primary grades must learn basic skills of word perception,

    [6] W. S. Gray, *On Their Own in Reading,* Scott, Foresman and Company, Chicago, Ill., 1960, pp. 10–13.
    [7] Bond and Wagner, *op. cit.,* pp. 135–173.

ways of grasping meaning from sentence patterns, and methods by which a single page and a story may be comprehended and evaluated. When a first grader laughs at the humor of a situation presented in a story and picture, he is indicating that comprehension has taken place. Also, the teacher knows that the primary-grade child understands the printed text when, in a very mock-serious voice, he orally reads the statement of the father when the children in the story are teasing and joking with him. The child who, after reading a story, exclaims "The same thing happened to me when I borrowed my brother's bike and didn't tell him!" may be indicating not only that he has recognized the similarities of the two situations but that he may be gaining some insight through the fusion of new ideas with old.

The teacher in the primary grades directs reading instruction so that each child is given the opportunity to learn to read in order to find answers to questions and to follow directions. Situations are planned that will give children experience in reading for specific purposes, such as: to follow a sequence of events, to note the necessary details in a passage, to draw conclusions, and to interpret personally. The teacher is aware that reading, as an idea-receiving component of the language arts, is supported by listening activities that are directed toward similar goals.

Typical situations Observable classroom situations reflect teaching objectives in the strategies and materials used by the teacher. In the following activities, try to assess the reasons for the various activities that are typically found in first-grade rooms. While observing that most of the activities deal with various facets of word perception and word recognition, note situations where children are reacting to the printed symbols of reading and combining new ideas with learned ideas.

1. Several children are working at a corner table matching word cards with word-shape cards. The tagboard cards they are using are cut to the basic configuration of the individual words. George has matched the cards

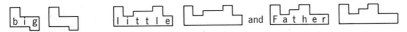

and he has discovered that the words

Father and Mother

have the same number of letters and the same shape, but are not the same words.

2. Nancy is using the dictionary at the back of her preprimer to write her own story about the characters in the book she has just finished.

3. Don and Bill are starting to play sentence dominoes. The teacher has prepared large tagboard cards on which are the written sentences from the stories these boys have read. As each boy matches his card with another, he reads the sentence. The game has progressed this far:

	I see him	Come here		Come here	Spot runs		Spot runs	I run
— see him / — see him								

4. A group of four children is sorting large mounted pictures of single objects or groups of similar objects into piles, according to words that begin with the same sound. So far the children have made two piles. In the first pile, there are pictures of a bicycle, some books, and a boy; and in the second pile, they have placed pictures of a car, three cats, and a cow. The children have just come to the picture of a pencil.

5. Linda and several girls are working at a pocket chart that is hanging on the wall. Using strips of paper with sentences written on them, they are placing the sentences in the pocket chart to show the order of incidents in a story.

6. With a small group of children, the teacher makes the following instructional statements in the directed reading lesson:

Read page 24 to yourselves and find the sentence that tells what Father did next. As soon as you find the sentence, put your finger on the first word and look up at me.

Look at baby sister's face in the picture on this page. Is she happy or sad? Do you ever look like that?

Even though we're not finished with the story, let's close our books for a moment. Mary, how do you think the story will end?

Turn back to page 11, and let's look again at the picture. Do you really think that the bicycle can be repaired?

Can you find the sentence on page 8 that tells what Jane said to her dog? Who can read the sentence the way Jane might have really said it? How would your voice sound if you were Jane?

Open your books to the Table of Contents. Can you find the title of the story we read yesterday? On what page does it begin?

Noting children's spontaneous comments The results of a well-organized program of instruction in reading during the primary grades can be heard in the comments of children. The wise teacher attempts to elicit necessary responses; however, he or she also listens to the unsolicited remarks of children in and out of the directed reading lessons:

Oh, I see! *Mary* and *Mother* both begin with capital *M*.

Red begins with the same sound and the same letter as *run*.

If you put the two words, *home* and *work*, together, you get *homework;* and my sister in high school has lots of that.

Sue's dress is blue. It's blue in the picture.

My brother in the fifth grade told me about question marks.

You get lots of different words if you use *p–t*. You get *put, pet,* and *pat*.

I used to get mixed up with *d* and *b* and *saw* and *was*, but I don't anymore.

I just put *-ing* on *play*, and I got the word *playing* for my story.

If you put *s* in front of *top*, you get *stop*. If you put it on the end, you get *tops*.

Instead of starting all our sentences with *We*, we could change *We went to the dairy today* to *Today we went to the dairy*.

During a free reading time, the primary-grade teacher observes the following explorations into the world of books and quickly notes in her class log:

Bill—continues reading in the book he selected yesterday. He seems most interested in comparing the picture of frogs and toads.

Sally—selected *The Cat in the Hat* by Dr. Seuss and asked if she could read part of this to the class. We'll meet after school today to talk further.

John—working at the science table library to see if he can find another experiment of magnetism that he can demonstrate to the class. Directed him to several books.

Mary and Sally—asked if they could read each other yesterday's story in the reader.

Pete—spent his time looking through a *Jack and Jill* magazine. After checking with me, he worked the puzzle page.

Randy—listened to Joe read his newest chapter in the *Space Man* book and offered some suggestions. The two seem to be collaborating on the illustrations for the book.

Library books The essence of the art of reading lies in the processes of comprehending, interpreting, and reacting. During the primary grades, there is the need for providing books of many kinds—picture books, folk tales, realistic stories, books to meet special interests. Lifelong attitudes toward reading and the values derived from reading are often learned during the first few years of school; and interested listening to portions of books read by the teacher, browsing through books, and intense pouring over specialized but easy-to-read books all are not only a part of the teacher's program of children's literature but represent a portion of the materials in the program of helping children learn how to read. The possibility that some children might learn best by departing on reading ventures of their own, in books they find rewarding and worthwhile, should not be ignored; and the classroom that provides time for teacher-pupil investigation of library books and supplementary reading materials creates a laboratory for learning through different avenues.

Basic instructional materials   As in the prereading phase, the teacher of the primary grades may have difficulty in the selection of appropriate materials to fit the needs of the children in a particular class. Until the 1960s, the beginning books of the basal reading series tended to feature a stereotyped family of core characters. The families, composed of Mother, Father, and several children, lived very comfortably in two-story frame homes, owned a car in which Father drove to work each morning, and possessed pets and play equipment in abundance for the children. In assessing the background of many children in the United States living in less physically ideal homes, who represent several racial groups and who may be members of extended families either in rural areas or in densely populated urban centers, some critics have found the conventional characters and home situations of the basal materials wanting.[8] For these reasons, the content of the basal materials for the young child gradually has been changing. There are several offerings for the urban child in which story characters may have experiences similar to his—in which Mother goes to work every day; city streets and apartment houses are the background for the pictures; and children of several ethnic and racial groups are depicted.[9] Other approaches to the development of reading materials have relied on common situations of play and common objects of the urban environment for story content and vocabulary development. In this approach, children's dialogues and accompanying photographs are used to provide beginning reading materials.[10]

Language-experience materials   The beginning reading programs for children living in rural and semirural areas of the United States have been met by the use of language-experience techniques. An example of a combination approach to language, reading and social studies for first-grade children is submitted by Mrs. Jane Myers.[11] During the summer preceding the entry of the

[8] Frank O. Wargny, "The Good Life in Modern Readers," *The Reading Teacher*, vol. 16, November, 1963, pp. 88–93.

[9] Note *Bank Street Readers*, The Macmillan Company, New York, 1965. See also *Holt Urban Social Studies Program: William, Andy, and Ramon* and *Five Friends at School*, Holt, Rinehart and Winston, Inc., New York, 1966.

[10] Note the *Chandler Language-experience Readers*, Chandler Publishing Company, San Francisco, Calif., 1964–1968.

[11] Teilman School, Fresno City Schools, Fresno, Calif.

children into the first grade, the teacher visits the homes of all of the children whose names are on the roster for her first grade. She becomes acquainted with the parents and the children, noting their interests and expectations for the first grade. She may learn of plans for the family to move before the opening of school, and hear of other families who have just moved into the neighborhood and whose children are not yet enrolled in school. After the initial parent contact has been made, the teacher asks permission to return to take photographs of the family and the child. During conversations, the teacher learns of skills of the mother, grandfather, father, uncle, or foster parent. She develops a list of family resource people who may visit the school later to talk informally with the class in the development of a home-community social studies unit.

By September, the teacher has become acquainted with the children in her room, has made initial parent contact, and has the photographs of the children and their families. The photographs and the visitors who may come to the room provide the basis for a language-experience approach to beginning reading. Individually dictated stories and class development chart stories provide the core of the reading materials for the class.

Coupled with sequentially developed readiness skills, a teacher can use this language-reading—social studies approach until the children seem to be ready to begin the basal reading program. Then, as the basal reading program is gradually initiated, teacher and children still employ the varied language and reading experiences that have been built into the social studies unit.[12]

Contribution of linguistics   Another problem to be considered in the early phases of the reading instructional program has been brought to the foreground by students of structural linguistics. In this section on reading, we have mentioned certain ways by which children are taught to attack words—by configuration clues, phonics, and structural analysis—and we have given examples of these approaches. As a result of overemphasis on the study of individual words, word calling rather than reading may occur. The teacher is cautioned against the overstressing of words in isolation at the expense of structural and meaning-bearing language patterns.[13] Since single words, spoken separately, tend to lose

---

[12] Dorris M. Lee and R. V. Allen, *Learning to Read through Experience,* Appleton-Century-Crofts, Inc., New York, 1963.

[13] Carl A. Lefevre, *Linguistics and the Teaching of Reading,* McGraw-Hill Book Company, New York, 1964, pp. 5–6.

their natural sounds, words need to be kept within a context as much as possible. However, the other techniques that we teach children—the context and the picture utilization clues—will help in giving sufficient balance to a program of reading instruction. In short, a combination of techniques in learning to read is essential; and the issues are not of *phonics* versus *sight word* and *word* versus *sentence*, but rather those of how best to use all of the available techniques, individually applied.

Reference material   During the first few years of school, the stage is set for the purpose of gaining information. While primary-grade children usually do not work extensively with reference materials, simplified dictionaries and encyclopedias are available and How to Make It and Why books are used for work in the social studies and science. Most important, the teacher's attitude toward *Let's find out the answer* and her use of selected reference books to obtain the clarification of a point at issue assist children in understanding that some books are designed to help in the solving of problems.

Individualization   Special interests of individuals are met by a range of supplementary reading materials, and teacher-child record keeping of books may provide incentives for further reading and investigation. A simple 3- by 5-inch box in which children's individual reading record cards have been filed—noting author, title, and reasons for liking the book—may be a prized possession for children. In the short conferences between child and teacher, the teacher can note the degree of comprehension attained and the special problems that may be presented. For the very young child, the teacher writes the comments dictated by the child, and future individual reading plans are considered together.

Reading in the upper grades

The reading program in the postprimary grades and in the classes of the junior high school must be based on the reading abilities that children have previously acquired, the changing needs of later childhood and early adolescence, the need for sequential development of the differentiated reading abilities, and the persistent reading requirements of the curriculum and out-of-school life.[14]

[14] David H. Russell, *Children Learn to Read,* Ginn and Company, Boston, 1961, p. 229.

Tasks In the intermediate and upper grades, Heilman suggests that the following reading tasks should be stressed:

1. Training in reading for different purposes
    a. Noting detail, possibly skimming for specific tasks
    b. Drawing conclusions or inferences
    c. Detecting author's mood and purpose
    d. Evaluative reading or critical analysis, which involves the weighing of facts, opinions, generalizations, analogies, and the like
    e. Problem solving through reading
2. Extension of word recognition skills—phonic analysis and structural analysis with emphasis on prefixes and suffixes
3. Practice in organization of data from reading
4. Development of general vocabulary and expansion of concepts
5. Development of all communication skills through integrating, listening, and composition
6. Broadening interests and reading tastes, helping to build a foundation for recreational reading and cultivating appreciation of poetry and good literature
7. Workbook exercises that develop skill in the use of the dictionary
8. Graded books and workbook exercises for use in reading diagnosis.[15]

The range of reading abilities increases and interests become more varied in later grades. A reading program recognizes the differences and makes provision for a sequence of learning. Children must have time for following established interests and for the discovery of new interests. The subject fields of the school curriculum necessitate facility in reading for specific purposes. A report on safety on the highways necessitates reading for specific facts and statistics that relate to a unit, "Problems of Modern Living." A different reading approach is needed to gain insight into life in the United States during the Civil War, as an upper-grade student reads the book of historical fiction by Harold Keith, *Rifles for Watie,* to supplement the history book outline. In the subject fields, the teacher operates as a guide in helping children adapt techniques and purposes of reading when meeting different kinds of reading materials.

Techniques must be expanded to meet the needs of the reading required in the content areas of the sciences and the social studies —in textbook, encyclopedia, the daily newspaper, and magazine. Work on the techniques of recognizing the printed word, on determining a new word in context, on using the root word and the

[15] Arthur W. Heilman, *Principles and Practices of Teaching Reading,* Charles E. Merrill Books, Columbus, Ohio, 1961, pp. 255–256.

prefix to unlock the meaning of a newly discovered word, on using diagrams and illustrations in the printed text are all concerns of the teacher.

Typical situations   Meeting the curricular and personal needs of the class, of groups within the classroom, and of individuals presents the teacher of the intermediate grades with critical issues in the selection of materials and activities, of pacing, and of helping children assess their own growth in reading. As you read the following situations, refer to the previous listing of reading tasks for children in the upper grades. What activities are designed to focus on reading for specific purposes and for organization of data? Are there evidences that word recognition skills are being extended? Are there situations where children are given an opportunity to broaden their interests and to sample various kinds of literary fare? The first set of situations might occur during the independent work period of the directed reading lesson.

A group of children is working independently, using the materials of the Science Research Associates Reading Kit.[16] Each knows his color level, the job to be accomplished, and the checking and recording procedures.

Using a page from their reading workbook, ten children are underlining statements of opinion and are circling statements of fact. They will work independently until all are finished; then they will compare their findings. In the meantime, several children are using reference materials to substantiate their judgments of fact statements.

One group is rereading a story in the basal reader to identify sections of the story that will be used as acts for a radio script the children plan to develop.

Using a teacher-prepared set of work sheets, some children are reading an unfinished story. When they have read a portion of the story, each will write his own conclusion. In discussion with the teacher and the group, each child will give his own reasons for his ending.

The teacher circulates about the room checking the children's most recent entries in their individual notebooks, which contain records of their independent reading. Through pupil-teacher reports and discussion, books too good to miss will be brought to the attention of the whole class.

Several children are working with the materials of a teacher-prepared file, which contains self-checking exercises designed to increase specific skills of word recognition and comprehension. Each child is concerned with the practice work he and the teacher have determined best suits his needs.

Four children, chosen by the class, are meeting to sort newspaper articles

[16] *SRA Reading Laboratory,* Science Research Associates, Inc., Chicago, Ill.

into categories for the current events bulletin board. The categories, which have been determined previously by the whole class, are Local Happenings, The National Scene, International Life, and Human Interest.

Directed class lessons   The directed class lesson remains a necessity for children in the intermediate grades. The teacher's instructional statements to the whole class, the group, and the individual continue to be important. While many of the examples in this chapter focus on group and individual activities, the need for total class instruction continues to exist. As the teacher recognizes common needs for instruction in reading for various purposes—for work in the more efficient use of the dictionary, for exercises in developing far-removed concepts in the social studies, for greater depth in using the skills of phonics and structural analysis—he uses the class instructional approach. In beginning new phases of reading—such as reading to detect propaganda, to weigh facts, to organize data—the teacher's motivation of the class gives added impetus to the excitement of a new dimension of learning. In committee work in the social studies and the sciences, the ultimate reason for the grouping is found in the sharing of a large sphere of understandings and insights by the group as a whole.

Beyond the reading period, during other periods of the school day, the following related language undertakings might be observed:

Some fourth-grade children are busy writing and illustrating a storybook for the first graders. This undertaking has been prompted because so many of these children have young brothers and sisters in that grade.

A fifth-grade class has gone to the school library for an hour. During this library period, the librarian is spending twenty minutes in discussing sources that might be used in the class study of "The Preservation of Our National Resources." During the remainder of the period, the children are invited to become acquainted with the references and to arrange with the librarian for times when special groups may come to the library for further study. As usual, the children check out books of their own choice.

A sixth-grade class is reading and selecting articles, stories, and poems submitted by the various classes in the school, in preparation for the publication of the first edition of the school newspaper.

The children in a seventh-grade class are enjoying a discussion of the elements of humor found in Richard Chase's *Wicked John and the Devil*, which has just been read by the teacher.

An eighth-grade class is discussing the role of the editorial page cartoon and is analyzing the symbolism used in several recent cartoons in the local paper.

A ninth-grade class is helping the librarian select representative books to have on special display for Children's Book Week. This requires reviewing new books and assessing books for all ages of children. The class is charged with helping develop the most exciting bulletin-board displays possible.

Individual differences   As has been stated, the provision for an adequate program of instruction to meet the needs of individuals remains a paramount issue. Meeting the needs of a gifted child in the intermediate elementary grades and during the junior high school means more than doubling his reading assignments. Perhaps the most seriously retarded readers, in terms of potential, are those who rank as mentally superior students. Special programs to increase the rate of reading demonstrate that remedial methods suited to the ability and interests of the students increase reading prowess of all children and thereby increase differences.[17] Beyond the mutual pupil-teacher assessment of skill attainment and the further development of research techniques, the child who is rated superior in his reading ability should be channeled in his exploratory reading to widen his vistas and develop new interests.

On the other hand, the poor reader faces constantly defeating situations as he progresses through school life. The skillful teacher seeks to diagnose the nature of the child's reading retardation to determine the type of training needed; to decide whether this could be best accomplished in the classroom or in a remedial reading laboratory; and to use the most efficient methods and materials to elicit the child's interest. The teacher further attempts to determine any physical or emotional problem that may block the child's actual growth, while acquiring pertinent information on the child's home and neighborhood environment that may impede his reading growth.[18]

Two potentially promising developments that may serve as aids to the teacher are the school volunteer corps and the reading counseling and teaching centers. Members of the volunteer corps in various communities are adults who have indicated special interest in reading to a child, listening as the child reads, discussing topics of interest with the child, utilizing special practice materials given to them by the child's teacher, providing books for the child to take home, and keeping a diary of events. Reading counsel-

[17] J. C. Cowan and R. W. Scheibel, "The Improvement of Reading in Gifted Children," *Educational Administration and Supervision*, vol. 46, no. 1, January, 1960, pp. 35–40.

[18] H. P. Smith and E. V. Dechant, *Psychology in Teaching Reading*, Prentice-Hall, Inc., Englewood Cliffs, N.J., 1961, p. 425.

ing and teaching centers, providing Saturday classes, are designed to utilize reading consultants, psychologists, social workers, and guidance counselors, who work together for changes in attitudinal and skill behavior in reading. The reading centers, preferably housed in community recreational buildings, offer an attraction to the program if reluctant children know they can participate in sports or take a swim before or after the work phase of the Saturday program. These two developments represent community effort and community involvement in the education of its children.[19]

Materials and organization in the teaching of reading The language arts are closely interrelated and reading is regarded as an integral component of all other language arts.[20] The conceptual approaches to reading instruction are varied. The use or nonuse of a series of readers, grouping procedures for reading instruction, and viewpoints regarding methods of teaching are being examined continually by educators.[21]

Basal reading programs Series of readers and their accompanying materials, workbooks, and teacher's guides generally are used to provide a framework for instruction in reading. These books and materials, developed by one or more authors, imply a basal reading system that usually includes a program of reading from the prereading phase through grade 6. Many publishing companies provide books, frequently in the form of anthologies, which continue a program of reading instruction through the junior and senior high school years.

The teacher's guides for reading series provide assistance in the use of readers and workbooks, in developing and maintaining needed reading skills, in planning informal evaluative measures, and in providing enrichment activities that relate reading to the other components of the language arts and to the other activities of the school day. For the beginning teacher, the suggestions for the organization of reading lessons and grouping procedures are probably the most significant contributions of the teacher's guide.

[19] Shelley Umans, *New Trends in Reading Instruction*, Teachers College Press, Teachers College, Columbia University, New York, 1963.

[20] Ruth G. Strickland, "Reading in Its Setting—The Language Arts," in J. C. MacCampbell and others, *Readings in the Language Arts in the Elementary School*, D. C. Heath and Company, Boston, 1964, p. 451.

[21] See Mary C. Austin and others, *The Torch Lighters: Tomorrow's Teachers of Reading*, Harvard University Press, Cambridge, Mass., 1961; and *The First R: The Harvard Report on Reading in Elementary Schools*, The Macmillan Company, New York, 1963.

Special grouping   The grouping of children for reading instruction traditionally has been undertaken by teacher observation-assessment of reading skills and abilities, by informal inventories, and by the results of standardized reading tests. For several decades, conventional grouping for reading has tended to be that of the three-group system—the above average, the average, and the below average achievers—often to the detriment of children who realize fully why they are in Johnny's group or group 3. Criticism has been leveled against the lockstep of the grouping system and the resulting attitudes developed by children. Grouping should not imply that each child in a particular group completes identical assignments and tasks at each point in the reading lesson. Grouping need not result in children's immobility, but should be characterized as a means by which direction can be given to learning while at the same time it serves as a flexible instrument for meeting special needs.

Russell has suggested four facets of grouping to facilitate learning: special needs grouping, research grouping, interest grouping, and partner or pupil-leader grouping. Special needs grouping brings together children who share mutual needs in word recognition skills, certain aspects of the reading study skills, encouragement of wide reading for recreational purposes. Research grouping is based on the special needs of individuals and committees in carrying out reports and projects in curricular areas, such as science and the social studies. Children sharing similar interests in reading form the basis of interest-grouping possibilities in which discoveries are shared through the use of a wide range of easy to difficult-to-read books. Partner grouping and pupil-leader grouping are based on the pairing of children to attack common problems that arise during the day in the various subject areas.[22]

Evaluation   The evaluation of a reading program is based on the objectives of the program and involves not only the teacher and the pupils in a given classroom, but the total staff of the school, which provides for the continuity of reading instruction and of necessity for its continuous appraisal. A concomitant school responsibility is the development of cumulative record cards or folders for each child, containing significant data relating to personal reading development, specific reading attainments, and interpretation of scores on standardized reading tests. Basic information on each child's attainments offers a starting point for instruction at the beginning of each school year and facilitates continuity and sequence through the elementary and secondary levels.

[22] Russell, *op. cit.*, pp. 497–499. See also Umans, *op. cit.*, pp. 59–104.

The teacher studies the problems arising in reading situations throughout the day; he analyzes children's responses in the directed reading lessons, and notes the individual differences in skill attainments in independent work phases. He seeks to keep adequate records of children's work and checklists of group and individual progress. He observes children's attitudes toward books and their abilities to use resources for information and for recreation. Through records and observations, the teacher may be able to adapt techniques, differentiate instruction, and provide meaningful materials to facilitate learning.

The teacher provides opportunities to children for self-appraisal of their growth by entering into a teacher-child partnership in which both use the results of informal reading inventories and tests for further work in special needs. As a child progresses through the grades, he should participate in the assessment of his progress in reading for specific purposes, as in content and rate. Results of comprehension and rate exercises and self-checking practice materials can be filed in his folder, or in the individualized or teacher-kept record box. Teacher and child use the results of interviews, questionnaires, inventories, and tests as springboards for further reading.[23]

Other reading approaches

The need to teach reading successfully to all children in the United States has never been so great. During the second half of the twentieth century, multiple approaches to the teaching of reading have been developed. The following discussion is intended to acquaint the reader with some of these diverse approaches, and to note sources that will more fully present the intent, the procedures, and the materials of these programs. Noting the similarities and differences of the various approaches, even in the capsule summaries that follow, may be of interest to the reader; and suggestions for making minor adaptations to the basal reading program heretofore described may emerge.

Individualized reading   The terms *personalized reading, extensive reading, individualized reading,* and *self-selection reading* have been used to name the processes of helping children to gain the desired attitudes, abilities, and skills of reading through an indi-

[23] Ruth Strang, *Development in and through Reading,* Sixtieth Yearbook of the National Society for the Study of Education, part 1, University of Chicago Press, Chicago, Ill., 1961, pp. 376–397.

vidual child-and-his-book approach rather than through the group-and-their-book approach to the basal reading program. Jeanette Veatch outlines the basic assumptions of her approach to individualized reading instruction. First, each classroom must have a great variety of reading materials. Second, reading instruction depends on children's own speech. Third, by investigating books in the classroom and library, children generally will make their own choice of books, thus developing incentive and self-motivation. And fourth, the teacher's conference with the individual child provides for both teacher and child understanding of reading progress.[24]

The main emphases of the individualized program lie in the self-selection of books by individuals, in the self-pacing concept of learning to read fluently and comprehendingly, and in the teacher's interest in the progress of individuals. Various programs in action provide flexible grouping arrangements for the children to facilitate skill learnings and the sharing of mutual interests. Inherent in this concept of reading instruction is the teacher's conscientious planning and organization of time for reading, for grouping, for pupil-teacher conferences, and for adequate record keeping.[25]

The language-experience approach   Based on the premise that reading is completely interwoven with all the other language arts, the language-experience approach to reading represents another departure from the basal reading program. As an exponent of the language-experience approach, R. V. Allen seeks to help children develop certain concepts about themselves and reading so that they will have a framework, of which meaningful skills may become a part. The conceptual framework is developed through a sequence that is, in part, represented by the following behaviors: first, what a child thinks about he can talk about; second, what he can talk about can be expressed in painting, writing, or some other form; third, anything he writes can be read; and fourth, he can read what he writes and what other people write.[26]

In this program the total interrelationship of the language arts—sharing, discussing, listening, reading, writing, and out-lining—is the major component of the instructional program.

[24] Jeanette Veatch, *Reading in the Elementary School,* Ronald Press Company, New York, 1966, p. 4.

[25] Nila B. Smith, *Reading Instruction for Today's Children,* Prentice-Hall, Inc., Englewood Cliffs, N.J., 1963, chap. 7.

[26] Dorris M. Lee and R. V. Allen, *Learning to Read through Experience,* Appleton-Century-Crofts, New York, 1963, pp. 5–7.

Dictated stories and group-created charts are the chief reading materials of the young child.

Linguistics and the teaching of reading Recently, linguistics has been used in making certain applications to the teaching of reading. Some of this work has been undertaken by the structural linguists, who are "primarily interested in discovering and describing as concisely as possible the interrelationships and patterns which make up the intricate structure of language." [27]

Certain other linguists have directed their attention toward the development of the mastery of the correspondence between the grapheme—a significant unit of graphic shape—and the phoneme —a significant unit of speech sound.[28] For example, in Bloomfield and Barnhart's *Let's Read,* children learn symbol-sound or grapheme-phoneme correspondence through regularly spelled words in reading materials. They learn the alphabet and read specific lists of words and sentences, at first utilizing only the *short* sounds of vowels, such as: *Ann had a bag* and *Nat had a nag.*[29]

Working from still another point of view, Lefevre presents an approach to reading through understanding the intonation patterns of American English. The oral-written relationship of language is again emphasized in the study of intonational shapes and patterns of utterances in statements, requests, and questions. Understanding of structural sentence elements (noun groups, verb groups, prepositional phrases, subordinate clauses, and of the structure or function words that mark such groups) is a part of this approach. Understanding of the four form classes (nouns, verbs, adjectives, adverbs) and their regular inflections completes the major considerations in comprehension of the relationships between the larger speech patterns and their printed representations. He indicates that a starting point for reading instruction lies in the use of children's comments on the experience chart.[30]

The reader is directed to the comments of McKee and Durr, "Notes on Linguistics," on various linguistic approaches and their applications to the teaching of reading.[31]

[27] Francis W. Nelson, *The Structure of American English,* Ronald Press Company, New York, 1958, p. 26.
[28] Leonard Bloomfield, "Linguistics and Reading," *The Elementary English Review,* April–May, 1942, pp. 125–130 and 183–186. See also C. C. Fries, *Linguistics and Reading,* Holt, Rinehart and Winston, Inc., New York, 1962.
[29] Leonard Bloomfield and C. L. Barnhart, *Let's Read, A Linguistic Approach,* Wayne State University Press, Detroit, Mich., 1961, p. 2.
[30] Lefevre, *op. cit.,* pp. xvi–6.
[31] Paul McKee and W. K. Durr, *Reading: A Program of Instruction for the Elementary School,* Houghton Mifflin Company, Boston, 1966, pp. 175–193.

Reading programs and the Initial Teaching Alphabet   In England, Sir James Pitman designed the Pitman Augmented Alphabet, which contains forty-four characters instead of the twenty-six letters that are in our conventional alphabet. This alphabet has become known as the Initial Teaching Alphabet, or i.t.a., and has been devised to present a more consistent printed code for the English language. The approach in the development and use of i.t.a. has been that of controlling the medium, alphabet and spelling, in which beginning reading books are printed.[32]

The i.t.a. attempts to make the correspondence of sound to printed symbol more regular for beginning readers, and it eliminates the use of capital letters. Materials printed in the Initial Teaching Alphabet have been in use in England since 1960. In the United States books, such as those by Mazurkiewicz and Tanyzer, are being used for the teaching of beginning reading.[33] On-going programs of teaching reading by the use of i.t.a. materials are being undertaken in various parts of the United States, and the reader is encouraged to read the reports that discuss current reactions and findings.[34]

In the sixties, the Cooperative Research Branch of the U.S. Office of Education supported separate coordinated research projects on beginning reading instruction. First-grade reading methods investigated and included are (1) basic reading, (2) language experience, (3) linguistic emphasis, (4) phonetic emphasis, (5) individualized reading, (6) initial teaching alphabet, (7) audio-visual approaches, (8) reading readiness, (9) approaches for the culturally different, and (10) inservice programs and other approaches. The prospective teacher is encouraged to read the reports of the studies that appear in educational periodicals. In summing up observations from the resulting data, Kerfoot noted, "One of the most important general observations to be drawn from the First Grade Studies is that teacher effect appeared to be greater than method effect."[35]

[32] John Downing, *The Initial Teaching Alphabet Explained and Illustrated*, The Macmillan Company, New York, 1964.

[33] A. J. Mazurkiewicz and H. J. Tanyzer, *Easy-to-read Series*, Initial Teaching Alphabet Publications, New York, 1963–1964.

[34] J. T. Howden, "Exploring the Initial Teaching Alphabet," *The First R*, California Elementary School Administrators Association, Burlingame, Calif., 1966, pp. 21–22. See also S. Tengan, "Initial Teaching Alphabet," in H. A. Robinson, *Recent Developments in Reading*, University of Chicago Press, Chicago, Ill., 1965, pp. 61–64.

[35] James F. Kerfoot, "Reading in the Elementary School," *Review of Educational Research*, vol. 37, no. 2, April, 1967, p. 123.

For your consideration

1   Review the teacher's guides for several series of basal readers
and compare the following: (*a*) the definition of the program;
(*b*) the components of reading instruction; (*c*) special considerations that have been incorporated into the series (child
growth and development principles, socioeconomic factors,
child-interest consideration, etc.); (*d*) the provision for a
sequential program of instruction from the prereading phase
through grade 6 or grade 9.

2   Select a grade or age level, and investigate a basal reading
program's offerings: teacher's guide, children's readers, accompanying workbooks, and other instructional materials.

3   Compare a current reader (content, illustrations, type style,
and format) with a reader of thirty years ago. What are your
findings?

4   Using a course of study, a reading methods textbook, or the
teacher's guide for a basal reading series, outline the procedures
that you feel are essential in any directed lesson.

5   Assume that it is the beginning of school and you wish to become acquainted with your children's reading interests, abilities, and skills as quickly as possible. List ways in which you
can assess the children's backgrounds in reading.

6   To discuss: Considering all the opportunities and necessities
for reading throughout the school day with any given group of
children, it is quite possible that some children will be over-
whelmed by the many tasks of reading.

References

ALLEN, ROACH VAN, AND CLARYCE ALLEN: *Teacher's Resource Book: Language
Experiences in Reading,* Encyclopaedia Britannica Press, Chicago, Ill.,
1966.

AUSTIN, MARY C., AND OTHERS: *Reading Evaluation: Appraisal Techniques for
School and Classroom,* Ronald Press Company, New York, 1961.

COHEN, S. ALAN: "Teaching Reading to Disadvantaged Children," *The Reading
Teacher,* vol. 20, February, 1967, pp. 433–435. Reviewed in the *Education Digest,* May, 1967, pp. 40–42.

CUTTS, WARREN G.: *Modern Reading Instruction,* The Center for Applied Research in Education, Inc., Washington, D.C., 1964.

DECHANT, EMERALD V.: *Improving the Teaching of Reading,* Prentice-Hall,
Inc., Englewood Cliffs, N.J., 1964.

DOWNING, JOHN: "The i/t/a Reading Experiment," *The Reading Teacher*, vol. 17, November, 1964, pp. 105–110.

FITZGERALD, J. A., AND P. G. FITZGERALD: *Teaching Reading and the Language Arts*, Bruce Publishing Company, Milwaukee, Wis., 1965, chaps. 4–7.

FRIES, C. C.: *Linguistics and Reading*, Holt, Rinehart and Winston, Inc., New York, 1963.

FROST, JOE L., AND OTHERS: *The Disadvantaged Child*, Houghton Mifflin Company, Boston, 1966, pp. 289–300.

GREENE, H. A., AND W. T. PETTY: *Developing Language Skills in Elementary Schools*, Allyn and Bacon, Inc., Boston, 1967, chap. 14.

HARRIS, A. J. (ED.): *Readings on Reading Instruction*, David McKay Company, Inc., New York, 1963.

HODGES, R. E.: "Linguistics, Psychology, and the Teaching of English," *Elementary School Journal*, vol. 66, January, 1966, pp. 208–213.

HUUS, HELEN: "Developing Reading Readiness," *The Instructor*, March, 1965, pp. 59–60.

LAMB, POSE: *Linguistics in Proper Perspective*, Charles E. Merrill Books, Inc., Columbus, Ohio, 1967, chap. 2.

LEE, J. MURRAY, AND DORRIS M. LEE: *The Child and His Curriculum*, Appleton-Century-Crofts, Inc., New York, 1960, pp. 310–340.

LEFEVRE, CARL A.: *Writing by Patterns*, Alfred A. Knopf, Inc., New York, 1965.

MC KIM, MARGARET G., AND HELEN CASKEY: *Guiding Growth in Reading in the Modern Elementary School*, The Macmillan Company, New York, 1963.

MARCKWARDT, A. H.: *Linguistics and the Teaching of English*, Indiana University Press, Bloomington, Ind., 1966, chap. 6.

NATIONAL SOCIETY FOR THE STUDY OF EDUCATION: *Development in and through Reading*, Sixtieth Yearbook, part 1, University of Chicago Press, Chicago, 1961.

STAIGER, RALPH, AND DAVID A. SOHN: *New Directions in Reading*, Bantam Books, Inc., New York, 1967.

STAUFFER, R. G. (ED.): *The Reading Teacher*, University of Delaware, Wilmington, Del., International Reading Association, vol. 20, 1966–1967.

TYLER, P.: "Linguistics in the Elementary School," *Elementary English*, vol. 42, December, 1965, pp. 843–844.

WITTY, PAUL A., AND OTHERS: *The Teaching of Reading*, D. C. Heath and Company, Boston, 1966.

7.

WRITING
LETTERS

With an agile thumb, forefinger, and wrist, inventive man has developed the stylus, the brush, the graphite pencil, and the ball-point pen to transmit his thoughts via graphic symbol systems onto clay, papyrus, parchment, foolscap, and bond paper. What do people write? At what place and at what time do we begin instruction in writing?

Preliminary considerations

Letters and invitations are likely to be the first kind of purposeful written language experiences in which children engage, aside from their signatures on written exercises and from labels and titles identifying pictures, objects, and written exercises. Before written work is begun, oral language has been used in and out of school for years as a means of communication. The children have built up a store of communicative experiences and ideas, and they have acquired the vocabulary, control of the sentence, and various other abilities and skills that make possible the oral expression of ideas for ordinary purposes.

Beginning written work; relation between oral and written

Primary emphasis is placed on oral work in the preschool, kindergarten, and first grade, but preparation for beginning written work is started very early. The children observe the teacher as she writes names, assignments of duties, records, and notes on the chalkboard. As soon as the children acquire a small, basic reading vocabulary, they begin to observe the written forms of words; they read sentences; they engage in class-cooperative enterprises such as making experience charts, which are dictated to the teacher for writing on the board; and they notice sentences, capitals, and periods. Individual writing must be delayed, however, until some progress has been made in spelling and handwriting. Writing begins with simple, purposeful, individual activities, such as signatures and labels. Then follows copying a simple communication dictated by the children and written by the teacher, such as:

> Dear Mother,
>> Please come to our party.
>>>> Louise

There seem to be several schools of thought regarding the written work of children. There are those who emphasize the mechanical correctness of written work from the beginning. On the other hand, there are those who deplore the limitations of overexacting standards in free expression and who urge children in the early primary grades to express themselves in writing with something of the same naturalness that they use in oral work. The teacher may set down children's stories as they are individually dictated.[1] For extensive individual writing, children are allowed to write freely, giving as much of a word as is required for identification—usually the beginning—or spelling the word as it sounds, and omitting marks of punctuation. Naturally, the children are held responsible for the technicalities they have already studied, but the teacher takes care of the other technicalities in putting the written work in final form. This general policy is used through the grades until the children have had opportunity to learn all the technicalities of writing. Conservative teachers are fearful of the persistence of careless errors habitually made in free writing. Less conservative teachers feel that the danger of persistent errors is smaller than the danger of cramping the child's thinking and restricting his satisfaction in the free use of vocabulary, sentence

[1] Alvina Trent Burrows and others, *They All Want to Write,* Holt, Rinehart and Winston, Inc., New York, 1964, pp. 36–41.

forms, direct discourse, figures of speech, and the like. The authors favor freedom of expression in early work and later, but on the condition that the children fully understand the situation and do not use their freedom as an excuse for careless work. The position on the point taken by a teacher will be clearly reflected in the character of written work that appears in the early grades. Habits and abilities developed in oral work will appear in written work with increasing vividness and clarity; and the teacher will find very soon that several phases of oral and written work are combined in various experiences and that to some extent growth in both proceeds simultaneously.

The friendly letter

Although the early written language of the children takes a variety of forms and serves a number of purposes, the friendly letter soon emerges as the most common form of written language and continues in importance through and beyond the school life of the child. As noted above, the beginning is a very simple form of communication, but it gains in wealth of ideas and in freedom and variety of expression with the years. The primary purpose of the friendly letter is to provide entertainment; a secondary purpose is to give information. The entertainment purpose gives the friendly letter its distinctive literary quality, characteristic of all creative work.

Specific objectives Friendly-letter writing draws largely from the general language objectives discussed in Chapter 4, Speaking and Listening, and shares these in part with other forms of written communication. Primarily important is attitude—willingness to write. For many people, writing a letter is a chore, not a pleasure. If the teacher can show children that letter writing is fun, he will set up conditions for initiating the experience and improving quality.

Closely associated with interest is pride and satisfaction in doing a good job. Some people obviously enjoy writing letters. For them, writing letters is a creative experience; they get satisfaction from the expression of ideas in appropriate language, such as one gets in writing a story or a play. It is possible that with proper instruction the number who derive this pleasure can be increased.

A third major consideration is courtesy. Courtesy should be assumed inasmuch as the letter is a *friendly* one, but children need instruction in specific points of etiquette and in proper attitudes toward other people. Courtesy appears in the choice of form of address and of a complimentary close suitable to the occasion. It also appears in the ideas expressed. In discussing the contents of a thank-you note, Applegate says: [2]

> Now let's plan the contents of the note. What shall we say? We can't, like the little girl, write: "Dear Grandmother, I have always wanted a pincushion for Christmas—but not very much." Nor as my nephew once wrote to his grandmother: "Thank you for the skates. They're nice, but I already had a pair." Of course you can be honest, but you don't have to blurt out all you know. Manners, remember, indicate thoughtfulness of others. How would you feel if you were a grandmother and had made by hand, perhaps with shaky fingers, a pincushion for your granddaughter, and she wrote that she'd always wanted a pincushion but not very much? How would you feel? Or about the skates? How will the grandmother feel if you tell her you already have skates? You see, we always tell the truth in a letter, but we leave out that part of the truth that would hurt the giver if we told it. That's what you're really thanking the giver for—for thinking enough of you to send you a present at all.

Fourth, the difference between the empty, fatuous letter and the richly entertaining one is primarily a matter of content. Difficulties appear in the choice of what to say and of too many or too few details. If one is on a trip and enjoying a variety of experiences, he may sum up the matter laconically by saying that he is having a marvelous time. At the other extreme, he bores his reader by giving a mere catalogue of places and dates. It is better to choose a single incident or event and to elaborate on it, giving the setting, what happened, and especially one's observations on and feelings about what happened. Perhaps there has been one big center of interest that will loom larger than anything else the class has been doing. If the children instantly pounce upon such a topic, by all means develop it at once. Should the whole letter center about this topic, so much the better. There will be opportunity for many interesting details.

The children should be encouraged to develop the topic, including, besides the mere facts, their opinions and emotional reactions. Stimulate them to think of vivid descriptive words. If something funny has happened, be sure to include it. Humor is usually appreciated in a social letter.

The following is a group letter written by a second-grade class to Shirley when she had the measles:

[2] Mauree Applegate, *Easy in English*, Harper & Row, Publishers, Inc., New York, 1960, pp, 405–406. Quoted with special permission of author and publisher.

Dear Shirley,

We have been studying about wool. We saw colored slides and pictures of sheep. One day we went to Mrs. Johnson's room to see a big loom, and what do you think she let us do? She let us finish weaving a rug which her class had started. Here in our room we have started weaving little rugs on hand looms. We are going to use the prettiest ones in our doll house. Several of the boys made looms of their own at home. Three of us are weaving woolen caps for our dolls.

We finished *The Eskimo Twins*. It was very funny at the end. The Angokok got so fat that the boys suggested pulling him behind the boat like a dead seal.

We hope that you can come to school again very soon.

Sincerely,
Your Class

Content is important in adult letters also.[3] The American public is mobile—families move from one location to another; an increasing number of students study abroad during one of their college years; Peace Corps volunteers leave the United States for two-year tours; men in the armed forces serve in many locations on the globe. Of these servicemen, Burgess says, "What they want in letters from home are the little household details: How the cat upset the can of milk all over the kitchen floor; how sister gave up smoking; how that cheeky Lester gal is still running after Bob Hale. Snapshots, that's what people want, in these intimate, friendly letters."[4]

In discussing letters, Amy Vanderbilt says:[5]

If you think of letter writing as conversation put on paper, it's much easier to produce a readable missive. We used to be told that it was ill-mannered to talk about ourselves and what we were doing, but to keep social letters on a high impersonal level is to make them dull. . . . Everyone likes to talk about himself and is usually more entertaining when he talks about what he's doing and what's going on around him, what touches and moves him, than he is if he struggles to keep his comments away from strictly personal matters. Gossip belongs in social letters, gossip in the friendly interested sense about friends in common, about births, deaths, successes, and little disappointments. These are the things you would tell a friend face to face, so why bore him with talk of the weather when what he wants to know about is you?

[3] Donald C. Peattie, "I've Been Meaning to Write," *The Reader's Digest*, May, 1963, 228D–228E.

[4] Gelett Burgess, "The Simple Art of Writing Letters," *The Reader's Digest*, May, 1948, p. 49.

[5] Amy Vanderbilt, *New Complete Book of Etiquette*, Doubleday and Company, Inc., Garden City, N.Y., 1963, p. 412. Quoted with special permission of author and publisher.

In the fifth place, language is important too. The language of the letter is the informal language of conversation; in fact, the letter is written conversation, if something of a monologue. The choice of vividly descriptive words and phrases, figures of speech, direct discourse, and transposed phrases and clauses give well-chosen ideas color and force. Slang is permissible. Usage, while free, should avoid offensive vulgarities and obscure meanings.

Finally, mechanics should be correct but not burdensome. The body of the letter is the important thing. In the lower grades, the teacher will take care of the heading and suggest the appropriate greeting and complimentary close. Capitalization, punctuation, spacing, and other technical details need not be discussed until later years. Drilling young children on the details of form takes the joy out of writing letters, and letter writing becomes a prescribed task. Gradually, in later grades, the children assume more responsibility, but the teacher continues to supply necessary technical information about which the children have not been instructed. Manuscript form, legibility, and neatness are treated as reasonable courtesies and as aids to thought giving.

It is necessary to give some attention to mechanics through the grades. Investigation has shown that punctuation errors head the list, constituting about half of all errors. Disturbing facts are the large number of errors per letter and the rather small amount of improvement from grade to grade. The most frequent errors in punctuation were in the use of the comma, period, and interrogation mark. Some encouragement is found in the fact that the errors involve only a few types, or failure in:

1 Placing the period after a declarative sentence
2 Correct use of the comma in a series, in direct quotations, in compound sentences, after appositives and introductory words, and after such words as *yes, no,* and *well*
3 Use of the interrogation mark after a question
4 Use of the quotation marks in direct quotations
5 Use of the apostrophe in contractions and in expressing possession

Situations The friendly letter by its very nature is an intimate, personal communication and loses some of its reality when submitted to class treatment. Most writing of a personal nature must be done in the seclusion of the home. If we cannot supervise the writing of intimate personal letters in the home, we can direct children's attention to the home situations that require letter writing, and we can give some school training in friendly-letter writing.

There are many school situations in which the writing of social letters is meaningful and purposeful. The following are illustrative and suggestive:

1. Writing to a sick classmate temporarily absent from school
2. Writing to a former teacher
3. Writing to a near relative
4. Congratulating a friend on a noteworthy achievement
5. Inviting a fireman or policeman to visit the class and explain his duties
6. Asking permission to visit a post office or dairy
7. Sending to railroads or chambers of commerce for illustrative material
8. Corresponding with a child in another country through the Junior Red Cross
9. Corresponding with a child in another area of the United States
10. Inviting a friend to a party
11. Inviting parents to attend a class or school program
12. Thanking school officials for materials and services
13. Inquiring about the duties of public officeholders

Anderson suggests that the teacher has a responsibility to help children understand that some letters should not be written—those in answer to some of the advertisements found in certain children's magazines in which stamps on approval are sent, or those that offer a bicycle for solving a puzzle. He further cautions that consideration be given to letters written to prominent people who may or may not be able to answer the many letters they receive.[6] In the case of favorite authors of books most loved by children, the knowledgeable teacher knows which author seems to make the effort to respond to children's letters and which publishers provide printed materials about their author that are sent to the youthful admirers.

The situation should be a real one in which the child has a natural reason for writing to a particular person for a particular purpose. If possible, all letters should be mailed. The general practice of choosing a single letter for mailing is often a practical necessity, but care should be taken that selected letters be chosen at various times as widely as possible from the class efforts so that as many pupils as possible may experience the satisfaction of having their letters mailed. Selecting the best letter for mailing often offers little motivation to the great majority of the class; therefore,

[6] Paul S. Anderson, *Language Skills in Elementary Education*, The Macmillan Company, New York, 1964, p. 365.

letter writing under this circumstance becomes a mere practice exercise for many pupils. Quality is more important than quantity of work. In some cases it is feasible to prepare composite letters using the best features from several individual letters. Some judgment must be exercised in selecting persons to whom to write. Certain adults do not appreciate receiving letters from children, and others are too busy or too infirm to reply.

Regular letters from a primary grade to a member of the group who was bedfast with rheumatic fever were stimulated throughout one winter by replies written by the little patient's older sister. In her letters, the seventh-grade girl was careful to thank the class for gifts; to tell how the patient was progressing, what she was able to do, what books she had read; and to include some message from the sick child to the group.

Following an excursion to a supermarket, a group of eight-year-olds wrote the following thank-you letter to the manager:

> Dear Mr. Kent:
>   We are glad that you allowed us to visit your store. We learned a great deal, especially about fruit and vegetables and how you keep food.
>   Thank you for inviting us.
>
> > Sincerely,
> > Grade Three

There is the caution against using the classroom post office as a device for stimulating letter writing; it may degenerate into silly note writing. With so many opportunities for writing real letters, it seems unnecessary to resort to an activity of such doubtful value.

Dallman lists and discusses several types of letters commonly written by children: (1) usual friendly letters; (2) letters of congratulation; (3) letters of sympathy; (4) letters of invitation, acceptance, or regret; (5) letters of apology; (6) letters of complaint; and (7) thank-you letters.[7]

Children naturally write about matters of most concern to themselves: personal experiences, school, animals, and objects. The weather seems to be a favorite topic with children as with adults. Disconcerting, if not surprising, is the small number of letters relating to thanks for gifts and services, greetings, congratulations, inspiration, and encouragement. Apparently children are not accustomed to thinking of other people and to taking advantage of many opportunities to express interest, concern, and appreciation. Fundamentally involved are social attitudes and

---

[7] Martha Dallman, *Teaching the Language Arts in the Elementary School*, W. C. Brown Company, Publishers, Dubuque, Iowa, 1966, pp. 71–73.

learning the means of observing social amenities that contribute to pleasant social relations.

An entirely different occasion is provided by the writing of letters such as might have been written by a historical character or by an imaginary person living in a particular period. Correlated with work in the social studies, letters of this type help students to think clearly about conditions, problems, manners, and customs of the past. The following is a part of such a letter written by a seventh-grade girl; impressed by her study of history, she pretends that she is living in New York City during the stirring times of the Revolutionary War and writes at length to her cousin in Boston:

> New York City
> November 25, 1776

Dear Cousin Kathryn-Bridget,

It frightens me so to think about the War, that I would like you to know exactly how I feel about it. Of course you have your own ideas about it but it is a relief to think that I can share with someone and you are my choice, because you I feel, are understanding. Around here people are forever talking about the war, but if you don't want an argument, you don't bring it up for there are Patriots, of which I am one, and there are Tories, too.

The worst of the war was fought around here. That is a terrible experience—to be right in the midst of war. You probably saw General Washington when he was in your city of Boston. I have seen him only once and that was when he rode by a forghtnight ago. . . .

It might be of interest to you that I am getting a new dark blue silk dress. It has rows and rows of white buttons and I think it is going to be simply stunning.

My sister Matilda-Jean is going to be married a year from Christmas to a very nice appearing young man, and mama and papa think he will make a good husband.

I wish you and Aunt Bessie and Uncle Tim, plus your twin brothers Tim Jr. and Jim a very merry Christmas and a very Happy New Year.

> I remain your dear cousin,
> Rebecca Adell Whiten

Suitable procedures   A suitable procedure for handling the friendly letter includes the following steps:

First, set up a real situation, a natural one arising in connection with one of the situations enumerated above, such as writing a letter to a sick classmate.

Second, examine models. If the activity is a first experience, considerable time will be needed. Examples are provided in textbooks, but much better are real letters, preferably written by children of the same age or grade level. In time, the teacher should accumulate a file of suitable letters. Possibly children can bring to class letters they have received. Certainly letters addressed to the class provide good material, if well written. Attention should be directed to both content and form, with the emphasis on content. Letter writing is not primarily a matter of drill on form. Ideas should be summed up in key points or standards and possibly checked with standards in the textbook. A few key points should be sufficient; clarity and force are lost by long enumerations.

The third step involves selecting a good topic and organizing and thinking through what one is going to say. In the class letter, this is a cooperative undertaking; sentences are suggested by the children, written on the board by the teacher, revised, and finally rearranged in sequence. In individual work, the child thinks about what he is going to say and the order in which he is going to say it. Older children may make notes in outline form. There should be one big center of interest, and this should be developed in sufficient detail to arouse interest, as shown in Shirley's letter above.

The fourth step is the actual writing. Attention is given primarily to thought and fluency. An attempt is made to formulate ideas and to clothe them in words and constructions that give clarity, vividness, and beauty. Mechanical difficulties of spelling and punctuation are reduced to a minimum if the teacher provides assistance suitable to the maturity of the pupils. Various methods are employed with young children. Some teachers pass around the class and give individual help as needed; others write words on the board as requested; others assist children in building up a vocabulary of useful words in the form of a vocabulary box or alphabetized notebook; and still others encourage children temporarily to disregard spelling and, to some extent, handwriting. It seems advisable to make a rapid sketch of ideas first and then to consider at more leisure the mechanical phases of the work. Of these procedures, it seems that giving individual help with single words and writing words on the board are the least productive because the amount of help that the teacher can give is limited and because the results are not made permanently available to the children. The preparation and keeping of alphabetized individual word lists in the form of alphabet boxes in the second grade and of notebooks in the third grade and beyond build up word lists that are permanently available to the child, and this method conserves the teacher's energy and time. Of course, in the later grades the children will make considerable use of the dictionary.

The fifth step is a critical evaluation of what has been written and subsequent correction. Again attention is given to content; the pupil asks himself such questions as, Have I said what I intended to say? Have I put it in the proper order? and Have I used well-chosen words and constructions? Attention is given also to correctness of expression and to mechanics: sentence structure, usage, punctuation, capitalization, spelling, handwriting, and placing and spacing the several parts of the letter. The teacher is faced for the first time, but not the last, with the problem of handling corrections. Researchers have little to say in favor of the teacher going over children's written work and marking mistakes in red ink. The only kind of correction that seems to have much value is self-correction; but how? Of course, going over one composition at a time with the child is ideal, but it consumes entirely too much time to be practical. Mass correction can be handled to some extent by presenting common difficulties to the class, preferably by using the chalkboard, discussing the errors, and correcting them. A composition that has very few errors is selected for class study. It is written on the board by the pupil-author exactly as originally written, or viewed by the overhead projector (depending on the rapport of the teacher with the whole class and on the prior approval of the pupil-author). The pupil makes as many corrections in his own composition as he can, and then other children are invited to make additional corrections. Several other compositions may be handled in the same manner. Following class study and correction of the sample compositions, each pupil turns to his own composition and makes similar corrections. Probably glaring and common faults will be discovered and corrected in this class procedure. Less common defects peculiar to individual compositions can be corrected individually. It is helpful to place a carefully selected list of key points on the board for the pupils' reference in checking their own work.

The final step is rewriting, with the necessary correction and revision of content, language, and form. Rewriting is an essential step in the early stages of learning and is useful later in writing important letters. It may be a valuable learning experience, if properly handled. Rewriting should not be used as a punishment; it should serve a learning purpose recognized by the child. Merely copying the teacher's corrected copy has little value. If a letter is to be mailed, and presumably it is, the teacher must finally assure himself that it is in proper form. This will require a check of the pupil's check and possibly some further revision.

Examples   Jessie Cooper, Fresno city schools, Fresno, California, reported a series of lessons in the writing of social letters by a sixth-grade class:

Situation   *A few weeks after Red Cross Christmas boxes were sent to Hawaii, a letter came to the class from a little Japanese girl living near Hilo. The class wanted to answer this letter.*

Objectives
1. To develop the ability to select content interesting to the reader
2. To recall and review the skill aspects of form
3. To develop further the attitudes of enjoyment in letter writing

General procedures
1. First day; discuss
    a. What makes letter writing interesting? Read examples of children's or adults' interesting friendly letters to the class, such as:

    Dear Boys and Girls,
            I am a little Indian girl. Just now, school is out, and I am having a good time.
            In the morning we go out to hoe the garden. We have a very nice garden. The vegetables are growing nicely, and we have plenty of lettuce and radishes.
            It takes many years for an Indian girl to speak English well.

                                With best love,
                                Maranita Perez
                                Pena Blanca, New Mexico
                                Cochita Pueblo

    b. What would we like to know about the Japanese girl?
    c. What would a Japanese girl living in Hawaii like to know about us? (List on board and evaluate suggestions.)
        (1) What we do at school
        (2) The games we play
        (3) What our parents do to make a living
        (4) What we eat
        (5) The clothes we wear
        (6) The trips we take in summer or winter
        (7) The kinds of homes we live in
    d. What shall we remember about the way we write letters? (List on the board.)
        (1) Heading
        (2) Indentation
        (3) Punctuation marks
        (4) Handwriting
        (5) Spelling
        (6) Using gcod sentences
        (7) Closing
        (8) Addressing envelopes
2. Second day:
    a. Recall form from preceding day.
    b. Each pupil thinks through what he wants to say. Some may tell the class orally what they expect to say in their letters.
    c. A class letter may be planned, on the board.
    d. Pupils make rough drafts of letters.

3. Third day:
   a. Teacher reads one or more letters to class for discussion.
   b. Any pupil who needs help on content and organization may receive it.
   c. Pupils correct their first drafts, using the checklists of content and form prepared the first day as guides. Pupils use language books to check doubtful points, and the teacher assists individual pupils.
   d. The pupils prepare final drafts from the corrected first drafts.
   e. Letters are finally checked, folded, and placed in envelopes.
   f. The manner of addressing envelopes is recalled and pupils address their own envelopes.

Means of evaluation
   1. Through discussion, the teacher and pupils can evaluate the progress in the selection of interesting content. Notes kept by the class secretary or topics dictated to the teacher (see Procedures 2c) can be evaluated by the group.
   2. Through reevaluation of the guidelines concerning form, discussion may reveal the extent to which the class-developed guides were used (see Procedures 2d). During the independent worktime, the teacher may observe individuals' use of the form guidelines.
   3. Follow-up discussions can help children vocalize their enjoyment of letter writing and letter receiving.

In a third grade a real situation was produced when Anastasia left for a visit to Greece. She had told the class about her trip and about her relatives in Greece; and she had shown folders and pictures of the ship upon which she would sail. During the days which elapsed after Anna said good-by and before she actually sailed from New York, the children wrote stories which they mailed to reach Anna on board ship. They also wrote her a letter:

Dear Anna,
   It seems strange in school today without you and we miss you very much. Our arithmetic average went down this morning. We think we needed you to help us.
   Today Alberta Wing came back. Perhaps you knew her when she was with us in first grade.
   Miss B brought the Shipping News from the Sunday paper. We saw that your ship will arrive in New York on Wednesday. We will be thinking of you on Friday when it is time for your boat to sail.
   We hope you will enjoy our stories and that you will have a pleasant voyage. Be sure to write to us.
                                        Your friends in Room 26

A month later, after the receipt of a letter and several postcards from Anna, the class sent the following letter. It was written much more easily than the first. There were many things to tell Anna, and the teacher helped the class make a selection or the letter would have been too long: "I wonder if Anna would really be interested in that? . . . When we write 'How are you?' or say 'I hope you are well,' is that telling Anna anything? . . . Let's choose just a few things to tell her and then explain them. . . . We don't want a lot of little short, choppy sentences, do we?"

Heading and salutation were written on the board by the teacher with only passing comment upon punctuation, capitalization, etc. The letter was then written by the teacher as dictated by the children. Some criticism, evaluation, and corrections were made by them. Three children who were considered good penmen made copies of the letter; and from the three copies, a committee of children chose the following one, which it considered especially well written. The envelope was addressed by the child who had transcribed the letter, and another pupil was chosen to mail it.

> Dear Anna,
>
> We received your letter and cards and like them so much that we have them on the bulletin board where everyone can see them. The program is there too. It was very interesting to know what people did on your ship. Did you go swimming on the ship?
>
> Since you left just about all the snow has melted. Many of the birds are back and crocuses are in bloom.
>
> Here in school we have started multiplication. So far it is very easy. The very first day our average went way up. We are now on page 61 in the workbook.
>
> Miss F, our new teacher, is very nice and we have two new girls both named Betty.
>
> We have found out many interesting things about ships. All around the room we have pictures of ships—from the very earliest kind to a modern one like you rode on. We heard a story about a baby whale and wondered if you saw a whale on your way to Greece.
>
> Write to us soon and tell us about the interesting things you are doing. You never told us your address so June went down and asked your father how to address this envelope.
>
> Charles wants to know which story you liked best.
>
> > Much love,
> > Your friends in Room 26

Because these letters were written to a real flesh-and-blood person from whom replies were expected, this sort of writing was fun. There was great enthusiasm and real spontaneity. How unfortunate it is that this joy in letter writing cannot more often be preserved to adulthood.

Problems   One problem that teachers face in the experience phases of all language work is setting up before the class tangible goals of achievement. Examples and models serve this purpose.

In oral work the model is heard and must be held in mind unless satisfactory recordings are available. Written phases are more tangible; samples of work that represent several degrees of merit for the grade can be chosen and examined at leisure. It is well in letter writing to make a judicious selection of samples representing less than satisfactory, satisfactory, and better than satisfactory work. These can be arranged in the form of a crude scale, from low to high or from high to low. The scale shows the children just what the class is working for and gives a means of evaluation which is as objective as is practicable. The scaling should emphasize content, with minimum standards of acceptability in mechanics set as a must. It is not too much to require that revised and corrected written work be free from glaring defects in usage, capitalization, punctuation, and manuscript form. Individual samples, selected from time to time, will be useful as a means of measuring progress.

The following letters illustrate the point. They were chosen by a sixth-grade teacher from samples of children's writings in past years, marked as *more than satisfactory, satisfactory,* and *less than satisfactory.*

More than satisfactory

Fresno 4, California
March 22, 1968

Dear Mrs. A,

We visited an art exhibit which had drawings by children of foreign countries. The oil painting "Seascape" impressed me more than any of the others. It was bright and ready to come to life. You could just feel yourself on the rock, and hear the waves dash against the rocks. The spray seemed fine and wet as it rose from the waves. The sky fitted in perfectly with the sea. It had so much action and realness in it. Indeed, the child who made this picture must have felt the sea.

Our newspaper is coming along nicely. The articles have been coming in faster. This time we will have more pages. Our newspaper is lots of fun as everyone can put in articles.

Your friend,

Satisfactory

Fresno 4, California
March 17, 1968

Dear Miss B,

We sure enjoyed you as our student teacher last semester.

I hope you like teaching in the fifth grade. You are probably the fifth graders' favorite student teacher, you were in our room with everybody.

I wish you would please come in and see us.

Love,

Less than satisfactory

Fresno 4, California
March 17, 1968
Dear Aunt C,
We are studying South America and we have broken up in groups and some girls and we have taken Uruguay and Paraguay.
I hope you can come down in Aprial somtime
Love

The letter-writing activity offers good opportunity for the enjoyment and study of letters of literary merit, such as Helen C. Washburne's *Letters of Chaney* and J. B. Bishop's *Theodore Roosevelt's Letters to His Children.* Reading these letters and others by distinguished persons is fun and provides a means of checking the desired qualities set up by the children as standards for their own letters. A survey of 150 letters of outstanding women shows the distinguishing characteristics to be courtesy, informality, humor, opinion, optimism, and good organization. Informality is revealed by using colloquialisms or conversational expressions; inventing expressions; including pen sketches and illustrations; eliminating overformal headings and conclusions; and supplying figures of speech humorously exaggerated. Courtesy is shown by giving due attention to the points in a letter that is being answered; never failing to express expected congratulations; never failing to acknowledge obligations; expressing good wishes; and adapting subject matter to the age and interests of the reader.[8]

The business letter

The business letter is like the friendly letter in many respects, but there are important differences. In the first place, unlike the friendly letter, the business letter is largely a school enterprise; occasional business letters are written at home, as in ordering goods from mail-order houses, but for the most part they are written at school for securing materials and services in various curricular activities. In the second place, an important difference is found in the purpose of the letter: the distinctive character of the friendly letter is entertainment, while the purpose of the business letter is expository. The third difference, a matter of tone and approach, grows out of these different purposes. The friendly letter is informal,

[8] Mauree Applegate, "Composition," in Verna D. Anderson and others, *Readings in the Language Arts*, The Macmillan Company, New York, 1964, pp. 112–139.

expansive, entertaining, and humorous; the business letter is brief, pointed, and formal—businesslike.

Past practice has placed the writing of business letters in the later grades, implying delayed social needs and an assumption of greater difficulty. The modern program, on the contrary, finds many occasions for writing business letters in the primary grades.

Specific objectives   Among the objectives of the business letter, courtesy receives a high rating. Convention prescribes a standard salutation (*Dear Mr. Smith, Gentlemen,* etc.) and a conventional close (*Yours truly, Yours sincerely, Cordially yours*). The familiarity of the corresponding forms of the friendly letter are to be avoided. The business letter, however, is always courteous in tone; requests are couched in gracious language, such as *Please send me. . . .* Brevity and directness are required, and the purpose of the letter is usually expressed in the opening sentence. The assumption is that businessmen are busy people whose time should be saved by clarity and directness. All essential facts are given. In an order for goods, it is necessary to describe exactly what is wanted, to give catalogue numbers if possible, and to figure the amounts of money involved accurately. When several items are ordered they are put in list form. Care is taken to observe the conventions in the arrangement of the parts of the letter. Spelling, handwriting, and punctuation should be correct, for businessmen are not tolerant of carelessness in these respects, and because accuracy in communication is necessary. The use of a colon after the salutation is regarded as good form. It is customary to refer to enclosures, such as checks, and to enclose a stamp if the letter contains a request for information. It is good practice to keep a copy of all business letters.

Situations   Opportunities for writing business letters arise frequently. One of the most common situations occurs in connection with ordering materials for use in various curricular areas, such as social studies, health, and science. These materials in part are supplied free by many firms and agencies. Included in this group are health booklets and posters, travel circulars, safety records and charts, exhibits of products, pictures and slides, and samples of materials. Children also have occasion to visit a farm, a dairy, a post office, a police court, a fire station, or a library, and arrangements can be made by letter. Often the use of public transportation facilities is involved in making trips, and children may write the necessary letters. Businessmen, professional men, and public officials are often invited to come to the school to present matters of interest to the class. In the later grades, children have occasion to write letters seeking temporary employment. Of course, letters of appreciation for special services and favors are in order.

Processes   At the seventh-grade level it may be assumed that the children have had considerable experience in both the content and the form of the letter. It is necessary to review both content and form, however, and to provide some remedial work. A project that involved presenting to the library a source book of authors of current literature at the junior high school level was under way. Committees were appointed to look up material in the library and make reports to the class. Some committees were unable to locate suitable material, and a suggestion was made that letters of inquiry be written to publishers. A series of lessons was devoted to the mechanics of form, capitalization, and punctuation. Sample business letters were studied. Standards were derived from the study of models and posted in the room for reference. Individual children prepared letters, and the better letters were chosen for mailing. Rough drafts were read to the class, difficulties noted, and remedial exercises provided. The replies of publishers were read and examined by the children.

The next step was writing letters to authors. This was recognized as a more exacting task, and added care was required in composing the letters. The children examined letters brought from home and other letters found in language and literature books. Possible adaptations to individual authors and proper forms of salutation and closing were considered. First drafts were prepared and read to the class for criticism. The children were not satisfied and felt the need for additional practice, particularly in the use of adjectives and in sentence variety. Monotonous sentences were written on the board and changes, such as using an inverted order, were suggested. Practice in transposing clauses was provided, and examples of forceful sentences were found and examined. The study of ways of expressing exact ideas effectively involved the study of adjectives. Discussions of the use of effective adjectives were found in books; dictionaries were consulted; and sentences were rewritten. The letters were finally rewritten and checked for form. Responses from well-known authors were gratifying. In their personal letters the children continued to use the skills that they had acquired during this undertaking.

The alert teacher is aware of incidental happenings that might necessitate the writing of formal letters. Yee [9] reports the directed letter-writing activities of a group of elementary school children who were interested in knowing why the transportation of certain small creatures, such as turtles, frogs, and fish, on a school bus was not allowed. Letters were sent to the state department of education; and, in return, replies were sent back to the children. In the course of the correspondence, the code was reinterpreted by the department of education to allow the transportation on school buses of harmless, nonmammal animals, properly confined in bottles, jars, and boxes.

The handling of the business letter in the primary grades is like that of the friendly letter described in the previous section. It is well for the teacher himself to remember certain aspects of courtesy when helping children learn how to write business letters. At no time should thirty-five identical letters be sent to any business, industry, or chamber of commerce requesting identical information. How this can be handled is a proper concern for teacher-pupil planning. The teacher may help the children to understand that, even though each child may write a get-well letter to an absent classmate, it is likely that one letter of reply will serve for the whole class.

Invitations, acceptances, and thank-you notes

Situations Schoolwork is largely concerned with preparing children to carry on activities in the home and community, but to some extent occasions that present immediate problems naturally arise in school. The class may be having a party, program, or exhibit, and decide to invite parents, school officials, or other interested persons. One class may entertain another class. A pupil may invite other pupils to a party at school or at home. A public official or businessman may be asked to address the pupils on some topic of current interest, or a visiting artist or entertainer may be invited to the school. In many of these situations invitations are in order; and in some cases, acceptances. Any special service or favor should be recognized by a thank-you note.

[9] Albert H. Yee, "Purpose and Motivation in Teaching Letter Writing," *Elementary English*, vol. 42, November, 1965, pp. 805–807.

Invitations, acceptances, and thank-you notes represent special forms of epistolary communication in which children receive training in social amenities, in recognizing occasions that require them, and instruction in the use of certain language forms. Of course, some of the experiences may be either oral or written; and certain characteristics, such as courtesy and appropriate language, are common to all. Here we are primarily concerned with written forms. The need and value of training in the written forms vary with school communities, increasing in those communities where social functions are frequent and high standards of social amenities are maintained.

The usual form of this type of letter is an informal note; less frequently, as in the case of wedding invitations and announcements, the notes are more formal in character. The child during his school life is mainly concerned with informal letters, and the training program should concentrate on these. The formal note will be used later, if at all, and the child can be referred to common sources of information, such as books on etiquette.[10]

Specific objectives   The invitation, acceptance, or thank-you note has a specific purpose and limited scope, in contrast to the generality of the social letter. The statement of facts should be clear and complete; in the case of an invitation, who, what, when, where— and possibly how to dress—must be included. Courtesy requires that the acceptance note show sincere pleasure and appreciation for favors anticipated. The language can be simple in style, but it should be formally correct. Proper forms are always observed in heading, salutation, and close. Suitable paper, ink, and longhand writing are requisites. Promptness in responding to invitations and in expressing appreciation is highly desirable. Certainly it is necessary to inform the hostess or guest promptly in case of necessary change in plans. The thank-you note has many of the same characteristics: sincere expression of gratitude for a gift or favor, promptness, appropriate paper with matching envelope, ink, and proper forms of salutation and close, such as *Dear Mary* and *Cordially yours*.

A group of primary school children were invited to see movies at the hour when they usually went to the library. A vote was taken, and a majority wanted to see the movie; but since the

[10] See, for example, Betty Allen and Mitchell P. Briggs. *Mind Your Manners,* J. B. Lippincott Company, Philadelphia, 1964, chap. 12. See also Enid A. Haupt, *The Seventeen Book of Etiquette and Entertaining,* David McKay Company, Inc., New York, 1963, chap. 22.

librarian had been very kind to them, the children felt that some explanation was due her. The word *tactful* was introduced to them; and it was pointed out that their note must not hurt Mrs. MacE's feelings or make her feel that the class came to the library only when there was nothing else to do. The following note was the result; it was copied and delivered to the librarian:

> Dear Mrs. MacE,
>   We have been invited to see movies in the auditorium this afternoon at 2 o'clock. They are supposed to be very good pictures. If you don't mind we would like to see them.
>   Next Friday we will come to the library as usual.
>   Sincerely,
>   Grade Three

Procedures   The procedures described above for written communication are generally applicable in the case of social notes. The writing experience should be initiated by a real situation. Models should be examined for ideas of form, tone, and language; and standards appropriate to the grade and class should be set up. Differences from other kinds of written communication may be noted, and some reasons for the differences discussed. The class may join in the planning of the note and in the writing of notes that concern the whole class. Samples of children's work may be collected and preserved for future use as models. Textbooks provide help in the form of samples and lists of key points.

There may be times, however, when motivation is great and the children feel a need or a desire to write *immediately*. In such a case, when they know what they want to say and how they want to say it, to examine models or textbooks would not only waste time but might result in frustration. An assembly program put on by a second grade pleased the third-grade children in the audience so much that, when they returned to their rooms, they suggested writing a thank-you letter to Miss B, the second-grade teacher. Although it was time for dismissal, the children wanted to wait and write the note; so the teacher turned to the board and wrote as the children dictated:

> Dear Miss B,
>   We enjoyed the Christmas play your children put on for us. It was lovely and very well done.
>   We wish you all a Merry Christmas.
>   Grade Three

This note was copied by a child and immediately delivered to the second-grade room. Because the moment was propitious, the work was all done eagerly in a few minutes, and the children derived deep satisfaction from it. Had the teacher suggested that the pupils wait until the language period next day, the enthusiasm would have dissipated, and writing the note might have been a real chore. How many adults are prone to postpone such simple tasks, with the result that they never do them?

Evaluation   The true test of the school's impact on its instruction in letter writing lies in the future, when the children have become adults and utilize both language skills and sensitivities. Yet, in the program of instruction in letter writing there are means that can be used to evaluate progress. Checklists for content evaluation and charts, indicating letter-writing form and mechanics, are developed by the teacher and the children; and they are used by the children, increasing their independence in self-evaluation. Models, illustrating special areas of letter writing at particular times, help illustrate certain social amenities and draw children's attention to the topics under discussion. The time the teachers and the children devote to developing, practicing, discussing, and evaluating the various aspects of letter writing is time well spent.

For your consideration

1   Discuss: Not all children have the same experiences and occasions to write letters in their out-of-school lives.
2   Collect samples of children's letters and notes. Comment on the content and form.
3   Collect samples of business letters that can be used as models for children's use in writing.
4   For two weeks keep track of the social letters and business letters that you write. What were the purposes of your written communications? If possible, keep a copy of each letter so that you can examine the contents after the need for writing the letter has passed.
5   List five qualities of good social or business letters and rank them in order of their importance.
6   Sketch a plan for teaching a lesson or series of lessons on letter writing in a particular grade. Outline your objectives, the procedures you will follow, the materials you will utilize, and two evaluative measures you will employ.

References

ARTLEY, A. STERL, AND OTHERS: *Interrelationships among the Language Arts,* National Council of Teachers of English, Champaign, Ill., 1964, pp. 4–12.

DALLMAN, MARTHA: *Teaching the Language Arts in the Elementary School,* W. C. Brown Company, Publishers, Dubuque, Iowa, 1966, pp. 63–74.

DAWSON, MILDRED A., M. ZOLLINGER, AND A. ELWELL: *Guiding Language Learning,* Harcourt, Brace & World, Inc., New York, 1963, chap. 14.

DREWES, RUTH H., AND OTHERS: *Practical Plans for Teaching English in Elementary Schools,* W. C. Brown Company, Publishers, Dubuque, Iowa, 1965, chap. 14.

HATFIELD, W. W.: *An Experience Curriculum in English,* Appleton-Century-Crofts, Inc., New York, 1935, pp. 185–191, 208–216.

LAMB, POSE: *Guiding Children's Language Learning,* W. C. Brown Company, Publishers, Dubuque, Iowa, 1967, chap. 6, pp. 348–358.

LEE, J. M., AND DORRIS M. LEE: *The Child and His Curriculum,* Appleton-Century-Crofts, Inc., New York, 1960, pp. 340–344.

MAC CAMPBELL, J. C., AND OTHERS: *Readings in the Language Arts in the Elementary School,* D. C. Heath and Company, Boston, 1964, chap. 6.

NATIONAL COUNCIL OF TEACHERS OF ENGLISH, *Language Arts for Today's Children,* Appleton-Century-Crofts, Inc., New York, 1954, pp. 209–219, 227–236.

STRICKLAND, RUTH G.: "The Contribution of Structural Linguistics to the Teaching of Reading, Writing, and Grammar in the Elementary School," *Bulletin of the School of Education,* vol. 40, no. 1, Indiana University, Bloomington, Ind., 1964.

——: *The Language Arts in the Elementary School,* D. C. Heath and Company, Boston, 1957, pp. 273–290, 309–328.

8.

STUDY, RESEARCH, AND REPORTING

Study and research commonly take the form of problem solving and follow the customary problem-solving procedure: (1) setting up a topic or problem that may be used for the study of a significant area of the curriculum, such as the westward movement, life in colonial times, how animals protect themselves, and form in music or art; (2) breaking down the topic or problem into significant subtopics, problems, or questions; (3) locating available information; (4) gathering information, possibly from several sources, and making memoranda of information pertinent to a particular topic; and (5) organizing into a coherent, orderly whole selected information bearing on one or more topics. It will be observed at once that this list represents a logical series of steps that mature students and adults use in the serious study of any topic or problem. It also represents the culmination of years of training, consisting of work on the specific abilities and skills that are the constituent elements of the total mature performance.

Just what contribution does language make and what part does language training play in the development of good habits of study? We are dealing here with informational phases of schoolwork, of course; and the principal methods of securing information are reading, observing, and listening. Because efficient study depends, in general, upon the ability to get information by means of these chief methods, it depends more specifically upon the ability to understand what is read, seen, and heard. Good reading, observing, and listening involve more than passive, uncritical absorption or comprehension; they require powers of selectivity, evaluation, interpretation, application, organization, and summarization—active processes of thinking. Language, as the primary means and form of thought, therefore, contributes to and determines these abilities. For example, the effort of putting into words just what takes place in performing and experimenting clarifies and deepens for the pupil his understanding of what he has seen and at the same time sharpens his language. An important contribution of language to study and research abilities is made in the imparting of information, whether that information appears in connection with problem solving or with some other kind of schoolwork, curricular or extracurricular.

Preliminary considerations concerning reading for information

Reading is a major consideration in the process of obtaining, organizing, and reporting the crucial elements of needed information. The research skills—reading study skills—need to be taught sequentially to children in an ever-expanding program of instruction. Whether these skills should be taught within the framework of the reading program or whether they should be taught within the framework of the social studies, the sciences, or any other curricular area is a matter of debate, but they must be taught. The curricular areas of the social studies, science, and others lend themselves well to the techniques related to problem solving.

The specialized vocabulary employed in the various subject areas needs to be developed by providing experiences that will introduce and clarify the essential concepts. Children need assistance in seeing the relationships between facts met in different contexts. Children need to be able to organize their findings for specific purposes with an increasing ability to read critically. Further, there is need for the increased emphasis in instruction relating to the skills, abilities, and attitudes necessary to use source materials effectively.[1]

Heilman, in noting the various topics to be studied in the reading study skills, suggests that the following areas are included: [2]

---

[1] Paul A. Witty, "The Role of Reading in the Social Studies," *Elementary English*, vol. 39, October, 1962, pp. 562–569.

[2] Arthur W. Heilman, "Teaching the Reading-study Skills," in A. J. Mazurkiewicz, *New Perspectives in Reading Instruction: A Book of Readings*, Pitman Publishing Corporation, New York, 1964, pp. 418–424.

1   Locating information
2   Evaluating relevant data
3   Organizing data
4   Retention of pertinent material
5   Ability to comprehend and adjust reading rate to purpose
     and nature of material

He further suggests that the skills and attitudes necessary for the
effective use of books in obtaining information are developmental
in nature and, as such, merit systematic teaching.

In locating information, a young adult ultimately must be able
to use reference materials intelligently (encyclopedia, atlas, world
almanac, dictionary) and also be able to use the internal aids
of these references (table of contents, index, maps, charts, tables).
He must be able to evaluate the contents of the data he has
found in order to assess its appropriateness to the problem to be
solved, its authorship, and its authenticity. Organizing involves
note taking, summarizing, and outlining, either as preparation for
reporting or as provision for retention. Further, the young adult
who has progressed through our schools should be aware of the
many purposes of reading, and should be able to recognize that
reading rate is dependent on both the purpose and the nature of
the printed content. Several good sources are available for further
reference in the provision of an adequate program of instruction
in the reading study skills.[3]

Scope of chapter

For practical purposes, the language experiences in study, research,
and reporting are here grouped and treated somewhat arbitrarily—
and with considerable overlapping—under the following heads:
(1) making records and charts; (2) preparing problems, questions,
outlines, and lists; (3) taking notes and writing summaries; (4)
preparing indexes and bibliographies; and (5) using the dictionary.
It will be noticed that the grouping follows to some extent the steps
in problem solving listed at the beginning of the chapter, but that
the order of treatment is not the same. An attempt has been made
to secure in the present list an order of treatment generally corresponding to actual use in school. This order is determined in turn by

[3] Guy L. Bond and Eva Bond Wagner, *Teaching the Child to Read,*
The Macmillan Company, New York, 1966, chap. 13; Paul McKee and W. K.
Durr, *Reading: A Program of Instruction for the Elementary School,* Houghton
Mifflin Company, Boston, 1966, chaps. 9–11; Nila B. Smith, *Reading Instruc-
tion for Today's Children,* Prentice-Hall, Inc., Englewood Cliffs, N.J., 1963,
chap. 10.

need in connection with various school activities and by the maturity and readiness of the pupils.

At this point it is suggested that the reader review Chapter 5, Giving Information Orally. The processes of the parallel aspects of preparing oral reports and preparing written reports should be recognized and considered.

Records and charts

Records and charts are means of compiling, organizing, and presenting the factual phases of schoolwork. Facts may be summarized in brief, pointed sentences, taking the form of a unified paragraph, log, or diary; or they may be put in the form of a table, chart, or graph. The nature of the material and the preference of the teacher determine the forms used. Various uses of record keeping include recording the results of experiments; recording observations of weather, birds, signs of spring, and the like; showing progress in the study of certain topics or problems; recording the results of an interview; making records of interesting events, such as a play day or the visit of a fireman; summarizing a survey of community needs and practices, as in a health report or a record of the uses of decimals; writing a receipt; and cataloguing information on interesting books. Information gathered and recorded will serve a variety of purposes. Some information may be used as resource material in the further study of a topic or problem, some may be used as the basis for a report to the class by a group or individual, and some may constitute a part of the study of a larger unit by a group or an individual.[4]

Scrapbooks often help organize ideas in a unit of work. Working singly or in groups children may make their scrapbooks large (newsprint size) or small, and include drawings, pictures cut from magazines, poems, original stories, pressed leaves, flowers, or whatever the unit study suggests. The pictures should be classified, arranged in an orderly fashion, and appropriately captioned. Descriptions may be added. Mapping the city or the school neighborhood requires labels. A table display of favorite objects may be brought by the children. This leads to appropriate labels and oral explanations of "Just why I like this."

Experience chart One of the study-research report forms that appears early in the grades is the experience chart. It is developed

[4] Edith M. Leonard and others, *Basic Learning in the Language Arts,* Scott, Foresman and Company, Chicago, 1965, part 2.

as a report of an observation or field trip, a summary of the study of a special topic or problem, or a record of a special event or experience. It is commonly used in the low first grade to provide a source of easy, meaningful reading material and occasionally for the same purpose in later grades when the children are retarded in reading.[5]

An example of the experience chart is provided by Cecelia Ham.[6] This unit centered on the study of bees, and the chart was used as a study guide and as a means of organizing and recording information gained. The title of the series of charts was "Our Bee Book." Beforehand, however, certain questions were set up for study:

1 Where there are no flowers, what do the bees do?
2 Does a bee go from one flower to another without first returning to the hive?
3 What are the enemies of the bee?
4 Why does a bee have a sting?
5 Why do bees swarm?
6 How many bees live in one hive?
7 What kind of bees are there in a hive?
8 What is the work of the queen?
9 What is the work of the worker and of the drone?
10 How many queens in a hive? Why? How did she get there?

As the study progressed, new words learned were listed on a class chart under its own title:

WORDS WE KNOW

wax	pollen	comb	honey
nectar	pollen basket	bee	drone
queen	workers	egg	larva
royal jelly	guards	water carriers	busy
housekeepers	sting	bee bread	dust
flowers	abdomen	hive	legs
tongue	buzz	head	six-sided
fanning	wings	eat	compound
hang	cradle cell	ventilation	farsighted
eye	hairs	near	gather
six	leg comb	nurse	gum

Information was gathered, formulated into sentences, and organized under several heads:

[5] Virgil E. Herrick and Marcella Nerbovig, *Using Experience Charts with Children,* Charles E. Merrill Books, Inc., Columbus, Ohio, 1964.
[6] Former demonstration teacher, second grade, College Elementary School, Fresno State College, Fresno, Calif.

OUR BEE BOOK

There are three kinds of bees in a hive.
The bees are the queens, the workers, and the drones.
The bees swarm sometimes.
The bees have six legs.
The bees have five eyes. Two of them are compound eyes to see far away.
The small eyes are hard for us to see because they are protected by little hairs.

The Queen

The queen doesn't work, but she does lay eggs.
The queen lays thousands of eggs a day.
The queen is fed royal jelly.
The queen has a sting, but she uses it to place the eggs.

The Workers

The workers are the busiest bees.
The workers gather pollen and nectar.
The workers make royal jelly.
The worker bees make wax.
The worker bees are nurse bees.
The workers fan the hive.
The workers make bee bread.
The workers make bee gum.
The worker bees make a cradle cell from wax.
The worker bees are guards.
The workers wash the queen.
The workers are water carriers.

For second-grade children, observing the natural phenomena of bee life; viewing study prints, filmstrips, and motion pictures; listening to the teacher's explanations; and taking part in discussions were activities most appropriate to the obtaining of information. Books, such as the following, assisted in the learning—by the teacher's reading to the class, by providing illustrations for individual perusal, and by determining whether bees, indeed, were insects: Glenn O. Blough, *Who Lives in This House?;* Illa Podendorf, *The True Book of Insects;* Ross E. Hutchins, *Insects, Hunters, and Trappers;* Dorothy Sterling, *Insects and the Homes They Build;* Su Zan N. Swaim, *Insects and Their World;* Edwin Way Teale, *The Junior Book of Insects;* and Herbert S. Zim, *Insects: A Guide to Familiar American Insects.*

The development of an experience chart is commonly a class enterprise with contributions from all the children under the direction of the teacher. The teacher solicits contributions on important points observed, helps children develop sentences, and writes the sentences on the board as dictated by the children. When the important points have been covered in satisfactory sentences, the teacher and the children review the sentences, eliminating duplications and combining similar sentences. Attention is then given to organization: What should be said first? What next? What would make a good concluding sentence? Recording the chart in its final form on a large sheet of tagboard provides a permanent record for future class use. This procedure was followed in developing the charts reported above.

In addition to providing training in some of the simpler mechanics of written expression—such as formulating simple sentences, using periods and question marks at the end of sentences, and using capital letters at the beginning of sentences and in titles—the experience chart offers opportunities for pupils to develop some understanding of more advanced qualities of good composition. Because the chart is primarily informational, basic concern focuses upon its accuracy and reliability. Conciseness is also recognized as an important factor. Such conciseness, clarity, and accuracy of expression require, in turn, the selection of precise and appropriate words and expressions. The importance of organization is emphasized in choosing a central theme or topic, in sticking to it, and in arranging sentences so that there is a logical sequence of ideas.

Tabular record charts Another common and useful form of record is the tabular chart, which is a brief catalogue of essential information about selected key items, showing comparisons, relationships, and possibly changes in time. Such a chart may be used in the first grade to record weather observations. The days of the week or month may be listed, and opposite each day are placed weather notes such as *clear, cloudy,* and *rainy* and information about temperature and wind direction.

In keeping a one-week record, primary children used the following words to describe the weather accurately:

February 21. Bitter cold, bright, snowy, crisp
February 22. Very cold, windy, drifting
February 23. Stormy, blustery, occasional sunshine
February 24. Light snow, dull, mild

The following record of weather conditions was kept by a fourth-grade child. It was well worded, concise, accurate, and descriptive enough to be interesting, and represents quite a mature form of expression:

Sunday, November 20th, in the afternoon, it started to rain and snow. At night the streets were covered with slush. All night it snowed. On Monday, November 21st, all the town was covered with snow.

In the second grade, possibly as an early-spring unit, the children may record observations of birds, noting name, date of appearance, place seen, and who saw the bird. Numerous uses for the tabular chart are found throughout the grades in areas of health and safety, science, the social studies, and mathematics.

In addition to providing familiarity with tabular forms, the chart furnishes training in certain specific language abilities and skills such as selecting important information, being exact in observing and in recording, using accurate, clear, concise, descriptive words, securing logical organization, writing dates and proper names, using appropriate written mechanics such as capitals, periods, colons, and semicolons, and writing neatly and legibly.

In the primary grades the tabular chart is commonly developed as a class enterprise; in the intermediate grades and in the upper grades, individual and group work is possible. Developmental procedure requires, in the first place, a worthy occasion for a record or chart that serves an immediate purpose in the activity. A study of the proper form of the record follows as a second step. In making a bird chart, for example, attention must be given to essential items, arrangement, and spacing. The form may be dictated by the teacher or developed with contributions from the class, depending on the maturity and experience of the pupils. Often models are helpful. If the record is an individual one for individual use, it is well to reach an agreement as to the exact form. After preparing the form, the pupil takes the next step by collecting and recording data. Key points in this phase of the experience are selecting important facts and arranging them in orderly form. In handling individual records, the teacher must, either through class discussion or through individual help, give his pupils some instruction in selecting and recording material. A checklist of goals serves to emphasize such crucial points, helps in locating weaknesses, and functions as a record of progress.

Diaries   Keeping a diary is a form of writing experience that may reasonably be considered under the general heading of study and research experiences. The classification is a logical one when the diary relates closely to some phase of schoolwork, whether class or individual. Thus a class, even as young as the kindergarten, may record in diary form significant experiences in building a post office, caring for a pet in the classroom, observing the behavior of a robin, or planting and caring for a garden. The record is still primarily a factual one when a class or individual writes a story of a bird or animal in the first person. The characteristics of the factual diary are similar to those of the record form treated earlier in the section.

Useful in social studies may be a diary of the progress of any new construction job which the children pass on the way to school. Keen observers, if encouraged to pool and share their observations of such projects as a new bridge, road, pavement, building, or dam, may provide the stimulus which will lead the children to a mine of information and acquaint them with new facts as well as new words and meanings. Fourth- or fifth-grade children may keep individual diaries in which they record the day when the excavation began, when cement was mixed and poured, when carpenters began work, etc. Terms such as *rivet, girder, beam, joist,* and *sill* may be listed and learned. Materials such as plaster, glass, copper, steel, and iron; and machines such as steam shovel, riveting machine, hammer, and screw driver may be named and studied. Young children may report information regarding all these matters to the teacher, who will keep the class diary on the board and add to it from day to day.

Considerable incidental learning takes place in a project like this. Much reading is necessary both by the children and the teacher to get essential information. It is the teacher's responsibility to provide practice to correct errors in the mechanics of oral and written expression. Music, art, spelling, science, health, safety education, reading, and mathematics will all find a way into the project if the teacher is alert and open minded—and he will find his own interests broadening with the experience.

A word of caution at this point may not be amiss. Once an interest has developed in a project such as the one described above, children in their zeal can become nuisances around the scene of construction. For this reason, it may be better for the teacher to appoint a committee who will report on the project or at intervals to take the group as a whole to observe progress in construction.

At times, the diary takes the form of an individual record of intimate personal experiences, and this form to some extent introduces elements of emotion and imagination that are characteristic of creative writing; but even the diary of personal experiences has some basis in facts. The following story by a teen-ager represents the recollection of a trip, which follows the on-the-spot diary or journal frequently kept by travelers:

> Last week I flew to Florida. When I left New York City the temperature was around zero. When I arrived in Florida the temperature was 78 degrees. Such a delightful change!
>
> The flight down was perfect! We flew non-stop so it took only three

hours. It was one of the most beautiful flights I have ever taken. The sky was a clear azure blue all of the way. At times cloud banks cut off our view of the earth, but most of the way the panorama of the country-side stretched out clearly below us in the bright, sparkling sun. It was a fascinating experience to watch the clean, white ground give way to bleak, barren terrain, which in turn became green and lush. We stepped into the plane in a cold, winter world and stepped out of it three hours later into a warm, summer climate. It was sheer magic!

My stay in Florida was just wonderful. I had such a good time! Our plane was met at the airport by a limousine which whisked us off to a swank hotel. As soon as we arrived we were invited to a reception on the terrace.[7]

Closely akin to the diary is the autobiography, which according to Don Wolfe represents the only democratic art capable of achievement in the schools at large.[8] Wolfe seeks to help students limit the topic of the autobiography to an introduction, five moments of an experience, and a conclusion. Autobiographies or portions of autobiographies, such as the following, are read to the junior or senior high school class: [9]

AUTOBIOGRAPHY

I squirm deeper into my seat as the bus races through the rain-soaked August night, its lights bouncing from the filmed highway and jutting into the mist drifting from the black Jersey swamps. I'm leaving behind a part of myself, a part that I'll never get back again. The asphalt ribbon is broken by the flaring neon mosaic of passing roadhouses and drive-ins, and as these patterns of light flash past me I wonder if that's all a man is: a series of sections scattered through the world with only memories to pull the threads together. Threads. Threads twining through time; threads of love, truth, and aloneness; the threads of one's self—wrapped by the elusive threads of dreams.

This is the last run from Washington to New York; the bus is almost empty. A few passengers occupy the red-covered seats; their heads roll against the chairbacks and nod with the lurching of the darkened bus. My leg jostles the seabag propped alongside me, leaving a smudge on my starched uniform. I move my hand slowly toward my knee, then stop and lean back in the seat. Why should I bother? Who's going to chew me out? I've got my discharge from the Navy; there's no need to worry about a clean uniform any more—no need at all—I'm free. I'm going home. I should be happy—that's for sure.

---

[7] James A. Smith, *Creative Teaching of the Language Arts in the Elementary School*, Allyn and Bacon, Inc., Boston, 1967, p. 35. Quoted with special permission of author and publisher.

[8] Don M. Wolfe, "A Realistic Writing Program," in Arno Jewett and others, *Improving English Skills of Culturally Different Youth in Large Cities*, U.S. Office of Education, Washington, D.C., 1964, p. 89. Quoted with special permission of author and publisher.

[9] *Ibid.*

But free for what?

A tired melancholy fills me as a I rest my head on the cool window glass.
Charles Bryan

As to uses in school, the teacher will recognize that the diary and autobiography are records not only of facts and experiences but of feelings too. The personal diary and the autobiography are the kinds of experiences that are closely related to the self and cannot be attempted without close teacher-pupil rapport. It is to be recognized that most interaction will be between the individual and the teacher.

Problems, questions, outlines, lists

Problem and questions In the beginning of a study of any large informational area of the curriculum it is necessary, first, to set up as a goal of study an important theme, principle, or generalization; and second, to break it down into subproblems or topics to provide a basis for systematic study, including gathering and recording information. Both phases of study bring into play important language abilities that are properly treated in this section.

The teacher naturally assumes the major responsibility for setting up major goals of understanding in the lower primary grades; but beginning with the third grade and increasingly beyond this grade, the teacher expects the children to share in that responsibility. Thus, in the third grade the children may help formulate and consider such questions as, What are the primary needs of primitive people, and how do they meet them? How do animals prepare for winter? How can we protect ourselves against colds? In a unit on "How Do Firemen Help Us?" the teacher and pupils listed the following questions for study:

1 What should one do in the case of fire?
2 What do firemen do at a fire?
3 What equipment do firemen use?
4 How is a fire department organized?
5 How do firemen live?
6 How are firemen trained?
7 How can we help prevent fire?
8 How much is lost in a fire, and how can we protect ourselves against loss by fire?
9 Who pays for the fire department?
10 How did people protect themselves from fire in earlier times?

In the later grades a class, in the study of a large unit, may be invited to set up a key problem such as, How can we account for the present emergence of African states? How do animals protect themselves against their enemies? What should be accomplished in a unit on safety or community health? Implied in the ability to set up large questions or problems for the study of a unit is some preliminary knowledge of the unit and the ability to search for and recognize large integrating issues. Discovering and formulating significant problems require thinking of a high order; and thinking, as we have found, is closely correlated to language. Sound thinking and the statement of an idea in clear, vigorous language are inseparably related. Whether the basic idea is expressed as a topic, problem, generalization, rule, or principle is not so important as the attitude of the learner—a state of mind rather than a linguistic pattern. However, the exact formulation of the problem in words is important as an indication of clear thinking.

Breaking down the large topic into key subtopics is a necessary second step in systematic study. Thus, in considering why Alaska is so sparsely populated and what opportunities are offered for settlement, an upper-grade class listed the following topics, among others:

1   Why more people have not gone there before
2   The type of people living there now
3   Opportunities for making a comfortable living
4   Climate
5   Social advantages

Requisite for logically listing topics is a sense of the importance of details and their relationship to the main problem, and the ability to formulate questions and statements in clear, thought-provoking language.

Outlines   Outlines commonly serve two purposes: to provide a guide to the study of a problem or topic, or to summarize the results of the study. Beginnings in outlining are made as early as the kindergarten, where the teacher and pupils list what they see on a trip in the neighborhood: people, automobiles, flowers, animals; or in the first grade, where they make a list of buildings commonly found on a farm: house, barn, milk house, tool shed. In later grades the outline becomes more pretentious, showing a grouping of related topics under a number of major heads.

The basis of good outlining and related activities is clear

thinking—comprehension and understanding of what is important and how it should be organized. Good outlining is based on
recognition of logical relationships among ideas. Related written
mechanics deal with the standard forms for outlining and listing,
including proper arrangement and spacing, and with the correct
use of capitals for items and of periods and colons as needed.

Essential requisites for teaching outlining are an occasion
when the pupils need to use it and possession of information that
can be put into outline form. Outlining is not to be taught mechanically as an isolated drill exercise. Children should not be required
to outline until they have something that requires outlining,
something presenting itself first in the experience of the child.
The outline then serves the purpose of ordering and organizing
children's experience and knowledge.[10]

The pupils will need help with the outline form, the use of
letters and numerals for topics, arrangement and spacing, and
capitalization and punctuation. Ideas of correct form may be obtained from the study of models or dictated by the teacher. The
significance of the form in showing relationships between ideas
should be emphasized. The teacher and class together may profitably prepare an outline for the study of a typical topic or problem,
or possibly several. Individual performance in outlining follows
a group assignment. Outlines are compared, differences noted,
and suggestions for improvement given. Opportunities for preparing outlines in all appropriate phases of the work should be
utilized.

An example of outlining experiences is provided by the work
of the children in a third-grade class at the W. B. Holland School
in Fresno, California, who, under the direction of Miss Irma Grosse,
undertook the study of the Pacific Rim of Fire—an earth science–
social studies unit. With samples of lava, pictures, diagrams, and
models, the teacher involved the children in a study and discussion
of volcanoes. As the work progressed, the children were led to
understandings of areas in the world where volcanoes can be seen.
In describing the Pacific Rim of Fire, certain areas such as Alaska,
various Pacific islands, and portions of Central and South America
were named. Setting the stage for visiting specific lands in the
Pacific Rim of Fire, the teacher arranged exhibits and displays to
depict various aspects of life, specifically in Alaska, Japan, and
Mexico. Discussion revealed to the class that a plan of attack

[10] Mauree Applegate, "Outlining," in Verna D. Anderson and others,
Readings in the Language Arts, The Macmillan Company, New York, 1964,
pp. 139–143.

would be needed to become acquainted with the people who live in such different parts of the Rim of Fire. General questions raised by the children were: What kinds of schools for children are there? How do the people dress? Is there farming? How do people earn their living? What kind of government is there? Do they have Christmas? The questions were listed on the chalkboard; and from them the children determined the following categories:

1	Location	6	Religion
2	People	7	Occupations
3	Homes	8	Government–history
4	Holidays	9	Trade
5	Education	10	Miscellaneous

Using these categories, the teacher labeled ten large envelopes with the main topics. The envelopes were attached to the chalk tray, and questions on each topic were put into the appropriate envelopes. The initial questions and those added later provided the details of the outline.

The first land area to be studied was Alaska, and it became apparent that much study and research would be necessary to answer the questions. Committees were formed to investigate the various topics. Filmstrips, motion pictures, study prints, realia, reference books, and persons in the community were all used as sources. The children frequently referred to the questions to determine their progress. In culminating this first phase of the study, the committee orally reported their findings about Alaska, using the major topics of the outline as their guide. The outline provided an approach to the next two phases of the study—Japan and Mexico —and the findings in each phase provided means by which various aspects of life in Alaska, Japan, and Mexico could be compared and contrasted.

The third-grade children completed their study of the Pacific Rim of Fire, which had started with Mt. Lassen in California, by going to Alaska and Japan, adding side trips to the Philippines and Hawaii, taking a brief look at volcanoes in South America, studying Mexico, and returning to California.

Lists Similar to the outline in form but simpler in organization is the list: a shopping memorandum, materials needed in a construction activity, items for a party, equipment for a field trip, the contents of a first-aid kit, a checklist of standards of reading. When a group of primary children were preparing to dramatize the story of Hansel and Gretel, they prepared the following list of stage properties and materials they would need:

Scenery for Act I. In the kitchen
Scenery for Act II. In the forest
Scenery for Act III. At the witch's house
Properties: Candy house, table, chair, fireplace, cage, oven

Notes and summaries

Note taking and summary writing are important phases of language-study experiences. With a list of guide topics or questions, the pupils consult various sources and make notes of significant information bearing on the topics. Summarizing may be regarded as bringing together material accumulated from various sources, selecting and validating what is needed, and arranging the pertinent information into an orderly, coherent whole. The unit in summarizing may be the whole topic or a single subtopic or question.

Note taking requires the judicious selection of material relating to a topic or problem on the basis of pertinency and validity. To recognize important material and to report accurately and concisely are important aspects. Statements may be quoted verbatim as facts, opinions, principles, and conclusions; or the content may be expressed in the pupil's own words. Copying is sometimes necessary, but pupils should never be allowed to quote verbatim without using quotation marks and crediting their sources. Summarizing requires digesting material; seeing important issues; reconciling conflicting authority; reaching conclusions, often one's own; giving sufficient detail to support the conclusions; and expressing conclusions in clear, concise language.

Pupils must be shown how to take notes and how to summarize. These skills can be taught best by dealing with real, immediate situations. At first the pupils should work out topics and questions as a class exercise. Having set the topics or questions, the pupils may study a common source, such as a textbook, and report or take notes on the material. Or each pupil may work with a separate source, a more difficult task; then he reports to the class the material pertinent to the topic, and class discussion follows. When developmental procedures of this type are mastered the pupils may be allowed to proceed independently, working on selected topics individually.

Language books may provide helpful suggestions, exercises, and illustrations. A more fully developed practice lesson in note taking, suggesting procedures that a teacher might use, is provided by Dawson for children at the sixth-grade level: [11]

Taking Notes
It is necessary to take notes on what you have been reading if you wish to remember and use what you learned. Study the notes which follow:
Undersea Cable
Compton's Pictured Encyclopedia, vol. 3, pp. 5–7
Characteristics of undersea cable
Copper core for transmission of electric current. Core surrounded by layers of insulating materials
Cable lasts 30–40 years
Laying the cable
Especially equipped cable-laying ship follows charted path
Guiding device feeds out cable
Check the model against the list of suggestions below. Be prepared to show that the student followed them.
How to take notes
Write the topic at the top.
Give the title of the book, the author, and the page.
Use abbreviations that are easy to interpret.
Group facts under major headings.
Record facts accurately.
Practice: Taking notes
Take notes on a topic of your choice from two or more sources of information. Follow the suggestions above.

The study-language experiences of note taking and summarizing are characteristic of those phases of the curricular, and to some extent extracurricular, program that deal with getting and understanding information. In the beginning grades the pupils make mental notes from observations and interviews and give them to the class orally; and they frequently combine several points in the form of an oral summary. Such brief summaries are common in the discussion of topics in health, social studies, and science—how we brush our teeth, why a rabbit lives in a hole in the ground, and what the milkman does for us. Written notes and summaries are made on the chalkboard by the teacher at the dictation of the pupils. Gradually the pupils assume individual responsibility for more comprehensive oral summaries and for writing notes and summaries. Though social studies, science, and the health program continue to provide the chief occasions for

[11] Mildred A. Dawson and others, *Language for Daily Use, Grade 6,* Harcourt, Brace & World, Inc., New York, 1964, p. 113. Quoted with special permission of author and publisher.

using the study-language experiences, pupils also prepare summaries of books and articles, program notes in music, community experiences such as a visit to the county fair, and procedures in a hobby such as making an airplane.

Indexes and bibliographies

The study of indexes and bibliographies involves both reading and writing techniques. In reading, the pupil uses the index or table of contents to locate information on a given topic. He uses bibliographic lists to locate promising sources of material. In written work, he prepares an index or table of contents of material in a comprehensive record, report, or summary, such as a bird book, an informational summary of a unit in the social studies, a classbook or magazine, a pleasure-reading guide in a library unit, or a newspaper. He also prepares bibliographies of source material on a given unit or topic, indicates sources of information or citations by reference, and prepares recommended reading lists, possibly arranged topically.

Apart from selecting references of suitable material, the writing factors are mainly mechanical in nature: choosing the proper form, as in arrangement and spacing of the title page; exhibiting accuracy in the author's name, title of book, page or chapter, and date of copyright; alphabetizing titles; emphasizing titles by the use of quotation marks or underlining; using proper punctuation marks; and demonstrating habits of neatness.

As in other phases of work in which matters of form are conventionalized, the study of models is the best approach. Attention may be called to the way indexes, tables of contents, and bibliographies are handled in sources consulted in the reading phase of research; or the textbook may provide models and directions. Careful checking of a pupil's work by himself and by the teacher is required for accuracy. Planning the form, as in blocking out a title page for arrangement and spacing, will improve final results.

Use of the dictionary

The dictionary is used largely for checking pronunciation and clarifying meaning in close connection with various information-getting subjects—reading, social studies, mathematics. Dictionary training for the interpretation of reading materials will not necessarily enable the individual to use the dictionary effectively in facilitating his own expression. Use for expression purposes must be taught as definitely and specifically as spelling and handwriting. The dictionary is a reference book containing much more material than the pupil will need at one time. The pupil consults the dictionary for a particular purpose, and he must learn to find and select the information he needs and to ignore other information. Some facts of permanent value, such as the spelling of a common word, are to be memorized at the time; other facts have a temporary use. Instruction should be arranged and graded in sequential steps and attention must be given to individual differences in readiness.[12]

Sequence of steps   Before pupils start to use a commercial dictionary, they should be fully familiar with the alphabetical order of letters. In the first two grades they begin memorizing letters and arranging small groups of words in order according to the initial letters. They next make their own dictionaries of useful words, employing the word box at the second-grade level and the notebook at the third. They become further acquainted with alphabetical lists in their readers and spellers. They use picture dictionaries. Alphabetizing by all letters is not learned, however, before the fifth grade.

A practical use of the dictionary by pupils is to check the spelling of familiar words. Preparation for this use has been made through employing their own dictionaries and the spelling lists in textbooks for the same purpose. Related to this experience, but coming in the fourth grade, is learning syllabication. Syllables are noted in reading and spelling. A practical need for such knowledge appears in written work when it is necessary to divide the word at the end of a line.

Use of the dictionary to verify the pronunciation of common words comes at about the fifth-grade level. Marks for the long and short sounds of vowels and the accent are learned first; other diacritical marks are learned as needed. Attention is also called to the preferred spelling.

The final use of the dictionary is to note the exact meaning of words that are vaguely familiar. Attention is called to the several meanings listed, and drill is provided in the selection of the mean-

[12] Robert C. Pooley, "Language, Linguistics, and School Programs," *Proceedings of the Spring Institutes,* National Council of Teachers of English, Champaign, Ill., 1963.

ing appropriate to the immediate use. The study of synonyms and antonyms may be used to enrich and vary pupils' expression at about the fifth- or sixth-grade level.

Language books provide exercises for use in the several grades. In them are exercises for accent, alphabetical order, definitions, use of guide words, pronunciation, and synonyms. Instruction on a particular step in dictionary study is provided for the class or group when there is an immediate need and when the pupils are ready for such instruction. Demonstrations and explanations are key procedures. Practice exercises may be provided as prepared by the teacher or selected from textbooks or workbooks. Advantage should be taken of opportunities to use the new skill in purposeful situations. Checking and supervision should be continued until mastery is attained. As in other phases of language work, sensitivity to quality of performance—a language consciousness—must be cultivated.

Evaluation   Study, research, and reporting imply seeing problems; observing, listening, reading; testing; and making use of findings. The understandings, abilities, and skills that can emerge from children's meaningful experiences develop an approach to thoughtful analyses of problems. The future for every child promises further rapid expansions of knowledge and technology and concomitantly necessitates that each possess the means by which social problems can be met.

Helping children to acquire the understandings of approach, the knowledge of the use of appropriate tools, and the needed organizing and synthesizing insights are major responsibilities of the teacher. Traditionally, the main devices to measure children's progress have been tests that measure the skills in the use of the tools—the encyclopedia, world almanac, dictionary—and the skills and mechanics of organization—note taking, outlining, summarizing. While these skills and abilities are essential, necessarily taught, and sequentially amplified, children's development in other aspects of study, research, and reporting must also be considered. Abilities in formulating questions for study, seeing issues, approaching reference materials, organizing, and synthesizing depend on the development of experiences in the language arts, the social studies, and the sciences. If children are not given opportunities to ask questions, to discuss issues, to offer varying points of view, and to draw conclusions, the evaluation of these abilities cannot be made. Evaluation of the attitudes of children toward study, research, and reporting can be made in terms of the teacher's goals, as he develops his objectives and the procedures and materials that will be used to accomplish his goals.

For your consideration

1   Attempt to recall when and how you first learned the use of the following tools: (*a*) index; (*b*) dictionary; (*c*) encyclopedia; (*d*) author, title, and subject cards in the card catalogue of a library; and (*e*) *The Reader's Guide* and *The Education Index.*
2   Attempt to recall when and how you first learned to carry out the following activities: (*a*) taking notes, (*b*) outlining, (*c*) summarizing, (*d*) making footnotes, and (*e*) preparing a bibliography.
3   Discuss: The techniques of study, research, and reporting vary according to the nature of the problems to be investigated.
4   Investigate a social studies or science course of study and report the provisions made for the development of children's learnings in study, research, and reporting.
5   Outline an appropriate study-research experience for a particular grade, such as an informational experience chart, a tabular record, an outline.
6   Investigate the teacher's guides of several language arts textbooks and several reading textbooks for a particular grade. Note any provisions made for guiding children's learning in order to locate pertinent, factual information and for guiding learning in organizing this information for presentation.

References

ANDERSON, VERNA D., AND OTHERS: *Readings in the Language Arts,* The Macmillan Company, New York, 1964, pp. 139–143.

ARTLEY, A. STERL: "Readiness for Dictionary Usage," *Elementary English,* April, 1964, pp. 348–350.

BURROWS, ALVINA T., AND OTHERS: *They All Want to Write,* Holt, Rinehart and Winston, Inc., New York, 1965, chap. 3.

DREWES, RUTH H., AND OTHERS: *Practical Plans for Teaching English in Elementary Schools,* W. C. Brown Company, Publishers, Dubuque, Iowa, 1965, chaps. 10–12.

GREENE, HARRY A., AND W. T. PETTY: *Developing Language Skills in Elementary Schools,* Allyn and Bacon, Inc., Boston, 1967, pp. 196–199, 268–270.

HATFIELD, W. W.: *An Experience Curriculum in English,* Appleton-Century-Crofts, Inc., New York, 1935, pp. 197–207.

MC KEE, PAUL: *Language in the Elementary School,* Houghton Mifflin Company, Boston, 1939, pp. 189–194, 202–208.

MAHONEY, SALLY: "Basic Study Skills and Tools," *Elementary English,* vol. 42, December, 1965, pp. 905–915.

PETTY, WALTER T.: *The Language Arts in Elementary Schools,* The Center for Applied Research in Education, Inc., Washington, D.C., 1962, pp. 48–60.

STRICKLAND, RUTH G.: *The Language Arts in the Elementary School,* D. C. Heath and Company, Boston, 1957, pp. 286–289.

TIEDT, IRIS M., AND S. W. TIEDT: *Contemporary English in the Elementary School,* Prentice-Hall, Inc., Englewood Cliffs, N.J., 1967, pp. 178–180.

9.

CHILDREN'S
LITERATURE

When there are so many places to explore—the near, the far, the realistic, the imaginary; when there are so many times to visit—the long ago, the now, the future; when there are so many friends waiting to be met—the make-believe, the real, the almost true; when there are so many adventures to be had, how can we best encourage children to become readers?

Children need to meet the world of books. Whether this world of reading should be described as *recreational, inspirational, empathy-directed,* or *personal-value-oriented* is a matter of definition. Certainly these values and others are found in children's literature.

The development of the habit of reading is an integral part of the language arts program. Burns and Lowe state: [1]

> Reading is a habit. Once you acquire the habit you seldom lose it. But you must somehow be exposed to reading early in life to have it become a part of your daily routine, like washing your face or breathing. Many an unfortunate elementary school child in our highly seasoned, electronic, picture-conscious age has never been exposed to the reading habit,

[1] Paul C. Burns and Alberta L. Lowe, *The Language Arts in Childhood Education,* Rand McNally and Company, Chicago, 1966, p. 110. Quoted with special permission of author and publisher.

and cannot, therefore, read without an effort. Some modern children seldom if ever read for fun.

Recognizing that the teacher is a key figure in motivating children to become acquainted with the world of books, this chapter develops the role of the teacher, book selection, and techniques for sharing books, stories, and poems, with specific reference to experiences in dramatization and verse choir.

The role of the teacher   The teacher must become increasingly aware of the variety of literature for children; he must be cognizant of the offerings of literature in his day-by-day work with children. There are the poems and the stories of traditional literature—ranging from Mother Goose to ballads, from folk tales to fables, myths, and epics; while modern books offer a variety of characterization, plot, theme, and style within the framework of humor, fantasy, and biography. Modern illustrations, created in many styles and through various media, enhance the picture-book story and poem, helping to develop new perceptions in children. The teacher himself must be enthusiastic about storytelling, poetry reading, and storybook reading.

For any teacher, one or two basic anthologies of stories and poems are requisites. Collections such as those by Arbuthnot; [2] by Johnson, Sickles, and Sayers; [3] and by Huber [4] create a right-hand source of selected literary offerings. To become familiar with stories, poems, and books—by delving into the needs and interests of children and by exploring the ever-expanding field of trade books for children—is a necessity. By developing a poetry file for those special occasions that seem to be continually cropping up with children, by learning to tell stories naturally and effectively, by building up stores of titles and authors to help the child who says, "I loved this book. Give me another one just like it!", the teacher is on his way to creating readers.

The provision of a balanced diet in literature is a main concern in planning a program in a preschool, kindergarten through junior high, or senior high school sequence. Young children need to hear the favorite "talking beast" tales of *The Three Little Pigs, The Little Red Hen,* and *The Three Billy Goats Gruff,* while they are being exposed also to other kinds of animal stories, such as

[2] May Hill Arbuthnot, *Time for Poetry; Time for Fairy Tales; Time for True Tales,* 2d ed., Scott, Foresman and Company, Chicago, 1961.

[3] Edna Johnson and others, *Anthology of Children's Literature,* Houghton Mifflin and Company, Boston, 1959.

[4] Miriam Blanton Huber, *Story and Verse for Children,* The Macmillan Company, New York, 1964.

Lynd Ward's *Biggest Bear,* Clare Newberry's books about her appealing cats, and C. W. Anderson's "Blaze" stories. They need the experience of seeing and listening to the reading of such books as Ezra Jack Keats's *The Snowy Day,* which is an adventure in viewing color and shape in relation to the realistic experiences of a little boy in snow country. Stories, poems, and books of the imaginative, the realistic, the humorous, the active, and the quiet need to be presented in the early years of school, for it is then that the book habit is started. Verse, from the themes of Mother Goose and Dr. Seuss to the poetry of Elizabeth Madox Roberts, Robert Louis Stevenson, and Harry Behn, presents examples of varied listening and perhaps opportunities for spontaneous re- peating experiences. The experiences of hearing, seeing, touching, turning pages, examining pictures, observing the printed symbols of language, and casually commenting on those elements found interesting are essentials in children's initiation to literature.

If we believe that interests are learned and that teachers are the agents for change, then the selection of books in the classroom and school libraries, the stories and poems read to children, and an active teacher as catalyst remain eminently important as chil- dren progress through school. Often after the first few years of school, there seems to be a slackening of interest in reading on the part of children. Too often, teachers stop the practice of reading to children when their classes have attained the educational level when all should know how to read. Perhaps the insistence on a written book report for every book read detracts from the fun of reading. Often the school district's central library services do not fit the needs of the expanding range of interests and reading abilities of the children. Far too often teachers complain that the overcrowded curriculum leaves no time for recreational reading; and in this setting the only time allotted to free reading in the elementary school is that time when the child finishes his math assignment or gets a perfect score on his spelling test.

For the teacher who is well grounded in the knowledge of literature, the continuous "selling" of books to his older pupils can be accomplished; the key is his interest in assessing his pupils and the field of literature. How exciting it is to hear portions of England's earliest history read from Rosemary Sutcliff's books of historical fiction, *The Lantern Bearers* and *Dawn Wind,* when one is attempting to learn about that period of history! How interesting to hear the way Benet's *A Book of Americans* characterizes famous Americans in verse! How fascinating to compare the motion-pic- ture versions with the books of . . . *And Now Miguel, Island of the Blue Dolphins, Mary Poppins,* and *The Story of Dr. Dolittle!* And, certainly, how reassuring to find a book one can read and enjoy for oneself on the bookshelf of the classroom or school library!

Book selection   In the understanding of children's needs and a knowledge of the spectrum of children's literature, the teacher, the school staff, and the school district can develop guidelines for book acquisition. The mushrooming of the trade book industry in the United States has made the evaluation of new publications a stupendous task. Nothing can ever replace the reading and evaluation of a current book, but the teacher needs assistance in directing his attention to the books, both of the past and present, which may have significance in his work with children.

To assess briefly the needs of children, which to some extent may be met through books as a part of life, May Hill Arbuthnot suggests that there are basic needs common to most peoples and to most times: [5]

1   Competence—the need to achieve
2   Material security—the need for physical well-being
3   Intellectual security—the need to know
4   Emotional security—the need to love and be loved
5   Acceptance—the need to belong

She further suggests that books rich in meaning for the child can help him in his search for balance between himself and society.

From Sam in Jean George's *My Side of the Mountain* to the tales of Robin Hood in the ballads, to the feats of Paul Bunyan, competence is mirrored. Material rewards are pictured as outcomes of the struggles of the folk-tale personages of Dick Whittington, Cinderella, and Snow White, as well as depicted by the Lechow family in *The Ark* by Margot Benary-Isbert and by Boy in Ester Wier's *The Loner*. The curiosity of the child indicated in his many *whys* can be encouraged, and it in turn can be developed into interests by the variety of informational books available from subject A—*animals, aerophotography, astronomy,* to subject Z— *zebras, zoos,* and *zero.* The families in the regional books by Lois Lenski, in Archie Binns' *Sea Pup,* and in Madeleine L'Engle's *Meet the Austins* may give some insight into families that meet problems together, thus providing a glimpse into the creation of emotional security. The need for change—to "get out of oneself"—may be realized in many ways, perhaps through the magic of George

[5] May Hill Arbuthnot, *Children and Books,* Scott, Foresman and Company, Chicago, 1964, pp. 3–10.

Selden's *Cricket in Times Square,* by the laughter provoked by Lorenzini's *Pinocchio,* or by scaling the mountain with Rudi in James Ullman's *Banner in the Sky.*

How best to select books to meet the needs of children is an important issue. Guides for selecting books with substantial theme, characterization, and plot, and with significant contributions of style are available to assist the teacher. In the bibliography following this chapter, sources are cited; but there are several that need emphasizing. *The Children's Catalog,*[6] updated yearly, is a subject-author-title annotated listing of books in which distinguished books are starred. *The Horn Book Magazine,*[7] published six times a year, reviews current books for children and is a good guide in keeping abreast with the field. For schools interested in developing a school library, *The Children's Catalog,* the American Library Association's *A Basic Book Collection for Elementary Grades,* and *A Basic Book Collection for Junior High Schools*[8] are essential tools with which to begin. The Children's Book Council, Incorporated,[9] is headquarters for National Children's Book Week and a year-round promotion and information center for children's books. The Council's *Calendar* is a quarterly publication, sent free of charge, in which is found current information on such subjects as new books appropriate for the season, awards and prizes for outstanding books, materials available from publishing companies, and Council material to use for Book Week and the motivation of vacation reading.

Sharing of books   Children and young people do "sell" books to each other, for librarians attest to the popularity of certain books as one child tells others about the riches found in a certain volume. How best to utilize this message system is a concern of the teacher.

The oral activities of creative book reporting, book talks and teasers, and riddles such as "Guess what book character I am?" are channels for sharing the excitement and the involvement in books. For children who enjoy painting, their cut-out characters and scenery of a favorite story backed by flannel or a bit of sandpaper, provide the props for a flannel-board presentation. The oral reading of a portion of action and suspense, pathos,

[6] Dorothy H. West and Rachel Shor, *The Children's Catalog,* H. W. Wilson Company, New York, 1961.

[7] The address of the publishers of *The Horn Book Magazine* is 528 Boylston Street, Boston, Mass. 02130.

[8] American Library Association, *A Basic Book Collection for Elementary Grades,* 1960; *A Basic Book Collection for Junior High School,* 1960.

[9] The address for the Children's Book Council, Inc., is 175 Fifth Avenue, New York, N.Y. 10010.

or hilarity by one child gives an opportunity for oral interpretation of the printed page. The making of murals, with each child contributing a figure of his favorite book character, may be another way of sharing reading pleasure.

To truly share books, there must be various avenues of expression; the written book report is one of them. These reports sometimes take the form of a brief outline, which initially may be presented orally and then filed in a classroom file of Books I Like Best, perhaps by subject, for future reference of others in the class. The following example by a fifth-grade girl represents such reporting:

Book Report—Caryl
1. Title—*The True Book of American Animals*
2. Author—John Wallace Purcell
3. Nonfiction
4. I liked the tickbirds best. They were a friend of the buffalo. These birds eat ticks. They also warn him of danger. In turn the tickbirds get a free meal and ride.
5. I liked the part when the mother hippo took her baby out to an island in the river. A crocodile almost got it. But his mother saved it in time.

The next book reports, representing a free form of reporting, are given here exactly as written by fifth-grade children, all members of the same group:

My favorite book is an Pueblo Indian story the name is "The Missing Kachina" the story is by Grace Moon. There are several other books by her too. but I like the Missing Kachina best. I like her stories because they are all exciting. There are parts in all her storys where the ones she writes finds gold or something. You may be able to find her storys most any library. I am sure you would enjoy her storys.

My favorite book is "Donald Duck and his Friends." The chapter I like best is the Fire engine and the hotel caught on Fire. if you read this story you would like it.

A book that I read and liked a lot is Heidi. It was written,—J. Spyri. And the main characters are, Heidi, the Uncle, Peter, and his Grandmother. The part I liked a lot was where Peter rolled the wheel chair down the mountain and if you want to know what happened to him and many other exciting things read the book.

This book is a good book and its name is Smoky. I like the part where he and another horse got in a fight, and the other horse got killed. I didn't finish it, boy I bet he didn't get kilt.

I read The Secret Garden by Frances H. Burnett. I think it was interesting because it started out with an ugly little girl named Mary.
Later in the story she goes to live with her uncle in a big house in London.
Lots of other things happened to her but if you want to know what happened read the book.

It may be noted that, while the children seemed to like their books because of some element of mystery or excitement, there is nevertheless a wide range in maturity of expression and in reading ability, as evidenced by the choice of books read and reported on. One child is acquainted not only with the author of her book, *The Missing Kachina,* but with other stories by the same author, and she has even discovered familiar characteristics of this author. The child is struggling for expression and needs considerable help in the mechanics of writing, but in spite of these difficulties she has written quite an acceptable report.

The reader of *Donald Duck* enjoyed the story; and the report, while immature, is after all a beginning. The *Heidi* report, though not long, is complete and seems almost literary in style. The writer has conveyed in these few lines the impression that she enjoyed the story very much and that she is a bookish little girl. On the other hand, the reporter of *Smoky* is obviously not a great reader and finds written expression almost too much for him. Though he enjoyed the excitement of *Smoky,* he probably needs additional reading experience before attempting further reporting. And finally, *The Secret Garden* shows quite mature sentence structure and vocabulary. Paragraphing, punctuation, and spelling are also unusually good; one feels that this child has a wide reading background and is quite capable of making the analysis necessary for a good book report.

Written reports such as these should be filed individually by the children to be taken home and shared ultimately with other members of the family. The wise teacher seeks to "publish" book reports in as many ways as possible before they are carried home, however. From time to time, to compensate for faulty handwriting, spelling, and mechanics, the teacher-typewritten reports of all of the children's work in book reporting may result in a series of room booklets entitled "Have you read these books?" or "Try these books for fun." These are useful for browsing by the children as well as for providing bait for encouraging further reading. Through the medium of a weekly room newspaper children's book reports, as well as their other writings, can be published further.

Dramatization

Dramatization is a natural way to share the fun and excitement of literature, and it also is a means by which learnings in the subject areas of the school can be clarified. Hence, the following discussion focuses on aspects of dramatization throughout the school day.

Dramatization experiences take several forms: finger play, dramatic play, pantomime, informal dramatization, puppets, and formal dramatization. These forms represent progressive stages in child development from egocentric to social behavior, and they challenge the child's increasing ability to handle complex experiences. The teacher naturally chooses the form that is appropriate to the level of maturity of the children, but he does not restrict the class to any one form; variety is desirable to avoid monotony, to fit particular situations in various phases of schoolwork, and to meet a variety of specific goals in language development.

Finger play   Finger play is a simple form of poetic dramatization, thoroughly enjoyed by children and used to good effect by teachers in the lower grades. The enjoyment of literature is deepened by listening and speaking, accompanied by dramatic action. Finger plays deal with animals—kittens, squirrels, rabbits, pigs—and with familiar household tasks. Many of the poems include numbers, counting, and concepts of size and position. Opportunities are offered for speech training such as the sounding of troublesome letters.

A finger play thoroughly enjoyed by kindergarten children is the story of the little ducks. The action accompanying the poem is indicated by numbers. The teacher recites the poem, inviting children to participate in the action and in reciting the words with her. In the final action, five children may move off toward an imaginary barnyard. The poem can be repeated several times, different children taking the part of the five ducks going to the barnyard.

Little Ducks

Five little ducks, and they were new
Big ducks, little ducks, and fat ducks, too. (1)
One had a feather curled over his back (2)
And he leads the others with a quack, quack, quack. (3)
And he leads the others with a quack, quack, quack. (3)
And he leads the others with a quack, quack, quack. (3)
Down to the barnyard
They did go
A wibble-wabbity all in a row. (4)
One had a feather curled over his back (2)
And he leads the others with a quack, quack, quack.(3)

Action

1 Hold up hand with fingers up for five ducks.
2 For feather curled over back, crook first finger over fist.
3 Put palms together, one hand on top of the other, and open fingers for quack.
4 Keep hands together, lean forward slightly, and move back and forth for wibble-wabbity.

Dramatic play Dramatic play is the chief occupation of early childhood. Children spontaneously imitate older people and their activities, such as the mother dressing and feeding her children, the policeman helping pedestrians across the street, the motorman, and the postman; and they dramatize incidents from stories, comics, and movies. Through these activities the child identifies himself with other people, interprets their actions, and possibly unconsciously prepares himself for the fundamental activities of later life. The interest aroused and the vital type of experiences derived from dramatic play suggest its suitability as an instructional medium in those phases of the curriculum that are rich in people and incident, real or imagined. Through dramatic play the children gain richer understanding, experience in social behavior and leadership, stimulation for the imagination, training in language, pure enjoyment, and emotional release.

Spontaneous, undirected dramatic play is used in the kindergarten and first grade. Children are provided with an environment that stimulates play—blocks, toys, costumes—and allowed to choose freely, the purpose being to discover interests and to develop independence and resourcefulness, the ability to think, and relations with other children. For the most part, however, some direction to play is given by pointing to a particular topic under study. In a unit on the airport, for example, after some discussion of the movements of a plane, the duties of workers, and the responsibilities of passengers, the children freely selected particular phases for representation. Some children represented passengers getting tickets, making reservations, weighing baggage, and giving the baggage to a porter. Other children showed the mechanics checking and servicing the plane and starting the motor. Observation of the children by the teacher revealed the children's knowledge of the subject and areas of interest, as well as personal traits and social relationships.

In a unit on home life, centering in a playhouse, the children in one class discussed the members of a family and their duties. In a free-play period children assumed the roles of father, mother, children, and playmates, and spontaneously acted out various roles. One child was the father, who prepared for work and drove off in his car after saying good-by to the family. Another child was the mother, busying herself with the breakfast dishes and hurrying the children off to school. A third child played the part of the daughter of the family who fed the cat, greeted a chum at the door, and left with the chum for school. Suggested poems that might well be considered for use in this unit are "Sh" by James S. Tippitt, "Shoes" by Tom Robinson, and "Automobile Mechanics" by Dorothy Baruch. Other ways of viewing houses, homes, and the people who live within such structures might be presented by the books, *The Little House* by Virginia Lee Burton and *The Snowy Day* by Ezra Jack Keats.

In connection with the study of transportation, a group of children dramatized a foggy day in the harbor. Characters represented were an ocean liner, a tanker, a foghorn, a tugboat, the sea, and various people. The ocean liner was trying to find its way out. The two ships called to each other, located one another, and finally passed safely. The foghorn sent its warnings from time to time. The tugboat made contact with the liner and pushed it safely into its berth. The sea provided the sound effects of *sssssshhhhh*. With the consideration of water, waves, tugboat, and bridges in the harbor, Hardie Gramatky's *Little Toot* and Norman Bates's *Who Built the Bridge?* are natural outgrowths. And for children who can see the harbor in its various moods, Laura E. Richards's poem, "A Song for Hal," is irresistible with its "Every little wave has its night cap on—."

Pantomime   In pantomime the child expresses ideas and feelings by action, gestures, and facial expression without speaking; any lines to be spoken or read are done so by another child. Pantomime demands less of the performer in oral expression but more in physical expression. It offers a useful variation of experience in the early stages of dramatic development, and is especially valuable for the shy child who finds oral expression difficult. Pantomime gives the child confidence in acting and prepares for the more natural and interpretative expression in other forms of dramatization.

For young children, simple two- or three-sentence stories printed on oaktag cards by the teacher and distributed to the class or to a group of children for acting out may provide fun and promote reading and physical expression. Such a story as "I am a cat; I drink some milk; and then I wash my face" may be interpreted by one child while the others guess what he is playing. Sometimes children dramatize their own stories.

The following Halloween poem, written by a group of children, was dramatized repeatedly by different individuals, each giving a different interpretation. Usually the class repeated the poem in unison with appropriately sepulchral tones.

Around the corner
Of my house
Came a weird-looking witch.
She wore a tall hat,
A black gown,
And on her shoulder
Perched a fierce black cat.
She rapped upon my window;
Then swiftly flew away.

At times the pantomiming of Mother Goose rhymes provides an excellent means by which all children can participate. Older children have similar opportunities in the pantomiming of favorite book characters, such as Tom Sawyer whitewashing the fence. Sometimes older children work in small groups with a minimum of props to pantomime specific sections of books—perhaps a portion of Beverly Cleary's *Henry Huggins,* Robert Louis Stevenson's *Treasure Island,* or Eleanor Cameron's *The Terrible Churnadryne.*

Informal dramatization   Dramatic play and pantomime gradually merge into a stage that may be identified as informal dramatization; that is, any informal acting out of a story, rhyme, or life situation involving a series of related incidents and produced by several members of the group. Informal dramatization is characterized by spontaneity, simplicity of organization, and natural expression. Speeches are not memorized, and dramatic action is not dictated or molded into a fixed pattern; variations in performance appear in each repetition. The acting itself may be done by one child or several. The teacher may be conscious of a secondary goal, but to the children the play is self-sustaining and it is self-sufficient. The initiation of a play may be suggested by the teacher or may be simply the spontaneous desire of the children to have a play. The values of informal dramatization are the development of fluency, spontaneity, imagination, originality, and a social spirit.

A primary group had dramatized "The Three Bears," "Little Red Riding Hood," and "The Three Billy Goats Gruff" when the teacher suggested that it might be fun to make up a play of their own and act it out. She appointed a committee consisting of two boys and two girls, with Ann as chairman. The teacher suggested that they have a meeting in the morning before school to make up their play and, if they needed additional characters, to choose them from the class. She gave no instructions as to what the play should be about; she did suggest, however, that it would be better to have only a few characters—four or five.

The next morning Ann was at school earlier than usual; and as her committee members arrived, they joined her in a far corner of the room, where they talked animatedly for a time. Then Ann asked two other children to join them. After another short conference, Ann came to the teacher to say that they had made up the play and would like to rehearse privately. The teacher took them to a small room on another floor and left them there. In about fifteen minutes the committee returned to the classroom with the announcement that the play was ready whenever there was time to put it on. They were told that at 2 P.M. there would be time; and this appointment was written on the bulletin board, causing a ripple of anticipation around the class.

When the time arrived, Ann took charge. Props consisted of school furniture arranged to suggest a schoolroom at one side of the room and a home at the other side. A bit of realism was added by means of a windowstick tree midway between the home and the school.

When all was ready, Ann announced, "We're going to give a play called 'Schooltime.' Alfred is the dog, Blackie; Garth is the cat, Spot; Marlyne and Susan are schoolgirls; Alice is the mother; I'm the teacher in the school." Ann then took her place at the school side of the room, and the play began.

MOTHER (*shaking the two schoolgirls*): Wake up, children. Wake up! Get ready for school.
MARLYNE: My, I'm sleepy.
SUSAN: I don't want to get up yet.
MOTHER: But you must. Come, get dressed. Here, eat your breakfast. (*Children dress and eat hurriedly.*)
CHILDREN: Good-by, Mother.
MOTHER: Good-by. Be good, children.
(*Dog barks and cavorts around. Cat mews and rubs against girls. Children walk to school—across the room—and stop to pick flowers on the way.*)
TEACHER: Good morning, children.
CHILDREN: Good morning.
TEACHER: Take your seats. We must get right at our work.

(*Teacher puts an addition problem on the board. Dog begins to bark on the school steps. Cat arrives and mews.*)

TEACHER (*goes to door*):   Go home! Go on home! You're a naughty dog and cat. Girls, why don't you shut your dog up?

(*Dog and cat go slowly across room toward home.*)

TEACHER: Marlyne, come and work this problem.

(*Marlyne goes to board and works the problem.*)

TEACHER: Susan, you may correct it.

(*Susan marks it C.*)

TEACHER: Now, girls, we will read.

(*Girls get books and read aloud. Dog and cat create disturbance at school door and are again driven home. Reading continues, girls taking turns.*)

TEACHER: School is over now. Put on your coats. Susan, where are your mittens?

SUSAN: In my pocket.

TEACHER: Better put them on. Good-by, girls.

GIRLS: Good-by.

(*Girls skip home, where dog and cat bark and mew their welcome.*)

MOTHER: Eat your supper now, girls, and go right to bed.

GIRLS: Good night, Mother.

MOTHER: Good night.

The class applauded, for they liked the play. In the discussion that followed, suggestions and criticisms were made: "I liked the way the dog, Alfred, stood on his hind legs." "I liked the way the cat kept trying to sneak out. That was funny." "Ann made a good teacher." "That was a good play. It was funny." "I think there might have been more talking." "I couldn't hear quite all that Alice said."

For this first attempt at original play production, the children had wisely chosen a simple theme with which they were familiar. There was nothing unusual about the vocabulary, sentence structure, story, or acting, but because the audience approved, the committee was pleased; and the teacher felt that the work as a committee—the feeling of responsibility, the sharing and pooling of ideas—had made the undertaking worthwhile. One of the characters was an extremely self-effacing little girl who had never volunteered for anything, but because she wanted to help Ann and the committee and probably because the theme was a simple, thoroughly familiar one, she did her part remarkably well. Imagination and ingenuity were taxed in setting and props, and in the end such great satisfaction was felt that another committee was appointed to make up another play for the next day.

A fifth-grade class that had been studying China, Japan, and California was asked to demonstrate the culmination of a unit of work in the social studies. Apparently quite disconnected, the three areas of the unit were brought together by means of a dramatization that took the form of a joint meeting of chambers of commerce of the three countries in the attempt to work out trade agreements. The representatives of each country were prepared to say what they wanted to buy and what they had to sell. Good sales talks required some explanation of the quality of their products and reasons for their superiority.

Often one finds one or two children who, if given free rein, will develop unsuspected powers of leadership or originality in periods of informal dramatization, and the class will be carried along by their enthusiasm. As long as the experience shows growth and steady improvement, all is well. Not only must enunciation, pronunciation, vocabulary, and usage be watched but also there must be steady improvement in dialogue, in the quality of subject matter chosen, and in acting. If and when the experience begins to degenerate into mere silliness, then of course it is time to stop.

Puppets   Puppets offer a variety of dramatic activity suitable for any grade level. In the primary grades clay animals, clothespin dolls, and cardboard figures are used as simple puppets; and the situations and stories are simple in plot. In the upper grades the puppets are more complex in construction, often dressed in costumes; a stage and stage settings are provided; and the play includes a number of scenes, several characters, and more mature dialogue. In the puppet shows the necessity for a pupil's personal appearance before the class and for bodily action is eliminated; the effectiveness of the production depends mainly on the use of the voice and the manipulation of the puppets. The extremely shy child who finds natural, face-to-face expression difficult or impossible may express himself quite freely when concealed behind the screen; even speech defects may disappear. With younger children puppetry provides opportunity to indulge in make-believe; for older children it motivates close study of factual material to portray accurately dress, customs, and language. It stimulates inventiveness, creativity, and individuality and provides some training in manipulative skills. It encourages clear enunciation and the vivid portrayal of feeling by the manipulation of the voice. It is adaptable to various phases of the school program, especially literature, social studies, and health.

A class of third graders decided, in the early winter, when colds became prevalent, to deal with the prevention of colds and use puppets in the dramatization. Puppets were made to represent Charles, Juanita, a school nurse, Mr. Germ, and his helper Mr.

Careless. Charles and Juanita were planning to go to a picnic, when Mr. Germ and Mr. Careless put in their appearance and tried to break up their plans. The school nurse appeared and saved the day by banishing Mr. Germ and Mr. Careless. Juanita and Charles went happily on their way.

Formal dramatization   Formal dramatization is characterized by more thorough planning of plot, characterization, lines, staging, and costumes. A play written by the children provides a good opportunity for the intensive study of a particular topic or theme as well as for dramatic experience. Producing plays prepared by others, although it provides an opportunity to study dramatic form and, of course, to interpret, lacks the richness of educative experience that writing plays provides. The occasion for formal dramatization is usually entertainment, and the teacher and pupils are often tempted to sacrifice educational values to entertainment values. The temptation is to use a few good performers, probably those who least need the training; to limit freedom of thought and expression; to waste time in repetition; and to waste time and money in preparing elaborate costumes. The ingenious teacher will find ways of minimizing if not eliminating these dangers, keeping the idea before the pupils and the public that the chief business of the school is to promote learning, not to provide professional entertainment.

Specific objectives   It must be apparent that dramatization presents highly motivated situations that create immediate needs for, and provide training in, many of the basic language abilities and oral skills. It is difficult to think of any of the fundamental aims of oral language which cannot be realized by means of dramatization. But dramatization places more emphasis on some aims than on others. First, performers must make themselves heard and understood; sufficient volume and clear enunciation are demanded. Second, flexibility of voice and emphasis is required to express different feelings and to portray characters. The class is quick to recognize that it is ever so much more fun if Father Bear has a great, big, gruff voice and Baby Bear has a tiny, squeaky voice. Third, dramatization on the higher levels requires attention to organization, dividing the play into scenes, and planning a natural sequence. Fourth, the representation of characters and the expression of mood require suitable bodily action and facial expression, desirable qualities in many forms of oral language. Mobility of expression adds vitality and interest. Participation in dramatization tends to loosen the bonds caused by repression and shyness. Fifth, if freedom of expression is allowed, children will use expressive language—vigorous, aptly descriptive words and phrases. In reproductions and in dramatization of original stories new words will appear. Sixth, dramatization provides opportunities for two specific kinds of language experience: conversation and discussion. Practice in conversation is provided by dramatic dialogue. Discussion is an essential part of the informal types of procedures, handled in a democratic manner, for planning and producing the play.

Opportunities for dramatization   The enjoyment of literature offers many opportunities for dramatization. A satisfactory story for dramatization (1) moves rapidly from one well-marked episode to another, (2) has three or four distinct scenes or acts, (3) has four or five speaking parts, (4) requires only simple stage properties, and (5) often includes repetition of rhyme or a bit of dramatic dialogue. At the kindergarten level, many Mother Goose rhymes are suitable for dramatization, such as "Little Miss Muffet," "Little Boy Blue," and "Jack Be Nimble." Appropriate stories for the primary grades are: "Peter Rabbit," "The Tortoise and the Hare," "The Three Bears," and "The Straw Ox." Children in the upper grades enjoy the dramatization of selections from such books as Sir James M. Barrie's *Peter and Wendy*, Lewis Carroll's *Alice's Adventures in Wonderland*, Howard Pyle's *Merry Adventures of Robin Hood*, Louisa May Alcott's *Little Women*, Mark Twain's *The Adventures of Tom Sawyer*, and Howard Pyle's *The Story of King Arthur and His Knights*.

Informal dramatizations are a natural part of the story hour and the reading period. Special occasions are offered by the celebration of special days, book week, and programs.

Many situations arise in the social studies, science, and health work in which dramatization is useful as a means of clarifying ideas and adding interest. In the primary grades children play house, operate an airport, manage a grocery, and play doctor and nurse; they show how to cross a street safely and how to choose a good lunch. In the upper grades the dramatizations are more complex, showing how the pioneers lived, how the westward movement progressed, how the Constitutional Convention was conducted. They may cover single incidents or situations or topics of considerable scope, and are an excellent means of vividly highlighting and tying together important phases of a unit of work; they are a culminating activity. For example, the children who had spent four weeks studying the westward movement studied models of wagons, guns, and other equipment, secured the necessary provisions for a journey, planned the route, dressed in appropriate costumes, made the journey, and dramatized activities and incidents along the way, such as setting up camp, fighting the Indians, crossing rivers, preparing meals, and singing and telling stories around the campfire.

Props and equipment Dramatization of the several kinds makes possible the use of a considerable variety of material, much of it obviously adaptable. As a general principle, elaborate properties and equipment are not necessary for informal types of dramatization, the most common types. Children's imagination clothes symbolic material with the cloak of reality. A yardstick serves as a shepherd's crook or a knight's sword; two boxes and a plank or a bench make a satisfactory bridge; a desk serves as a bridge under which the troll hides; a wastepaper basket becomes a peddler's pack; a three-cornered hat improvised from newspaper supplies a Colonial soldier's costume. Puppet characters made from paper bags fastened to a stick or strip of cardboard may be shown by the children above an overturned card table. Stand-up characters may be made from large envelopes or folded pieces of stiff paper and shown as above. Puppet characters cut from cardboard, colored and attached to strings, may be used as string puppets or marionettes by older children. Old stockings or socks, stuffed and painted with faces, make workable puppets. The leg of the sock makes a convenient cuff to hide the puppeteer's hand. Yarn hair may be added as well as button eyes.

Formal dramatizations, which are often used as entertainments for the public, require more elaborate stage sets, costumes, and properties. The annual or semiannual show put on by the school is a tradition in many small communities. Often teachers invite parents on some special occasion—for a special day celebration or at the completion of a large unit of work. Impressing the public with the importance of the activity itself may justify the time and effort devoted to elaborate staging. The teacher will naturally try to tie the construction phases of dramatization into work in art and industrial arts so that the children will receive the maximum benefits. Often the construction of scenery, properties, and costumes motivates close study and the gathering of exact information. Teachers should not be required to waste the time of children in educationally unproductive enterprises intended solely for entertainment.

Teaching   The first step in dramatization, as in other language experiences, is to set up a present, worthy occasion—a story, incident, or situation that is appropriate to the work under way and appealing to the children. If it is a story, the second step is to bring the children to an understanding of the narrative, which is told or read by the teacher or read by a pupil. The reading and enjoyment of the story may lead to a request or suggestion for dramatization. The third step involves planning the dramatization, and therefore often requires a rereading of the story, in whole or in part, one or more times in the course of planning. It is likewise necessary to divide the story into scenes or acts, determined by place, time, or incident, and to arrange a natural sequence. The parts to be played are identified, and actors are chosen for them. The children who try out may be selected by the class or by the teacher. A stage manager or announcer is chosen, and possibly his duties are discussed. Staging and properties are planned. The group or several groups meet to discuss, plan, and prepare their parts. The play is then presented by the group. Audience evaluation follows. Because the whole class, presumably, is familiar with the basic source of the play and has engaged in preliminary planning, all members are ready to judge the fidelity of content, dialogue, setting, and general interpretation. Suggestions for improvement and demonstrations of these suggestions are sincerely sought. Representation of the dramatization for enjoyment or for improvement of the performance may be desired by the class as a final step; the same group or another group may perform.

The procedure just described is suitable for an informal type of group dramatization at the intermediate-grade level. It must be simplified considerably for use in lower grades and must be adapted to the requirements of particular situations at any grade level. Formal dramatization follows the same general steps, the chief differences lying in thoroughness and polish.

Verse choir

Verse choir, choral speaking, unison speaking, choric work, and speaking choir are all names for the same thing—a group of voices speaking poetry or rhythmic literature together, with unity and beauty. In many ways it is like a singing choir. However, in a singing choir emphasis is on tone quality, and words are often blurred. In a speaking choir, although there must be good tone quality, the main emphasis is on enunciation; every word must be clear and expressive. A really fine verse choir shows a singing quality of voice, and the blend of many voices can bring out unsuspected melodies of poems.

Speaking poetry in unison is not new. It was done in ancient Greece, where plays were odes chanted by a chorus, or later with a leader; but the chorus was always important. The Old Testament is full of passages that were probably rendered in this way, and in our modern churches we still carry on the chant or responsive reading, which is choral speaking. What can be more stirring than the Twenty-fourth Psalm read by a solo reader and chorus! The old ballads were recited by a leader carrying the narrative, while the chorus thumped and chanted the response. Certain American Indian ceremonial chants followed this solo-chorus pattern.[10]

Specific objectives   In addition to the enjoyment of literature (the primary outcome) and other literary and general social values, the chief values for language training relate to improving voice and speech. Requirements of clear enunciation and pronunciation are exacting if the total effect is to be distinct and pleasing, not blurred. Richness and fullness of tone are essential. Flexibility of voice is required for force and pleasing effects. These qualities of speech are not attained through the mechanical direction of the teacher, but through an effort at intelligent interpretation and an attempt to express by tone, pitch, and modulation of voice ideas and feelings that are clearly understood and felt. The material dictates its interpretation. The necessity of getting desired effects through the use of the voice provides opportunities for giving some understanding of and training in the mechanics of speech—use of the speech organs, voice placement, breathing, sounding letters, and use of pauses and modulation as indicated in part by punctuation.

Approaches   The approach to choral speaking is rich and extensive enjoyment of poetic and dramatic literature read by the teacher. Enjoyment in listening leads naturally to, and sets the stage for, active participation for further and richer enjoyment. The choice of selections in beginning work is important. Professor Mary Gwen Owen says, "Choose something which has a terrifically 'unpoetic' sound when read, something which will appeal to the boys. If the boys like it, the girls will too." [11]

---

[10] Paul S. Anderson and others, *Language Skills in Elementary Education,* The Macmillan Company, New York, 1966, pp. 65–71.
[11] Mary Gwen Owen, *So You Don't Like Choral Reading,* A Monograph of Language Arts, no. 52, Harper & Row, Publishers, Inc., New York, n.d., p. 3.

The first step is an impressive reading of the whole selection by the teacher or by some gifted pupil prepared for the job. Re-reading may be requested by the class. Pupils may then be invited to participate in the reading.

When a decision for class participation has been made, the second step involves noting the mood, thought, or particular feeling that the selection creates. Then follows casting and the arrangement of parts. Casting a poem means simply deciding how to read it—in unison, in solo and chorus, a line a child, a line a chorus, antiphonally; and then deciding how the particular lines shall be distributed. Once the children have an idea of what is expected, they will help with the casting, and many variations may be tried out. A simple arrangement is to divide the class into three groups—high, low, and medium voices—with eight to twelve members in each group. In addition, there may be one or more solo parts. The high voices usually ask questions and take the lines suggesting delicacy, lightness, or fun. The low voices answer questions and carry the lines suggesting gloom, sorrow, mystery, and solemnity. Medium voices carry the narrative, give explanations, and introduce characters. A solo voice may speak from either group or may move a little apart from the group when speaking, but there should never be too much moving.

The teacher should study the selection beforehand for possible arrangements, but the children should be allowed to make suggestions. Often surprisingly good ones are made. By sharing responsibility children learn to make earnest efforts at understanding the selection and to make intelligent use of dramatic techniques to get desired effects; they also derive a sense of proprietorship, which stimulates them to reach high standards. The complexity of arrangement varies with the age-grade-maturity level. In the primary grades the work is largely concert reading. In the intermediate and upper grades elaborate arrangements are fun. Care should be taken in selecting children for the solo parts; several children should try out. Sometimes children are grouped and reseated according to the pitch of their voices—low, medium, and high.

Preliminary, tentative groupings and arrangements are followed by evaluation of results and revisions of procedure, a possible third stage. Each part of the selection is studied to discover its particular mood, feeling, or idea; and attention is given to the best way to express it. Variations are tried and the better procedures selected. Listening to recordings of good verse choir renditions helps. Also, evaluation and suggestions for improvement can be obtained by comparing recordings of class productions with high-level recordings.

When a satisfactory interpretation has been reached, the selection may be repeated for enjoyment and practice. The number and timing of repetitions are determined by the enjoyment of the children. A growing repertory of familiar selections can be used again and again throughout the year.

Problems   A problem may exist in getting choral speaking under way. A beginning can be made by simply reading together or by reciting a familiar poem together. An easy variation is to add an occasional solo voice. As satisfaction and confidence build up, group work can be added and increasingly ambitious arrangements can be attempted. A beginning can well be made in the kindergarten or first grade. Here, and possibly in the second grade, children should learn to appreciate poetry and to build toward a choir but should do no formal choral speaking. They should be allowed to hop, skip, beat, and act out Mother Goose and other poems in different rhythms. Because the children will imitate the teacher, she must exercise great care in her rendering of poems and guard against singsong; and when the children, after hearing a poem a few times, begin to say it along with her, she must keep their tones light, maintain the tempo, and discourage loud voices and extreme dramatics. She should help them cultivate an ear for rhythm and for the music of the poem.

A first grade or kindergarten may begin with a simple two-part dramatization. In the following little poem, one child may act the part of the cat responding after the group addresses him: [12]

ALL: Little cat,
       Little cat,
       As you sat
       On the mat
       Did you dream
       Of a mouse
       Or a great big rat?
SOLO: Oh no!
       Not so!
       For I always dream
       Of a dish
       Full of fish
       And a bowl
       Full of cream!

[12] From *I Have a Song to Sing You*, by Laura E. Richards, copyright, 1938, Appleton-Century-Crofts, Inc., New York, 1938. Reprinted by permission of the publishers.

The following is a poem written by eight-year-olds and used for verse speaking many times. Different castings were planned by the children and used, but they seemed to like this one best.

JACK FROST

ALL:	Jack Frost will be coming soon.
FIRST VOICE:	He'll kill the flowers that are now in bloom.
SECOND VOICE:	He'll spill his paint on bushes and trees.
THIRD VOICE:	He'll stiffen the grass and the ground will freeze.
FOURTH VOICE:	Our gardens will soon be wilted and dead.
FIFTH VOICE:	We'll have to put hats upon our heads,
SIXTH VOICE:	And wear our scarfs, our rubbers, and mittens,
ALL:	And play indoors with our three little kittens.

The children had so much fun with the little rhyme that they made music for it; but it was soon noticed that, even when they sang it, they unconsciously took parts, speaking instead of singing.

In a more formal type of choral speaking program, to relax the body and speech organs and to develop breath control, children are put through a series of preliminary exercises such as sounding the vowels with full, rich tones; breathing deeply and blowing an imaginary feather; extending the tongue and flexing the lips. It seems to be wise to subordinate such formal training exercises to the actual speaking and reading of selections and to use exercises only as needed for more effective results. The formal procedure seems a little artificial, and possibly its results may not carry over into the activity that follows.

With young children it is sometimes difficult, at first, to get the class to pay attention to the leader and, in unison work, to keep the voice quality uniform. One or two children in a group will try to make their voices heard above the others. Anticipating this difficulty, one primary teacher sought and gained permission for her class to listen in from the balcony while a large college chorus rehearsed. The children saw how intently the college people watched their leader and how they responded to her signals. It was noted that, except in solo parts, no one voice was heard above the others but that all blended in harmony. It was explained to the children that although this was a singing chorus and theirs was a *speaking* chorus, the same rules prevailed for both. From this experience the children seemed to gain some understanding of what unison work was all about. Any church or adult chorus or choir can be visited in this way.

Memorization is a by-product of choral speaking. There is no need for formal memorization, particularly in the lower grades. Actually, children unconsciously learn many poems and parts of poems simply by repetition in choral speaking. However, the purpose of choral speaking is to enjoy poetry, not to learn it by heart.

One winter morning a lower-grade teacher remarked that, because drivers could not control their cars on slippery streets, children should be extra cautious about crossing. A child told of having stopped a kindergartner who was about to dash out into the street.

"I had to yell at him two or three times. A car was coming and it was slipping all over," explained the boy.

"Let's each pretend we are stopping a little brother or sister from crossing the street," said the teacher. "What would we say? How would we say it?"

She turned to the board and in a few minutes the following lines were written as the children suggested them.

> Don't cross! Don't cross!
> A car is coming.
> Don't cross! Don't cross!
> A car is coming.
> It's skidding and sliding.
> It's slipping and gliding.
> Don't cross! Don't cross!
> *Wait!*

Several individuals read it from the board with slightly varying interpretations, but all emphasizing the important words "Don't cross" and "Wait." Then it was read in unison, becoming more exciting with each reading until the final word became a lusty shout. The children were actually saving a little brother or sister.

On succeeding days the poem was experimented with until the children decided they liked it best as follows:

FIRST VOICE:	Don't cross!
SECOND VOICE:	Don't cross!
ALL:	A car is coming.
THIRD VOICE:	Don't cross!
FOURTH VOICE:	Don't cross!
ALL:	A car is coming.
FIFTH VOICE:	It's skidding and sliding.
	It's slipping and gliding.
SIXTH VOICE:	Don't cross!
SEVENTH VOICE:	Don't cross!
ALL (*shout*):	*Wait!*

The solo voices were scattered about the room, and each child became increasingly dramatic with his "Don't cross." On the final "*Wait!*" the group invariably leaned forward or made some involuntary gesture to add emphasis.

From time to time suggestions were offered by children or teacher, changes were made, and there had to be a bit of drill on final *t*'s and *ing*'s.

Given an assembly before first and second graders, this spontaneous little project became a real contribution to the school safety-education program. Throughout the year, many such opportunities are offered. It is for the alert teacher to recognize and take advantage of them.

Examples   Following are simple poems,[13] which have been found to work out well in choral work. The castings indicated are merely suggestions; numerous variations are possible.

The first poem, for primary children, should be spoken at a marching tempo. One-half of the class says the first four lines; the other half, the last four lines, picking up in perfect rhythm. Or, the class can try beginning softly, growing louder, and then fading away.

The Grand Old Duke of York (Mother Goose)

The grand old Duke of York,
    He had ten thousand men.
He marched them up a very high hill
    And he marched them down again.
And when he was up, he was up,
    And when he was down, he was down,
And when he was only half way up
    He was neither up nor down.

Blow Wind Blow (Mother Goose)
Blow, wind, blow, and go, mill, go,
That the miller may grind his corn;
That the baker may take it,

[13] May Hill Arbuthnot, "The Grand Old Duke of York," "Blow Wind Blow," and "A Farmer Went Trotting," *Time for Poetry*, Scott, Foresman and Company, Chicago, 1951, pp. 170, 311, 224; quoted with special permission of the publisher. Rose Fyleman, "The Goblin," *Picture Rhymes from Foreign Lands*, J. B. Lippincott Company, Philadelphia, 1935; copyright, 1935, by Rose Fyleman, reprinted by permission of the publisher. Kate Greenaway, "Little Wind," *Under the Window*, Frederick Warne & Co., Ltd., London, n.d. p. 155. Langston Hughes, "African Dance," *The Dream Keeper*, Alfred A. Knopf, Inc., New York, 1932; reprinted by permission of Alfred A. Knopf, Inc. E. H. Sechrist, "Is John Smith Within?" *One Thousand Poems for Children*, Macrae Smith Co., Philadelphia, 1946; by permission from E. H. Sechrist.

And into bread bake it,
And bring us a loaf in the morn.

The Goblin (by Rose Fyleman)

ALL OR HIGH: *A goblin lives in our house, in our house,*
in our house,
A goblin lives in our house all the year
round.

GIRLS OR LOW: *He bumps*
And he jumps
And he thumps
And he stumps.

BOYS OR MEDIUM: *He knocks*
And he rocks
And he rattles at the locks.

ALL OR HIGH: *A goblin lives in our house, in our house,*
in our house,
A goblin lives in our house all the year
round.

Little Wind (by Kate Greenaway)

FIRST: *Little Wind, blow on the hilltop.*
SECOND: *Little Wind, blow down the plain.*
THIRD: *Little Wind, blow up the sunshine.*
ALL: *Little Wind, blow off the rain.*

A Farmer Went Trotting (Mother Goose)

FIRST: *A farmer went trotting upon his gray mare,*
SECOND: *Bumpety, bumpety, bump!*
FIRST: *With his daughter behind him so rosy and fair,*
SECOND: *Lumpety, lumpety, lump!*

FIRST: *A raven cried, "Croak!" and they all tumbled down,*
SECOND: *Bumpety, bumpety, bump!*
FIRST: *The mare broke her knees, and the farmer his*
crown,
SECOND: *Lumpety, lumpety, lump!*

FIRST: *The mischievous raven flew laughing away,*
SECOND: *Bumpety, bumpety, bump!*
FIRST: *And vowed he would serve them the same next day,*
SECOND: *Lumpety, lumpety, lump!*

African Dance (by Langston Hughes)

LOW: *The low beating of the tom-toms,*

The slow beating of the tom-toms
Low—slow
Slow—low
Stirs your blood.
HIGH: *Dance!*
A night-veiled girl
Whirls softly into a
Circle of light.
Whirls softly—slowly,
Like a wisp of smoke around the fire.
LOW: *And the tom-toms beat,*
And the tom-toms beat,
And the low beating of the tom-toms
ALL: *Stirs your blood.*

Is John Smith Within? (Mother Goose)
FIRST: *"Is John Smith within?"*
SECOND: *"Yes, that he is."*
FIRST: *"Can he set a shoe?"*
SECOND: *"Aye, marry two."*
ALL: *Here a nail and there a nail,*
Tick, tack, too.

For older children, a poem such as the following may prove challenging. A possible casting is suggested, any one of several that might be used.[14]

A Prayer in the Time of Need
ALL: *Give us, O Lord, we pray thee,*
A breed of men like mountains,
Who lift their foreheads freely to the sun;
FIRST VOICE: *Crown them with loving kindness*
And with gratitude that they are sons of thine;
SECOND VOICE: *Robe them, we pray, with true majesty*
Which wears the ermine clean and undefiled,
Constant in service for the common good,
As glaciers feed the rivers and the soil.
ALL: *Raise up, O Lord, we beg thee,*
A breed of mountain men.

In the lilting lines of the "Skating Song" there is fun and ac-

---

[14] By permission from Marjory Medary, *Horn Book Magazine*, vol. 26, July, 1950, p. 299.

tion. The repetition of the sound words makes possible a delightful choric expression.[15]

Skating Song (by Nancy Byrd Turner)

ALL: *Zinng! Zanng!—we're up and we're gone,*
Faster and faster. The world spins on
Under our feet, and the cold air sings.
SOLO: *Who would bother to be a bird*
When the long, keen note of the ice is heard
And the hard steel whines and rings,
ALL: *And zinng, zanng! zinng, zanng!*

Evaluation

The keystone in evaluating experiences with literature is the children's receptivity to the world of books. If poems, books, stories are a natural part of each school day, if books to suit the immediate interests of children are available, if the teacher sparks an interest in the sharing of the riches gained from reading, the development of the reading habit may be started or even nurtured. The teacher guides the exploration of the varied reading fare for children, helps develop new interests and outlooks, and provides occasions for browsing, reflecting, listening, and even for the sometimes intense and uninterrupted reading made necessary by a "special" book. Each teacher's awareness of the relationships of children and books is the dynamic school-life force that may affect lifelong attitudes toward reading and books, the ultimate evaluation.

For your consideration

1 Visit a school library or the children's room of a public library to talk with the children's librarian. If possible, plan for the librarian to acquaint you with some of the current offerings of books for children. Plan subsequent visits for the purpose of reading as widely as possible.
2 Review *The Children's Catalog*, noting the possible ways in which teachers can utilize this tool.

[15] Nancy Byrd Turner, "Skating Song," in B. R. Buckingham, *The Children's Bookshelf*, Ginn and Company, Boston, 1934.

3   Study several anthologies of story and verse. Note the selection of contents and the organization of each collection.

4   Outline plans for the dramatization of a story or portion of a book you have found in your reading that might be appropriate for children in a particular grade.

5   Make a collection of verse and prose selections suitable for verse choir experiences for children of a particular age range.

6   Consider possible ways by which literature can be made an integral part of the school day.

References

ANDERSON, VERNA D., AND OTHERS: *Readings in the Language Arts*, The Macmillan Company, New York, 1964, pp. 97–104.

DALLMAN, MARTHA: *Teaching the Language Arts in the Elementary School*, W. C. Brown Company, Publishers, Dubuque, Iowa, 1966, chap. 12.

DAWSON, MILDRED A., M. ZOLLINGER, AND A. ELWELL: *Guiding Language Learning*, Harcourt, Brace & World, Inc., New York, 1963, chap. 6 and pp. 365–373.

FROST, J. L., AND OTHERS: *The Disadvantaged Child*, Houghton Mifflin Company, Boston, 1966, pp. 301–315.

GUILFOILE, ELIZABETH, AND OTHERS: *Adventuring with Books: A Book List for Elementary Schools*, National Council of Teachers of English, Champaign, Ill., 1966.

JACOBS, L. B., AND OTHERS: *Using Literature with Young Children*, Teachers College Press, Teachers College, Columbia University, New York, 1965.

LAMB, POSE: *Guiding Children's Language Learning*, W. C. Brown Company, Publishers, Dubuque, Iowa, 1967, chap. 3.

OGILVIE, MARDEL: *Speech in the Elementary School*, McGraw-Hill Book Company, New York, 1954, chap. 5.

RASMUSSEN, CARRIE: *Let's Say Poetry Together*, Burgess Publishing Company, Minneapolis, Minn., 1962.

SAWYER, RUTH: *The Way of the Storyteller*, The Viking Press, Inc., New York, 1962.

SHANE, H. G., MARY E. REDDEN, AND MARGARET C. GILLESPIE: *Beginning Language Arts Instruction with Children*, Charles E. Merrill Books, Inc., Columbus, Ohio, 1961, pp. 140–146.

SIKS, GERALDINE B.: *Children's Literature for Dramatization*, Harper and Row, Publishers, Inc., New York, 1964.

STRICKLAND, RUTH G.: *Guide for Teaching Language in Grades 1 and 2*, D. C. Heath and Company, Boston, 1962, chap. 7.

TIEDT, IRIS, AND S. W. TIEDT: *Readings on Contemporary English in the Elementary School*, Prentice-Hall, Inc., Englewood Cliffs, N.J., 1967, pp. 205–264.

TOOZE, RUTH: *Storytelling*, Prentice-Hall, Inc., Englewood Cliffs, N.J., 1959.

TRAUGER, W. K.: *Language Arts in Elementary Schools*, McGraw-Hill Book Company, New York, 1963, chap. 12.

WALTER, NINA W.: *Let Them Write Poetry,* Holt, Rinehart and Winston, Inc., New York, 1966.

WOODS, MARGARET S.: "Learning through Creative Dramatics," in Iris M. Tiedt and S. W. Tiedt: *Readings on Contemporary English in the Elementary School,* Prentice-Hall, Inc., Englewood Cliffs, N.J., 1967, pp. 36–43.

10

STORYTELLING AND CREATIVE WRITING

Much of the language training of the school, and much of the language of life outside the school, necessarily involves getting and giving information essential to the business of living. In this category would fall the oral communication activities discussed in Chapter 4 and such experiences as giving information, study, and research, topics treated in Chapter 8. The creative writing experiences treated in this chapter—stories, plays, articles—clearly belong in a different category. They are not concerned with the giving of information but with the expression of thoughts and feelings for their own sake or for the entertainment of others. The differentiation is found partly in the ends served and partly in the content and the handling of various language elements. Ghiselin has proposed that the "measure of a creative product may be the extent to which it restructures our universe of understanding." [1] Bruner, on the other hand, regards "effective surprise" as the sign of creativity; the purpose and even originality are secondary. [2] Con-

[1] Reported in Calvin W. Taylor, "Introduction," *Creativity: Progress and Potential*, McGraw-Hill Book Company, New York, 1964, p. 6

[2] Jerome S. Bruner, "The Condition of Creativity," in H. E. Gruber, *Contemporary Approaches to Creative Thinking*, Atherton Press, New York, 1962, p. 3.

tent is largely concerned with the expression of personal feelings and thoughts; and imagination enters prominently, but not exclusively. Originality is an important factor; that is, the child must express his own mental or emotional reactions, not simply report the thoughts and feelings of others. But the concept of originality requires some examination. Very few thoughts are original in the sense that they are expressed for the first time; originality consists to some extent in the selection, appropriation, and adaptation of the thoughts and feelings of others. Sincerity, conviction, and personal acceptance are thus involved.

It must be recognized at this point that originality of expression is a desired quality of nearly all language work and that some authors and teachers regard originality as the sole quality that identifies creativeness. To these people, creativeness is a quality of all expression; it does not serve to identify a particular group of language activities. The authors agree that originality is important in much, if not quite all, of language work, but they take the position that some forms present to a greater degree than others opportunities for personal growth and for developing the qualities of language peculiar to creative expression. For practical purposes of organization and treatment in this book, it is well to identify and treat these forms as a group. Many of the experiences in the present group tap resources of feeling and imagination, but thought as well is included as a proper field for creative effort. Vivid expression and original, clear, accurate thinking are important in problems that are largely intellectual.[3]

Can children be creative?   A little observation of children's expression in the preschool and even early school years should convince a skeptic that children are original and vivid in the expression of ideas peculiarly their own. In their stories and verse we find freshness and vividness. Children's interests are varied, and their naïve impressions appear in refreshingly original words: the *crust* on a banana; the *bone* inside an olive; *snapple* galoshes; *befront* is the opposite of behind; *tonow* means right now. Creativeness is the birthright of children, and it will flower and mature with the years unless stunted by unimaginative teaching. The examples of children's work in this chapter and elsewhere in the book should prove the point.

[3] Walter T. Petty and Mary Bowen, *Slithery Snakes and Other Aids to Children's Writing*, Appleton-Century-Crofts, Inc., New York, 1967, pp. 6–7; and Ruth H. Drewes and others, *Practical Plans for Teaching English in Elementary Schools*, W. C. Brown Company, Publishers, Dubuque, Iowa, 1965, chap. 2.

Storytelling

If children are to be at all verbally creative in the early years, it must be through oral language; individual creativeness in written work awaits the mastery of the mechanics of written expression. Of the oral language experiences, storytelling offers the best opportunities. In storytelling that deals with familiar, personal events, the child relives his experiences, interprets them, and has opportunity to give expression to his own thoughts and feelings about them.

Kindergartners' stories usually belong in the category of familiar experiences. Five-year-old Martha, in the following story, started out with bear characters but having no personal knowledge of bears, she almost immediately switched to something familiar— a trip she had taken.

MARTHA'S STORY

Once upon a time there was a little Daddy bear. His name was Adam. And the Mommy bear was Eve.

One day they went on a trip to Watertown. When they got there, who do you think they saw? It was the people they were going to meet, and it was the mother and father of their grandchildren—and the little boy grandchild was named Larry, the little girl grandchild was Chris. Then all of them went over to, from the station, to the grandmother's house.

After they got there they looked at the time on the clock and it was time to get supper. After it was all ready they all sat down to supper and ate. After they ate they turned on the television, watched it, looked at the clock. It was time to put the children to bed.

She had a loose tooth, and while she was in bed at night the loose tooth came out, and in the morning she found the tooth and brought it down to Mommy and showed it to her.

Then they got dressed and went to play and had fun.

And the story is done.

John, on the other hand, did not stick to a personal experience and soon found himself more or less involved:

JOHN'S STORY

I won't puff you up. Except the little clown was happy I think I hear another train coming.

I'll try if I can and I will if I try. Puff, puff. I almost got up.

Tracy expressed himself in rhyme—a simple experience story, but delightfully told with quite a lilt:

TRACY'S POEM

I'm not going to
Sit in a chair.

I'm just going to
Sit in the air.

In imaginative stories—reproductions or originals—the child identifies himself with the characters in their adventures, suffers with them, and shares with them elation in success or escape. Vivid experiencing of the real or imagined type stimulates the imagination; quickens observation; gives exercise to the emotions; develops sympathy and understanding for people and animals; leads to free, natural, imaginative expression; and may contribute to emotional stability.[4] This little story told by a first-grade child is quite typical of imaginative stories:

> Once upon a time there was a little fairy named Tinkerville. She went out in the garden one morning and she saw a butterfly. He was caught in a spider's web. Tinkerville asked him if he was caught. He said, "Yes." So she helped him out.

Specific objectives   All the general oral language objectives operate in storytelling, but particularly important are selecting a familiar experience or incident with some unusual or dramatic feature; keeping a point for the last; using concrete details and exact words; expressing feeling by voice and manner; showing sincerity; telling events in sequence; speaking directly to the audience; showing interest in one's story; and if the story is humorous, allowing the audience to carry the burden of laughter.

Occasions   A situation suitable for storytelling, as for other creative work, is one that arouses strong, vivid thoughts or feelings requiring expression. Activities at home, school, and in the community provide opportunities for creative thought and expression. Children can be creative in the way they express ideas about the sensory world of their environment—the look of the toad, the smell of the rain-soaked ground, the sightlessness caused by fog, the scream of the fire engine's siren, the movements of an industrial machine. Or, the mood for creative expression may be set by witnessing a current event or a special occasion, such as the launching of an earth satellite; by reading or hearing a story or poem; by listening to the recounting of personal experiences by the children or teacher; and by incidents and situations in learning about other people in the social studies.

The child must have something to say and the desire to express it; participation must be voluntary, invited but not forced.

[4] National Council of Teachers of English, Commission of the English Curriculum, *Ends and Issues: 1965–1966*, Champaign, Ill., 1966, pp. 12, 15.

Individual differences must be recognized and respected, because the creative impulse is stronger in some children than in others. Enthusiasm is contagious and will stimulate the apparently phlegmatic, unimaginative, shy children, if anything will. Various examples will be found in the pages following.

Materials Storytelling is a natural part of the literature-appreciation phase of language work in so far as it concerns the reproduction of children's classics. In the integrated program, opportunities arise for including stories appropriate to a unit, such as the life of desert Indians, Colonial life in the Middle Colonies, and the scope of UNICEF. Occasional storytelling periods, largely concerned with personal experiences, occur in the language class. Stories for reproduction should be suitable to the grade in content and have some of the following characteristics:

1. Familiarity
2. Clear, natural sequence
3. Repetition
4. Simple plot
5. Few characters

Readers, language books, courses of study, and children's storybooks provide suitable selections for reproduction; and textbooks provide examples of stories of personal experience that can be used as models and as means of motivation. Anthologies of children's literature and library lists of stories and books provide literary source material for enjoyment and for reproduction.

Handling storytelling lessons In handling a storytelling lesson or series of lessons, the teacher will first set up a situation in which storytelling is appropriate and enjoyable. He may take advantage of situations arising in the course of work in other subjects, such as the social studies, science, health, and safety; he may introduce a special storytelling period; or he may take advantage of some spontaneous contribution of a child. Several examples will serve to illustrate the points.[5]

On an icy morning quiet little Dorothy raised her hand and said she would like to say a poem she had thought of on the way to school. ("I have one, too," remarked Jimmie.) Dorothy's story was:

When the trees
Are bent low

[5] Paul S. Anderson, *Language Skills in Elementary Education,* The Macmillan Company, New York, 1966, pp. 297–303.

With a coating of ice
On their branches,
I don't think
They feel very pleasant,
Do you?

"Dorothy has made her poem different by ending it with a question," the teacher might remark. Jimmie's story was:

The trees with their crystal
Coats of ice
Are sagging and heavy.
But, if the sun came out
They would sparkle
Like fairyland.

"I like Jimmie's descriptive words—'crystal,' 'sagging,' 'heavy.' That's the way the trees look this morning, isn't it?" said the teacher.

On a windy morning when the children arrived at school, blown and breathless, there was a discussion of the strength of the wind. Questions were asked: "How does the wind make you feel?" "What are some of the things it does?" "How does it sound?" The following two poems resulted:

THE WIND

The wind comes roaring
Down from the sky.
It sweeps the snow
And piles it high.

It whirls around the corners
And nearly knocks us down.
It gets behind and pushes us
And dances round and round.

THE WIND

Last night the wind
Howled wild and loud.
"Whoo-oo-o," he cried
And made me hide
Under my blankets
All safe inside.

As the second step in directing a storytelling experience the teacher may provide for further stimulation. The situation normally arising may be stimulation enough, but often the teacher finds it desirable to intensify the desire for expression by emphasizing the thought, feeling, or mood of the situation and by giving it specific direction. Thus when the subject of trees arose in a sixth-grade class in connection with the study of Joyce Kilmer's poem, the teacher had the children recall favorite trees and experiences with trees; he called attention to some pictures of trees studied by the class; he told of his observations and experiences; and he read excerpts from other poems, noting ideas and descriptive words. The direction of thinking, the mood, and appropriate words and phrases laid the basis for the pupils' own efforts. In stories relating to personal experiences of loneliness, the teacher may ask, Were you ever left alone? How did you feel? What did you do? Or the teacher may stimulate the children by showing them pictures or by giving beginning sentences and allowing them to continue the story.

A teacher's possible approach might be something like this: "How would you like to make a story? If we all work together we might make a long story. What could our story be about?"

The teacher would list on the board suggestions as children give them: fairy, witch, boy or girl, rabbit, pet, circus, etc.

"We must have a good beginning sentence. One that makes us want to go on and read the rest of the story."

If no work has been done with beginning sentences, it may be well to take time out at this point to examine a few. The teacher may collect several readers, primers, preprimers, etc., and read a few beginning sentences from different books. Children will quickly label some baby stories, while stories beginning with more provocative sentences will be admired. Perhaps this is as far as the lesson can go at the time. The teacher might then say, "While you walk home this noon, try to think of a good beginning sentence for our story." The following story was started in the manner just described:

RABBITVILLE

In the long time ago in Rabbitville, a little white rabbit was hopping down a crooked path wondering how he was going to get his Easter eggs.

As he neared the little blue river, he came around a bend and there, right in the middle of the path, stood Johnny Skunk.

"Good morning, Johnny," called Billy Rabbit in surprise. "What got you up so early?"

"Oh, I was over at Farmer Brown's henhouse early this morning when I heard a dog bark. That hound chased me until I was all tired out, so I was just sitting here resting," explained Johnny.

"You're going to get caught one of these days, Johnny Skunk," warned Billy Rabbit. "I've told you and told you to stay away from that henhouse."

On down the path hopped Billy Rabbit. Suddenly he remembered his Easter eggs. "By the way, Johnny," he called back, "do you know where I can find some Easter eggs?"

"Of course," answered Johnny. "At Farmer Brown's henhouse."

"Wonderful! How did you ever—Johnny Skunk, did you say Farmer Brown's henhouse? I'm not going there. I might get caught myself," answered Billy Rabbit, and he hopped slowly on down the path.

"Oh, wait a minute!" cried Johnny Skunk. "Maybe if you'd go to Mrs. Duck, she would give you an egg or two. She's nesting behind that clump of brambles near the riverbank."

Billy called over his shoulder, "Thank you," and scampered off to find Mrs. Duck.

When he got to the river, Mrs. Duck was not at home, but there in her nest were three downy, yellow ducklings and, as Billy looked at them, they opened their mouths and said, "Quack! Quack!"

"Oh my!" said Billy to himself. "I'd better get out of here fast. Besides, I'm too late to get eggs from Mrs. Duck."

Billy had scarcely gotten the words out of his mouth when he heard a familiar voice, "Why Billy Rabbit! What are you doing with my children?" and there looking at him stood Mrs. Duck.

"Wh— wh— I just came to ask if you had a couple of eggs to spare, but I see your eggs have hatched."

"I can have an egg for you tomorrow but you will have to come after it, for I can't leave my ducklings alone," suggested Mrs. Duck. "In the meantime, you might ask Mrs. Bluebird and Mrs. Robin. Perhaps they will give you some eggs."

"Thank you, Mrs. Duck," and off hopped Billy.

"Hello there," called Mrs. Bluebird when she saw Billy coming. "Have you your Easter eggs yet?"

"No," replied Billy. "That's what I came to talk to you about."

"I'd be proud to have some of my eggs used for Easter eggs," said Mrs. Bluebird, "but three are about all I can give you for I want some left to hatch."

"That is wonderful!" exclaimed Billy happily. "I won't have to color your eggs." He took the pale-blue eggs and hopped off toward Mrs. Robin's home.

He found Mrs. Robin beside her nest. She was swinging back and forth in the gentle breeze, singing a gay little tune.

"Good morning, Mrs. Robin," called Billy. "Do you happen to have any extra eggs?"

"Why, yes," chirped Mrs. Robin pleasantly. "I just laid some fresh ones, and I can let you have a couple."

That pleased Billy Rabbit so much that he gave a great hop and landed, plop—right in a puddle of soft mud.

For a minute Billy was frightened. "My eggs!" he cried. But his precious pale-blue eggs had landed safely in the brown mud beside him and were not even cracked.

Slowly Billy pulled himself out of the puddle, wiped his eggs on some long, clean grass, and then called to Mrs. Robin, "Have you your eggs ready? I must be going now."

With his arms full of eggs Billy hopped slowly down the path.

He reached the river just in time to see Mrs. Turtle burying her eggs in the soft sand. He watched her as she clawed sand over the little white eggs and then, just as she started slowly toward the water, Billy called, "Oh Mrs. Turtle! Mrs. Turtle! Please wait a minute. May I have a few of your eggs for Easter?"

"Of course!" replied Mrs. Turtle. "Help yourself. There are plenty of them."

"Oh goody, goody!" cried Billy. "You are very generous."

Quickly Billy uncovered the hard-shelled little eggs, took as many of them as he could carry, and happily hopped down the path toward home.

Later in the day he dyed the eggs all beautiful rainbow colors. There were brilliant yellows, dark forest greens, pale lavenders, and rosy reds. On some were stripes and on one egg he even made a little bunny carrying an Easter egg.

When, at last, the eggs were all dyed, Billy gave a big sigh of relief and yawned sleepily. "I can't go to bed yet," he said to himself.

Then, from the highest shelf in the cupboard, Billy took down his special Easter basket. Carefully he placed all the precious eggs in the basket. He put the tough turtle eggs in the bottom and arranged the others on top. "There, I'm all ready to go," he thought as he gazed proudly at the basket of eggs.

Gently, he took the basket on his arm, opened his squeaky little door and hopped off through the dark forest to deliver his Easter eggs to the children of the outside world.

"I'm so glad I got the eggs finished so the children will have them on Easter morning," he thought, as he hopped along.

In telling stories young children often find conversation difficult. It is likely to consist mostly of question and answer or senseless bickering. This story, however, seems rather unusual in both quantity and quality of direct quotations, and there is evidence of steady improvement and growth in vocabulary and sentence structure as the story progresses. It will be noticed that, though the story grew out of a language period, science and nature-study facts were generously introduced.

After the situation has been set up, and after the preparatory step of giving specific direction to thought and feeling has been taken, the children may be ready for individual creative effort. If so, of course, they begin preparing their stories at once; but, if not, there will be further presentation and study of models. The children note and make a list of such desirable qualities as a particular thought, feeling, or mood for emphasis; words that tell exactly what one wants to say, in an interesting way; and the expression of personal thoughts and feelings.

Finally, the pupils prepare their stories, giving attention to the key points noted above. Expression is followed by discriminating criticism with primary emphasis on the major objectives of the experience: "Did you enjoy it? What contributed to the enjoyment? Could the enjoyment of the story be increased in any way?" Continued experience and practice in creative effort should result in growth and increasing maturity in the use of special techniques. Acquired abilities and skills should be consciously employed in various phases of the program whenever storytelling is appropriate.

Possible difficulties The greatest difficulty in beginning creative work is to overcome natural reticence in giving expression to intimate thoughts and feelings and hesitancy about experimenting with new forms of expression. Children may not have previously been encouraged to be original and natural in expressing their thoughts freely at home and in the school. Effective means of overcoming the barrier to originality and freedom of expression include stimulating the children by the procedures noted above, so that they have something to say; setting a pattern of originality and freedom for the class as the normal and expected thing; and providing a sympathetic and appreciative audience.

Another difficulty may be that of the attitude of the teacher in accepting nonschool vocabulary and terminology in some of the original stories and thoughts of children. One of the authors had the opportunity of working with a class of post first- and second-grade children in a summer school program designed to investigate the means by which children of deprived experiential backgrounds could best be motivated in school. The class had undertaken the study of pets and animals and their relationship to man. Conversation and discussion periods had been initiated; books, filmstrips, motion pictures, study prints, and room pets were incorporated into the unit. Planning sessions for trips and feedback sessions by class and individuals were recorded in a series of charts for reference. After most of this work had been accomplished and a field trip to the zoo had been undertaken only two days before, under the guidance of a sensitive and capable teacher-participant in the summer program, three children came laughing into the room. During a session with their teacher out under the trees, each had developed an oral story, which he insisted should be recorded by the teacher. The stories were of such nonsense that the entire class was breathless with laughter. They were read by the children with expression and enthusiasm.

> Hey, Mom! I got a seal.
> Take the thing back to the zoo! Want me to call the cops? (Darlene)

The neighbor looked over the fence. He ran to the doctor. "Hey, man! I'm going crazy! I just saw a hippopotamus in the yard!" (Maurice)

Carolyn brought a camel home for a pet. Mom said, "What a pretty thing! What you going to do with it?" "Hang it on the wall." "How?" "With a pin." (Carolyn)

Whether indeed these stories could be called "stories"—creative or original—is a matter of interpretation. Perhaps this occasion for laughter fulfilled a need that has been expressed by Applegate: [6]

> Children are willing to go through much of what to them is mumbo jumbo in order to please a teacher who has time in her daily program for fun. I think it's actually too bad if bottled-up children aren't allowed to pop their spirit corks often enough so that when they are released they don't figuratively hit the ceiling. Little pop-off's are better for growing youngsters than powerful explosions.

At any rate, these stories helped to bring laughter to everyone; and it was reassuring to note that one of the heartiest recipients of the humor was a second-grade boy who, at the beginning of summer school, had written laboriously:

I hate animals.
They make me sick.

When Nancy, a flighty third-grade child who had never contributed anything to the story hour, gazed out of the window and then rather solemnly pronounced this poem, she was highly complimented by the teacher, and the children signified pride in her achievement and in the fact that she had at last helped the class:

When the snowflakes
Come dancing down,
They look like
Little winter fairies.

Appreciation of sincere effort of whatever degree of merit should be spontaneous and freely given. Criticism should be constructive; and it may come in part from the children, if informality prevails and if children's judgments are respected. Real worth should be recognized; too much attention should not be given to minor flaws. The emphasis should be placed on, "What did you like about Jim's story?"

The shy child deserves special consideration. He should not be forced. Perhaps the teacher can give him special help outside

[6] Mauree Applegate, *Easy in English*, Harper and Row, Publishers, Inc., New York, 1964, p. 495. Quoted with special permission of author and publisher.

the class, so that his first efforts will be reasonably successful. Patience is required. Approval should be generous.

This first attempt at poetry by a nine-year-old child was complimented, but members of the group tried to help by pointing out that although it was a good story, it might have been longer; for example, the mouse could have found some cheese or built a little nest:

> *Im a little*
> *mouse. and when*
> *I nose around. I*
> *see a little house.*

The following poem, while not a masterpiece, has rhythm, and the repetition of the word "splashes" gives a distinct feeling of a rainy day. The teacher might remark that the use of the word with its *sh* sound "really makes us hear the rain."

> *I like to walk*
> *In the rain,*
> *And hear it patter*
> *On the window pane.*
> *Its rhythm is like a song*
> *As it splashes, splashes*
> *All day long.*

An informal atmosphere is favorable to creative effort. Such an atmosphere is effected largely by the attitude of the teacher and by the resulting attitude of the children. Seating is important too; if possible, the children should be seated in a compact, informal group on the floor or in chairs facing each other.

Occasional help may be given to the child who is halting for a word or phrase to express an idea exactly. Rewording a sentence to give force, clearness, or variety may be suggested. Correction of gross crudities must not detract from the effectiveness of the story.

As a variation of procedure in the primary grades, the class may work out a story together. Contributions are volunteered, evaluated, selected, and possibly written on the board. The written form requires close attention to organization. Another device is for the teacher to tell part of a story and allow the children to finish it.

Young children sometimes have difficulty in distinguishing between the real and the make-believe. The teacher may ask, "Did that really happen, or are you making it up?" Also, suggestible children may tend to copy the successful story pattern of others. Originality can be encouraged by suggesting to the children that they tell about things that really happened to them and by helping them pick out of their experience incidents worth telling about.

Creative writing

A feeling for and capability in creative expression, begun in oral storytelling, sooner or later comes to maturity in creative writing in the form of stories, poems, plays, and articles. In both written and oral creative endeavor the same purposes are served: intensive experiencing, close observation, originality and freedom of expression, and the enjoyment of ideas that are beautifully expressed. Creative writing, moreover, broadens the acquaintance with, and lays a foundation for, the enjoyment of literature; it increases sensitivity to and capacity for the enjoyment of beauty in people and things and adds somewhat to the ability to express oneself in clear, vigorous, descriptive, and entertaining language. Not many children will become artists, although it is worthwhile to discover the few who have unusual artistic capacity.[7]

Poetry may be tailored to fit a great variety of feelings and moods—about the whole range of human emotions. Poetic expression aids the child in understanding himself as well as assisting him in seeing more vividly the world of senses and events.[8] On a morning following a night of terrific wind, the children were in a mood for expressing themselves. They worked quickly until the last line was reached. No one could think of a word to rhyme with *papers,* so the teacher gave them the word *capers:*

MISCHIEVOUS WIND

Last night the wind
Was whistling round.
It screeched and howled
All through the town.
It tore at the doors
And whirled the papers.
It blew the snow
And played great capers.

[7] Mauree Applegate, *Freeing Children to Write,* Harper and Row, Publishers, Inc., New York, 1963, pp. 14–16.
[8] Eve Merriam, *What Can a Poem Do?* Atheneum Publishers, New York, 1962, p. 1.

One beautiful autumn day a primary grade watched the brightly colored leaves fluttering from the maple trees and composed the following poem:

I am a little leaf,
A red and yellow leaf.
High up in a tree
I held tightly
While the wind tugged at me.
Then one windy day,
I could hold no longer.
Gently I floated
Down, down, down.
The other leaves
Made a place for me,
And we all went to sleep
Until spring.

The children liked their poem and gave it chorally again and again. Each time they involuntarily made some gestures to indicate the tugging wind or the floating leaf. They had really captured the feeling of the leaf in their story.

When something was needed for an American Education Week assembly program, the children suggested that they would like to give their poem. Then someone suggested that music be made for it, and all agreed. The program was finally presented in the following way:

FIRST CHILD: This fall we watched one of the maple trees in front of Clarkson change color. Then, one day when the leaves were falling, we pretended we were leaves and wrote a story. It doesn't rhyme, but we call it a poem.
(*Children gave poem as choral speaking.*)
SECOND CHILD: We liked our story so well that we decided to make it into a song, and so we made original music for it. (*The word* original *was mentioned by a little boy, thought very grown-up, and its use was insisted upon by the class.*) We will sing it for you.

In the following poem a fifth grade told the robin's story quite faithfully. It shows observation and their first words, "red breast robin" instead of the traditional "robin red breast," is quite interesting. The children were highly satisfied with their product, which was made into a poster, appropriately decorated with a robin swinging on a branch, and given a place of prominence on the wall. It is very evident, however, that these children lacked poetic experience. They had probably heard very little poetry read and so lacked appreciation for *real* poetry. In this period of transition from jingle to poetry, they need to hear many fine poems read and read well—poems on every subject to help them realize that there is more to a poem than mere rhyme. The poem:

SPRING BRINGS A ROBIN

Little red breast robin
On a fence she's a-bobbin
She comes to us every spring,
When she makes her nest she likes to sing.
She lays her eggs in the nest
And that's what she takes care of best.
When the mean old jay comes by,
You ought to hear that bird cry.
When the bird flies out of its nest,
She goes down south to join the rest.

Halfway through first grade Freddie, whose background was rich in story lore, was writing chapter stories. In a 7- by 8½-inch paper-backed notebook, he wrote of his own accord the following series of stories. It will be noted that, though much longer than would ordinarily be expected from a first grader, his stories are about familiar incidents. A few of his shorter stories are of the imaginative type, and one longer story is about Abraham Lincoln, whose lowly childhood seemed to have caught his interest. However, most of his stories, as well as the illustrations, are from his own experience. Since Freddie lives in a part of the country where deep snow affects all winter activities, it is no wonder that he carries the snow theme throughout. Notice his use of descriptive words and the interesting variety of sentence structure. Nothing has been changed except spelling and punctuation.

This story is just a story.

One winter day some snowmen came because it was good packing. There were ten or so. It was a snow day. And it was a school day. But it was stopping to snow. The name of the day was Friday, so wouldn't you think that it was a school day? It was in the afternoon. It was snowing good and hard. Cars could not start their G.E. motors because it was so very cold. So everybody had to wear ski pants.

Chapter 2

Ten snowmen were on the world. The snow was so deep too. But Christmas was coming, so they had a Christmas tree. Everybody had a Christmas tree. One of the family got an old funny man and ice skates and a pig dog and four games.

Chapter 3

"Ten presents for me," said Jack.
"Twelve presents for me," said Jane.
"Three presents for me," said Daddy.
"Four presents for me," said Mommy.

Chapter 4

It had been snowing very hard and some children were making a snowman—Jane and Jack and their friends. The snowman was named; Whitey-Pretty was his name. But Whitey-Pretty didn't like the snow. It is cold, you know, so he didn't like the snow. But the children liked him anyway.

Chapter 5

Spring was coming. Whitey-Pretty was melting.
But birds were coming back, yes, and robins were coming.
After school Jack and Jane saw a robin that had a red breast.
It was their bird. His name was Reddy.
They had a long way to get home but they had a good time.

The End

According to Eve Merriam, poetic experiences lie all around us—in the changing seasons, in the sound of machinery, in the movement of the tides, and in daily and life experiences.[9]

When a third-grade child produced the following poem, its maturity caused the teacher to question its authorship, but the presence and condition of the particular shoe was soon verified by other members of the group who had seen it lying in an alley frequently used as a shortcut. Other children seemed to have taken a poke or a kick at it; but on this one child, who did not often have new shoes, the sight made a deep impression:

I saw an old shoe
On the street.
So old, worms were
Crawling out of it.
The sole was ripped,
And the laces rotted.
No one looked at it.
What a shame
To lose a shoe!

Children often identify themselves and their own emotions with the stories they write. Nancy was one of those quiet, pathetic children who, for no apparent reason, seems a social nonentity. The other children did not dislike her; they just overlooked her. When, during a story-writing period, she produced the following story, it seemed to indicate the depth of her hurt and her feeling of loneliness:

[9] *Ibid.*, p. 1.

THE FROG

Once on the edge of a pool lived poor little me, the green frog. I was sad and lonely and no one would play with me.

One day I was playing and all of a sudden I heard something say, "Little frog, would you play with me?"

I looked up and saw a little boy. I said, "Yes, I will play with you. No one before would play with me. I will be glad to."

And so the boy and I played together after this and I had more friends.

Specific goals   While the primary outcomes of creative writing are enriching experience and enjoyment of literature, creative writing also makes distinct contributions to language development. Satisfying work requires, in the first place, a particular idea, thought, feeling, or mood worthy of expression. In the second place, the form of expression requires particular attention. Colorful words and phrases express thoughts and feelings clearly and beautifully; comparisons and figures of speech add vividness; balanced sentences, inverted constructions, direct discourse, repetitions, and rhyme are used to good effect. Organization and interesting details add clarity, completeness, and vividness. In mechanics, there is much use of quotation marks.

Themes   A vivid experience requiring expression is even more important in writing than in storytelling. To be avoided are the traditional, general, vague, abstract, literary themes on which the children have little to say and in which they have little interest. The primary sources of material are found in the lives of the children, in incidents and events that affect them personally, about which they have some knowledge, and in which they are interested.

In discussing the subjects that seem to bring poetry from children, Mauree Applegate suggests the following:

1   Children like to write about themselves—their thoughts and feelings.
2   Children enjoy writing about their pets.
3   Children beg for a chance to be humorous.
4   Children make poems of action—any kind.
5   Children enjoy writing of quiet lovely things.
6   Children love to write what their senses tell them.
7   Nature appeals to children.
8   Adolescents, especially, characterize the people they know.
9   Children love jests, spaceships, and things to come.[10]

[10] Mauree Applegate, *Easy in English*, Harper and Row, Publishers, New York, 1964, pp. 251–262. Quoted with permission of author and publisher.

Torrance comments that, although imaginative functioning as a developmental phenomenon during the high school years has received little attention, there seems to be a decline in imaginative functioning between the sixth and seventh grades and on into the eighth. He suggests that the beginning of the high school period marks new pressures to conformity. Although there seems to be a fairly steady growth in imaginative functioning through the high school period, there is a leveling off or a decline at the end of this time. Laboratory and field experiments of the maturing of creativity are needed.[11] Perhaps the sensitive components of the language arts are the means by which creativity for young people can be nurtured best.

A sensitive eleven-year-old, entering this self-analytical period, wrote:

INSIDE MY HEART

Deep inside your heart
Where your dreams are
You think to yourself
"I am in a great palace
With all the riches I
Could wish for."
But suddenly your
Dream fades away.
And there you are
In the same old place.

Notice the confusion about the future in the poem of this fourteen-year-old girl:

Maybe sometime,
Maybe sometime,
All my wishes will come true.
Will I be a lady in a fine home?
Will I be a working girl?
Will I marry young?
Will I marry old?
Will I marry at all?
Never! my wishes all include just one thing
That is you.

Here another fourteen-year-old goes to nature for inspiration:

[11] W. Paul Torrance, "Education and Creativity," in Calvin W. Taylor, *Creativity: Progress and Potential*, McGraw-Hill Book Company, New York, 1964, p. 112.

For the rocks and the hills,
For the birds and the mills,
We should be grateful.
For autumn leaves bright,
For the snow on wintry nights,
We should be grateful.
For the summer and the spring,
When the birds and robins sing,
We should be grateful.

A junior high school girl proposes one way of meeting difficulties:

DAYDREAMING

The most pleasant thing I can imagine is daydreaming my life away. It is one way to cope with problems that seem almost unbearable. You know that you will probably never see far off lands and meet important people, but you can always dream.

A fourth grader describes a familiar experience thus:

I like to watch the fire
In the big fireplace.
I never seem to tire
Looking for a face.
I like to see the flames
Jump up and down and creep,
As if they're playing games—
Games of hide and seek.

Next in importance to personal experience as a source of inspiration for creative writing is the study of literature, especially poetry. Reading and listening to well-read stories and poems often provide the spark that sets fire to the imagination and the urge to create. Literature provides a mirror in which the child can see and interpret his own experience, suggesting phases of his own experience, real and imagined, that are adaptable to creative expression. Moreover, literature provides ways of treating topics and patterns of words that the child can adapt to his own ends.[12]

Steps in development The same general instructional procedure used in storytelling is appropriate for creative writing. In the first place, an occasion that provides an immediate purpose for writing is helpful. The occasion may arise naturally in

[12] May Hill Arbuthnot, *Children and Books*, Scott, Foresman and Company, Chicago, 1964, chap. 19.

the course of related work in some other phase of the school program; or it may be created by the teacher, who can often take advantage of fortuitous circumstances. For example, on a particularly foggy morning a sixth-grade teacher asked the children whether they had noticed on the way to school how objects, such as trees, houses, and approaching cars, looked in the fog. During the discussion she showed pictures, read stories and poems, and recalled experiences of persons who became lost in a fog. As an outgrowth of this preliminary work, each child drew a picture of some fogbound scene or incident and then wrote a few words or lines that vividly described the scene or incident. An inconspicuous beginning in poetic expression was thus made. Later the children reviewed and extended their descriptions; some of them used verse form.

The point is that children cannot create something out of nothing. If the children do not have a background of ideas, thoughts, and feelings, the teacher must help create such a background. The teacher does not say, "Now close your eyes and think," but, "Open your eyes and see."

The use of models—usually of literary merit, but sometimes the work of other children—is necessary to suggest ways of dealing with the topic, appropriate words and phrases, and literary devices; but such models should not be copied or followed slavishly.

Class consideration of productions provides the opportunity to give genuine approval, when approval is due; to unveil falsity, cant, and plagiarism; and to suggest improvements in thought and form. All the children profit by this critical discussion. Individual differences should be recognized here and approval given to the less able child who comes forth with a sincere, if mediocre, product, as well as to the few talented children. This is the first attempt at written expression by a slow fourth-grade child and, as such, should receive commendation:

Tom had a toothache once day he wants too go out and play but he couldnt.

Some hurdles Perhaps the greatest problem is to get the reluctant child to make an effort to express himself. To a natural lack of interest in written expression may be added, in such a case, a resistance to any requirement of effort. The problem is not solved by urging the child to express himself, but by helping him find something to say and an adequate motive for saying it. To meet this problem, Petty and Bowen suggest varying approaches, such as (1) arousing interest by choice of appealing topics; (2) citing characters and incidents from familiar stories and books; and (3) using stimulating objects and exciting events from familiar activities.[13]

Semantically the terms *expression, self-expression,* and *experience* need to be developed in the context in which they occur. The era of "happenings" and "experiences" is with us in all fields of the arts—poetry, sculpture, films, painting, music, and dance. Sylvia Angus suggests that, while experience is basic to any art form, art ultimately implies control—the opposite of random occurrence; and she defines art as "the controlled structuring of a medium or material to communicate as vividly and movingly as possible the artist's personal vision of experience."[14] To bring about self-expression and self-control of ideas, the teacher of creative expression sets out in this role with certain cautions in mind:

1. Teachers themselves must see in each unit a wealth of possibility before they suggest such an assignment.
2. The atmosphere of the classroom will in large measure determine the success of the units.
3. The materials used in the classroom to stimulate response should be vividly and compellingly pertinent to pupils' own experience.
4. The pupils should be familiar with simple patterns which they can adopt and adapt for their own purposes.
5. The pupils should be trained to catch an inspiration when it comes and to work it out then so far as time and present insight permit, and to revise carefully.
6. Publication and public praise are advisable only when they are necessary to destroy an inhibiting group attitude.

An older child occasionally finds the writing of limericks a good beginning and becomes quite clever at this form of expression. A good limerick usually denotes a keen and rather mature sense of humor and is certainly deserving of commendation. However, the child and class must realize that it *is* a limerick and not necessarily a true poem. An eighth grade enjoyed the nonsense rhymes contributed by Joyce, such as the following:

> *There was a young fellow named Jones,*
> *Who rattled and rattled his bones.*
> > *And when he would snore,*
> > *He would rattle some more,*
> *And now he is covered with stones.*

[13] Petty and Bowen, *op. cit.,* pp. 17–37.
[14] Sylvia Angus, "It's Pretty, but Is It Art?" *Saturday Review,* September 2, 1967, p. 15.

A second problem arises from the limits placed on creative expression by the mechanics of writing. The teacher must either limit written work to the child's range of mechanical ability or allow the child freedom of expression with the consequence of having to deal tolerantly with a number of mechanical imperfections. The policy of encouraging free expression is favored by the authors. The teacher then must correct the child's written work for him, insist that he correct it, or use a combination of both methods. Unquestionably the child should assume responsibility for the mechanics in which he has been trained; to do otherwise would encourage careless and slovenly work. However, since the child's ability to think and his power of oral expression far exceed his ability to use the proper mechanics of writing, the teacher should take over when the child's expressional needs exceed the limits of his responsibility or knowledge in matters of mechanics. The relative share of responsibility between child and teacher will vary with the grade level. In the lower grades, compositions, individual or class, are dictated to the teacher. Later the child begins individual work, and then he is gradually introduced to and assumes responsibility for mechanical phases, including spelling, capitalization, punctuation, paragraphing, and neatness. Work worthy of publication should be corrected by the pupil to the utmost extent possible and then checked and finally corrected by the teacher.

Sometimes, before the children start writing their first completely independent stories, the teacher may explain to them that spelling "won't count today." She may instruct them to write their stories as fast as they can think of them and if there are words they cannot spell, to put down just enough of the word so that they will know what it means. She may say, "Later I'll help you correct your misspelled words." In correcting these papers the teacher will find many stories which she cannot read at all but which the writer will have to translate for her. Then the story may be written correctly by the teacher and recopied by the child. This method takes time, but it gives the teacher an insight into individual difficulties, and the child is very proud of his corrected and recopied story. As an added incentive the teacher may type a few of the best stories for the class storybook.

The following story, written by a third-grade child, does not mean much in the original, but after it was correctly rewritten by the teacher, the child was pleased and proud of his creative efforts.

Mother, said Bobby May I go toapoupar to night at the sevicksenker. the little boy next Door siad thot IT was abuort fairys. yes you my. that night Bobby touk jum. the garting rose and the play begain. there was a man and he was to telly the story. once opan a time he bagain in a dark agoom forest there lived 24 little dawrfs and fairts. one day one of the dafrws said to another darwfe wood you like to take a walk in the forest today. just as they reht the forest they hared a qyer sound It was not very far off. They both soated towords the woods and what should they see bat a geart big gante sanding befor him. he killed thim and went spun his way. The gerttine went down and the peole sarted home. that night Bobby dream of the play.

the end

In the following story a fifth-grade girl shows the influence of TV and the space age.

SUPER GIRL

When I was little I used to watch Super Man all the time. When it was over I used to tie a towel around my neck and pretend like I was Super Man.

One day a boy who was about my own age and I were trying to fly. He said that he jumped off his porch and flew over to the neighbor's house. It was impossible but I believed him. He told me to jump from a branch about seven feet up in a tree. So I did. That was the last time I ever played Super Girl.

In the following composition an eighth-grade girl shows real promise in creative poetic expression. Confused by her emotions and the very profusion of her pictures, she needs guidance and constructive suggestions; but one feels that with sympathetic criticism she may develop into a good writer.

MAGIC FINGERS

The springtime was beautiful, clear, and mild,
Flower's in bloom and the trees were wild
And wet with dew—the sun had not yet ris'n.
While the little blades of green grass
Whispered and rustled of days gone past.
There was magic in the air.
The bushes and trees seemed to echo it,
As the sun rose, bit by bit,
Shedding its glory and all its might,
Dispersing the shadows and fears of night.
And, as the first rays of the sun were a signal,
The birds began their morning concert, setting the rays to
*   dancing,*
Brushing past trees, whirling and prancing.
Little fluffy white clouds played tag with the giant orb of light,
As if to contest their strength and might.
The magic was at its greatest peak,

But tho it waned, and acquired a meek
And docile attitude,
'Twould never leave our latitude
Of fair and calm feelings.
And now, tho 'tis winter, the trees are shrouded in white
*   blankets,*
And the brook tinkles merrily
While ice attempts to muffle its joy in its cold heart.
The magic ever lingers,
Pauses and bursts with all its glee again,
As spring nears.

Writing plays   Writing plays is a special form of creative writing
in which the children find opportunity to use the language abilities
peculiar to all creative work and the specialized techniques developed in dramatic experiences. Writing plays thus combines
two types of training in language and provides for further development of each.

The play may be a product of the imagination, dealing with
topics and problems of a fanciful nature—an esthetic experience
indulged in for its own sake. In school, however, dramatic writing
is usually the outgrowth of some phase of curricular work in which
there is a serious purpose of presenting important information,
such as an event in history—the raising of the Bear Flag in California in 1846. The writing of the play here serves a dual purpose:
vivifying an important occasion or event and training in a particular kind of language experience.

Writing plays provides opportunities for developing a great
many different language abilities. Particularly important are such
abilities as choosing significant topics worthy of, and adapted to,
dramatic presentation; emphasizing important phases of a topic
to accomplish a particular purpose, such as showing that Virginia
territorially was the mother of many states; using vivid, terse
dialogue; building up to a dramatic climax; and using the form and
written mechanics of play writing.

The procedure in handling a play-writing experience follows
the general steps of all creative experiences. The occasion should
be a real one, impelling in its immediate purpose. The class should
thoroughly understand the purpose of the play and should select
some overall idea, feeling, or mood to be expressed. The planning
stage is handled according to the pupils' experience in dramatization and play writing and according to the maturity of the children.
In the lower grades, the play, if used, is dictated to the teacher.

Presumably, however, most play writing will be done in the intermediate and upper grades. The teacher may use a whole-class or group procedure, or a combination. The preliminary purposing and planning are likely to be done by the whole class; the detailed writing of the script, by group work. In beginning play writing, it is necessary to acquaint the children with the dramatic form. This is done by studying plays, either commercial or textbook.

Usually the writing of the script is done by selected committees working on the several scenes. Proposed scenes must meet the approval of the committees, of course, and must be presented to and passed on by the whole class.

This form of writing is fun for many children and is valuable both for developing an understanding of important phases of curricular work and for cultivating important language abilities. The values of play writing may be enhanced by the study of dramatic literature, good movies, and TV and radio programs.

This radio skit was written by an eighth-grade girl working independently, and shows the strong influence of the popular commercial programs:

Characters: Jean Mannon, Eva Mannon, Announcer
ANNOUNCER: Ladies and Gentlemen. Are you nervous and upset? Do you jump at the least little noise? If so try "Nerves" for the nerves. One drop and you'll never try another. Now, dear people, "Nerves" brings you part one of "The Jewel Mystery."
(*Slight pause*)
ANNOUNCER: It was a cold winters night and the house was creepy as ever at the old Mannon home. Jean and Eva Mannon were in their room while their Aunt Jessie was downstairs going over some important papers.
JEAN: Eva, how come you didn't do your homework?
EVA: Oh, I have a terrible headache. I feel as if something dreadful is going to happen.
JEAN: That's silly. What could possibly happen?
(*Sound effect—a shrill, sharp scream*)
JEAN: What was that?
EVA: I knew it! I knew it! I just knew something would happen.
JEAN: Don't be silly. That was just a stray cat or something? It must have been.
ANNOUNCER: Slowly the girls got up and went downstairs. As they reached the bottom, Eva called.
EVA: Aunt Jessie! Aunt Jessie! Are you there?
JEAN: Aunt Jessie!
ANNOUNCER: Just then they flung open the doors to the study and there, on the floor, was lying Aunt Jessie with a crumpled note in her hand. The note read: "I gave you your chance. I want those jewels." Signed X.
EVA: Is she dead? Has she fainted?
JEAN (*crying*): She's dead—she's dead. Murdered!

EVA: No! No! Who could have done such a thing?

ANNOUNCER: Jean walks slowly to the phone picks up the receiver and calls the police.

JEAN: I want to report a murder. At 551 Park Avenue. Please, please hurry.

ANNOUNCER: Jean fainted. Eva was crying and screaming. Ladies and gentlemen, who murdered Aunt Jessie? Will the police get there in time to prevent another murder—perhaps the murder of Jean or Eva? Folks, you can't afford to miss the next part of "The Jewel Mystery." Remember, folks, "Nerves" for the nervous!

Articles   The writing of articles is ordinarily a part of the larger project of publishing a newspaper or magazine, although articles may be prepared separately for local papers. Only a small number of the items in a school paper can strictly be called articles; for the most part they are news reports, poems, stories, and the like. The actual article presumes an idea or issue in which the writer is vitally interested, from the point of view of either bringing conviction to others or airing a grievance. The article has the creative qualities of expressing an individual point of view and of developing it in language that is clear, forceful, and convincing to the reader. There is more exposition and argumentation in articles than in other kinds of creative writing.

Many issues arise in connection with the school life of the child in which he is vitally interested and on which he has something to say. Such issues include playgrounds, report cards, safety, hobbies, and various curricular activities. If permitted freedom of expression, children will find in writing articles a means of presenting their views on personal, school, and community matters. From writing articles the children gain a sense of responsibility for community behavior; crystallize their thinking on important issues; obtain training in the use of an expository form of writing; and prepare for reading the informational parts of newspapers and magazines.

In handling the writing of articles, the teacher should emphasize choosing a worthy issue, sincerely expressing one's own views, writing clearly and forcefully, avoiding offending others by impoliteness, and avoiding dogmatism and narrow prejudices.

The following article was written by an eighth-grade boy for an imaginary newspaper, *World Press*, during the French Revolution. It shows unusual maturity in both ideas and form.

EDITORIAL

In the past few years the world has stood aghast observing the horrors of the French Revolution. Let us all hope that mankind will never again have to endure an eternal struggle such as this has been. The people of France are not completely to blame for this mayhem and murder for they had a legitimate complaint against the tyranny imposed upon them by the aristocrats of France. An inevitable revolution took place but has slowly been turned from its main idea into a thrust for power and the wanton slaughtering of all who oppose whatever mob that makes that thrust. Any sensible leader who arises in France is either shouted down or murdered. Thousands of Frenchmen and women have met their death on the guillotine. At this point the people have drawn blood and like it. A mania has developed, "kill or be killed," the motto. Let us hope that France will awaken to the peril in which she is slowly pushing herself and develop a firm basis of leadership to build herself into the nation she was meant to be.

Evaluation   In school, children speak when there are opportunities for speaking and write when there are times provided for writing. The nature and quality of the speaking and writing that emerge from school activities reflect teacher expectations and planning. For a child to express himself personally, there must be time for the necessary ingredients of discovering and reflecting; experimenting with sounds, words, and patterns that best express crucial thoughts; and grasping the necessary conventions of language to convey the meaning. Time to explore the many possibilities and to select a means of expressing the thought is essential. If the teacher provides opportunities only for "pat" oral and written responses during the school day, then little attempt at assessment of the originality of speaking and writing can be made, except to note that children's comments give a glimpse of the original and fresh. By providing opportunities to develop curiosities, to explore relationships, and to become increasingly sensitive, the teacher encourages the child in the confrontation of his own perceptions.

For your consideration

1 If possible read or tell a story, recording your oral interpretation by the use of a tape recorder. Note the following: (*a*) voice quality, (*b*) use of voice for dramatic emphasis, (*c*) pacing, (*d*) pronunciation, and (*e*) breath control.

2 Select a grade level and list as many opportunities for oral and/or written creative work as you can.

3 Outline a storytelling lesson or series of lessons, briefly stating objectives, motivating techniques, procedures, and the methods of evaluation.

4 Collect samples of creative writing from the children in one class. Assess the range of topics and compare them in the development of content.

5   Demonstrate for your class a motivating activity which you might use with children to initiate a lesson in creative writing.
6   Set aside thirty minutes for the following task: Assign yourself a topic and write the best story or poem you can within your time limit. After this exercise, compare your writings and your reactions with the class.

References

BROENING, ANGELA, AND OTHERS: *Conducting Experiences in English,* Appleton-Century-Crofts, Inc., New York, 1939, pp. 140–192.

BROWN, DOROTHY L., AND MARGUERITE BUTTERFIELD: *The Teaching of Language in the Primary Grades,* The Macmillan Company, New York, 1941, chaps. 2, 10, pp. 110–116, 129–138.

BURNS, PAUL E., AND ALBERTA L. LOWE: *The Language Arts in Childhood Education,* Rand McNally and Company, Chicago, 1966, pp. 87–90.

BURROWS, ALVINA, AND OTHERS: *They All Want to Write,* Holt, Rinehart and Winston, Inc., New York, 1964, chap. 4–6.

DALLMAN, MARTHA: *Teaching the Language Arts in the Elementary School,* W. C. Brown Company, Publishers, Dubuque, Iowa, 1966, pp. 81–90, 94–98.

DAWSON, MILDRED A., M. ZOLLINGER, AND A. ELWELL: *Guiding Language Learning,* Harcourt, Brace & World, Inc., New York, 1963, chap. 19.

DREWES, RUTH H., AND OTHERS: *Practical Plans for Teaching English in Elementary Schools,* W. C. Brown Company, Publishers, Dubuque, Iowa, 1965, part 2.

MAC CAMPBELL, J. C., AND OTHERS: *Readings in the Language Arts in the Elementary School,* D. C. Heath and Company, Boston, 1964, chap. 3.

MAY, FRANK B.: *Teaching Language as Communication to Children,* Charles E. Merrill Books, Inc., Columbus, Ohio, 1967, part 4.

MEARNS, HUGH: *Creative Power: The Education of Youth in the Creative Arts,* Dover Publications, Inc., New York, 1958.

MERRIAM, EVE: *What Can a Poem Do?* Atheneum Publishers, New York, 1962.

NATIONAL COUNCIL OF TEACHERS OF ENGLISH, *Language Arts for Today's Children,* Appleton-Century-Crofts, Inc., New York, 1954, pp. 211–213, 218–219, 234–236, 242–245, 274–282.

PEASE, DON: *Creative Writing in the Elementary School,* Exposition Press, New York, 1964, chaps. 4–5.

PETTY, WALTER T., AND MARY E. BROWN: *Slithery Snakes and Other Aids to Children's Writing,* Appleton-Century-Crofts, Inc., New York, 1967.

SHANE, HAROLD G., AND OTHERS: *Improving Language Arts Instruction in the Elementary School,* Charles E. Merrill Books, Inc., Columbus, Ohio, 1964, chap. 15.

TIEDT, IRIS M., AND S. W. TIEDT: *Readings on Contemporary English in the Elementary School,* Prentice-Hall, Inc., Englewood Cliffs, N.J., 1967, pp. 154–158.

WALKER, NINA W.: *Let Them Write Poetry,* Holt, Rinehart and Winston, Inc., New York, 1966.

PART 3

ATTITUDES, SKILLS, AND ABILITIES

I I.

ATTITUDES, COURTESIES, CONTENT, AND ORGANIZATION

In Chapter 2 an attempt was made to identify the chief lines of growth in language and to recognize thereby the kinds of experiences that the school should provide. A comparison was made between growth in language and growth in other areas of the curriculum, such as music, industrial arts, social studies, and health. A distinction was made between language experiences (conversation, dramatization, reporting) and the elements or factors that condition the experiences (willingness to participate, finding something appropriate to say, using acceptable mechanics of oral and written expression). Comparable phases in the game of football were noted. It was pointed out that a properly balanced language program requires both participation in natural, lifelike experiences and instruction and training in component abilities and skills.

We have dealt with language experiences in the immediately preceding chapters. We now turn to those parts of the language program that concern instruction and training in attitudes, abilities, and skills.

The child in the oral phases of language—talking, reporting, conversing, etc.—necessarily selects something to say, uses words, forms sentences, and vocalizes. In written phases of the work—

reports, story, verse, letters, summaries—the child is concerned with content, words, sentences, sticking to a point, paragraphing, punctuating, capitalizing, spelling, and the like. In both oral and written expression the child grows in ability and skill elements as he grows in experiences. If the oral and written experiences are sufficiently frequent, and if sufficient attention is paid to the ability and skill elements in the experiences while they are under way, it is possible that no separate instruction and training on elements will be required. This will be recognized as an extremely well-integrated program. Reading takes place in the development of experience charts, by reading the class-developed newspaper, through researching a social science or science problem, and by reading books that lend themselves to interpretation and depth understanding of an era or event.

The development of abilities and skills in connection with real language experiences is, of course, ideal—the instructional goal toward which teachers are striving. But the observation of teaching indicates that some specific, separate attention to abilities and skills is common. Courses of study and textbooks devote considerable space to these parts of the language program, implying a necessity for definite instruction. Just how much of the time devoted to language can profitably be given to directed work on abilities and skills in separate periods depends on a number of things: the amount of time given to real experiencing in language, the utilization of opportunities in other areas of schoolwork for language development, the recognition of language goals, the skill of the teacher, and the accepted philosophy of education.

In this chapter we are concerned with the elements of attitudes, courtesies, content, and organization. These elements are recognized at once as basic in all language experiences. They provide motivation for experiences and other elements; they are concerned with *what* is spoken or written.

Attitudes

Willingness to participate and a desire to achieve fluency are generally regarded as basic dynamics of expression—the means of securing voluntary and free participation. Willingness to participate is important in all language work, particularly in the creative phases. Noteworthy is the striking contrast between willingness to speak outside the school and reluctance to speak inside the school.

Too often the school inhibits rather than encourages free expression. There must be a real desire to speak and write in the school, and children must find satisfaction in the expression of ideas. The teacher seeks to utilize the many situations requiring purposeful expression in order to stimulate willing participation. Hilda Taba says, "In classrooms with open networks of interpersonal relations the lines of communication are open." [1]

Closely related to willingness to participate is the desire for improvement. The desire to say something leads naturally to the desire to say it effectively, to note and correct deficiencies, to profit from criticisms and suggestions—in general, to work for improvement. Desire to improve operates in both oral and written language experiences.

Processes, conditions, and means   What can the teacher do to help his pupils develop good attitudes in language? The primary attack is to set up conditions in the class that invite and entice children to participate. Attitudes are elusive, caught by suggestion and environmental stimulation; they are by-products of the total language program. Interest is caught, not provided on demand. One can require a child to learn the correct use of *lie* and *lay;* one cannot require that he *want* to tell a story or write a poem. Again Hilda Taba says, "Communication and interaction generate a task orientation which makes it possible for one individual to stimulate another or to extend the ideas offered by another." [2] The teacher himself should be attentive and sympathetic, aware of his responsibility to help create an effective social climate in his classroom.

Approval, to be helpful, must be genuine and hearty, but also discriminating in holding the speaker to reasonably high standards of performance. Here again individual differences must be recognized. The shy child needs the encouragement of generous approval; the overaggressive, loquacious child profits by learning the techniques of self-evaluation. Consider, for example, the case of eleven-year-old Erwin, who had never produced even the simplest kind of written expression. When, after profound effort, he managed to write the following story, the teacher and classmates alike realized that something remarkable had happened, and they were quick to compliment him without calling attention to the shortcomings of his story:

[1] Hilda Taba, *Curriculum Development: Theory and Practice*, Harcourt, Brace & World, Inc., New York, 1962, p. 164.
[2] *Ibid.*, p. 2.

The Tarkey Farm
Is running out of tarkey
and he is happy
and   the end

A second fundamental condition for free, fluent participation is *having something to say.* Topics chosen for conversation, discussion, storytelling, and the like should tap sources of familiar experiences concerning which children have knowledge, ideas, and interest. The alert teacher finds a wealth of suitable topics in children's hobbies, in current experiences outside the school, in curricular activities, and in in-school experiences. Individual freedom of choice within a suggested area is important. The subjective areas of personal living are too often excluded from the school curriculum. Feelings about oneself and others, attitudes toward the natural world and existence, and tastes in leisure activities have been suggested as features of essential content or subject matter in the language arts.[3] Specific procedures will be required at times to stimulate discussion and help recall information, such as the use of pictures for young children and children with language handicaps.

The third obvious factor in developing a good language attitude among children is a strong reason for expression, a situation that presents a real, immediate occasion for speaking or writing. Strong purpose increases clarity of thought and fluency and conviction of speech; it decreases the inhibiting effect of shyness by making the child idea-conscious rather than people-conscious.

Involved in several of the points made above is the implication that reasonable standards should be set in terms of individual capacities. The goals should be sufficient in breadth and depth to stimulate every child in the class to make his best effort; but it would be folly to set the same standards for every child. Nothing is more discouraging than continually being required or urged to attempt the impossible. Each child should be encouraged and expected to strive for the goals of which he is capable. Comparisons with other children may be harmful. Differences are natural and to be expected. In setting standards, the crux of the problem of school learning is pinpointed. Too often there is no match between the goal of the teacher and that of the individual child. Blanket goals, assignments, teacher expectations and assumptions lead to a minimizing of the desired learning. Dealing with the

[3] W. W. Hatfield, "Humanizing the Language Arts," *Elementary English,* vol. 44, October, 1965, pp. 673–678.

tenet of individual differences in rate of learning, Suppes says, ". . . I consider it the most important principle of learning as yet unaccepted in the day-to-day practices of subject-matter teaching in the classroom." [4]

An imaginative child may write about a simple happening; but if he is earnestly trying to express himself, commendation should be forthcoming. Such a child was Patricia, who wrote the following:

THE CARDS

Last night my friends came to my house and we played a game of cards and they played some of their tricks yts the cards and at 8 o'clock I went to bad and they went home   the end

The teacher remarked, "Patricia has told us what a pleasant time she had with her friends last night, hasn't she?" and let it go at that. When opportunity arose she would emphasize run-on sentences and hope that Patricia would benefit without direct criticism of her work.

In the same group Peggy, a much more mature child, wrote the following story, prompted no doubt by a blind man who, with his Seeing Eye dog, visited the school:

A DOG

I am a German Shepherd Seeing Eye Dog. My name is Rover.

One day I was leading my master down street. We went to cross the street when a car was coming. I stepped in front of my master too fast and pushed him down. He struck his head on a cement curb. I barked but he did not get up. Some people heard me and came running. When they saw what I had done a couple of men picked my master up. One woman called the doctor and ambulance.

The ambulance took my master to something called a hospital and a tall kind man took me to his home.

The house was big and white with green grass all around it. I was very lonesome.

One day the man got out of his car. He told me to get into it. The man had my harness in his hand. I thought something was wrong but when the man stopped the car in front of the hospital and I saw my master I jumped quickly out of the car and right into my master's arms. After that I was more careful.

Freedom *not* to participate in an experience is important.

---

[4] P. Suppes, "Modern Learning Theory and the Elementary School Curriculum," *American Educational Research Journal,* vol. 1, 1964, p. 79. Reported in Ira A. Gordon: "New Conceptions of Children's Learning and Development," *Learning and Mental Health in the School,* 1966 Yearbook, Association for Supervision and Curriculum Development, National Education Association, Washington, D.C., p. 70.

The predicament of the child who is forced to take part is vividly described by Ethel H. Ludin: [5]

> So many times when children hear that the English lesson is to con- sist of short talks, a chill of sudden dread strikes them. Talk? What about? Why? Stand up before the class and make a speech? Oh, joyless English lesson! The typical youngster visualizes himself standing before his classmates, blundering on, and looking into maliciously twinkling or solemnly critical eyes—or, even worse, gazing with a semi-hypnotic stare at nothing at all and somehow getting through. The announce- ment, therefore, that no one would have to speak unless he had some- thing to say was greeted with joy. It was evident that our plan of pro- cedure should be based on this note.

Not every topic will prove stimulating to every child. The teacher may very well give attention to the child who never has anything to say. If lack of participation is caused by not knowing "where to start," guidance in special preparation is in order; if due to excessive shyness, the teacher will take occasion to stimulate and encourage. Individual assignments are often the means of giving the reluctant child the necessary push to participate.

The importance of maintaining reasonable standards in all phases of the school program can be noted in its effect on attitude. The language of a casual conversation differs from the language of a formal document. The short story differs in form and content from a chapter in a social studies textbook. Language used at a baseball game differs from the language used in a formal debate. Thus, by helping children develop a framework of standards for varying situations, the teacher can best serve as an agent through which the utility, the beauty, the concise or expressive qualities of language can all be explored.

Courtesies

In handling courtesies, as in handling other phases of the language program, it is impossible to disassociate development in the area from the larger social development of which it is naturally a part. Development of courtesy is fundamentally development in sympa- thetic understanding and sensitivity to the thoughts and feelings of others, a desire to please, and growth in desire and ability to use language that will show understanding, consideration, and interest

[5] Jess S. Hudson and others, *Language Arts in the Elementary School,* Twentieth Yearbook, National Education Association, Department of Ele- mentary School Principals, Washington, D.C., 1941, p. 296. Quoted with spe- cial permission of the publisher.

and will avoid unintentional hurt or offense. Courtesy is evidence of social maturity. Language is both a means and an end of social adjustment.

Objectives An analysis of courtesy shows at least three key components: attitudes, such as a desire to please and to avoid offense; knowledge and understanding, such as competence to make a guest feel welcome and to disagree tactfully in a discussion; and the ability and skill to use proper language expressions and forms, in part fixed by conventions.

In Chapter 2 the essential courtesies were listed under three heads: listening attentively, giving and taking criticisms pleasantly, and behaving amiably in speaking and writing. This analysis is clearly inadequate as an indication of the wide variety and scope of work involved in training in courtesies. A complete listing is also quite impractical. Although there are certain general characteristics of courteous behavior that are common in many experiences, each one sets up its own particular requirements. It is desirable for the teacher to consider the specific kinds of courteous behavior for any given experience. For example, carrying on a conversation includes such matters as giving others a chance to talk, listening attentively, disagreeing tactfully, not interrupting, acting graciously when interrupted by another, and avoiding harmful gossip. In letter writing important constituents of courtesy are using appropriate greeting and close, adapting content to the interests of others, answering letters promptly, and showing concern for others.

Situations and processes Because training in courtesies is mainly training in many specific kinds of behavior peculiar to varied experiences, it is best provided in actual situations. Thus courtesy is seen by pupils not as an end in itself, but as a means of adequately meeting these situations. Ideas, attitudes, and abilities that define and characterize courteous behavior in general may then evolve. Situations for the practice of courtesy arise constantly.

A primary group suggested the following letter of appreciation and apology to a neighboring teacher who weekly invited them to see films in her room:

Dear Miss LaVerne,
    We appreciate the invitation to movies on Fridays and we enjoy the films that you show. We hope it does not bother the other children when we come in late.

Sincerely,
Room 15

The meaning of and need for courtesy can be explained and developed by discussion. Standards appropriate to the grade level and maturity of the children can be set, along with other standards concerning content, organization, speech, written form, and the like. The examination of good models is similarly helpful, as in letter writing or introductions. Explanation and discussion are useful in handling the knowledge phases of the work, such as those concerning what to say when introducing one's mother to the teacher or how to address a distinguished visitor. Because children's crudities are often due to ignorance, negative examples may profitably be studied in comparison with good examples. Examples of discourtesy can be cited from children's experience and observation, or a file of typical incidents may be built up by the teacher. Discussion should center on better forms of conduct. Children should not be embarrassed by having common shortcomings critically analyzed before the class.

Another approach begins with hypothetical problems rather than with negative examples. How would you meet such situations as dealing with an annoying solicitor, greeting unexpected and unwanted guests, being interrupted in work by an overeager friend, and answering the telephone when you are planning to go out? Discussion of problems can be supplemented at times by role playing, the children acting out the situation as realistically and vividly as possible.[6]

The development of feelings of sensitivity and the desire to be pleasant, like other attitudes, must be approached and guided indirectly by suggestion and example. Prevailing patterns in the home and social circle have a vital influence; a teacher can do little about them directly. He can, however, suggest and exemplify desirable patterns in the classroom and school. In addition to noticing and approving the good behavior of the pupils, the teacher may drop pertinent hints from time to time by saying that people are generally friendly, and we do not knowingly offend our friends; that people do not like us when we are discourteous; and that discourtesy is not the best way of meeting discourtesy—"A soft answer turneth away wrath."

Content

Next in importance to attitudes and courtesies as a factor in a vital language program and a logical next step in its development is

---

[6] John Jarolimek, *Social Studies in Elementary Education*, The Macmillan Company, New York, 1967, pp. 204–206.

evaluation of content. The primary purpose of communication—the saying or writing of something important and interesting to another—needs to be recognized and stressed early. Content is fundamentally important in all language experiences, but its nature naturally varies with the experience. The teacher should help his pupils to distinguish the content peculiar to a particular experience or situation.

Specific objectives   Certain general characteristics or qualities of content are identifiable and provide points of attack in the achievement of specific goals or objectives. The first point concerns the importance of selecting a suitable topic. Perhaps much of the irresponsiveness of children in language situations is due to a feeling of not having anything to say. This helplessness is commonly caused not by lack of worthy experiences but by failure to identify and recall phases of experience suitable for expression. The teacher needs to stimulate and encourage children and to provide help in selecting good subjects by revealing to them resources of which they are unaware. Material is found in children's personal experiences in the home and community—play, trips, pets, and hobbies—and in the school in both curricular and extracurricular endeavors. In these various activities there are incidents that have interesting, unusual phases which arouse in the child some mental or emotional response worthy of expression. It is the expression of such personal thought or feeling that has value and that adds the spice of interest. The teacher will need to probe for these reactions, recognize them, and encourage the children to express themselves freely. At times he will need to discourage the mere cataloguing of events and to train the children to avoid the trivial, the commonplace, and the sensational. In such work the teacher is training the children not merely to use language but also to observe closely, to be keenly sensitive to feelings and moods, and to think clearly. Examples may serve to clarify this point.

Jean described a commonplace experience, but her use of the descriptive words *fat, gray,* and *jiffy* made this little story worthy of commendation:

ON THE WAY TO SCHOOL

One day as I was going to school I saw a fat gray squirrel. When I was coming home there was the same squirrel I had seen before. I ran home, got a nut and was back in a jiffy. When I gave it to him, he took it and ran away.

Robert's story, though containing only three sentences, seemed quite complete. It was written independently during a story-writing period by a quiet, slow boy.

THE MAGIC POOL

> Once upon a time a girl and a boy were sitting by a pool. The boy said, "This is a magic pool. Look, I can see my face."

"I like Robert's use of the word *magic* to describe his pool," complimented the teacher. "Having the boy really say something helped to make the story interesting too."

Helen, age eight, also has undoubtedly drawn upon a real experience. She is seeing tadpoles in a brook or pool; but by adding an imaginative touch, she has given her story a charming quality. Helen's story has no name.

> Once upon a time some baby tadpoles and fish were rolling little tiny stones to each other when their mothers called them to come in and go to bed. So they ran everyway. "Good night! Good night," they cried.

The teacher commented favorably: "I especially liked Helen's last sentence. Can you see the little tadpoles as they scurry quickly home?"

Partly because he chose an unusual theme, fourteen-year-old Alf's short poem rose above the commonplace:

> *Did you ever walk*
> *Along a street*
> *And gaze at*
> *Other people's feet?*
> *Listen to their*
> *Steady beat,*
> *While on your*
> *Way to school?*

The possibility of making a successful composition or talk is increased by limiting the scope to a single incident or phase of an experience—not the whole trip through Yellowstone Park but the incident of the bear getting into the parked car and stealing a loaf of sliced bread.

The favorable effect of a composition is enhanced by including interesting details and information necessary to complete and vivify the picture, story, or report.

In the primary grades the teacher frequently needs to help the children distinguish between the real and the make-believe. The temptation to make a good story better by fictional embellishments is quite common and is not limited to children. Both fiction and facts have a place, but they should not be confused. The teacher may well ask, "Did that really happen, or are you making it up?"

Subjected as they are to radio, TV, movies, and comics, children are frequently uncertain as to whether or not a story—even one of their own making—is true or simply *might* be true. The following combination of skill, imagination, and comics was written without assistance by an eight-year-old during a free period in school. When it was read to the group and someone asked, "Is it true?" the reply was, "Well, it *might* be." And who knows!

Nothing has been changed except the spelling.

WUMBO'S ADVENTURE

Once upon an African night, a strange glowing object raced across the sky. It went over some tall trees and disappeared. A band of natives saw the strange "thing."

The next morning they went out on a searching party to look for the "thing." They thought it was an evil god. They split up and went in different directions.

Now a certain man named Wumbo went one way. After a while he heard voices in a strange language he did not understand. He was so busy listening that he did not hear the man from Outer Space creep upon him.

Before Wumbo heard a sound, he was caught.

The Space Men took him to their Space Ship which looked like a giant turtle shell.

The Space Men looked like, to Wumbo, the most horrible things he had ever seen. They all had three square heads, five eyes, and their mouths looked like loud speakers.

Near the Space Ship the monsters had set up strange "Gadgets."

All of a sudden one of the monsters started jabbering in that strange language and pointing to an instrument. The instrument looked like a diamond with a half moon in it.

The other monsters looked at the instrument and made a rush for their Space Ship and then they took off and were never heard of again.

As for Wumbo, later in the day the other natives found him, untied him from the tree and all was well.

Originality and independence in thinking are desired qualities. The young storyteller is often inclined to follow the pattern of an approved classmate. In the later grades the tendency to report undigested material verbatim also needs to be dealt with.

The teacher may well collect from the children's work and elsewhere compositions that illustrate good and bad points of content. The following are compositions from the fifth and sixth grades, illustrating content. How should they be rated? In what respect are they good or not so good? The first pair is on "Citizenship," and the second pair on "My Occupation." The fifth composition, on "The Squid," is more informative in type. The spelling, punctuation, and paragraphing are original.

CITIZENSHIP

A good citizen must not forget important things. We shouldn't run on the corridors, or carelessly throw balls and bats. When using a bat, we should be in front of a backstop only.

Try not to throw paper around, and if we find some on the payground let's pick it up. Our playground should be clean.

At noon remember to wash our hands. While in the cafeteria use our best manners, and don't talk loudly.

Fights cause us to get hurt. We might also lose our best friend. Therefore, we whould try to stay out of them.

Don't run in our rooms. While in the bathroom be quiet and sure the the water is off, when we're through using it. We shouldn't throw papers in the bathroom either.

CITIZENSHIP

Citizenship to many boys and girls doesn't mean much. Citizenship is really one of the most important duties in life. Everyone, including myself, should try to be a better citizen.

When I go out for recess I see good citizenship and some not so good. Some of us don't remember to throw the papers in the cans, but throw them on the floor.

On the playgrounds, sometimes boys start fights which dont get them anything but a black eye, bloody nose, or something like that. It is less painfull to cooperate.

"Play Fairly at All Times," is a good rule.

MY OCCUPATION

When I grow up I am going to be a surgant-physician. I will need language very much.

In permoring an operation I must be able to speak clearly and correctly, if I made a mistake and got the wrong instrument, it would take time to get the right instrument, and operations must be done quickly.

As a physician I need to give prescriptions to people and give them advice on how to cure themselves.

MY OCCUPATION

When I grow up I am gowing to be an airplane pilot. When I am an airplane pilot I will have to use language in a manner that other people can understand me I will have to talk to the other pilot and get in contact with the ground. I will have to talk to the passengers I will have to talk with the flight instructor

THE SQUID

The squid belongs to the class Cephalopoda (the highest of mollusks).

It has ten tentacles, two of which are longer than the others and are used to catch its prey. The other tentacles transfer its victim to the beak for dinner.

The squids eyes are very well-developed.

Its body is tinted and spotted with changeable colors.

It can discharge an ink-like fluid to cover its movements while being chased by an enemy. Also from the same tube it discharges ink it can discharge to make it go backwards at a higher rate of speed.

The giant squid measures about fifty feet in length.

Flying squids leap across the water sometimes landing on ships.

Opportunities Opportunities to emphasize the importance of good content, to clarify understanding of what constitutes good content, and to train in specific abilities are offered in every experience in the language program—in fact, in all phases of the curricular and school-life program where language is used. Good language habits often result simply from general good teaching and good learning. But in spite of the many opportunities pupils have to use language effectively in real situations, teachers find that special attention needs to be given, in definite training lessons, to specific problems. The training lesson, however, should never be far removed from the particular language experience in which the need for the training is revealed.

Training lesson The first step of procedure for a training lesson is to recognize a specific language need in some purposeful experience. This need is revealed by an evaluation of the children's work by both teacher and children; the need may be limited to a small group or may be common to the whole class.

A second step is to clarify the children's ideas of the desired quality. If the point at issue, for example, is selecting suitable topics, the teacher helps the children identify in their experience those aspects which have potential interest for a listener or reader and about which they have some knowledge and strong feeling. Children can suggest suitable topics for illustration and class discussion, or the teacher can present examples illustrating good qualities and weaknesses. Good topics should be interesting and definite rather than vague, vapid, and wordy. Titles are often used to suggest topics. Such a title as "Where I Went" or "What I Saw" is too broad. "An Experience I Wouldn't Want to Repeat" or "Why Pigs Have Tails" immediately arouses in the listener or reader a feeling of anticipation.

If the point at issue is expressing personal feelings and ideas, the teacher may well present for study samples from the children's work or from other sources. Compositions may be presented in pairs, good and bad, so that children can get a feeling for the personal quality desired.

The third step is to have the children prepare original examples embodying the particular quality under study, such as lists of topics that are personal, definite, and brief; a composition dealing with a limited topic or single experience, and a composition showing interesting details. These, of course, should be presented and considered by the class.

The fourth step or stage is to have the children prepare and deliver their talks or compositions, concentrating on a particular point.

In comparison with the wealth of explanatory material and exercises on the mechanical phases of writing, usage, and pronunciation, current textbooks offer little help to the teacher in setting up special training exercises in content and in organization. This is difficult to understand, in view of the general recognition of the primary importance of content and organization for good composition. There may be the implication that content and organization are adequately learned incidentally through speaking and writing, which is very doubtful; the omission may be due to oversight; or training exercises in content and organization may not be so easily fitted into conventional patterns as are exercises in capitalization, punctuation, and usage. Under the circumstances, the teacher is faced with the necessity of building up his own procedures and exercises when the need for them appears.

Organization

Organization and content are closely related. The primary concern in a study of content emphasizes choice of topics and material that are interesting to others. The primary concern in a consideration of organization stresses the presentation of the material in such a way as to make it clear and forceful.

The following compositions from the social studies, fourth grade, show good content; the differences appear in organization.

> The Indians didn't wear many clothes. The woman wore skirts made of bark, and they wore capes. The men wore pieces of animal skin tied around the waist.
> Their food consists mostly of corn, fish, and deer meat.
> Their houses were made of very heavy wood, about 4 inches wide, and 9 feet high. The horses were covered with leather, and tied with a strip of leather at the top.
> For transportation they used horses, canoes, and their feet.

> For food the early Indians hunted. when they hunted they wear masks, and the women gathered nuts. Their homes wer made of tule, and they had a sweat house. they had the sweat house so they could get owt the gwims. another way to get food was to fish.

In discussing man as a self-organizing system, Ira Gordon says: [7]

[7] Gordon, *op. cit.*, p. 68. Quoted with special permission of the author and publisher.

This "push for order" can be seen as a basis for concept-building and categorization. The very nature of the child, neurologically, requires of him that he process information in such a way that categories emerge. What particular concepts, and at what levels of abstraction, depend, of course, on input. Schooling which utilizes the child's endeavors to structure his world contributes to competence. Schooling which either tries to impose an order when the child cannot grasp it, or presents masses of data expecting the child to order them as the adult does, may lead to mental indigestion and feelings of incompetence.

Specific objectives Primarily important is sticking to the point, achieving unity. Selecting a suitable topic and limiting its scope to a single aspect of the topic make sticking to the point easier; there is only one point to stick to. A second feature of good organization is the presenting of material in an effective sequence. The sequence may involve cause and effect relations, a series of incidents or events in which there is a time factor, or directions to be followed in a prescribed order as in a recipe or game. Other basic considerations are the beginning and ending sentences, especially in short compositions or talks. The beginning sentence—the topic sentence—catches interest and frequently introduces the topic, question, or problem. The significance of the beginning and ending sentences is best shown in concrete examples. Compare some of the following beginning sentences:

> Grade 1: This story is about a flying house.
> Grade 2: Little Star was an Indian boy.
> Grade 3: Here comes old Gray Turtle down the road—step! step! step!
> Grade 3: It was sunset when Mother brought the clothes in and, as she stepped in the door, she heard a thump, thump, thump. Something was in the attic!
> Grade 6: "There she goes!" exclaimed Jim Land as he watched the X-5 take off.

The good ending sentence brings the story or incident to a prompt close, holding interest to the last and providing a satisfactory conclusion or a neat turn.

Even young children may, with training, be made aware of these important elements in good story writing. The following story, written independently by a nine-year-old girl, has an interesting beginning and shows cause and effect relations. Events follow each other in natural sequence, and the story is satisfactorily concluded.

FLUFF

Fluff was two days old when Nancy found her in a basket near her mother. "Oh, what a cute little white kitty," said Nancy. "What shall we name her, Mother?"

"I don't know, Nancy," her Mother said. "Fluff might be a good name."

"Yes, Fluff would be a good name," so they named the little white kitty Fluff.

Day by day Fluff grew bigger and bigger. She grew into a big cat. You could tell she was happy by the merry twinkle in her green eyes.

Then, one day, Nancy forgot to feed her. Nancy grew crosser and crosser until, one day, Fluff could stand it no longer. She went to a better home where she lived happily ever after.

The writing of longer compositions introduces the necessity of paragraphing—the dividing of a theme into topical thought units. Here again the purpose is the achievement of logical clarity. Paragraphing requires maturity as well as study and experience, although a beginning can be made in the primary grades.

Steps Organization concerns knowledge factors and can be handled by the direct procedures used in teaching content. The training lesson follows the same steps: purposeful occasion; models, possibly standards; individual performance followed by evaluation; practice, concentrating on specific difficulties; deliberate use; and estimation of progress. Illustrative material will be found very useful. Possibly more or less formal practice exercises in organization and sequence, provided in textbooks and workbooks, may offer some help if the immediate contributory purpose of such exercises is recognized.

Regarding the development of organizational abilities, Burrows and others state: [8]

> It is very interesting to observe some of the manifestations of a dawning sense of order. Even quite immature children often want to divide a report or a story into chapters in an effort to satisfy their need for some sort of dividing line. The word "chapter" may seem a bit humorous to the staid adult, but it is by no means to be laughed at. Let the young writer divide his little offering on, perhaps, the fruit fly into chapters if he wishes. In short order he sees that some of his items really belong in another chapter, maybe a new one that should be written about the damage the fly does the world over. This bundling of material to put like things together is one of the first stages of logical and coherent writing.
>
> As children mature it is easy to point out, usually following their own discovery of the matter, that within a chapter is a sequence of ideas—smaller divisions within the larger one, the basis of paragraphing. That each different idea—each part of the chapter—stands out better if seen in a separate paragraph is about as far as it seems reasonable to go with the elementary school children in the debatable matter of paragraph

[8] Alvina T. Burrows and others, *They All Want to Write*, Holt, Rinehart and Winston, Inc., New York, 1964, pp. 70–71. Quoted with special permission of the authors and publisher.

division. Certainly much of the trouble in paragraphing arises from forcing the use of a form before the need for it is understood. . . .

Later on, children become aware of another factor of organization, infinitely more involved than the grouping of like ideas and frequently conspicuous by its absence even in adult writing. This is the active principle in sequential arrangement. The marshaling of functional material toward a real goal implies the beginning of a dynamic organization.

Evaluation   It must be apparent that in the area of attitudes, courtesies, content, and organization the chief evaluative instrument is the teacher's judgment, supplemented by individual pupil and class checking; and that much use is made of samples and lists of standards or goals—more or less detailed—taken from pupils' work.

For your consideration

1   Visit a class during some phase of oral work and evaluate in terms of observable attitudes, courtesies, content, and organization.

2   List the courtesies—social amenities—that need to be developed with children in one of the following activities: (*a*) writing a friendly letter or a business letter; (*b*) taking part in a conversation or a discussion.

3   Evaluate for content and organization several samples of children's work.

4   List the possible techniques that a teacher must use to motivate the improvement of content of children's written work.

5   Discuss: Training in organization is training in thinking.

References

ANDERSON, PAUL S.: *Language Skills in Elementary Education*, The Macmillan Company, New York, 1966, pp. 72–80.

APPLEGATE, MAUREE: *Easy in English*, Harper & Row, Publishers, Inc., New York, 1963, chap. 1.

BONNEY, MERLE E., AND R. S. HAMPLEMAN: *Personal-Social Evaluation Techniques*, The Center for Applied Research in Education, Inc., Washington, D.C., 1962.

DAVIS, DAVID C.: "Whatever Happened to . . . ?" *Elementary English*, vol. 43, March, 1966, pp. 240–244, 302.

DAWSON, MILDRED A., M. ZOLLINGER, AND E. ELWELL: *Guiding Language Learning*, Harcourt, Brace & World, Inc., New York, 1963, pp. 214–215.

EVANS, ROBERT: "A Glove Thrown Down," *Elementary English*, vol. 44, May, 1967, pp. 523–527.

GROTHE, BARBARA FORD: "A Study of Spelling Conscience," *Elementary English*, vol. 43, November, 1966, pp. 774–776, 784.

HORROWORTH, GLORIA L.: "Listening: A Fact of Oral Language," *Elementary English*, vol. 43, December, 1966, pp. 856–864, 868.

MAY, FRANK B.: "The Effects of Environment on Oral Language Development," *Elementary English*, vol. 43, Oct.–Nov., 1966, pp. 587–595, 720–729.

MC KEE, PAUL: *Language in the Elementary School*, Houghton Mifflin Company, Boston, 1939, pp. 56–59, 85–86, 99–105, 110–112, 124–125, 147–150, 170–171, 214, 312–316.

NATIONAL COUNCIL OF TEACHERS OF ENGLISH, *Language Arts for Today's Children*, Appleton-Century-Crofts, Inc., New York, 1954, pp. 229–235, 246–247.

PETTY, WALTER T., AND ROBERTA J. STARKEY: "Oral Language and Personal and Social Development," *Elementary English*, vol. 43, April, 1966, pp. 386–394.

STRICKLAND, RUTH G.: *The Language Arts in the Elementary School*, D. C. Heath and Company, Boston, 1957, pp. 37–42, 189–190.

WOOD, DOROTHY A.: *Test Construction*, Charles E. Merrill Books, Inc., Columbus, Ohio, 1961.

12.

SPEECH

Speech in the language program   The primary concern of the language teacher is developing children's ability to find something to say and their desire and willingness to say it. But to this training must be added instruction in the manner of speaking. What is the place of speech as one element in the total program? By attention to the speech of social and business associates one notes marked differences in quality and is impressed with the tremendous social value of clear, correct speech. Good speech is good business. The significance of speech as a factor in the total personality of the individual may not be so outwardly apparent. Psychologists tell us that good speech generates confidence and a feeling of security in relations with others, while poor or halting speech lessens confidence, causes worry, and leads to withdrawal types of behavior. It would seem, then, that speech training deserves attention as a factor in communication.

The teacher is concerned with the speech of all his students, not only of the obvious few who have serious defects. It follows, then, that he must give attention to all the factors that contribute to effective oral expression. Among the several factors are articulation, voice, rhythm, and delivery. Articulation is concerned with the clear and accurate production of speech sounds. Examples of common difficulties are the omission of sounds, as in *pay* for *play;* the distortion of sounds, such as the overarticulation of the *s* in *whistling;* and the substitution of sounds, such as *wun* for *run.*[1] The primary attributes of voice are pitch, volume or loudness, and quality. Rhythm relates to the flow and stress of language and the grouping of words into phrases. Delivery includes such elements as animation, relationship with the audience, facial expression and gestures, posture, and mannerisms.[2]

Preliminary survey of pupils' needs   The aims of a survey of pupils' needs are to formulate standards, to estimate individual accomplishments with reference to the standards, and to note factors that may contribute to further development. Standards of normal expectancy vary with the age-grade-maturity grouping and with the social background of the pupils. There can be no hard and fast definition of standards suitable for all grades or for the same grade in all types of schools. There can be no substitute for the judgment of the teacher. Estimates of individual accomplishments require the exercise of judgment over factors requiring attention. The general goal is satisfying self-expression and effective communication. Any factor that causes failure to achieve this goal may be listed as a speech deficiency. A rough yardstick is offered by Johnson, ". . . a child's speech is defective when most listeners pay as much attention, or more, to how he speaks as to what he says." [3] To be avoided are complete indifference to careless, inadequate speech habits and overconcern with precision and perfection, which inhibit free speaking and attach an exaggerated importance to the mechanics of oral language. The teacher's understanding of the nature of language; of regional, acceptable pronunciation; and of levels of usage affect his work with children.[4] Teachers are cautioned against having standards that are too high or too low.

A practical procedure for the teacher to use in planning a preliminary survey of pupils' needs is to make a checklist of items similar to the checklists described previously, using as the main

[1] Charles Van Riper, *Speech Correction: Principles and Methods,* Prentice-Hall, Inc., Englewood Cliffs, N.J., 1963, pp. 19–23. See also Dorothy K. Marge, "The Social Status of Speech-handicapped Children," *Journal of Speech and Hearing Research,* vol. 9, June, 1966, pp. 165–177.

[2] Verna Anderson and others, *Readings in the Language Arts,* The Macmillan Company, New York, 1964, pp. 76–78.

[3] Wendell Johnson and others, *Speech Handicapped School Children,* Harper & Row, Publishers, Inc., New York, 1956, p. 4.

[4] Jon Eisenson and Mardel Ogilvie, *Speech Correction in the Schools,* The Macmillan Company, New York, 1963, pp. 40–64.

topics the following: articulation, voice, rhythm, and delivery. There may also be a number of subtopics under each head, varying according to the preference of the teacher. The teacher will probably at first make general observations about areas of strength and weakness. This general survey may lead to listing specific difficulties.

A general survey should be thoughtfully devised and observations of the children's speech should be made over a period of time, in varying situations. In considering articulation, checklists are necessary.[5] To assess articulatory disorders, the teacher must possess:

1. A knowledge of the general age at which children tend to produce speech sounds successfully.
2. An understanding of the differences found in speech sounds in different regions of the United States, especially if he teaches in an area where the population is mobile.
3. An understanding of the differences in sound systems between American English and other languages which children may speak at home, if he teaches in an area where English is a second language to some of the children.

Checklists and observational notes combine to give the teacher an assessment of voice control, rhythm, and delivery in several situations—playtime and classtime, informal conversational moments, and structured mathematics discussion.

In voice control, the teacher needs to observe the persistence of inaudibility, overloudness, nasality, which may be observed in children. Rhythm difficulties of unduly slow, irregular, or high-speed speech need to be noted in the settings in which they occur. Delivery qualities, such as manifestations of nervous mannerisms, must be assessed. By considering the multiple components of the children—their past experiences and their present needs, the nature of the various school tasks in which they are called upon to function, the teacher's expectations and understandings of them—the teacher can begin to see the persistent speech needs of the individuals in his classroom.

The preliminary survey will not give the teacher all the information he needs for a complete instructional-correctional program. It will acquaint him with the general levels of language

[5] See, for example, inventories such as those found in Alan W. Huckleberry and E. S. Strother, *Speech Education for the Elementary Teacher*, Allyn and Bacon, Inc., Boston, 1966, pp. 133–136; and J. C. Bangs, "Speech and Hearing Centers: Syllabus," *Voice and Speech Disorders: Medical Aspects*, N. M. Levin (ed.), Charles C Thomas, Springfield, Ill., 1962, p. 924.

development of his pupils, identify pupils of outstanding ability or those in need of correctional aid, suggest general types of deficiency, provide a basis for outlining a general program of constructive work, suggest areas that need further intensive study, and provide a basis for estimating progress. The teacher who is too correction-conscious may overlook possibilities for the further development of the gifted pupils. The capable children have as much right to opportunities for growth as do the handicapped children. While sympathies are properly aroused by the handicapped pupil, teachers should not fail to offer the gifted pupil a chance for the greatest development in oral expression of which he is capable.

General conditions   A sound, practical basis for speech development is setting up conditions in the classroom that are favorable to the cultivation of desired speech abilities and skills. Generally speaking, the conditions favorable to the development of good speech are equally appropriate for the handicapped child and the capable child; and the conditions favorable to speech are those favorable to other phases of the language program.

A primary condition is that the teacher's speech should set a pattern and a standard for the children. Children are with a teacher many hours during the day, and they consciously or unconsciously imitate him or her in voice quality, pitch, and inflection. It is not unusual to find a peculiar quality of nasality or shrillness appearing in children's speech. The quality of speech is contagious, and imitation may nullify direct efforts at retraining.

The classroom should be free from tension and nervous strain. The children should be conscious of and sensitive to quality of speech, but not unduly anxious or worried. Difficulties are to be faced with frankness, good will, and optimism. Individual differences are recognized and accepted naturally. A spirit of interested, pleasant helpfulness stimulates all children, especially the shy child; encourages the attainment of the highest standards of which the individual is capable; and gives a feeling of satisfaction for worthy effort and progress, not for superior performance only.

Purposeful experiences   The classroom offers a wealth of real experiences in which the quality of speech is important. Purposeful experiences provide incentives for clear, impressive presentation, situations in which need for specific abilities and skills is revealed, and real opportunities for the immediate use of newly acquired skills and abilities. All purposeful oral language experiences contribute to the development of desired speech skills—the individual experiences of making talks and reports and of telling stories, and the social ones of engaging in conversations and discussions and of making introductions and telephone calls. Some experiences make special as well as general contributions to the development of speech skills.

Dramatization offers opportunities for participation of a type in which expression is especially important and in which the shy child can participate with less feeling of self-consciousness. In the spirit of play, children speak naturally, as they do at home or on the playground. The need for clear expression is apparent and immediate; the dramatization fails unless the actors make themselves heard. Several children working together gain confidence from each other. An interest in playing a part well helps to overcome self-consciousness.

Dramatization may also provide an incentive for correcting faulty or careless habits of speech, as in the case of John, age eight, in the third grade. John desired above all else to be chosen for a certain part in the marionette show. But he had cultivated several unpleasant means of calling attention to himself; among them was the habit of sounding *w* instead of *l* or *r*. Thus, light bulb was *wight bowb*, worked was *wowked*, and lend was *wend*. In this sort of baby talk he apparently had been encouraged by his mother. Each time John asked to be in a play, someone in the group objected because he did not talk plainly. John undoubtedly was hurt, but the teacher felt that he was able to take the criticism and that nothing less would break his bad habit of speech. In private she tried to show him where to place his tongue to sound *l* and *r*. When at last John was convinced that he would never be chosen as an actor until he corrected his speech, he suddenly began speaking as correctly as anyone and was immediately commended and given a part in the play.

The use of marionettes and puppet shows has some distinct values. Facial expression and bodily movement are not so important as in dramatization, but more exacting requirements are made on the oral expression of ideas. The extremely shy child, even the stammerer or the stutterer, may participate freely and effectively when concealed by a screen.

Training in voice quality, pitch, volume, and enunciation is one of the values of choral speaking. Also, the shy child who hesitates to speak by himself gains courage from group participation. It is possible that choral speaking has special value for children with foreign-language backgrounds, where little opportunity is offered for using English in the home and possibly in play groups. The manner of handling choral speaking is a factor to be considered. Some teachers feel that the extensive reading together of much material is superior to the memorized, program type of work. Other possible speech-training values in choral speaking are bringing imagination to bear on the improvement of voice quality and articulation and training in phrasing and breath control by means of reading or reciting poems adapted to the purpose.[6]

Similar to the language experiences in purpose and value are oral experiences in other fields, particularly oral reading and singing. Efforts at effective interpretation of poety and prose aid in the development of voice quality, pitch, volume, inflection and emphasis, rhythm, etc. Interpretative reading and poetry recitation are especially valuable for cultivating desired abilities. Singing involves attention to voice projection and tonal quality, and it is possible that the training carries over into speech to some extent.

The motivation for speech training that comes from purposeful expression is strengthened by the occasional use of various devices. For example, in a dramatization behind a large make-believe TV which has an ample screen for the viewers, the play element appeals to children at primary-grade levels, and of course the importance of clear speaking becomes immediately apparent. Another device is the tape recording of children's oral work. The handling of oral work has been handicapped in the past by the impermanence of the spoken word. With the recorder it is possible to preserve and study objectively the child's story or report, to discover deficiencies in various speech and language elements, and to observe progress in overcoming specific difficulties. Deficiencies that pass unnoticed in speaking are recognized at once in the reproduction. Teachers claim very satisfactory results when the recording is fairly true. Fidelity of recording depends on the quality of the instrument and the skill of the operator.

Incidental training   In proceeding from general conditions favorable to speech development to specific measures for bringing about improvement, one is impressed in the first place with the incidental training that accompanies the various purposeful experiences. In such experiences the need for improvement is immediately revealed and accompanied by the desire for clear, effective expres-

---

[6] Huckleberry and Strother, *op. cit.*, pp. 141–158. See also Henry A. Bamman and others, *Oral Interpretation of Children's Literature*, W. C. Brown Company, Publishers, Dubuque, Iowa, 1964, pp. 3–16.

sion and definite corrective effort. Attention is called to a factor of prime importance (such as talking loudly enough for everyone to hear) in the preliminary preparation period or in the follow-up evaluation period. A brief discussion or demonstration of a particular point may be in order. The teacher naturally does not interrupt; corrective work is not permitted to interfere with freedom of expression. The amount and timing of such incidental attention to speech factors vary with age, with the class, with the temperament of the individual, and with the type of disability. Group corrective work with young children is mainly of the incidental type; wisely handled, it contributes to satisfaction in good performance rather than to discouragement.[7]

Place of training lessons and exercises Training lessons and exercises provide a direct, intensive attack on various speech elements. Habits of speaking may be so firmly established as to fail to respond to general classroom conditions, however favorable, and even to incidental treatment. Several decades ago Raubicheck was firmly convinced of the need for a vigorous, direct attack. She pointed out that children coming to school have already had four or five years of experience in speaking, and that the teacher's problem is often one of attempting to change patterns already well established. It is a problem of *re*education. Passive imitation is not sufficient to bring about changes; a direct attack is necessary.[8]

As a working principle it may be stated that special training lessons should supplement other measures when the latter fail to bring about the desired improvement. To be effective the training lesson must have a purpose apparent to the child, and the exercise must be closely related to the expressional activities. The danger in this type of training is the danger that threatens all practice work: isolation and formalism.[9] In situations where children have language deficits, understandings of the alternative usages of the language of the future school, social, and business worlds must be provided to give these children the necessary techniques for adequate speech functioning.

Organization for training lessons Since the value of the training lesson depends largely on the recognition of need by the learner,

[7] Paul S. Anderson, *Language Skills in Elementary Education*, The Macmillan Company, New York, 1964, p. 52.

[8] Letitia Raubicheck, *How to Teach Good Speech in the Elementary Schools*, Noble and Noble, Publishers, Inc., New York, 1937, p. 47.

[9] Verna Anderson and others, *op. cit.*, pp. 80–83.

an effort must be made to determine individual needs and to provide training suited to those who need it.[10] This adaptation requires an inventory of speech deficiencies, such as was described earlier. The children who need a particular type of training are brought together into a small, homogeneous, temporary group and given the necessary instruction and practice. Possibly individual instruction should be used at times. The language program must be sufficiently flexible to allow such specialized group and individual work.

Handling a training lesson   In handling a training lesson for a class, group, or individual, the teacher must make provision for the learner to (1) discover a need, (2) develop an idea of correct form, (3) practice the correct form, and (4) use the correct form in real situations. Need is revealed best in purposeful experiences, but at times special exercises may be useful to test certain abilities. Since the work deals with oral expression the child must get the correct idea of form by oral demonstration, usually by the teacher but occasionally by other pupils. The teacher must assure himself that the sound is correctly heard; failure to reproduce a correct sound may be due to faulty hearing as well as to faulty speech. The idea of correct form is not secured until the child can produce the desired sound or effect—get the "feel" of it. Practice may be distributed over several periods. Sufficient drill must be provided to impress the correct form upon the child and to make it habitual in speech.

An example of a training lesson in the correction of the sound "*th*" in an initial position is given by Mary L. Smith in the following quotation. The adaptability to an individual or small group and the importance of teacher instruction-demonstration should be noted.

> TEACHER: "Watch my mouth. See if you can tell me what number I am saying. (Without voice, say *three*. Children respond, "Three.") Watch how my tongue spreads lightly along the edge of my teeth when I say the voiceless *th* sound. Another number that starts the same way as *three* is *thousand*. What other words do we know that start the same way as *thousand?*"

The following sentences may help them think of the *th* words that start voicelessly. (If they mention voiced *th* words such as

[10] Ruth I. Golden, "Ways to Improve Oral Communication of Culturally Different Youth," in Arno Jewett and others, *Improving English Skills of Culturally Different Youth in Large Cities*, U.S. Office of Education, Washington, D.C., 1964, pp. 100–109.

those, they, them, tell them we will study these words in a later lesson.)

>When we receive a present, we say —————— (thank you)
>When we want to give the right answer, we have to —————— (think)
>If someone is very slender, we may say he is —————— (thin)
>The opposite of thin is —————— (thick)
>In counting, the number after twelve is ——————(thirteen)
>When you want a drink of water, you are —————— (thirsty)
>We are apt to eat a big turkey dinner on what holiday —————— (Thanksgiving)
>When we sew, what do we put in the needle —————— (thread)
>Jim batted the baseball that Tim —————— (threw)

"Let's say the words we have been talking about. I'll say the word while you watch my mouth. Then you say the word and feel what your tongue is doing as you start the word. What was your tongue doing at the beginning of these words?" (Class should respond, "It was spread along the edge of our teeth.")

Note: The difference between voiceless and voiced *th* is the same as the difference between the sounds of the letters *t* and *d*. The *t* sound is voiceless. The *d* sound is made the same way except that it is voiced.[11]

Children with foreign-born backgrounds   In many areas of the country, teachers find in their classes children who come from homes in which a foreign language or a strange (to the teacher) English dialect is spoken. The children's efforts to think and to communicate in a new language present difficulties, but the difficulty is more than one of communication. Inability to communicate tends to develop lack of confidence and a feeling of insecurity, which may cause withdrawal within the classroom and on the playground. Foreign-born children are often regarded as shy, quiet, and unresponsive, but in their own group they are cheerful and loquacious. The foreign child may become isolated and suspect to the other children. He may have a tendency to be ashamed of his background and parents.

A large part of the teacher's task is to make such a child feel comfortable and confident in the school group. The teacher can do this by personally making the child welcome and by enlisting the cooperation of other children in making friendly advances. He may point out to the children the advantages of speaking another language and the efforts required by older children and by adults to learn a foreign language. He may emphasize the real, often

[11] Mary Louise Smith, *Listening Habits and Speech-sound Discrimination Developed through a Multiple Sensory Approach,* Alameda County School Department, Hayward, Calif., 1962, pp. 26–27. Quoted with special permission of author and publisher.

rich, cultural heritage of the national or ethnic group the child represents, and may even invite adult representatives of the group to visit the class to talk about their accomplishments. The class may learn some common phrases from the foreign language or learn to sing a song in the language. English-speaking children in this way may come to appreciate some of the difficulty in learning to speak another language.

The teacher should realize, also, that the difficulty of participating in class discussions is due in part to the lack of a common background of experiences. The normal home life of the foreign-born child may not provide the common experiences shared by other children. The total school program should be rich in varied experiences providing the foreign child with thoughts and feelings to share with the others.

While personal and social factors operate in the background of the child's efforts to adjust to his American environment, the key problem remains one of communication. Communication in English is hampered by lack of vocabulary, by pronunciation, and by the difficulty of putting words together into acceptable phrases and sentences. The inflection of the voice and the rhythm of speaking may also present problems. Each foreign language presents its peculiar problems. The French child will always slip on *th* and *wh* and will stumble often on *ch*. The German child will find his greatest problem with *wh, th, j,* and short *u*. Hebrew-speaking children cause their playmates much merriment in saying *sink* for *sing, lem* for *lame,* and *vot* for *what*. Spanish-speaking children have trouble with words like *chair, yellow, think, hill, bird, book,* and *woman* because they contain elements foreign to the Spanish tongue. A teacher from Hawaii reports that her children have a tendency to memorize whole sections of contextual material due to the fact that language training is not carried over into other fields.[12]

The teacher naturally will adjust his instructional measures to the particular child and situation. The child may know little English and come from a home in which all conversation is in a foreign language; or he may have acquired at home and in the community an American English characterized by structural, articulatory, and intonational elements that differ from those of the teacher's speech.[13] Or, recently arrived from a foreign country, he

[12] For assistance in determining American sounds absent from or distorted in European languages, see L. Sipin, "A Comparative Analysis of the Phonetic Systems of Certain Modern European Languages, with Applications to the Correction of Foreign Dialects," M.A. thesis, State University of Iowa, reported in Huckleberry and Strother, *op. cit.,* table VI, pp. 110–111.

[13] Jane Beasley Raph, "Language and Speech Deficits in Culturally Dis-

may have had no experience at all with the language of his new environment. A few points may be noted: (1) It is important that the child speaking a foreign language should hear much acceptable English to accustom his ear to the sound of the language. (2) With a beginner, the method must be direct—concrete, objective, and dramatic. (3) Emphasis should be placed on common experiences and common words, as *door, table, chair, see, give.* (4) For young children, a toy kit is helpful. (5) Sets of pictures dealing with familiar home experiences or topics under study at school are useful. (6) Words should be put into phrases, and pronounced separately as necessary. (7) A phrase or sentence must be accompanied by action: *I pick up a pencil, I go to the window, I give you a book.* (8) With older children, difficulties are noted and attacked directly, with much emphasis on hearing and practice in pronunciation. (9) Incidental correction in talking or reporting is helpful in a later stage, such as giving a child the precise word needed to express himself and helping with the pronunciation of a troublesome word.[14]

Speech correction   In the preceding pages of this chapter an attempt has been made to outline a comprehensive program of language development suited to all members of a class; a program in which the orally expressive child has the opportunity to perfect his speech abilities and the immature or defective child receives some of the specific retraining he needs. General measures for discovering needs and general procedures for meeting the needs have been presented. The teacher will soon identify the superior and the noticeably deficient children and will observe that between these two groups are a considerable number of children who have such minor difficulties as not speaking loudly enough to be heard, speaking indistinctly, and mispronouncing common words. General and incidental measures usually serve the needs of superior children and those with minor difficulties. Now particular attention is directed to those children whose speech is conspicuously poorer than that of most children and whose difficulties require specific remedial treatment.

It is stated that approximately 10 percent of every class has speech difficulties serious enough to justify specific corrective work. Defects vary in degree or seriousness; some are the result of habits

---

advantaged Children: Implications for the Speech Clinician," *Journal of Speech and Hearing Disorders,* vol. 32, August, 1967, pp. 203–214.

[14] For specific principles and processes of teaching English to children of other language groups, see Mary Finocchiaro, *English as a Second Language,* Regents Publishing Company, Inc., New York, 1965.

that may be changed by retraining, while others have deep-rooted causes in physical malformations of the speech organs or in emotional attitudes. The beginning teacher might well consider the suggestions offered by the guide, *Speech Activities in the Classroom: Grades K–8*, when faced with the problem of helping children with their speech development.[15]

What I would like the Speech Consultant to do:
  Test students for speech defects.
  Explain the speech defects to me.
  Suggest remedial aids for correcting the defects.
  Give group demonstrations, stressing correction of the most common speech defects.
  Give special help to those students who have serious speech defects.
  Suggest and obtain resource materials for me to use in the classroom.
  Assist in establishing rapport with the home on more serious speech defects.
What I can do after the Speech Consultant has visited my room:
  Give students ample opportunity to express themselves.
  Provide varied experiences to aid vocabulary growth.
  Provide a relaxed, secure room atmosphere.
  Encourage the children to want to talk.
  Have some understanding of the emotional problems and how they are reflected in the student's speech pattern.
  Through classroom speech activities, help the students who have speech problems.

The teacher's responsibility in the correction program   It is apparent that certain kinds of speech deficiencies can be handled by an experienced teacher directly. He must make an inventory of the speech difficulties of his pupils, provide time and place for remedial work in the total language program, secure the necessary materials (some of which are available in textbooks), and develop instructional procedures and exercises suited to particular defects.[16]

The experienced teacher has a responsibility, also, in the handling of the deep-rooted defects requiring the services of the professional correctionist. The time that a correctionist can give to a particular case is necessarily limited, but the teacher works with the child throughout the day. The correctionist will give specific directions and exercises for the teacher to carry out, and he will give advice on the general handling of the particular child. The effectiveness of the total program depends largely on the teacher.

[15] Orange County Board of Education, *Speech Activities in the Classroom*, Office of the Superintendent, Santa Ana, Calif., 1965, p. 25. Quoted with special permission.
[16] Verna D. Anderson and others, *op. cit.*, pp. 80–87.

In general, the teacher can help the speech-defective child by assuming a direct, calm, objective attitude; by recognizing that the speech defect may reflect an insecure concept of self and by helping the child to adjust himself socially to the group; by keeping the child from situations in which the difficulty is aggravated, but not by pampering him; and by protecting the child from the thoughtless ridicule of his classmates.

Much can be learned about the nature, cause, and treatment of particular defects. In the few remaining pages of this chapter will be offered a bare sampling of the material available in standard books on speech correction.

Disorders of articulation   Disorders of articulation are very common, constituting from 75 to 85 percent of all types treated by correctionists. From 5 to 10 percent of all school children have some articulatory difficulty. Types of disorders include (1) substitutions, occurring initially, medially, finally, or in blends, as in *yady* for *lady,* *wadon* for *wagon,* *pat* for *path,* and *bwidge* for *bridge;* (2) omissions, occurring also initially, medially, finally, or in blends, as in *anksgiving* for *Thanksgiving,* *li'n* for *listen,* *too* for *tooth,* and *pay* for *play;* (3) additions, occurring when a person goes from one articulatory adjustment to another, such as *gulad* for *glad;* this in certain cases may be considered regional pronunciation rather than an articulatory disorder; (4) distortions, described as sounds which an individual produces, not conforming to any other elements of the language—associated with lisps and tongue placement.[17] A child may make one or more of these types of errors, and the error may vary with words and with the position of the sound within words.

Most articulatory defects are the result of faulty learning. Organic conditions such as poor tooth structure or abnormal palate and tongue development may contribute to the difficulty, but they are not the primary cause. The majority of difficulties cannot be removed by surgery. Faulty learning is attributable to the speech patterns set by others, often by parents; to the persistence of infantile speech habits because of lack of stimulation for maturing; and possibly, in some cases, to emotional maladjustments caused by various social factors, such as tension in the home. Conditions during the school life of the child—anxiety and frustration in speech situations—may maintain or aggravate the difficulties.

[17] Darrell J. Mase, "Disorders of Articulation," in N. M. Levin, *op. cit.,* pp. 605–606.

The treatment of an articulatory defect begins with an exact definition of the difficulty and the determination of contributing factors. Some evidence is obtained by close observation of the child's speech. This information is supplemented by results of speech-test exercises (such as those given in textbooks and in speech-correction books) and by data assembled from hearing tests, physical examinations, and intelligence tests.

A general procedure for handling articulatory speech disorders is suggested by Johnson: [18]

1. Eliminate, or minimize the effect of, factors causing the disorder.
2. Create vivid auditory impressions which will enable the child to recognize readily both the error and the correct sound, and to discriminate between the two whenever he hears them.
3. Teach correct production of the sound in isolation.
4. Strengthen the production of the sound so that it can be produced easily and at will.
5. Secure transfer of the correct sound into connected speech in a small nucleus of commonly used words.
6. Make the production of the correct sound, instead of the error, habitual in all connected speech.

Each of these steps is developed in some detail by Johnson. In discovering and eliminating contributing factors, the teacher may find it necessary to investigate home conditions and secure the cooperation of the parents. In carrying on the corrective work through the several stages, the teacher will draw on his knowledge of general teaching procedures and utilize such resources in the way of special materials and procedures as may be available.

Retarded speech development   Some of the children participate little or not at all in oral work because of shyness and lack of confidence; but they can and do talk on occasion, under favorable conditions. Other nonparticipants have never learned to talk and speak freely under any conditions; they have a limited vocabulary, may use baby talk, and may give little indication of comprehension. Contributing factors may be mental retardation, defective hearing, or environmental factors such as parental pampering, isolation, jealousy of another child, feeling of rejection by parents, severe illness, and a foreign-language background.[19]

It is obvious that extreme cases of delayed speech may have deep-rooted causes and that the advice of a psychologist or speech correctionist would be valuable to the teacher. Without such pro-

[18] Wendell Johnson and others, *op. cit.*, p. 118.
[19] *Ibid.*, chap. 6.

fessional help the teacher may attempt to discover the causes himself by visiting the home to observe home conditions and to find out how much the child talks at home. At school the teacher may promote a wholesome classroom atmosphere and begin a training program with very simple words which the child has occasion to use. Pictures related to familiar home and community activities are stimulating, particularly to the child who is learning to speak English as a second language. Development may be very slow; patience is required of both pupil and teacher.

Disorders of voice   Voice disorders, less common than defects of articulation, contribute only a small fraction of the cases with which the correctionist must deal; but the treatment of some of them presents greater difficulty.[20]

A good voice is loud enough to be heard in the situation in which a person is speaking and is adequate in pitch, pleasing in quality, and sufficiently flexible to give emphasis to important ideas and to express deep feeling. Disorders are variations from the qualities of a good voice that are great enough to distract the attention of or prove unpleasant to the listener. Normal differences of age and sex must be recognized and considerable latitude allowed for individual differences. In general, the seriousness of a disorder is determined by the extent of variation from the normal. Specific speech disorders include:[21]

Pitch: "Pitch levels which are unusual, or inappropriate to their age or sex"; too high or too low.

Loudness: Too low because of habit, disease, or deep emotional or personality disturbance; or too loud because of habit or hearing deficiency.

Voice quality: Nasal, breathy, hoarse, or harsh.

Flexibility: Monotonous, lack of expression.

Some of the causes are organic in nature, and the teacher will do well to refer such cases to a qualified physician. For example, extreme hoarseness may be caused by a pathological condition of the larynx; the child with adenoids has difficulty in producing sounds that require nasal resonance. However, "most voice problems cannot be accounted for in terms of organic causes. For various reasons, the *functioning* of the voice mechanism may be deficient, and a voice problem may exist, even though the structure is entirely adequate."[22] Some voice problems are the result of habit or imitation. It was difficult, in one case, to account for the guttural

---

[20] C. Van Riper, *op. cit.*, p. 154.
[21] Wendell Johnson and others, *op. cit.*, pp. 174–179.
[22] *Ibid.*, p. 181.

voice quality of a college student until the instructor had occasion to visit the home and found that both parents and four other children had the same quality.

Another group of significant factors is that of psychological disturbances or maladjustments. Johnson says: [23]

> Psychological maladjustments may cover the range from deep-rooted emotional disturbances to the shyness and timidity that seem to be characteristic of a considerable number of children. We have noted the rather common belief that vocal characteristics reveal personality traits. This belief is substantiated by a rather large accumulation of clinical observations and some systematic research investigations. . . . Cases could also be described to illustrate the relationship of other types of voice problems to personality factors. For example, chronic feelings of anxiety and insecurity may result in excessive bodily tensions which in turn may produce vocal disturbances, such as harsh quality or high pitch. Deficient loudness may come from excessive shyness, and so on.

Other contributing factors, according to Van Riper, are hearing deficiency; delayed sexual development; voice change at puberty; sluggish articulators—palate, tongue, lips, and jaws; physical strain, frequently caused by overstrenuous play; and general tenseness, caused by emotional states of fear, excitement, and rage.[24]

Correction begins with convincing the speaker that he has a defect. This is not easy because ordinarily a person is not aware of his difficulty. It may be possible to lead the speaker to observe the reaction of others to his voice or to make a recording for reproduction and study. If the disorder has a physical or emotional basis, it is necessary to determine the cause and to adopt suitable measures. Specific disorders may be handled in various ways, depending on the training and skill of the teacher. For example, in treating disorders of pitch it is desirable to determine the natural pitch of the voice by determining total range and pitching the voice at or near the middle register. Treatment for impaired flexibility may include overcoming shyness and timidity; training in oral reading, with emphasis on expressiveness; and giving practice in normal, purposeful speaking situations.

Stuttering   Stuttering is relatively infrequent, occurring in possibly 1 percent of a school population; but of course it is a serious problem for the child of school age. It is observed that many children, if not all, are hesitant in speech during their early years. Ninety-nine percent acquire satisfactory fluency in the course of normal development. Stuttering, which appears in the unfortunate

[23] *Ibid.*, p. 182.
[24] C. Van Riper, *op. cit.*, pp. 164–175.

1 percent at about the age of three, is a condition of speech acquired as a result of environmental influences, chiefly the over-
anxiety of parents. The child can be retrained into habits of fluent
speaking if the work is begun early. The help of a specialist is
desirable, but the classroom teacher can do much for the child.
Johnson outlines and discusses at length a program for dealing
with the stutterer. Included are the following measures: [25]

1 Encourage the child to talk more.
2 See to it that the child has as much feeling of success as
   possible in speaking.
3 Stimulate the stuttering child's interest in good speech and
   effective speakers.
4 Encourage the child to talk about his stuttering and his feelings about it.
5 Help the child to develop a more realistic attitude toward his
   stuttering.
6 Help the child to develop a realistically good opinion of
   himself.
7 Help the child to see the best in others.
8 Help the stuttering child to participate more fully in school
   activities.
9 Encourage the child to enjoy learning and to cultivate worthwhile interests.
10 Build the child's confidence in his basic physical ability to
   speak normally.
11 Train the stuttering child to observe his stuttering, to view it
   as his own behavior, and to modify it.

Impaired hearing Another type of pupil with whom the teacher
must deal is the child with impaired hearing. The extent of impairment will vary from very slight to total loss of hearing. Hearing
may be suspected, before conclusive evidence is revealed through
suitable tests, by the child's inability to follow oral directions; by
difficulties in spelling and reading; and by behavior traits such as
listlessness and unresponsiveness or belligerency and unhappiness
in group activities. The handling of the deaf and extremely hard
of hearing requires the training of the specialist. The teacher can
do much to facilitate the learning of the child with relatively slight
impairment. Johnson suggests the following practical measures: [26]

1 Having him sit as near as possible to where he is likely to be
   most of the time.

[25] Wendell Johnson and others, *op. cit.*, pp. 271–293.
[26] *Ibid.*, pp. 379–380. See also Wendell Johnson in Verna D. Anderson
and others, *op. cit.*, pp. 88–97.

2   Allowing him to move freely about the room in order to hear what is going on.
3   Being sure, when giving a direction, that the hard of hearing child is following what is being said. One effective way to check is to ask him occasionally to stand and repeat the direction to the rest of the class.
4   Finding a time to explain the problem of the hard of hearing child to the other pupils.
5   Helping him to understand and to acknowledge his hearing problem. This is one of the most important aspects of any handicapped child's problem, but it is especially important for the hard of hearing.
6   Allowing him to recite and to read orally just like any other member of the class. Some hard of hearing children have speech problems as a result of the hearing loss.
7   Seeing to it that he is included in all sorts of extracurricular activities participated in by his classmates. Frequently a hard of hearing child will be a bystander when a group game is being played because he didn't hear the rules and doesn't want to ask.

Evaluation   The teacher is concerned with providing children with opportunities for taking part in conversations and discussions, making oral reports, giving explanations and directions, and engaging in storytelling and dramatizing. Within these major speaking activities, the teacher notes by listening and by checklisting special problems of articulation, voice, rhythm, and delivery. Decisions involving both incidental and direct instruction in the speech mechanics are based on the teacher's understanding of language growth principles and awareness of the regional-standard use of the human speaking apparatus to produce the sounds of speech. The teacher is alert to speech difficulties that can be cared for in the regular school program, and he also works with the speech correctionist, who gives specific assistance to children with serious speech disorders. The teacher's attitudes, reflected in the creation of a classroom climate for speech improvement and in the specific techniques employed, will determine children's progress in the skills of speech.

For your consideration

1   If possible, make a preliminary inventory of the speech-training needs of a particular class.
2   Outline a general program of speech training suited to the observed needs as revealed in your preliminary inventory.

3 Talk with a kindergarten child and then with a child in a fifth grade. What differences in articulation do you notice?
4 Make a list of the serious speech disorders that would seem to require special correctional work.
5 Plan a lesson for a specific speech difficulty that a teacher may properly handle.
6 If possible, visit a speech correctionist as she works with a small group of children or interview her about her grouping procedures, instructional techniques, ways in which children are referred to her, and methods by which the classroom teacher supports her work with individual children.

References

ARTLEY, A. STERL, AND OTHERS: *Interrelationships among the Language Arts,* National Council of Teachers of English, Champaign, Ill., 1954, p. 29.

CORBIN, RICHARD, AND MURIEL CROSBY: *Language Programs for the Disadvantaged,* National Council of Teachers of English, Champaign, Ill., 1965, pp. 74–98.

DAWSON, MILDRED A., AND G. C. NEWMAN: *Language Teaching in Kindergarten and the Early Primary Grades,* Harcourt, Brace & World, Inc., New York, 1966, pp. 143–155.

———, M. ZOLLINGER, AND A. ELWELL: *Guiding Language Learning,* Harcourt, Brace & World, Inc., New York, 1963, chap. 20.

EISENSON, JON, AND MARDEL OGILVIE: *Speech Correction in the Schools,* The Macmillan Company, New York, 1963, chaps. 3–4, 10–13.

GREENE, H. A., AND W. T. PETTY: *Developing Language Skills in the Elementary Schools,* Allyn and Bacon, Inc., Boston, 1963, pp. 502–510.

LEE, J. MURRAY, AND DORRIS M. LEE: *The Child and His Curriculum,* Appleton-Century-Crofts, Inc., New York, 1960, pp. 304–310.

MC CARTHY, DOROTHEA, AND OTHERS: *Factors That Influence Language Growth,* National Council of Teachers of English, Champaign, Ill., 1953, pp. 11–12.

NATIONAL COUNCIL OF TEACHERS OF ENGLISH: *Language Arts for Today's Children,* Appleton-Century-Crofts, Inc., New York, 1954, pp. 128–141.

OGILVIE, MARDEL: *Speech in the Elementary School,* McGraw-Hill Book Company, New York, 1954, chap. 4.

PRONOVOST, W. L.: *The Teaching of Speaking and Listening in the Elementary School,* Longmans, Green and Company, New York, 1959.

SMITH, NILA B.: *Areas of Research Interest in the Language Arts,* National Council of Teachers of English, Champaign, Ill., 1952, pp. 20–27.

STRICKLAND, RUTH G.: *The Language Arts in the Elementary School,* D. C. Heath and Company, Boston, 1957, pp. 88–89, 204–206, 209–214, 216–218.

——— AND OTHERS: "Needed Research in Oral Language," *Elementary English,* vol. 44, March, 1967, pp. 257–264.

TRAUGER, W. K.: *Language Arts in Elementary Schools,* McGraw-Hill Book Company, New York, 1963, pp. 45–47, 75–85, 139, 156.

13.

VOCABULARY
AND
SENTENCES

Work on vocabulary and sentences may be approached from two points of view: mere correctness and clear, accurate, vivid expression. The first approach is largely a negative one, eliminating errors. The second approach goes directly to the heart of the effective use of language—clear thinking—in searching for words, phrases, and sentences that express ideas clearly and vividly and in changing usable but commonplace expressions into interesting ones. Traditional teaching has been concerned, and possibly satisfied, with mere correctness. Modern teaching faces and attempts to meet the challenge of the broader concept. A child's words and sentences may be substantially correct but still flat, dull, and inexact. Says Pooley:[1]

> Language free from error is not necessarily good language. It becomes good as the child develops a feeling for the bright, sparkling word or phrase, the exact word for his needs, the sentence which says exactly what he wants to say as economically and clearly as possible. This feeling for the fitness of words in their uses is the positive side of usage instruction, the side to receive much more attention than has been given to it.

Another sidelight on this issue is Dale's comment, "Does it matter

[1] R. C. Pooley, *Teaching English Usage*, Appleton-Century-Crofts, Inc., New York, 1946, p. 187.

whether something *not worth reading* is written correctly? I would prefer a misspelled something to a correctly spelled nothing." [2]

The positive approach is developed in this chapter. Recognizing that vocabulary and sentences reflect experiential background, the chapter seeks to give insight into language development and the approaches the classroom teacher may use to give children these vehicles, needed in speaking, writing, listening, and reading.

Vocabulary

Vocabulary development of the child   The development of vocabulary in the early years of the child's life is a part of the process of growing up. From one or two words at one year of age, the vocabulary increases to thousands as the child progresses through elementary school.[3] Nouns develop first. Relational terms, qualifying terms, and complex sentences come later. Vocabulary development is determined by environment, by life patterns, and by the influence of parents, teachers, peers. The teacher's problem is to explore children's language backgrounds, to broaden and deepen experiences, and to help develop new words and linguistic patterns with which to deal with new ideas. Children delight in new words. The opportunities are challenging and rewarding.

Clues to handling vocabulary development in school are found by observing more closely how vocabulary develops in the young child. It will be found that words grow out of needs for meeting real-life situations, and that vocabulary increases in range and complexity as experiences become rich and varied.

The close relation of vocabulary to experience is shown clearly in the language development of the child. The word *dada* comes to be associated with the man about the home and *mama* with the female person, who takes care of his needs. The word *car* is picked up as a means of referring to the family automobile and to a toy. *Wawa* is the means of expressing the idea *I want a drink*. In due time *all gone, bye-bye,* and *Tommy fall down* appear as means of thinking and expressing simple ideas. Words appear as a convenient medium for expression of thoughts and feelings, first expressed through inarticulate sounds and bodily movements. Lan-

---

[2] Edgar Dale, "Vocabulary Measurement: Techniques and Major Findings," *Elementary English*, vol. 42, December, 1965, p. 895.

[3] Irving G. Lorge and Jeanne Chall, "Estimating the Size of Vocabularies of Children and Adults: An Analysis of Methodological Issues," *The Journal of Experimental Education*, vol. 32, Winter, 1963, p. 154.

guage increases in complexity and exactness as the child's ideas and feelings are differentiated and more clearly defined in the process of maturing and discovering the means for adjusting to an increasingly complex social environment. The environment extends in time to include books, radio, and television, as well as people and things, but vicarious experience does not alter the close relation that naturally exists between ideas and words. Direct experience continues to be the chief source and means of vocabulary development. Children receive direct experience in the form of clues and signals from family, friends, and teachers relevant to the meaning and use of words that reflect abstract concepts and ideas not present in the immediate environment. In discussing the need for considered thought in the teaching of words and ideas, Hayakawa says of children: [4]

> They are trained to respond in specific ways to certain signals: "Christianity" (a fine thing"), "the Constitution" ("a fine thing"), "Shakespeare" ("a great poet"), "Benedict Arnold" ("a traitor"), and so on. But, especially in the elementary and secondary schools, they are taught very little about how not to respond.

To proceed *from* experience *through* language *to* meaning is clearly to recognize the function of language in communication. To develop vocabulary is to train children to observe, to interpret experience, to discover nuances of feeling and mood, and to find words that express exactly what they think and feel. Ideas and feelings, initiated by perception or thought, progress from a vague, nebulous form to exact definition in the process of finding words to express them. The order is experience, interpretation, and finally words. Perhaps one should repeat the term *experience* at the end of the series to complete the cycle, inasmuch as words actually lead to further experience and enrich the original one. Vocabulary work throughout the school life of the child should be a means of clarifying and expressing ideas and feelings. It should grow out of real, vivid experiences and the desire to put them into words.

These general statements may take on more meaning as we explore various possibilities for developing vocabulary in school first in meaningful experiences in the content areas of the curriculum, and then in language experiences and in special exercises.

Meaningful experiences　If growth in vocabulary is to proceed naturally, as a correlate of experience, it is obvious that most of the

[4] S. I. Hayakawa, *Symbol, Status, and Personality,* Harcourt, Brace & World, Inc., New York, 1963, p. 24. Quoted with special permission of author and publisher.

growth will take place in those areas of the curriculum that offer opportunities for real, vital experiencing—in the content subjects of social studies and science. Particularly conducive to vocabulary development is the direct observation of people, things, and processes provided by excursions and field trips and by the examination of objects, specimens, and models in the classroom. In an excursion to a house under construction, for example, the children observe materials, processes, and workmen; they make a list of terms identifying and summarizing what they see, such as *floor, joist, studding, window sash, pitch, rafters, cornice, insulation, air conditioning, floor plan, carpenter, plumber, architect, builder, pouring concrete, laying bricks,* and *bungalow.* In conversation, discussion, and the making of experience charts and diaries following excursions, the children clarify ideas through expression and acquire new words.

Observation in the classroom is no less productive of ideas and words. A live rabbit was housed in the classroom for several days before a nature-study lesson. The children fed the rabbit and watched it eat. In the discussion that followed the teacher pointed out that the rabbit lives naturally in a hole in the ground and asked the children to observe whether the rabbit is well adapted to such a home. They noticed the warm fur, the claws for digging, the food and water supply nearby, the protective coloration, etc. To describe a Promethea moth just hatched, children listed such terms as:

delicate	velvetlike	spotted
silent	soundless	fuzzy
dainty	dull reddish brown	cream markings
cloudlike	silver lines	lovely
colorful	soft	dotted
graceful	spidery body	fragile

Projects are not ends in themselves; they are defensible as a means for extending experience and clarifying thinking, processes that stimulate vocabulary development. Thus cooking, building simple models to specifications, developing an aquarium, studying working models, attempting to make adobe bricks, and following instructions in making puppets all train the child in observation, stimulate research, clarify ideas, and extend vocabulary. In setting up an electric current to produce light in a small lamp, the child will have occasion to use the terms: *lamp, filament, wire, dry cell battery, conductor, electricity, current, positive* $(+)$ and *negative* $(-)$, *terminals, switch, series circuit, parallel circuit.*

Pictures and other instructional aids provide a near-real type of experience, and they have the advantage of practicability when it is impossible to take children on field trips or to bring objects into the classroom. In connection with a farm unit in the first grade, it is possible to secure class-size pictures showing buildings, animals, implements, fields, and some of the activities. Distant lands and people, industries, physical features, buildings, and technological developments can thus be brought into the class-room. Pictures are useful in nature study, by portraying flowers, birds, and animals; in music, by showing instruments; and in art. Of course, it is recognized that pictures do not take the place of firsthand experiences; indeed, the latter are the basis of getting meaning from pictures. Vocabulary development, however, is readily promoted by their use. Discussion of illustrations in children's books not only leads to greater appreciation but may add many new words to the vocabulary. Children should recognize the difference between photographs, pictures that are true to life, and purely imaginative illustrations. Motion pictures, filmstrips, especially prepared transparencies, mockups, models, specimens selected to develop concepts and their concomitant vocabulary are essential tools in guiding children's thinking and understanding.[5]

Third-grade children gathered around the teacher, examining storybooks which had not been read to them, described the pictures variously as:

shadowy	silly	funny
queer	peculiar	unusual
could be true	blurry	old-fashioned
gives real pleasure	looks far back	bright color
clear	dull	dim
attractive	not well colored	clouded
exciting	distinct	different

Reading material, particularly imaginative literature, suitable in content and vocabulary to the maturity of the children is a rich source of ideas and words. From reading, both oral and silent, the children get ideas and also words for expressing them. Noticing new words, particularly well-turned and beautiful expressions, adds to the enjoyment and understanding of literature and provides a limitless source of fresh ideas for use in various language experiences. This development is immediately utilized in the introductory phases of creative expression. It must be remembered that the

[5] Edgar Dale, *Audio-Visual Methods in Teaching,* Holt, Rinehart and Winston, Inc., New York, 1959, chap. 1.

value of incidental word study can be lost by formal, pedantic handling.

Meaningful experiences inevitably promote growth in vocabulary, but definite guidance in word study is necessary to secure maximum growth. Children can be led to an exactness and extension of the meanings of words that they could not achieve unaided. At times new words are observed and studied for exactness of meaning, appearing in a new context. Sometimes the meanings of familiar words of general and varied application are extended, as *bow,* used in greeting and as part of a ship. Sometimes children are led to examine their own experiences and to express meanings more precisely, as in the use of *neat, terrific, great.*

Vocabulary development in language experiences   All work in language experiences is necessarily training in vocabulary. In conversation and storytelling the teacher may suggest an appropriate word as the child hesitates. New, effective words and phrases are recognized and receive favorable comment; the achievement of a particularly well-turned phrase is sometimes greeted by the applause of the class. On occasion the teacher may make such comments as "How did the puppy sound when he *yelped?* Who can make a yelping sound? It isn't like a bark, is it? . . . What did the selfish pig do? Are we sometimes selfish? Can you say the word *self-ish?"*

A story by Clyde was well received because of the *sound* words —"He makes us hear that motorcycle," said the teacher.

THE NOISE

As I was standing in the street there was an awful roar. Put! Put! Crash! Crash! Boom! It sounded like a hurricane. But just as I was turning around the corner, down the street came a motorcycle.

Of the following story the teacher said, "Ann has used some very good descriptive words. Can you see Jack Frost's painting on her window?"

> One crispy, sunny morning,
> When it was awful cold
> I woke up very suddenly
> And found that it had snowed.
> Jack Frost had painted pictures,
> Upon my window pane
> A garden full of sparkling flowers
> Which grew beside a lane.

Sometimes a child who has unusual creative ability cannot

get his stories on paper because of mechanical difficulties. Here such a child, working with another child who could write and spell very well, produced the following story. It was well received by the class because of the expressive words that the two children had chosen. "Gee, that little mouse was scared."

FLUFFY

Fluffy was a big gray cat. One day she got in a pile of leaves. She jumped around and around until she was all tired out. It was a nice warm day and Fluffy curled up and went to sleep in the soft bed of leaves.

Soon a little mouse crept softly through the leaves but the rustling sound awakened Fluffy. The little frightened mouse scampered away with Fluffy chasing after him. He ran for his house in the stump of an old tree where Fluffy couldn't reach him.

Then the mouse turned around and chuckled to himself while Fluffy angrily walked back to the pile of leaves.

In reporting, there is need for accuracy. Children should be sure of their facts, and they should express their ideas in their own words. When they use words that they do not understand, the children are advised to go back to the context or to refer to a dictionary.

In creative experiences there is need for vividness and beauty of expression as well as for accuracy. A group of eight- to nine-year-olds decided to write a story jointly. Beginning sentences were submitted by different children. The sentences were written on the board by the teacher. After some discussion, a vote was taken, and the following sentence was chosen: "Twilight was at hand and the dainty little fairy folk were getting ready for their dance."

Silence followed. Having chosen their sentence the children could now think of nothing to follow it. At last the child who had contributed the sentence added, "Wee fairy ladies went to and fro putting on bluebell gowns, while little men dressed themselves in yellow suits." This was written on the board and read by the teacher with emphasis on the word *went*. "Wouldn't *hurried* be a better word?" suggested a little girl, and immediately someone else said, "*Scurried* sounds faster"; all agreed. Then someone suggested *glossy* bluebell, and other children gave the little men *golden* yellow *tulip* suits. The third sentence came quickly, but then a lull followed. The fairies were dressed; now what?

The teacher suggested that, since the story was well started, the children might think about it until the next day. In the meantime she advised them to try to find some good words that would describe fairies, and she marked off a section of the board where they might list unusual words which they found or thought of.

In spare time during the rest of the day there was much quiet excitement as the children found fairy stories and poems in the library corner or in books brought from home at noon. Each child was anxious to find an appropriate word and write it on the board. By morning the list showed such words as *fluttered, flickered, gauzy, excitedly, quivering, gnome, sparkled, gasped, joyfully, pitiful, elfin, gently, twinkled, firefly,* and *robe.* The words were read aloud and commented upon. There was a brief discussion about the use of descriptive words and the reasons for their use. Then the teacher wrote on the chalkboard the following: "The fairy danced."

"That sentence doesn't say much, does it?" she remarked. "Can you use some of your words to give us a picture of the fairy dancing?" As words were supplied by the children they were written under the sentence until it looked like this:

The		fairy	danced	
little				quickly
golden-haired				and skipped
little curly-haired				and skipped nimbly
tiny				and skipped about
wee				to and fro
rosy-cheeked				and glided
nimble little				merrily
excited				joyfully
white-gowned				and fluttered

Using different combinations of words, the children made up sentences to picture the real fairy dancing.

Some discussion now took place about the plot. What was the fairy going to do beside dance? What would be a big incident? "Let's make it exciting," pleaded a boy; and a little girl immediately said in a hushed voice, "Suddenly the Queen of Fairies called them all together and said, 'Three of our fairies are missing.'"

From this point the story progressed rapidly. When an owl was introduced a short pause was allowed to list words appropriate to describe an owl—his appearance, habits, etc. When it was decided that the owl would open the petals of a tulip, a picture of a tulip was brought by a child to prove just how the owl might do this, for although the story was make-believe, certain facts had to be true to nature. When the story was finally completed there was considerable satisfaction. Many illustrations were drawn, and these, along with copies of the story, went into the children's storybooks. Following is the story:

> Twilight was at hand and the dainty little fairy folk were getting ready for their dance. Wee fairy ladies scurried to and fro putting on glossy bluebell gowns while little elfin men dressed themselves in golden, yel-

low tulip suits. At the toe of each pointed shoe was fastened a tiny silver bell which tinkled with every step.

Suddenly the Queen of Fairies called them all together and said, "Three of our fairies are missing! We must look for them at once!"

Quickly two little elves ran to call the fireflies. "Come! Come!" they cried. "We need your light."

In a twinkling, swarms of fairies and elves scattered through the thick woods, each with a sparkling firefly leading the way.

On, on they went past the Crystal Pool, past Friendly Gnome's house and beyond Giant Cricket's home, but still there was no sign of the missing fairies.

At last Peach Blossom, a tiny rosy-cheeked fairy, came to Mr. Owl's house. Gently she flew to the door and knocked.

The door opened and Old Mr. Owl said kindly, "Come in please. What do you want?"

"Three of our fairies are missing," answered Peach Blossom. "We've been searching since sundown but have found no sign of them. Will you help us?"

"Whoo-oo!" hooted the Owl as he nodded his wise old head. He cocked his head on one side, folded his wings across his breast, closed his big round eyes, and thought. Then, said he, "I hear a sound." Putting the tip of his wing up to his ear, he listened carefully. Peach Blossom held her breath.

For some time she patiently waited and then, at last, Mr. Owl rolled his big brown eyes, wrinkled his brow, and said solemnly, "I hear the sound of muffled cries in the distance. Fairies! that's what I hear—little fairies in distress."

Peach Blossom was terribly excited. Her wings quivered as she cried, "Where, oh, where are they?"

"I don't know exactly," replied Mr. Owl rubbing his chin thoughtfully, "but if we follow the sound we may discover them."

"Let us go," said Peach Blossom eagerly.

"Whoo-oo! Whoo-oo-o!" cried Mr. Owl as he swept into the air. Peach Blossom fluttered at his side while the firefly flickered close by.

Over the treetops they flew. Mr. Owl was in the lead now, his ears wide open to follow the sound. Plainer and plainer came the sound until Peach Blossom could hear it too.

Then Mr. Owl swooped low and circled over a garden shadowed by trees at the edge of the forest. Louder and louder grew the cries until Peach Blossom knew they were coming from right beneath her. She drifted slowly down beside a big, red tulip which drooped heavily.

"Help! Help! Let us out!" came the pitiful cry from the tulip.

"It is our fairies," cried Peach Blossom, excitedly looking up at Mr. Owl as he landed beside her. "They are in the tulip!"

"Help is here. Be patient," called Peach Blossom to the fairies in the tulip.

"We are suffocating!" gasped a weak voice.

Mr. Owl was thinking fast. With one stroke of his powerful wing he pulled the tulip lower and lower until it touched the ground. Gently he put one foot on the tulip and pressed lightly on the closed petals. A tiny hole appeared in the end of the tulip. Peach Blossom put her face to the hole and cried, "Come! Come out here."

Joyfully, one by one, the three fairies slipped out of the flower, and then, how they danced for joy.

Suddenly Peach Blossom looked at the horizon. "Quick," she cried, the sun will soon be up. We must hurry to the Queen."

Politely the fairies thanked Mr. Owl who was drowsy and nodding by now, motioned to the firefly who was standing near, and they all flew away to the fairy castle.

Special training lessons and exercises As just shown, vocabulary growth takes place best in natural situations in which there is a thought or feeling requiring definition and expression. It is the task of the teacher to take advantage of the situations for definite guidance at the time they arise. The question remains, Can time be profitably devoted to lessons and exercises in word study apart from the immediate situations requiring purposeful expression? Such training lessons and exercises have figured prominently in the traditional language program in the form of preparation of word lists on given topics, dictionary exercises in defining words, completion exercises in filling blanks from given lists of words, preparation of lists of synonyms and antonyms, and the study of etymology. Such procedures require reevaluation. The danger is that training lessons will be so artificial and so far removed from actual situations that they will make little permanent contribution to children's thinking and expression. There are better ways of handling training lessons.

Although it may be treated in a separate period, the training lesson is one in which the purpose is to clarify and enlarge children's ideas and use of words. It will grow out of an immediate, recognized need—for example, the need to substitute definite words for vague expressions in stories. The teacher may call attention to such omnibus words as *good, nice, cute, swell.* He will discourage the use of expressions like *a good time, a good day,* and *a good dinner.* When you say a *"good" day,* just what do you mean? The teacher may well solicit suggestions, supplement them, and write them on the board: *sunny, warm, bright, springlike, summery, brisk, windy, calm, balmy, quiet.* Discussion is naturally followed by attempts to use the more vividly descriptive words in storytelling and in other language experiences.

An occasion may arise for helping children to express bare ideas more vividly. For example, a pupil may say, "The boy went down the street." A clearer picture is developed if one states *how* the boy went down the street. Did he run, walk, stroll, skip,

[6] Mildred A. Dawson and others, *Guiding Language Learning,* Harcourt, Brace & World, Inc., New York, 1963, pp. 66–78.

stumble, shuffle? What kind of boy was he—noisy, redheaded, big, frightened, happy, freckle-faced? By combining the proper words, we get a clear picture: *The ragged, freckle-faced boy scampered down the street.*

Instead of starting with a sentence, the teacher may begin with a bit of dramatic behavior. As part of a dramatization or as a special assignment a pupil may be asked, for example, to cross the room in some distinctive manner. How did she walk? The pupils may informally dramatize different ways of crossing the room; and the class can be asked to find appropriate words for describing them.

Making lists of words may be made significant by having the children prepare them with a particular purpose in mind—for use in a story or poem or for a social studies summary or report. In one project, before starting Halloween stories, appropriate descriptive words were listed on the board and left there for reference. Two poems that resulted were given in chorus with a solo voice taking the part of the moon in the first one:

One spooky, Halloween night
Witches and goblins were out.
Scary ghosts were in sight
And shadowy owls flew about.

The moon peeped from a black cloud
And winked at a pumpkin yellow,
He laughed and laughed aloud
And said, "You're a mighty fine fellow."

Dry leaves lay in a heap
That rustled as children ran past
From door to door for a treat
Until they went home at last.

HALLOWEEN SPOOKS
Look up at the sky
And see the witch!
Look at the tail
Of the black cat twitch.
Look at the goblin
Flying around
On this spooky
Halloween night!

Exercises in finding words that aptly describe a picture, selection, or poem may be used profitably to promote clear thinking as well as to develop vocabulary. Occasionally a teacher may write a word on the board and ask children to give words suggested by it:

Noise: bang, crash, shout.
Taste: sweet, delicious, spicy.
Music: soft, rhythmic, sleepy, lullaby.
Squirrel: flurry, scampering, nimble, chattering.
Color: bright, brilliant, gay, dull, somber.

As another vocabulary-building exercise, the teacher may orally discuss and write on the board the names of animals, asking the children to give the names of the young, as:

bear	cub	cat	_____
sheep	_____	frog	_____
dog	_____	chicken	_____
duck	_____		

In the same way sounds can be matched:

lions	roar	cows	_____
sheep	_____	crows	_____
elephants	_____	geese	_____
frogs	_____	hens	_____
ducks	_____	owls	_____

As a slight variation, the teacher may write:

To provide shelter we build a
doghouse	for dogs	_____	for sheep
_____	for chickens	_____	for rabbits ·
_____	for pigs	_____	for fish

Or the teacher may write:

We call a group of
cattle a	herd	wolves a	_____
sheep a	_____	bees a	_____
fish a	_____	horses a	_____

The children may be asked to give examples of favorite smells, providing appropriate descriptive words, as in the following:

Smells We Like Best

Maple sap boiling: sweet
Smell of violets: woodsy
Freshly broken pine needles: spicy
Steak frying: appetizing
Brownies baking: delicious

The following group poem shows the use of expressive *sound* words, in this case, *windy* words:

A WINDY NIGHT

The wind was howling through the trees.
It knocked down branches and blew off leaves.
It whistled and screeched all through the night,
And shook the windows with all its might.

"Autumn Trees," on the other hand, makes use of *sight* words:

AUTUMN TREES

The trees outside our window
Are turning yellow and red,
And leaves are floating slowly down
To their winter bed.

Fifth and sixth grades sometimes like to make up riddles or tell ones they have heard. As a variation, the riddles may be written on small cards or pieces of drawing paper which the children will exchange, illustrate, and color. This procedure may be adapted for primary children as in the following:

It is long and pointed.
It is larger at one end than at the other.
It grows in the ground. We eat it.
Color it orange.

The study of synonyms and antonyms, exercises in the selection of best descriptive words, and exercises in substitution can be helpful when related to purposeful expression. This adaptation usually requires, of course, that the teacher select or prepare a list for a particular purpose rather than use exercises in textbooks and workbooks indiscriminately. Exercises in books are useful as models rather than complete lessons.

The study of etymology has some value in the later grades and for pupils in the intermediate grades.

The individual word box or notebook is used by teachers effectively from as low as the second grade until children are able to use the dictionary effectively.

Children can search for and list manufactured words, such as *Socony, Nucoa, Kodak, rayon, dacron.*

Similes can be studied, such as *restless as the sea, dark as the night, quiet as a mouse, hard as a rock.* Children enjoy finding new ways in which to convey the meanings of these timeworn expressions.

Multiple word meanings can be noted, as in *pitch, fall, clear, lean.*

Children can list words to describe sensory experiences:

Sounds of mother getting dinner; cleaning house
Smells in a bakeshop; in the woods after a rain
Feel of different kinds of cloth: cotton, velvet, wool, silk
Sights on a snowy morning; of a building going up
Taste of apple pie, rice pudding, hot dog, Jello

A group of eight-year-olds listed the following:

Lovely Things We Know
A deep red rose
The color of maple leaves in the fall
Soft, fluffy snow on the trees
An apple tree in full bloom
A pink peony
The brilliant colors of a Monarch butterfly
The color of a hummingbird

Books for children are available to help sharpen interest in words, their uses and their meanings. The teacher is advised to review books of this nature and to incorporate them into his language program.[7]

Sentences

Many preschool children have acquired not only a large stock of words but also a practical command of sentence forms. They express their meanings and adapt various forms of expression to their purposes by pauses and inflections of the voice. At six years some children use every part of speech and every form of sentence. The basic patterns of expression are those set by persons in the social environment. Individual differences as well as class differences are marked. The habitual forms of expression that children bring to school may or may not be acceptable to the teacher. The teacher often faces difficulties in readjusting his own attitudes and in determining realistic standards and procedures for reeducation in the basic patterns of speech.

A functional program places emphasis on the thought that may be expressed by one or more sentences. The emphasis on the sentence is not on How did you say it?, but on What are you trying to say? and Did you say what you meant to say? The attack of the school strategically follows the natural stages of language development: (1) clear thinking and expressing ideas, (2) thinking

[7] See end-of-chapter references, Children's Books for Language and Words, for a selected listing.

and expressing relationships between several ideas, and (3) giving emphasis to expression and adding interest through the use of a variety of sentences.

Clear thinking and expressing ideas   It may be observed that the child of one year begins to express himself in ideas, first in gestures, grimaces, and sounds, and later in words. At first one word serves to express an idea, then phrases and finally sentences are used. It is in later preschool years and in the early grades that confusion in thinking and expressing single ideas seems to arise as a result of the multiplicity of ideas to be expressed. Then it appears necessary to take measures to develop what we commonly call *sentence sense,* the ability to recognize and to express an idea. The child may have the fault of (1) saying too little, in phrases that do not convey complete ideas, or (2) attempting to say too much, by combining unrelated ideas in a series of unrelated sentences joined by *and, then, so,* or commas.

Children also often attempt stories that are too mature for them. In trying to be grown up or to make a good story, they select a subject quite foreign to their understanding, with the result that the story is a muddle of phrases that may be clear to the writer but are meaningless to the audience. Susan, an imaginative child, wrote the following story during a period when all the children were writing independent stories:

> Once upon a time there was a lovely lady who thought she wanted to be a mermaid so she went to the wicked dwaft man by mistake. At this time there was in the land a beautiful prince who knew and loved the lovely lady. The wicked dwarf may was trying to prevent the lovely lady from being a mermaid. But he finally did prevent it. But she did not care and she went and married the prince and they lived happily ever after the lovely lady was a princess.

It will be seen that she had had wide experience with reading and with listening to stories. To her the story was a good one, and she read it to the class expecting to be complimented. Instead the children looked mystified. "What's a mermaid?" "Why did she go to the dwarf?" "You said he prevented it and then you said she got married. I don't understand." The teacher was careful to compliment Susan on her grown-up words and phrases. "Susan has used a grown-up word, *prevent,* and I like her phrase, 'At this time there was in the land.' Did you notice her descriptive words like *wicked, lovely lady,* etc.? Could we help Susan rearrange two or three of her sentences so we could understand her story better?"

The teacher may help her pupils to develop sentence sense

by pointing out that they use sentences in speaking when they show thought units by pauses and inflections; by calling attention in reading to sentences, capitals, and punctuation marks; by writing sentences on the board; by writing on the board a story composed and dictated by the class; and by listening to and interpreting each other's oral contributions.

If these means fail to serve the purpose, that is, if the children continue to use obscure sentence fragments in speaking or writing, the teacher may make a more determined attack on the difficulty. Obscure oral statements may be examined for clarification. A more formal approach is to write a paragraph of undivided material on the board and allow the children to discover the convenience of sentence division and to gain insight into sentence structure. Still more formal is the use of textbook or workbook exercises in identifying phrases and sentences, changing phrases to sentences, and writing sentences from phrases. The value of formal exercises is determined by the pupils' recognition of the purpose of the corrective exercise and its relation to his own composition. Corrective work, of course, should be limited to those who need it.

In discussions and in exercises the word *sentence* is used as a convenience in referring to an idea, although a formal definition may not be attempted. Also, the ideas and possibly words *subject* and *verb* or *predicate* are useful as a means of labeling key ideas. Such conceptions and terminology may be acquired in the business of distinguishing phrases from sentences. Dramatization—acting out a sentence—may clarify the subject-verb relationship.

A difficulty that the children experience in expressing simple thoughts appears in the run-on sentence construction. This fault appears in the narrative type of composition in which the child relates a series of incidents or happenings. Examples are:

> When he woke up, he saw a whale and it was looking at him so he swam as fast as he could and the whale started after him then Hector hid behind a rock and then he saw his mother and they lived happily ever after.

> His father stopped the car and got out and went to the other car and three men got out and hit him on the head.

> After we went on more rides we went to another place where they had little cars and there was a car that had police on it it was painted black and white.

Children seem to have difficulty in keeping ideas distinct. The attempt to meet the difficulty by limiting the number of sentences (as formerly advocated) hampers thinking and makes children sentence-conscious rather than thought-conscious. The admonition not to use so many *ands* leads to the conviction that *and* is a bad word and should never be used. A sounder but more difficult approach is to lead children to discriminate between ideas that form a close continuity and those that do not. In contrast to the misuse of *ands* in the examples above, a little story written by Arthur is cited:

> My cat follows me upstairs and downstairs and when I go to bed he comes too.

The teacher's comment:

> A teacher in correcting this might ask Arthur to omit one of the *ands* and to divide the material into two sentences. However, it seems that such a change is not only unnecessary but would also make commonplace a story that in its original form has something of art within it. As the sentence flows along, we visualize the cat as it tags Arthur upstairs and downstairs and going to bed at night.

The teacher may ask the children whether the incidents happened close together, and he may suggest other connectives when appropriate, such as *if, when, for, which,* and *because.* Proofreading exercises in textbooks and workbooks may have value when a child recognizes his difficulty and sees the purpose of the exercises.

The mastery of the sentence idea is a gradual growth and is not achieved in any one grade. It presents a persistent and recurrent problem for both teacher and student throughout the grades, and even into college—a problem whose solution requires patience and individual work.[8]

Thinking and expressing relationships between ideas   The development of the single-sentence sense logically precedes and forms a necessary basis for advancement to the stage in which compound and complex sentences are effectively handled. Educators formerly concentrated on the simple sentence in the primary grades and began work on the complex sentence in the intermediate grades. The tendency was to discourage the use of complex sentences by children of six to eight. However, it is recognized that many children in the primary grades use the complex sentence spon-

---

[8] See, for example, research reports by Ruth G. Strickland, "The Language of Elementary School Children: Its Relationship to the Language of Reading Textbooks and the Quality of Reading of Selected Children," *Bulletin of the School of Education,* vol. 38, no. 4, Indiana University, Bloomington, Ind., 1962; Walter D. Loban, *The Language of Elementary School Children,* Research Report, no. 1, National Council of Teachers of English, Champaign, Ill., 1963; Kellogg Hunt, *Grammatical Structures Written at Three Grade Levels,* Research Report, no. 3, National Council of Teachers of English, Champaign, Ill., 1965.

taneously and effectively. Thus a kindergarten child, explaining his Easter picture, said, "This is an Easter basket almost like the one I made yesterday, but it has more eggs in it." Enlightened practice places the emphasis on an individual rather than on a grade basis. The requirement of using simple sentences only hampers the free thinking and expression of many children; when individual children are ready to use complex sentences, they should be so encouraged and directed. The following sentence, given by an eight-year-old as a beginning for a group story, shows a maturity which certainly should not be bridled: "Very far away, in a land which you have probably never heard of, lived two children and their cruel stepmother."

A story, "The Old Woman and Her Geese," was written by two children working together. One child was extremely imaginative, while the other was good at the mechanics of writing. They have used unusual variety in sentence structure:

> Once upon a time there was a crookedly old lady and her geese. She lived in a little red house upon a high hill. There were green shutters on the house and a tulip bed beside it. All around the yard there was a high white fence.
>
> One sunny morning when the old lady had done her work, she came out of the house and found four white geese drinking out of the rain barrel.
>
> As the geese flapped their wings to fly off the rain barrel, one big white goose slipped and fell into the water.
>
> "Honk! Honk!" cried the goose loudly as he splashed around in the water.
>
> Quickly the old woman hobbled over to the rain barrel, pulled the goose out and put him on the ground.
>
> He flapped his wings and waddled off. "Next time I'll go to the pool to drink," he said to himself.

The use of complex sentences indicates a maturity of thinking and an ability to sense relationships between main and subordinate ideas. Hopefully, the era of teaching the definition of the complex sentence with ensuing page-by-page practice in recognizing such sentences is terminated. Experiences that will present ideas and their interrelationships are the starting points for study.

A basic problem in the mastery of complex sentences is choosing the proper connectives for indicating relationships. Connectives serve as guideposts for the direction of thinking. Examples may be discussed with the children to illustrate changes in meaning with different connectives: "Mother says you may go out to play *when* you have wiped the dishes, *if* you return promptly at five o'clock, *because* you have finished your work, etc." Training in connectives has more value than the stating of grammatical rules and definitions, and more vital influence on habits of expression.

Giving emphasis and interest through variety Variation of sentence structure is used in order to gain emphasis and interest. When the basic mechanics of expression have been mastered, attention can be given to finer distinctions of meaning and form. This type of work is characteristic of the mature pupil-writer in the upper grades and possibly in the lower grades where freedom of expression is encouraged.

The following story, written independently during a story-writing period in school, shows unusual maturity of plot and structure. The boy, an eight-year-old, was a great reader. The story is reproduced here exactly as written by the child:

hans and his surprise

once in a little green house in Sweden there lived a little boy by the name of hans. Now hans mother had a good many sheep and hans had to watch them. every day, he would sit on the hillside with his staff and rod for hans lived in the 17th Century. And every night he would sit in the most comfortable chair and read. He had just a few books but he new them very well and loved them all by heart.

now, I am sorry to say that hans took ill one morning and he could not tend the sheep so his mother thought and thought and at last she found an idea. she went down stairs picked up her worn shawl and went scurrying out the door. she took all the sheep and started down the street toward the town yelling sheep for sale sheep for sale. she got into the town and kept on yelling sheep for sale sheep for sale

the people of the town crowded around her and at last she got the last sheep sold she walked into the pet shop and said holding out her money I would like 8 kittens and mind you there baby kittens the storekeeper gave her the furry kittens and she went home yelling kittens for sale.

Again the people of the town crowded around and after she sold all the kittens but one she went home. she gave hans the kitten that was left. the mother took the money from the kittens and they lived happily after that.

The most effective work will be done in connection with the creative effort of the children in whom there is a keen desire and immediate motivation for effective expression. Much of the work will be necessarily individual, but problems of expression relating to emphasis or clarity may arise that are interesting to a group or even to a whole class. The problem may be presented orally by the teacher or may be written on the board for close study. The children should experience the thrill of discovering better ways of expressing an idea.

At times specific exercises, arising preferably in some individual child's problem of expression, may be given. One profitable exercise is practice in changing sentence beginnings—by inversion of clauses, for example—to emphasize important ideas. Such a sentence as, "The Indian boy took a nap while the dog watched the thief," may be studied for variety of expression. Another profitable exercise is practice in combining choppy sentences. The teacher may put on the board a group of such sentences and have the children combine them. Training of this type, arising because of an immediate need, may be very valuable.

The twelve pattern practice techniques suggested by Nelson Brooks show promise as means by which children can develop insights into language patterns.[9] Using the concept that children learn language by analogy rather than by analysis, these practice exercises are designed to elicit certain specific responses. Recognizing that these responses—or utterances—do not of themselves represent communication, each could be part of person-to-person communication. For example, in the replacement pattern practice, "Helen left early" has the directed response "She left early." In integration, two separate utterances are integrated into one, so that "They must be honest. This is important," becomes "It is important that they be honest." In rejoinder, the child is asked to make an appropriate response to a given utterance, being told ahead of time the attitude to assume—being polite, answering the question, agreeing—on a continuum to that of completely failing to understand. A polite response to "May I take one?" results in "Certainly"; the question, "Where did it happen?" results in "In the middle of the street"; in previously determining that regret should be expressed, the utterance, "He missed the bus," elicits "What a shame!"

Working with the underprivileged   Attention has been focused especially on the environmental factors that influence language development. By studying and researching the language of underprivileged children—whether in city-ghetto or isolated rural area—certain factors of language development have been noted. The sociological and linguistic implications are important in planning for maximum language growth of all children with extreme language deficits, and for again recognizing the individual differences found in all classrooms.

In reviewing the language of children who, by several definitions, emerge as underprivileged, meager vocabulary is frequently

[9] Nelson Brooks, *Language and Language Learning*, Harcourt, Brace & World, Inc., New York, 1964, pp. 152–164. Used with special permission.

listed as a characteristic. Often a meager vocabulary is a result of the lack of preschool experiences. Inadequate syntax is another characteristic frequently listed. Children with impoverished language backgrounds do not use a variety of tenses commonly used by other children. Omission of articles and little awareness of conjunctives indicating causal relationships—*for, or, so*—are other characteristics that teachers must note.[10]

Evaluation   A rich program of meaningful language experiences in which objects and items, processes and results are named, internalized, and used by children is essential. Special techniques and planned experiences to assist in the development of sentence sense and sentence usage are of immediate importance.

The teacher records children's comments and uses the tape recorder for the analysis of both planned and spontaneous speaking occasions. Realizing that effective writing is dependent on such factors as control of vocabulary and syntax, the teacher at all grade levels provides primary opportunities for varied experiences in speaking and listening, in considering words, and in experimenting with the expression of thoughts. Written practice and exercises grow out of understandings that have been developed in oral language situations, in and out of class and individual needs. Ultimate appraisal of the effectiveness of the work in the choice of the word, the turn of the phrase, and the meaning of the sentence is reflected in children's spontaneous conversations, organized discussions, creative stories, and specialized reports.

For your consideration

1   If possible, visit a classroom to observe an on-going unit in science or social studies or a lesson in mathematics. Note the specific terminology used during the period. Later, list the words and analyze them in the following ways: (*a*) their specific use in the study of the subject, (*b*) the understanding of the words that were indicated by the children, and (*c*) the meanings that the words might have in other sentences and contexts.

2   Sample the technical vocabulary of a unit in a textbook for health, science, or social studies for any grade level. To determine a technical term, use the criterion that the word represents a concept crucial to the study of the subject. List the terms

[10] Edgar Dale, "Vocabulary Development of the Underprivileged Child," *Elementary English,* vol. 42, November, 1965, pp. 779–785.

and determine how best children could understand the word and its meaning.

3 Observe a classroom during a lesson in which children are involved in some major speaking activity—conversation, discussion, oral reporting, storytelling. Record the variety of sentences used. If possible, obtain written samples of this class and compare the written sentence structures with your recordings of the variety of orally expressed sentences.

4 Plan a series of lessons or experiences designed to remove one sentence difficulty found in your observations noted in (3).

References

APPLEGATE, MAUREE: *Easy in English,* Harper & Row, Publishers, Inc., New York, 1963, chap. 11.

BEREITER, CARL, AND SIEGFRIED ENGELMANN: *Teaching Disadvantaged Children in the Preschool,* Prentice-Hall, Inc., Englewood Cliffs, N.J., 1966, chap. 5.

BROOKS, NELSON: *Language and Language Learning,* Harcourt, Brace & World, Inc., New York, 1964, chaps. 11 and 13.

COBRIN, RICHARD, AND MURIEL CROSBY: *Language Programs for the Disadvantaged,* National Council of Teachers of English, Champaign, Ill., 1965, pp. 221–231.

DALLMAN, MARTHA: *Teaching the Language Arts in the Elementary School,* W. C. Brown Company, Publishers, Dubuque, Iowa, 1966, pp. 101–110.

DREWES, RUTH H., AND OTHERS: *Practical Plans for Teaching English in Elementary Schools,* W. C. Brown Company, Publishers, Dubuque, Iowa, 1965, chaps. 15–16, 20.

HERRICK, VIRGIL E., AND LELAND B. JACOBS: *Children and the Language Arts,* Prentice-Hall, Inc., Englewood Cliffs, N.J., 1955, chap. 14.

LEONARD, EDITH M., AND OTHERS: *Basic Learning in the Language Arts,* Scott, Foresman and Company, Chicago, 1965, part 4.

MC KEE, PAUL: *Language in the Elementary School,* Houghton Mifflin Company, Boston, 1939, pp. 89, 107–108, 302–312.

PONDER, EDDIE G.: "Understanding the Language of the Culturally Disadvantaged Child," *Elementary English,* vol. 42, November, 1965, pp. 769–774.

RUSSELL, DAVID H.: *Children's Thinking,* Ginn and Company, Boston, 1956.

SMITH, NILA B.: *Areas of Research Interest in the Language Arts,* National Council of the Teachers of English, Champaign, Ill., 1952, pp. 7–11.

STANLEY, J. C.: *Measurement in Today's Schools,* Prentice-Hall, Inc., Englewood Cliffs, N.J., 1964, chap. 7.

STRICKLAND, RUTH G.: *Guide for Teaching English Is Our Language, Grades 1–2,* D. C. Heath and Company, Boston, 1950, chap. 8.

TIEDT, IRIS M., AND S. W. TIEDT: *Contemporary English in the Elementary School,* Prentice-Hall, Inc., Englewood Cliffs, N.J., 1967, chap. 3.

TRAUGER, W. K.: *Language Arts in Elementary Schools,* McGraw-Hill Book Company, New York, 1963, chaps. 8–9.

CHILDREN'S BOOKS FOR LANGUAGE AND WORDS

ALEXANDER, ARTHUR: *The Magic of Words,* Prentice-Hall, Inc., Englewood Cliffs, N.J., 1962 (grades 4–6).

APPLEGATE, MAUREE: *The First Book of Language,* Franklin Watts, Inc., New York, 1962 (grades 6–9).

ASIMOV, ISAAC: *Words from the Myths,* Houghton Mifflin Company, Boston, 1961 (grades 6–8).

EPSTEIN, SAM, AND BERYL EPSTEIN: *First Book of Codes and Ciphers,* Franklin Watts, Inc., New York, 1956 (grades 4–8).

————: *First Book of Words: Their Family Histories,* Franklin Watts, Inc., New York, 1955 (grades 4–6).

FERGUSON, CHARLES W.: *The Abecedarian Book,* Little, Brown and Company. Boston, 1964 (grades 9–).

FRASCONI, ANTONIO: *See and Say: A Picture Book in Four Languages,* Harcourt, Brace & World, Inc., New York, 1955 (grades 3–5).

FUNK, CHARLES: *Heavens to Betsy and Other Curious Sayings,* Harper & Row, Publishers, Inc., New York, 1955 (grades 5–7).

HOFSINDE, ROBERT: *Indian Picture Writing,* William Morrow and Company, Inc., New York, 1959 (grades 3–5).

HOGBEN, LANCELOT T.: *Wonderful World of Communication,* Garden City Books, New York, 1959 (grades 6–9).

KAUFMAN, JOEL: *The Golden Happy Book of Words,* Golden Press, Inc., New York, 1963 (K–3).

LAIRD, HELENE, AND CHARLTON LAIRD: *Tree of Language,* World Publishing Company, Cleveland, Ohio, 1957 (grades 7–9).

LAMBERT, ELOISE, AND MARIO PEI: *Our Names: Where They Came from and What They Mean,* Lothrop, Lee & Shepard Co., Inc., New York, 1960 (grades 6–9).

LUDOVICI, L. J.: *Origins of Language,* G. P. Putnam's Sons, New York, 1965 (grades 7–9).

O'NEILL, MARY: *Words, Words, Words,* Doubleday & Company, Inc., Garden City, N.Y., 1966 (grades 5–7).

OSMOND, EDWARD: *From Drum to Tickertape,* Criterion Books, Inc., New York, 1960 (grades 5–8).

RADLAUER, RUTH S.: *Good Times with Words,* Melmont Children's Press, Chicago, Ill., 1963 (grades 3–6).

RAND, PAUL, AND ANN RAND: *Sparkle and Spin,* Harcourt, Brace & World, Inc., New York, 1957 (grades K–3).

REID, ALASTAIR: *Ounce, Dice, Trice,* Little, Brown and Company, Boston, 1968 (grades 3–5).

ROGERS, FRANCES: *Painted Rock to Printed Page,* J. B. Lippincott Company, Philadelphia, 1960 (grades 6–8).

RUSSELL, SOLVEIG P.: *A Is for Apple and Why: The Story of Our Alphabet,* Abingdon Press, Nashville, Tenn., 1959 (grades 3–6).

SAGE, MICHAEL: *Words inside Words,* J. B. Lippincott Company, Philadelphia, 1961 (grades 4–6).

WALLER, LESLIE: *Our American Language,* Holt, Rinehart and Winston, Inc., New York, 1960 (grades 4–6).

WEST, FRED: *Breaking the Language Barrier,* Coward-McCann, Inc., New York, 1961 (grades 6–9).

14.

USAGE
AND
GRAMMAR –
LINGUISTICS

Usage

Usage should be considered in relation to other factors contributing to performance in language, and should take its proper place in the hierarchy of attitudes, abilities, and skills. It is certainly not the chief end of language instruction; far more important are willingness to participate, content, and adherence to the point. Work on usage should contribute to the development of more important abilities as well as to total performance. If properly handled it will do so. In fact, the more fundamental language attitudes and abilities will provide motivation and set the stage for work on acceptable usage.

As background for this chapter's consideration of the problems and procedures of teaching usage, it may be well to review briefly related material in other sections of the book. In Chapter 2 certain principles concerning the place of usage in the curriculum were developed. As a basic assumption, it was observed that the English language is changing, that some traditionally objectionable forms of expression are now accepted, and that the general trend is toward a direct, vigorous, idiomatic form of expression. However, there are certain forms that are recognized as crudities, and they are objectionable. Excess use of crudities should be attacked vigorously and consistently. It was recognized in Chapter 2 that standards of acceptability vary in communities and that it is unwise for the teacher to be insensitive to usages demonstrated in a particular community and its several social groups. A third principle stated that different types of speech suit different situations, and that the teacher and children must recognize these situations and the kinds of language appropriate to them.

Chapter 18 provides grade lists and suggestions for a sequence of work. This information, supplemented by the observation of children and by the study of the local course of study and textbook, should be useful to the teacher in determining relative importance of usage difficulties.

Observation shows clearly the persistence of crudities through the grades. The teacher should understand that acceptability of expression is a gradual growth, individual in character, extending over a period of years and not achieved in any one grade; and that the habits of expression reflect the social environment of the children, the language used at home and in the community. The teacher faces at times the problem of changing deeply rooted habits of unacceptable expression and of overcoming indifference and even social prejudice against change. It is a difficult problem.

Conditions favorable to acceptable expression: motivation   What can the teacher do to facilitate the habits of acceptable expression? He may make a beginning, at least, by establishing conditions in the classroom that are favorable to good expression. As a bare minimum, he can set an example of clear, vigorous, acceptable English, providing at least one social situation in which acceptable language is heard. He may go further and show that he expects the children to use some care in the choice of words by insisting on reasonable acceptability and by expressing approval at favorable times. He may make good language the fashion through skillful motivation.

Primary motivation comes through experiences. Language habits, like other habits, serve in helping people attain recognizable goals. The great drive for improving language from infancy on is to make oneself understood by others—to express needs, to give information, to persuade, to gain approval. Children of school age especially desire approval by the group, and find that acceptable language is one means of winning this approval.

Further motivation is provided by the phases of a thoroughly sound language program that gives oral language experiences for young children in which they employ the dialect of the social class language they already speak. The emphasis rests on the expression of feelings and emotions and the use of language to develop the powers of reason. Through listening experiences, gradually introduced to focus attention on sounds and later attention on the many dialects of the English language, the upper elementary school child is led to the understanding that he must learn also the standard dialect found in the language of the teacher and the textbook, which is useful in future school and job requirements.[1]

Another primary requisite for improvement of usage is enriched language experiences. Acceptable forms of expression must be repeated sufficiently to cause the acceptable forms to *sound right*. All phases of the oral program make a contribution here— both experiences and training lessons. Practice exercises, if written, should be read aloud, and an abundance of oral practice in using acceptable forms must be given.

Setting reasonable goals Definite, reasonable goals should be set for a particular class. A feeling of futility may occur in the pupils if the teacher goes to either of two extremes: neglects to set any definite goals or scatters effort among all the mistakes made by the pupils of the class. A few crudities should be listed for attention: those that are made by a number of pupils, those that represent recognized crudities of expression in a particular social group, and those that fit into the total program as outlined in the course of study or textbook. Priority should be given to basic crudities attacked, but not eliminated, in earlier grades.

Recognizing the range of latitude in standards, Pooley lists the following crucial elements:

1. The elimination of all baby-talk and "cute" expressions.
2. The correct use in speech and writing of *I, me, him, she, her, they, them.* (Exception, *it's me.*)
3. The correct use of *is, are, was, were* with respect to number and tense.
4. Correct past tenses of common irregular verbs such as *saw, gave, took, brought, bought, stuck.*
5. Correct use of past participles of the same verbs and similar verbs after auxiliaries.
6. Elimination of the double negatives: We don't have no apples, etc.
7. Elimination of analogical forms: *ain't, hisn, hern, ourn, theirselves,* etc.
8. Correct use of possessive pronouns: *my, mine, his, hers, theirs, ours.*

[1] Walter Loban, "A Sustained Program of Language Learning," in Richard Corbin, Muriel Crosby, and others, *Language Programs for the Disadvantaged,* the Report of the NCTE Task Force on Teaching English to the Disadvantaged, National Council of Teachers of English, Champaign, Ill., 1965, pp. 221–231.

9. Mastery of the distinction between *its*, possessive pronoun, and *it's*, it is.
10. Placement of *have* or its phonetic reduction to *v* between I and a past participle.
11. Elimination of *them* as a demonstrative pronoun.
12. Elimination of *this here* and *that there*.
13. Mastery of use of *a* and *an* as articles.
14. Correct use of personal pronouns in compound constructions: as subject (Mary and I), as object (Mary and me), as object of preposition (to Mary and me.)
15. The use of *we* before an appositional noun when subject; *us* when object.
16. Correct number agreement with the phrases *there is, there are, there was, there were.*
17. Elimination of *he don't, she don't, it don't.*
18. Elimination of *learn* for *teach, leave* for *let.*
19. Elimination of pleonastic subjects: *my brother he, my mother she, that fellow he.*
20. Proper agreement in number with antecedent pronouns *one* and *anyone, everyone, each, no one.* With *everybody* and *none* some tolerance of number seems acceptable.
21. The use of *who* and *whom* as reference to persons. But note, *Who did he give it to?* is tolerated in all but very formal situations. In the latter, *To whom did he give it?* is preferable.
22. Accurate use of *said* in reporting the words of a speaker in the past.
23. Correction of *lay down* to *lie down.*
24. The distinction between *good* as adjective and *well* as adverb; e.g., He spoke *well.*
25. Elimination of *can't hardly, all the farther* (for *as far as*), and *Where is she (he) at?* [2]

Pooley continues:

This list of twenty-five kinds of corrections to make constitutes a very specific standard of current English usage for today and the next few years. Some elements in it may require modification within ten years; some possibly earlier. Conspicuous by their absence are those items which were on the usage lists by which many of us were taught and which survive today in less enlightened textbooks:

1. Any distinction between *shall* and *will.*
2. Any reference to the split infinitive.
3. Elimination of *like* as a conjunction.
4. Objection to the phrase "different than."
5. Objection to "He is one of those boys who *is.*"
6. Objection to "The reason . . . is because . . ."

[2] Robert C. Pooley, "Dare the Schools Set a Standard in English Usage?" *English Journal,* vol. 49, March, 1960, pp. 179–180. Quoted with special permission of author and publisher.

7. Objection to *myself* as a polite substitute for *me* as in "I understand that you will meet Mrs. Jones and myself at the station."
8. Insistence upon the possessive case standing before a gerund.[3]

Determining individual needs The necessity of a program of corrective work adjusted to individual needs has been consistently recognized. In 1929, Lyman stated, "The remedial work which follows revelations of language weakness must be largely, if not exclusively, individual." [4] Later Ingrid Strom concluded that, since growth in control of language is part of the total growth pattern of the child or adolescent, the teacher should expect different rates of growth, with errors being best attacked through individual instruction.[5]

A practical question arises: How is the teacher to determine individual needs? Since the list of crudities attacked in any one grade is not large, the checklist is a usable device. The teacher lists the crudities across the top of a ruled sheet of paper and the pupils' names down the left-hand margin. A record for each pupil is shown by checks in the proper columns. As a means of determining crudities, the teacher may listen to oral work or give a diagnostic usage test. The test may be taken from the textbook or prepared by the teacher as a dictation or proofreading exercise; it may be a standardized test.[6] By observing language usage for several weeks a working list may be compiled.[7]

Incidental correction of crudities Something can be accomplished in the elimination of crudities by suggesting proper forms as children engage in such various language experiences as conversation, storytelling, and reports. When a child hesitates in his search for the proper form for expressing an idea, the teacher may supply it; or, when the child has completed his talk, the teacher may suggest a correction. The teacher should be warned against interrupting the child and emphasizing correctness to the point at which

---

[3] *Ibid.*, p. 180. Quoted with special permission of author and publisher.

[4] R. L. Lyman, *Summary of Investigations Relating to Grammar, Language and Composition.* University of Chicago Press, Chicago, Ill., 1929, p. 133.

[5] Ingrid Strom, "Research in Grammar and Usage and Its Implications for Teaching Writing," *Bulletin of the School of Education,* vol. 36, no. 5, Indiana University, Bloomington, Ind., 1960, p. 14.

[6] H. A. Greene and H. L. Ballenger, *Iowa Language Abilities Test, Test 3, Language Usage,* Harcourt, Brace & World, Inc., New York, 1946–1948.

[7] Amelia Rock, "Audio-lingual Approach to Correcting Language Patterns," *The Instructor,* vol. 77 December, 1967, pp. 110–111.

freedom of expression and interest are lost. The integrity of the composition as an experience for self-expression should be preserved.[8]

Use of training lessons and exercises   Training lessons and exercises provide a direct means of attack on a difficulty; they take the form of oral or written instruction and practice or drill. Much work of this type has been futile in the past; and it will probably continue to be futile, unless the teacher observes faithfully certain basic principles. Of first importance is the child's understanding of just what is to be learned and the purpose of learning it; the child must see some connection between a blank-filling exercise and his speech habits. For a child who wants to adjust, practice is natural and acceptable. The training lesson should be an outgrowth of a purposeful experience that reveals need for a particular skill. This recognition of specific need plus the desire to improve motivates and sets the stage for the training exercise.

2. A second principle is that certain usage forms should be considered mutually, clearly labeled to indicate that some show standard dialect and some do not. For example, Loban suggests that after directions have been understood by children, the teacher might read a list of expressions, having the children mark the standard or school expressions to distinguish them from such expressions as: "She is my friend" and "Him a happy fellow." The teacher is cautioned that, if the second example represents a valid expression to children, the teacher should not label this expression *bad* as opposed to *good,* but state rather that they are different and are used in different situations.[9]

3. The third principle, already stated, is that much oral work should be provided so that the correct form will *sound right* in a particular situation.

4. The fourth principle is that the practice periods should be short, intensive, and frequent.

5. The fifth principle is that the teacher should determine, if possible, the cause of a mistake and make a clear explanation suited to the maturity of the learner. Since the young child develops his language often by analogy, it is not surprising that he will say, *The clown danced, The girl laughed,* and *The wind blowed.* Further, the teacher should be aware of the existence of bidialectism, that is, the difference between school language and life usage. In

[8] John M. Kean, "Schools, Children, and Communication," *Educational Leadership,* vol. 24, April, 1967, pp. 618–623.
[9] Loban, *op. cit.,* pp. 227–228.

assessing the usage patterns in children's out-of-school life, the teacher will receive clues that will aid in determining future instructional plans.[10]

To be effective, instruction must be brought down to the level of individual needs, though not necessarily individual instruction. The preliminary inventory of needs, suggested above, provides a point of departure. Those common to the whole class can be profitably taken up with the class. It is likely, however, that for the most part needs will vary considerably. The teacher, then, may take one of two courses. He may treat each child as an individual learner, or he may group children with similar needs. The second course offers the advantage of simplification of instruction without sacrificing the individual. The teacher can teach several groups; he cannot teach thirty or forty pupils on an individual basis. The grouping is temporary and has a specific purpose: overcoming a specific language difficulty. An individual plan of work is useful as a supplementary procedure, adaptable to the extreme variants found in all classes and particularly in the small school.

The cycle of learning experience in developing a single skill, whether class, group, or individual, includes (1) discovery of need, (2) recognition of the proper form, (3) practice, and (4) use in context, preferably in original material. The first two phases imply the necessity for positive instruction; the pupil cannot be allowed to attack his remedial work blindly. It is reasonable that the necessary instruction must be handled by the teacher, who directs it to a specific problem. Printed materials—textbooks and workbooks—help, but they cannot displace a competent teacher. The third phase and part of the fourth can be handled as seatwork exercises, carried on individually under the general supervision of the teacher. The contextual part of the fourth phase involves using a particular skill in free writing, a follow-up experience.

Specific training experiences take a considerable variety of forms adapted to particular grade levels. At the first-grade level the children may engage in exercises such as substituting an acceptable for an unacceptable expression. For example, in a show-and-tell period a child may say, "I brang this toy." In a training lesson in a language period, the teacher may give the acceptable expression and have the children use it in reporting what they brought. Similarly, the correct use of *throw* may be taught in connection with a beanbag game. This type of exercise, providing practice in

[10] David DeCamp, "Dimensions of English Usage," in Gary Tate (ed.), *Reflections on High School English,* The University of Tulsa, Tulsa, Okla., 1966, pp. 186–187.

needed language forms in more or less interesting but isolated situations, is suggestive of the old, widely used language game. It provides opportunity to hear and to practice proper forms, but its value is lessened by its separation from experiences and the failure on the part of the pupil to comprehend the purpose of the exercise. Some primary teachers insist that their children are mature enough to be made aware of immediate language goals and to share in the responsibility of meeting them.

A more direct line of attack, increasingly valuable throughout the grades, is to take a particular language difficulty from the children's oral or written work, write it on the board, and present it to the children as a problem of expression. The nature of the difficulty should be noted, the acceptable form contrasted with the unacceptable, and some practice immediately given in a variety of sentences. Group or class correction exercises of this type are profitably followed by having each child improve his own work.

Use of materials   Formal types of exercises are provided abundantly in textbooks and workbooks. Teachers may also compose their own exercises, including blank filling and multiple choice, error recognition and correction, crossing out incorrect forms, question-and-answer exercises, original sentences, short talks and essays featuring correct usage, and games. The best kind of exercise involves choice of construction. The convenience of making assignments in work of this type leads to its overuse as a form of busywork; but in spite of this abuse, formal exercises may have some value when the purpose is clearly conceived by the pupil, when immediate need is recognized, and when practice is preceded by a well-handled preparatory period of instruction.

Suppose, for example, that a pupil, group, or class is having trouble with the use of *we* and *us* in such expressions as *we boys* and *us boys*. A recent textbook contains a section dealing with the difficulty. It explains that both forms are correct at certain times but are sometimes confused. It lists some examples of correct form: "*We boys* are going home. The teacher asked *us girls* to clean the room. Share the pencils among *us boys*"; then provides a series of sentences in which the correct form is to be supplied: "—boys cannot solve the problem. Give it to—girls. Stop teasing—girls." [11]

The use of workbooks is not always dependable as a means of bringing about improvement in usage. The selection of material may not be appropriate to the needs of a class; explanations and rules

[11] Mildred A. Dawson and others, *Language for Daily Use: Book 5*, Harcourt, Brace & World, Inc., New York, 1964, p. 215.

may be beyond the comprehension of the children; and the important difficulties of a particular class may not receive sufficient emphasis. Practice work, unless closely supervised, may result in the continued use of unacceptable forms; and practice is likely to be silent and detached from real communication. Usage practice, to be effective, should be spoken and heard.

These criticisms may be taken to suggest a discriminating use of textbook and workbook material rather than to recommend the complete abandonment of such material. Proper instructional materials may be an aid to the teacher, especially in the handling of problems of extreme variability. Instructional aids explaining difficulties and showing acceptable and unacceptable forms supplement the oral instruction of the teachers. Diagnostic tests and practice exercises can be used effectively if there is a recognized purpose in the mind of the learner. The value of the materials depends in large part on the way in which they are used. The indiscriminate assignment of lessons to whole classes and progression through the book page by page are not the best ways to use the material. If the teacher uses a group or an individual plan in remedial work, recognized as inescapable, it is helpful to inventory the contents of workbooks and textbooks according to type of language difficulty treated. An index of available material in textbooks, workbooks, and supplementary books can be provided for the use of children in the intermediate and upper grades without too much difficulty. Materials in the form of exercises on key difficulties may be selected from several sources, reproduced or mounted on paper, provided with answer keys, and housed so that they can be secured by the children without the help of the teacher. This equipment is useful in group work and practically mandatory in individual types of instruction.

Self-evaluation records A final essential feature of the training program in usage is provision for recording individual goals and progress. Each child may keep a list of the usage goals, such as the teacher keeps for the whole class. Possibly a master list, constituting a single page in the language or general goal book, can be duplicated and distributed to the children. Each pupil should make a record of his language difficulties on this sheet early in the term. As specific difficulties are mastered, that is, as acceptable forms are used reguarly in free speaking and writing, the pupil should record progress by checks on the goal sheet. The tangible evidence is a proper and powerful incentive for improvement. Further tangible evidence may result from pattern practice exercises recorded on tape by individuals in the class. Playback listening can provide the speaker-listener with a new dimension for his personal usage evaluation.[12]

Grammar—linguistics

Relation of usage to grammar   In the everyday language of the community and school, the terms *usage* and *grammar* are made synonymous. Usage, however, properly refers to habitual forms of expression—the language one actually uses. Grammar, on the other hand, properly refers to the structure and science of language—classes of words, their inflections, their relationships to each other singly, in phrases, and clauses, and the functions of these in the sentence. In the sentence *Mary lost her book*, one may use the word *lost* correctly without knowing the large class of words to which it belongs and without being able to state exactly its relation to other words in the sentence. On the other hand, one may be able to state definitions and rules without being able to apply them to words in a sentence, even in the correction of errors. The primary emphasis in language teaching today is on usage, but grammar still requires consideration. Investigations have failed to present proof of the value of grammar as a means of improving expression, yet linguists and teachers believe that there should be some kind of grammar somewhere in the program. The fact that there is disagreement on kind and place somewhat weakens the argument.

Functional grammar   The nature of grammar is obviously related to the purpose or value it is assumed to have. Functional grammar in the traditional sense is derived from a study of the errors of usage, and includes training in those definitions and principles that may assist pupils in the correction of errors. The study of linguistics has created a much broader concept of grammar, making a positive rather than a negative approach; the emphasis is on effective expression rather than on correction of errors. In the process of grasping thought and building sentences and paragraphs to express ideas adequately, the children discover classes of words, notice changes in meaning with changes in form, learn the proper placement of modifiers and the skillful use of phrases and clauses, and discover how meaning is affected by change in the position of various parts of a sentence. The children learn appropriate terms for labeling ideas with which they deal, and make generalizations to

[12] Ruth I. Golden, *Improving Patterns of Language Usage*, Wayne State University Press, Detroit, Mich., 1960, pp. 148–157.

describe observed changes in words and to express relationships they discover. The concepts and generalizations gradually crystallize into a body of conceptions regarding language which in themselves give a certain degree of satisfaction and which are useful in comprehension of thought and in expression of ideas. The emphasis is on thinking and relating ideas, understanding the structure of language, gaining clarity and force of expression through choice of words and manipulation of sentence elements in a variety of forms, and on avoiding common mistakes.

It will be observed that acceptable usage appears as a part of the broader grammar—linguistics program, but it does not dominate the program. As was pointed out by Pooley in 1946, teaching functional grammar should free the child for creative expression, not hamper him; show him what to do and how to do it, not emphasize the negative. Grammar should expedite communication.[13] At another point, in relation to the teaching of grammar in the high school, Pooley states, "Grammar supports usage at the point when the child can grasp a generalization and apply it accurately to particulars."[14]

Sequence in functional grammar   Grammar work of the functional type is obviously not concentrated in any grade or presented in a series of isolated lessons. It represents the building of a body of concepts and understandings that begin to take form in grade 1 and develop gradually throughout the elementary school years, growing in detail, clarity, and organization with the pupils' increasing maturity and expanding expressional needs. The sequence is a series of ideas and understandings, proceeding from large concepts to details. The basic concept of the sentence will develop very early; the recognition of different classes of words will come soon after in the search for depth, vividness, and accuracy. Foundations of understanding are laid in the lower grades, but the formulation of principles and definitions will come in the junior and senior high school years. Instruction should be placed on a class or individual basis rather than on a fixed grading basis. What should be taught depends on the language experiences and the needs of the children. Continuity in the growth of the learners is the important consideration.[15]

[13] Robert C. Pooley, *Teaching English Usage*, Appleton-Century-Crofts, Inc., New York, 1946, pp. 207–208. See also Don M. Wolfe, "Grammar and Linguistics: A Contrast in Realities," *English Journal*, vol. 53, February, 1964, pp. 73–78, 100.

[14] Pooley, *op. cit.*, p. 224.

[15] *Ibid.*, pp. 126–128.

Processes   The procedure for handling grammar concepts and principles in the functional program is informal in character; grammar is taught as opportunity and need arise in connection with some communication experience. The situation may be one of making the meaning clear, as illustrated in the following composition (part of a friendly letter) and the discussion following:

> Dear Miss Nelva,
>   When are you going to write again? I wish you would write to my house and also send your picture. My aunt loves to see your picture. When I heard that you had something in the paper about you, I looked for your picture, but I could not find it.

In discussing the third sentence a problem arose: an incorrect tense.

> TEACHER: Has your aunt ever seen Miss Nelva's picture?
> CHILD: No, but she would love to see it.
> TEACHER: That's how you should write the sentence—to show Miss Nelva that your aunt *will* look at the picture when you get one.

The next sentence had another kind of difficulty in it:

> TEACHER: What did you hear about Miss Nelva?
> CHILD: That there was something in the paper about her.
> TEACHER: Then you should write, "When I heard that there was something in the paper about you, I looked for your picture, but I could not find it."

Such discussion with the writer helps to make inductively taught grammar function as a tool of facile expression. Gradually, more and more responsibility can be placed upon the pupil to apply his knowledge of grammar in revising his writing. There will, however, continue to be occasions when only a conference with the teacher will clarify for the pupil how to correct his error without losing his idea.

Another situation may be one of attaining "speed and ease in narrative by combining sentences with the same subjects into sentences with compound predicates," as in the sentences *John fell down* and *John hurt his ankle.* Or it may be a matter of securing variety in sentences for interest and emphasis by shifting modifying clauses, as in the sentence *I found I was dreaming when I woke up.* Or it may simply be the refining of an unconventional, crude type of expression.[16]

The learning situation takes up a problem—how to express a given idea—and suggests a problem-solving type of attack, somewhat as follows: (1) The first step of the problem is to define a spe-

---

[16] Harold Newman, "Toward a New Perspective of Grammar and Composition," in J. C. MacCampbell, *Readings in the Language Arts in the Elementary School,* D. C. Heath and Company, Boston, 1964, pp. 200–210.

cific idea to be expressed in answer to the question, Exactly what am I trying to say? (2) Next, information is gathered on the proper form of expression. The kind of information varies with the maturity and the language background of the child. If the problem is new to him, he will profit from the study and comparison of good forms for expressing similar ideas. Erroneous forms may be studied profitably for contrast. If the problem of expression is similar to one previously studied, the child naturally recalls and applies relevant generalizations. The teacher provides the amount and kind of guidance needed by the child. (3) The child organizes and clarifies his thinking by adopting the new form of expression and possibly experiments with it in expressing similar ideas in the same manner. (4) A generalized statement of the principle or rule may be formulated and checked with the textbook. (5) Opportunities should be seized for applying the new principle or rule both in oral and written expression and in reading.

Certain general characteristics of the informal procedure may be summarized: (1) Grammar is taught as needed in expressional activities. (2) New concepts and rules are learned inductively through the study of live language and therefore have meaning for the learner. (3) Terms and statements of rules follow ideas and understandings. (4) The observation of language plays an important role. (5) Familiar generalizations, recalled and applied as needed in meeting new problems, gain increasing clarity and breadth of application. (6) The direction and rate of growth are determined by the teacher according to plan; development is orderly, systematic, and planned.

Implications of grammar   Linguists regard oral language as the primary basis for the study of language. Oral language provides the approach to reading, writing, spelling, and other language arts and skills. The analysis of speech shows meaning revealed by intonation patterns, combinations of stresses, pitches, and junctures. Reading is translating visual symbols into speech; punctuation marks reveal appropriate speech patterns. Spelling is translating sounds of words and letters into conventional written forms. Oral language also provides the basis for the study of syntax—patterns of word order, the functioning of the several parts of speech, and the identification of and use of various classes of words, parts of speech.[17]

[17] W. K. Trauger, *Language Arts in Elementary Schools*, McGraw-Hill Book Company, New York, 1963, pp. 149–150. See also G. H. Owen, "Linguistics: An Overview," in Verna D. Anderson and others, *Readings in the Language Arts*, The Macmillan Company, New York, 1964, pp. 19–25.

Some basic principles and concepts, related to clear thinking and expression, can be noted. Fundamental, of course, is the understanding of completeness in the expression of a single idea, the sentence idea—the basic unit of meaning. Clear thinking and clear expression proceed in a sequence; the order of words is important. Obscuration of thought is noticed frequently when words are out of their natural order and when sentences lack subjects or predicates, mere fragments. Confusion is found when ideas not closely related are connected by *and, so, then*—run-on sentences. Reconstruction of a sentence involves rethinking. The teacher should remain aware that the sentence is the chief unit of speech, defined as a minimum complete utterance that occurs between two pauses and that inevitably shows some kind of arrangement, construction, or syntax.[18]

In time it is found that a talk may be tiresome and a composition may be boring if composed entirely of simple sentences— mere subject, predicate, complement. Variety of sentences adds interest. Children in the lower grades soon find that simple sentences fail to satisfy them and they are ready to experiment with more mature forms—combining closely related ideas with *ands*, putting together compound sentences, and varying sentence forms to show relationships among ideas.

The principles of modification and subordination are recognized as means of gaining clarity and vividness. They appear in sentences as various connectives are used; in the form of adjectives, using words that add detail and vividness when describing persons and things; and as adverbs, when adding to the meaning of verbs and adjectives.

For example, the sentence "John fell down and dropped the ball" expresses very simply the action at a crucial point in a ball game. Vividness is added by recasting the sentence, telling more about John and reporting how John happened to drop the ball. Thus, "John was the most eager and capable player on the team, but the ball slipped out of his glove when he stumbled over a stone." Instead of using a sentence to describe John, one could use single adjectives: *reliable, dependable, sure-footed*. Or, one could tell how he ran: *swiftly with abandon*. Emphasis is given to the cause of the mishap by placing the dependent clause first in the sentence: "When John stumbled over a stone, he dropped the ball," etc. The problem is one of clear, vivid expression, not one of correctness. Situations will arise for expressing time relationships; such con-

[18] Simeon Potter, *Language in the Modern World*, Penguin Books, Inc., Baltimore, 1966, p. 78.

nectives as *when, since, before,* and *after* will be found useful. Other situations will provide opportunities to use words expressing causal relationships, such as *because, since, inasmuch as;* and words expressing conditions and concession, as *though, even if.*

Emphasis is on choice of words in lower grades. Later, such terms as *modifier, adjective, clause, dependent clause,* and *connective* appear in the course of discussion as convenient labels for ideas. Occasions will arise at the secondary level when it will be necessary to point out that in the matter of agreement, English verbs rarely change form to agree with subjects; that the forming of plurals of nouns is accomplished by adding *s* or *es* to the singular, but that verbs drop the *s* in forming the plural; that the use of pronouns for nouns provides economy of expression and avoids the monotony of repetition; that pronouns have special forms for showing possession without using the apostrophe; and that certain verbs need auxiliaries to express variations in time, such as *gone, seen, done, begun.*

Contributions of linguistics During the decade 1950–1960, certain linguistic specialists sought to provide a structure for programs in the teaching of English that would overcome the inadequacies of the traditional grammar, "drilling on the eight parts of speech." Two particular approaches—the structural approach and the more recent transformational-generative approach—are recognized as present forces in shaping this portion of the language arts curriculum.[19]

Dr. Charles C. Fries is one who has been identified with the structural approach to teaching English. In his book, *The Structure of English,* he states that "the grammar of a language consists of the devices that signal structural meaning." [20] He classifies four parts of speech among the words with lexical meaning, designated class 1, class 2, class 3, and class 4, and further differentiates 154 function words. Describing "parts of speech" as functioning patterns, he identifies the four classes of present-day English by various examples: [21]

[19] For further study of the contributions of linguists, see Harold G. Shane, *Linguistics and the Classroom Teacher: Some Implications for Instruction in the Mother Tongue,* Association for Supervision and Curriculum Development, National Education Association, Washington, D.C., 1967.

[20] Charles C. Fries, *The Structure of English,* Harcourt, Brace & World, Inc., New York, 1952, p. 56. Quoted with special permission of author and publisher.

[21] *Ibid.,* pp. 65–85.

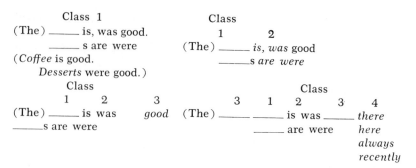

Function words are identified as words not included in these four classes.[22] Noam Chomsky, associated with the transformational-generative approach, describes this grammar as "a device that will generate all of the grammatical sequences of a language and none of the ungrammatical ones."[23] Working from the "kernel sentence" (sentences that are simple, active, and declarative), all other sentences are built by transformations, by introducing new elements (for example, adjectives) into the kernel sentence, or by rearranging the kernel (for example, developing passive, negative or interrogative sentences).[24] Kernel sentences are composed of a noun phrase and a verb phrase:

> Bill throws the ball.
> The dog chases the cat.
> The girl had lost the doll.

Numerous transforms of these kernel sentences are possible, among which could be:

> The ball was thrown by Bill.
> The dog doesn't chase the cat.
> Had the girl lost the ball?

In discussing this approach, Roberts says:

> Obviously, what we learn when we learn English is not a set of sentences but a sentence making machine. We learn a mechanism for generating sentences according to the requirements of the circumstances through which we move, and for understanding such sentences—the grammar of English (or of any language) is now thought to be viewed as a small set of sentences, called kernel sentences, plus a set of rules for transforming these into more complicated structures. Given a finite set of kernel sentence structures plus a finite set of transformational rules, we

[22] *Ibid.*, p. 88.

[23] Noam Chomsky, *Syntactic Structures*, Mouton and Company, The Hague, 1957, p. 13.

[24] Owen Thomas, "Generative Grammar: Toward Unification and Simplification," *English Journal*, vol. 51, February, 1962, pp. 94–99.

can generate infinitely many sentences, including infinitely many never produced before.[25]

Although space prohibits the outlining of the sequences of learning desired by the various proponents of the structural and transformational-generative approaches, the reader is advised of textbook series that have been developed for the elementary, junior, and senior high schools.[26]

Evaluation

In the teaching of usage, learning language through experience predominates. As with the development of vocabulary and sentence sense, the teacher listens and records. Assisting children in learning their own *hard spots*, the teacher helps them to set up record systems to appraise progress toward realistic goals. In work on syntax, children and teacher work to create sentences that most adequately express the desired meaning. The discovery approach to the structure of language is the focal point of the modern language program.

For your consideration

1   If possible, tape the spontaneous conversations of several children of different ages. Note specific language usages.
2   Examine samples of children's written work at any grade level and note difficulties of expression.
3   Suggest lines of attack on the difficulties found in 1 and 2.
4   Analyze several language textbooks, noting the various usage exercises given. Use the index of the book to guide your analysis.
5   Try to recall your experiences in elementary and secondary school in learning the terminology of technical grammar and the structure of sentences. What do you remember about learn-

[25] Paul Roberts and Mary M. Ross, *Supplementary Manual—Transformational Grammar: Background for Teachers* (Roberts English Series), Harcourt, Brace & World, Inc., New York, 1966, pp. v–vi. Quoted with special permission of author and publisher. See also Paul Roberts, *English Sentences*, Harcourt, Brace & World, Inc., New York, 1964.

[26] H. Postman and others, *New English Series*, Holt, Rinehart and Winston, Inc., New York; D. Conlin and G. Herman, *Modern Grammar and Composition Series*, American Book Company, New York; and P. Roberts, *Roberts English Series: A Linguistic Program*, Holt, Rinehart and Winston, Inc., New York.

ing the parts of speech? When did this work begin? Did you
have specific practice in diagraming sentences?

References

ALLEN, H. B.: *Readings in Applied Linguistics,* Appleton-Century-Crofts, Inc.,
New York, 1964, chaps. 36–44.

CHOMSKY, NOAM: *Syntactic Structures,* Mouton and Company, The Hague,
1957.

DAWSON, MILDRED A., M. ZOLLINGER, AND A. ELWELL: *Guiding Language
Learning,* Harcourt, Brace & World, Inc., New York, 1963, chaps. 1 and
20.

DREWES, RUTH H., AND OTHERS: *Practical Plans for Teaching English in Elementary Schools,* W. C. Brown Company, Publishers, Dubuque, Iowa,
1965, chaps. 17–18.

EVERTS, E. L.: "Linguistics and the Elementary Teacher," *The Instructor,* vol.
76, December, 1966, pp. 21 and 108.

FRANCES, W. N.: *The English Language: An Introduction,* W. W. Norton and
Company, Inc., New York, 1965, chap. 6.

GLEASON, H. A.: *Linguistics and English Grammar,* Holt, Rinehart and Winston, Inc., New York, 1965.

GOLDSTEIN, M. B.: *The Teaching of Language in Our Schools,* The Macmillan
Company, New York, 1966.

GREENE, H. A., AND W. T. PETTY: *Developing Language Skills in Elementary
Schools,* Allyn and Bacon, Inc., Boston, 1965, chap. 12.

GUTH, H. P.: *English Today and Tomorrow,* Prentice-Hall, Inc., Englewood
Cliffs, N.J., 1964, chap. 1.

HODGES, R. E.: "Linguistics, Psychology, and the Teaching of English," *Elementary School Journal,* vol. 66, January, 1966, pp. 208–213.

HUNT, KELLOGG: *Grammatical Structures Written at Three Grade Levels,* National Council of Teachers of English, Champaign, Ill., 1965.

JEWETT, ARNO, AND OTHERS: *Improving English Skills of Culturally Different
Youth in Large Cities,* U.S. Office of Education, Washington, D.C., 1964,
pp. 35–82.

LAMB, POSE, AND OTHERS: *Guiding Children's Language Learning,* W. C. Brown
Company, Publishers, Dubuque, Iowa, 1967, chap. 9.

MAC CAMPBELL, J. C., AND OTHERS: *Readings in the Language Arts in the Elementary School,* D. C. Heath and Company, Boston, 1964, pp. 200–229.

MARCKWARDT, ALBERT H.: *Linguistics and the Teaching of English,* Indiana
University Press, Bloomington, Ind., 1966, chap. 2.

MAY, FRANK B.: *Teaching Language as Communication to Children,* Charles E.
Merrill Books, Inc., Columbus, Ohio, 1967, part 2.

NATIONAL COUNCIL OF TEACHERS OF ENGLISH: *The English Language Arts,*
Appleton-Century-Crofts, Inc., New York, 1952, chap. 12.

———: *Language Programs for the Disadvantaged,* Champaign, Ill., 1965, pp.
216–220.

PETTY, WALTER T.: *The Language Arts in Elementary Schools,* The Center for
Applied Research in Education, Inc., Washington, D.C., 1962, chap. 5.

ROBERTS, PAUL: *Patterns in English*, Harcourt, Brace & World, Inc., New York, 1956.

SHANE, HAROLD G., AND OTHERS: *Improving Language Arts Instruction in the Elementary School*, Charles E. Merrill Books, Inc., Columbus, Ohio, 1962, chap. 7.

STANLEY, J. C., AND OTHERS: *Measurement in Today's Schools*, Prentice-Hall, Inc., Englewood Cliffs, N.J., 1964, chap. 7.

STRICKLAND, RUTH G.: "The Contribution of Structural Linguistics to the Teaching of Reading, Writing, and Grammar in the Elementary School," *Bulletin of the School of Education*, Indiana University, Bloomington, Ind., 1964.

———: "Teaching of Grammar," *National Elementary Principal*, vol. 45, November, 1965, pp. 58–62.

15.

FORM
AND
MECHANICS
IN
WRITTEN
WORK

Form and mechanics in written work include capitalization, punctuation, arrangement of work on a page (manuscript form), and neatness. They are specific skills, closely related to speaking and thinking but governed by conventions and rules. They can be taught mechanically or meaningfully. When the skills are taught mechanically, they are identified, presented as isolated elements, and learned by rule and by practice in formal exercises. In meaningful teaching, on the other hand, the skills are developed in close association with the language activities of which they are a necessary part. The significance of and reason for the various conventions in clarifying meaning are made apparent to the learner. Practice may be required to establish habits, but the practice follows meaningful development and has an immediate, recognizable purpose.

Form and mechanics frame the thought and make the meaning clear. For example, sentence division, indicated by capital and period, shows the separation of ideas into thoughts; the nature of the thought is indicated by the final mark: period, question mark, or exclamation point. The colon indicates a series to follow; the comma indicates sentence elements out of their usual order, separates interrupters to the main thought, and makes clear the members of an enumeration. Proper handling of the learning of mechanics is an aid, not a block, to thinking and expression.

Specific skills   The form and mechanics skills to be included in the language program are obviously those that are needed by children in their language experiences. Needs will vary with age, grade, maturity, cultural background, and type of language program in the school. Manuscript form includes margins at the left-hand and right-hand sides of the paper, spacing at top and bottom, indention of paragraphs, and correct placing of titles and dates. Common uses of capitals are in the first words of sentences, lines of poetry, direct quotations, and titles; in names of particular persons and places; in the word *I;* and in topics in an outline and important words in titles. Neatness in written work relates to cleanliness, corrections, and handwriting. The chief punctuation marks and their uses are as follows:

Periods:
After statements and most commands
After an initial
After a common abbreviation
After letters and numerals in outlining

Question marks:
After questions

Exclamation points:
At the end of any group of words that expresses strong feeling

Commas:
Between day and month of year
Between city and state
After the salutation and complimentary close of a friendly letter
To separate words in a series
To set off direct quotations
After expressions or clauses of introduction
Between parts of a compound sentence
Before and after appositives
Before and after parenthetical terms

Quotation marks:
Around direct quotations
Around titles of articles

Hyphens:
After part of a word divided at the end of a line within compound
    terms

Apostrophes:
Within contractions
Within possessives

Colons:
After salutations in business letters
Before a long series
To separate the hour from the minutes

Semicolons:
To replace a comma and conjunction in separating two ideas of
   a compound sentence

It will be well for the teacher to note the common difficulties
of his pupils. Among them he may find many of the difficulties reported by McKee:

1   Omitting the period at the close of a sentence
2   Using a comma in place of a period at the close of a sentence
3   Omitting the apostrophe in the possessive
4   Omitting the quotation marks surrounding direct quotation
5   Using a period for a comma in sentences
6   Omitting a question mark at the end of a question
7   Failing to use a comma to set off words of direct address
8   Failure to use a comma in a date
9   Omission of a comma to separate a series
10 Omission of comma after introductory expressions such as
    "Yes" or "No" [1]

Following is a fourth grader's description of a model, good in
content but weak in mechanics:

> We want to show how the Indians of California live.
> I made the house it is made of grass and sawdust the real house are
> made out of tules and wild hemp plants and milk weed plants and other
> plants.
> They used the house for sleping and storying food and for cooking.
> We made the trees out of brown paper and pipe cleaners.
> We made the lake out of colored sponges we made the back gron out
> of blue pant and chalk and wite pant also.

Emphasis in particular grades   The teacher faces the practical
problem of setting up goals in mechanics for a particular class.
Practical assistance is offered by textbooks and courses of study.
These are designed to meet general needs in a school system or an
even larger area, and serve only as a guide to the teacher. However,
since classes within a single city vary widely in language maturity
and needs, the teacher should make a study of the language ex-

[1] Paul McKee, *Language in the Elementary School*, Houghton Mifflin
Company, Boston, 1939, p. 322. Quoted with special permission of the pub-
lisher. See also Paul S. Anderson and others, *Language Skills in Elementary
Education*, The Macmillan Company, New York, 1966, pp. 399–401.

periences and skills of his pupils and set up goals in terms of specific needs.

Determining class needs is only half the job. It is necessary to consider the level of language maturity and needs of each pupil and to provide a varied program sufficiently flexible to promote desired growth in all.

In studying the needs of individual pupils it is desirable for the teacher to recognize the stages of language development through which children normally pass. This understanding aids the teacher to determine the sequence of and proper emphasis on the several items. Typical handling of sequence in various phases of the language problem—particular experiences, general abilities, and specific skills—may be found in Chapter 18. Any detailed course of study or analysis of contents of a textbook series provides the same information.

Readiness for writing   Preparation for writing is made in oral language and in reading before children actually begin to write. Writing is closely related to speaking, not only in such items as content, organization of ideas, and vocabulary, but also in the use of pauses, the juncture, and the intonation of the voice to show the division and the relationship of ideas. Thus, in speech the intonation of the voice shows whether one is making a statement, asking a question, or expressing strong feeling; long pauses indicate complete breaks in sentences, and short ones indicate the grouping of related words into phrases within the sentence; direct discourse is indicated by the inflection of the voice. In oral reading also the child learns to bring out meaning by the use of the context and his oral speech background; he identifies and learns to use punctuation marks as clues to what to do with his voice. The skills of speaking and oral reading are not learned mechanically, of course, but in connection with the expression of ideas. When the child begins to write, he is recording his thoughts in written symbols; and in using punctuation, he indicates certain elements of the ways he uses his voice. In discussing the "conventions" of punctuation, capitalization, and word division, linguists such as Gleason caution that these conventions do not provide the identical clues that are provided by the intonation signals of spoken language.[2]

A carefully developed program in speaking and oral reading helps to lay a foundation for the meaningful learning of written mechanics. Further, Gleason suggests that the teaching of com-

[2] H. A. Gleason, *Linguistics and English Grammar*, Holt, Rinehart and Winston, Inc., New York, 1965, pp. 182–186.

position must involve helping students to become increasingly aware of the differences in the basic functioning of the structure signals of oral and written language.[3]

Mechanics in language experiences The primary approach to teaching the mechanics of written work is made in purposeful experiences. In the first grade the child has occasion to sign his name to papers, to write labels and headings, and to help compose class records and charts. In these experiences he learns to use capital letters in writing certain words, to put the salutation of a note at the proper place on the page, to indent, to begin sentences with capitals, and to close them with periods or question marks. In class compositions, written on the board at the dictation of the children, the teacher is careful to use proper forms and to call the children's attention to them. New mechanics are introduced as needs arise in communication experiences. In time, children begin to write compositions of several sentences, social and business letters, outlines, bibliographies, and the like. Each new experience provides an opportunity for the introduction of new mechanics, as well as for the continued use of the old. Experiences serve to give meaning to mechanics and to provide motivation for learning them.

Problems arise with the precocious child whose language development far surpasses that of the body of the class and whose creative efforts demand mature mechanics for which he and the class are not ready. The power of oral expression of the imaginative child so far exceeds his command of written mechanics that he has difficulty putting his thoughts on paper. The following is by Dorothy, an eight-year-old third-grade child, who voluntarily wrote this continued story of seven paragraphs:

A MERRY CHRISTMAS

"Merry Christmas, everybody, Merry Christmas" shouted Janet Christmas morning.

Cousin David from Washington was with her for Christmas, so they ran down stairs together. "I've got a game" "Here's some iceskates," "A dress for my doll," "An electric train.

These were only a few of the many cris that arose. But at last Janet fell over something near the back of the tree, it had a card on it that said "Janet." She tore the thin peice of paper that was over it and screamed. "A desk, a great big desk" "A what" asked David because Janet was making so much noice jumping up and down that he couldn't hear what she said.

---

[3] *Ibid.*, p. 172.

At last the two succeeded in getting it out, and Janet at once started to put things on it in a very untidy fashion.

"Children, Children this will never do!" said Mother when she came down, (as she put her hands over her ears,) "You soud like a cyclone." It was pretty hard for her to get the children dressed and have them eat their breakfast, But they were soon ready to go to Grandmother's, the idia of chicken pie and turkey struck them.

At Grandmother's they played many games. But at last came the time for that dinner. David acted as if he liked Grandmother's dinner's.

After awhile Grandmother brought out the toys of her own children for her grandchildren. The girls liked to help with the dishes, but the boy's liked the book's about trips the moon and such thing's. they were sorry that they couldent read them all right away.

But it was a very merry Christmas.

What should the teacher do with this child? Should he require Dorothy to confine her expression within the limits of manageable mechanics or allow her freedom of expression? If the latter, some compromise must be made with mechanics. The authors advise the teacher to let the child express herself freely, to give her such individual help as time allows by supplying needed mechanics, to value the freshness, vividness, originality of expression, and to avoid trying to make the composition mechanically perfect. Mechanics are subordinate to freedom of expression.

Class development lessons It is generally agreed that new mechanics should be approached through purposeful experiences in which they are needed for the clear expression of ideas; in common practice this is a simultaneous, whole-class approach. The new skill must be highlighted in some manner, either as an incidental part of the writing experience or in a special developmental lesson. The choice of procedure will reflect the teacher's philosophy and his judgment of the abilities of the particular class. In the incidental treatment, the teacher (1) calls attention to the need for the new device by emphasizing the relation to clarity of expression, (2) sets models or directs attention to models in the textbook, (3) helps children develop a generalization, and (4) possibly provides a brief practice in the form of original composition or exercises in the textbook. The teacher does not take much time for specific instruction, relying largely on the high motivation of the situation to gain vividness of impression. The children are allowed to begin writing soon, and of course the written work is checked. The account below concerns a language experience growing out of a real situation:

When a moth hatched in a third-grade room, the children

wanted to invite other classes to see it. The following notice was dictated to the teacher, who wrote it on the board. It was copied and sent to two rooms.

Would you care to come to Room 15 to see our Promethea moth? It came out early this morning. If it is convenient you might come between 11 and 11:20 A.M.

Room 15

In the afternoon it was suggested that some first-grade children might like to see the moth. Rather than take time to write another note, Mary was dispatched with an oral announcement of the moth's arrival and an invitation to see it. The first-grade children were greatly interested and expressed a desire for a cocoon of their own. The next morning one of the third-grade children suggested that, since they had two more cocoons, they might share them with the first grade. This was unanimously agreed on, and Frank was sent across the hall with a cocoon and a note:

Dear Boys and Girls,
    We heard that you wanted a cocoon and so we will share with you. Here is a Polyphemus for your room. When it hatches may we see it?
    We hope that you will enjoy it.

Sincerely
Room 15

In the afternoon a messenger arrived with a thank-you note from the first grade:

Dear Boys and Girls,
    Thank you for the cocoon. We will watch it. When the Polyphemus comes out, we would like you to see it.

Room 18

To some people it might seem that too much time had been given to note writing and that a very simple and relatively unimportant occurrence had been overworked. To the children, however, the hatching of their moth was the prime interest of the moment; one child described it as a miracle. They were anxious to share the experience with other children. True, the invitations and presentation could have been given by word of mouth, but in this case only one child, the messenger, would have benefited by the experience.

All through life there are repeated occasions for the writing of thank-you notes and invitations. How many adults procrastinate in these little courtesies simply because they are not quite sure of what to say or of the correct form. It would seem, then, that the earlier the training and the more abundant the experience, the better equipped these children will be for adult responsibilities in such matters.

In the longer developmental lessons, the need is recognized in the purposeful experience, and this need sets off a more or less elaborate series of training exercises. The first three steps are similar to those in the incidental treatment outlined above: calling attention to the need for the new device and its relation to clarity of expression; setting live models or directing attention to models in the textbook; and deriving from the study of models some basic understandings and principles. Following these steps, practice work is provided in the form of workout examples, recognition exercises, proofreading exercises, dictation, and copying. The following is a study-dictation exercise, which can be followed up by proof-reading: [4]

> Study the punctuation and capitalization in the conversation below. Then close your books and write the conversation correctly as your teacher dictates it to you:
>> Bill asked, "Why is there no such thing as a whole day?"
>> "Every morning, day breaks," answered Mary.

A third, very systematic plan used by some teachers for establishing mechanical skills consists of (1) copy work, (2) studied dictation, (3) unstudied dictation, (4) the unfinished story, and (5) independent writing. This series of graded steps is brought into use after specific needs have been revealed and may be related to an immediate activity, such as the preparation of a language booklet. Copy work is preceded by directed study of the elements of manuscript form, punctuation, sentences, and spelling. Pupils are advised to write a phrase at a time rather than a word or letter at a time. A high degree of accuracy is required. In dictation work, the teacher reads the whole paragraph while the children listen closely, and then he rereads the selection phrase by phrase. Unstudied dictation follows. No previous preparation is given, although difficult words may be written on the board. The selections used are brief, with simple spelling and sentence structure. The unfinished-story stage provides some control of content and mechanics but introduces a measure of freedom. Independent writing involves the free use of mechanics, although naturally the compositions are checked for items under immediate study.

[4] Mildred A. Dawson and Jonnie M. Miller, *Language for Daily Use*, Book 5, Harcourt, Brace & World, Inc., New York, 1964, p. 149. Quoted with special permission.

Making mechanics meaningful   Either in the incidental handling
or in the more systematic treatment of the developmental lesson,
the teacher will adopt measures to make mechanics meaningful
to the child. Mechanics take on new significance as the child's
thinking and demands for expression become more complex. Opportunities arise for developing the desired understanding of the
importance of mechanics in connection with the children's composition work. The handling of the comma serves as an illustration
of meaningful procedures in the excellent treatment of this topic
several decades ago by Nila B. Smith: [5]

> Apart from the heading of letters, in which the comma usually indicates
> an omission, and such independent expressions as *yes* or *no* and the
> name of the person spoken to in conversation, commas are used to clarify
> meaning when sentence elements are out of their usual order, to separate
> interrupters from the main idea, and to make clear the members of an
> enumeration. It is obvious that after end-of-sentence punctuation, the
> the simple uses of the comma in dates and addresses, with *yes* and *no*,
> and with the name of the person spoken to in conversation will come first
> in the child's experience. The teacher, writing at the children's dic-
> tation, uses commas in these ways, explaining their usefulness as
> the pupils read back to her what she has written. From the be-
> ginning the purpose of punctuation is to help interpret meaning.
> Gradually, the child has occasion to enumerate: *Mary, John, and Henry
> came to our party. We had popcorn, cookies, and lemonade for refresh-
> ments.* Later he will be more ambitious in his enumerations. *We wrote
> the play, made the scenery, and acted the parts for our visitors.* In the
> upper grades he is using more formal enumerations still: *We have
> studied Mexico from three points of view: its geographical setting, its
> products and business enterprises, and its social customs and arts.*
>   Interruptions follow the same pattern of gradually maturing with
> thinking:
>
>> John, my cousin, came to our house for Christmas.
>> The gauchos, having been driven out, roamed the broad fields
>> to the south.
>> My Uncle Bill, who is in the Navy Air Corps, has been around
>> the world three times.
>> My Aunt Caroline, since she went to New Mexico, has sent us
>> some colorful Indian beadwork.
>
>   In each case the purpose is to keep the main idea clear—what we are
> talking about and what we are saying about it—by setting off the inter-
> rupters. The two commas act as hooks by means of which to lift out
> whatever interrupts the main thought. It is interesting to note that the
> punctuation bears no relationship to the particular grammatical con-

[5] M. R. Trabue and others, *Teaching Language in the Elementary School*,
Forty-third Yearbook, National Society for the Study of Education, University
of Chicago Press, Chicago, 1944, part 2, pp. 89–90. Quoted with special permission of the publisher.

struction of the interrupter. It is the *fact of interruption* that creates the need for the commas.

When children grow in power to vary the order of elements in their sentences, they find increasing need for punctuation.

When we were eating, Spot sniffed around our feet.

There is danger of eating Spot if the comma is omitted. Similar problems arise in such sentences as the following:

By the way, I wore the costume you had when you were a clown.

Racing like a mad dog, around the corner bolted Jack.

As children mature in their ability to sense the effect of connectives, they learn the importance of the comma to make the meaning clear:

We went disguised, as Mrs. Broderick asked us to.

We met Bill and Jack at the corner, and Mary got on further down the street.

We had hoped to reach the gate to Yellowstone by night, but the flat tire made it impossible.

Growth in ability to punctuate cannot outrun the child's grasp of meaning. For example, time and again teachers labor to explain the formation of the possessive case with the apostrophe, only to find their instructions carefully followed when no possession is indicated by the meaning.

The boys' raced to town.

The light gleaming on the houses' shone in our eyes.

Meaning, *the fact of possession*, must be established first.

With these examples as a guide the teacher may be able to devise procedures for other items of form and mechanics.

Discovering pupils' difficulties   The developmental work incident to the introduction of a new item of form or mechanics will be adequate to serve the needs of some, perhaps many, pupils of the class; but it cannot be assumed that no further attention needs to be given to items once introduced. There is abundant evidence of the persistence of common errors. Growth in control of the mechanics of written work is a gradual process and one in which individuals vary widely. A systematic program of discovering and dealing with pupils' difficulties is necessary. The first step in such a program is discovering these difficulties.

In looking for weaknesses to be corrected, the teacher naturally concentrates on those elements of form and mechanics appropriate to his grade and class, including of necessity those items that have been taken up in preceding grades. A list of these items should be prepared and used as a checklist to record individual competencies and deficiencies. The form is the familiar class record sheet.

To determine pupils' difficulties, the teacher analyzes samples of children's work from time to time, notes errors when giving individual help, and possibly gives diagnostic tests. Tests may take a variety of forms, such as dictation exercises and proofreading exercises. They should include the specific items for which the class may be held responsible. Teacher-made tests are most likely to be adapted to the needs of the class; next in order are the tests found in textbooks; and finally, there are carefully chosen standard tests. One type of test is a letter that covers many skills, including capitals and punctuation marks. The children rewrite it. It is advisable for the teacher to keep a record of pupils' difficulties.[6]

Organization for remedial instruction It is a well-established principle that one of the most effective types of drill is corrective work applied at the point of error. This means simply that the pupils who need drill get it. The class record sheet shows the teacher the kind of corrective work needed by each pupil. Each pupil, also, should have a record of his own competencies and deficiencies. Students needing the same type of corrective work are brought together for work on a particular difficulty; the class is regrouped for each specific difficulty. The necessary instruction, including oral instruction by the teacher and study of textbook material, is given; and practice exercises are assigned. Soon after the completion of a given amount of practice work, a test may be given or compositions checked to see whether the difficulty has been corrected. Records of progress are kept by the teacher on the class record chart and by the pupil on his own goal sheet. This procedure in itself provides a powerful incentive for corrective work.

Procedures in remedial instruction Generally, procedures in remedial instruction follow the steps used in developmental lessons, as outlined above. It should be emphasized that the child with a mechanical difficulty frequently needs instruction, not only practice. The assignment of practice exercises often fails to get at the root of the difficulty, a faulty comprehension of the basic principle of usage.

In the reteaching, attention should be given to the right and

[6] H. A. Greene and W. T. Petty, *Developing Language Skills in the Elementary Schools,* Allyn and Bacon, Inc., Boston, 1967, pp. 210–218.

wrong forms; the contrast between the ambiguity or confusion resulting from the wrong form and the clarity of the right one demonstrates the reason for the latter. Examples of the right form are to be clearly and vividly presented, and of course practice must be provided.

Practice exercises may involve (1) choice of construction, where several forms are given and the child chooses and sometimes writes the best; (2) proofreading of prepared material, in which corrections are made or copied in correct form; (3) writing from dictation; and (4) original writing, in which designated forms are used.

EXAMPLE OF A PRACTICE LESSON, UPPER GRADE

Situation   *In a social studies lesson the national parks of California were discussed. Possibilities of obtaining pictures and pamphlets of the parks were discussed also, and important names were written on the board. The class was divided into groups, each of which had selected a particular park about which material was to be procured. In a preceding lesson, first drafts of the letters were written.*

Lesson   *Correction of the first drafts of letters; rewriting of letters.*
Objective   *To review use of capitals.*
Procedures

1. "Today we are making the final drafts of letters. In going over the first drafts I found some mistakes. A large proportion of the mistakes were individual ones and can be corrected individually. There was one kind of mistake, however, that was rather general—the use of capital letters. We should have special preparation to correct these mistakes on our first drafts."

2. "I shall pass out some work sheets that will help us. Notice that the work sheet has some examples of the use of capital letters. The examples show the common mistakes that were made; they are the uses of the capitals that we have discussed this year. First, study the examples, and if there are any questions I will help you. When you receive the first draft of your letter, check to see that you have capitalized words correctly. Please put this work sheet in your style book, when you have finished using it." The work sheets are distributed; discussion follows study.

Capitalization Helps—Work Sheet

A. *Names of special places*
   I am interested in learning more about Sequoia National Park.
   We are studying parks in California.
Why is the word *park* capitalized in the first sentence?
Why is the word *parks* not capitalized in the second sentence?
B. *Book titles*
   We have used such books as *Our Country's National Parks*, by Irving R. Melbo in our study.

> I liked the book, *National Parks: A Guide to the National Parks and Monuments in the United States*, by Paul Jensen.

Why are all the words capitalized in the first book title?

Why are some of the words in the second book title not capitalized?

C. *People's titles*

> I would like to know what kind of work the Park Ranger does.

> We have talked about the work that the Ranger Naturalist does.

Why are the words *Park Ranger* and *Ranger Naturalist* capitalized?

> Why did you capitalize the word *Superintendent* when you addressed your envelope?

3. "First drafts of letters will be returned together with clean sheets of paper. Before beginning new drafts, correct errors in your first drafts. If you do not know how to correct them, let me help you. Look for other errors. Be reasonably sure you are prepared to make a perfect copy before making the final copy. If in doubt, ask for help."

4. "When you have finished your new draft, look it over for mistakes. Correct them. Ask questions if in doubt."

5. "Fold letters per directions; address envelopes or practice addressing on slips of paper."

6. Letters are collected according to park groups.

7. Selected letters are revised and checked by groups acting as committees.

8. The children file copies of their letters in their individual log of the social studies unit.

Evaluation   *In the group discussion about capitalization, the teacher notes the responses. By checking the work during the rewriting period, individual progress in all areas of proofreading can be noted. Anecdotal notes made by the teacher or the use of a check sheet facilitate planning for future group and individual work in punctuation, capitalization, form.*

Textbooks and workbooks A casual examination of language textbooks will show that they are not designed for the individualized grouping procedures which authorities assert must be used in the effective handling of the mechanics of writing, particularly in the remedial phases. They are planned for a whole-class procedure, with occasional extra work for the more capable children and some extra practice exercises for the slow learners. To carry on a thoroughgoing type of group or individual work the teacher must adapt the material at hand and possibly provide supplementary material. Kinds of material needed are instructional, that is, practice exercises and explanations and examples of the form of new mechanics. The most readily available material is found in textbooks. The teacher should prepare an analysis of the material in the text, listing by topics—such as the use of the comma in a series—those pages on which instructions, study examples, and practice exercises are provided. It is possible, of course, that the textbook provides a sufficiently detailed index, but the teacher may wish to cross-reference exercises and note single exercises in which several skills are practiced simultaneously. The complete index, covering all essential mechanics, may be inserted in the textbooks or placed in a language notebook for reference. The teacher may prepare separate work sheets for each skill, listing material from the class textbook and from other sources—supplementary texts, workbooks, and teacher-made exercises—on a single sheet. These can be passed out by the teacher in making assignments, or the children can secure them from a convenient filing cabinet at the teacher's direction.

A source of material outside the regular text is found in workbooks and in supplementary textbooks. This material could be indexed and handled in the same way as the class textbook material. Supplementary material should be selected carefully; much of it is not usable.

It would be decidedly helpful, also, if the teacher were to prepare check-out tests for each topic or for a group of related topics. These tests can be duplicated and conveniently filed.

Material of the types described above requires time-consuming preparation, but it is essential in any corrective individual-group work that is to be corrective. However, the material is relatively permanent and may be accumulated gradually.

Handling errors in written work   One important topic remains to round out a program for teaching form and mechanics: the handling of errors in written work, or proofreading. Experts agree that the only correction that has any considerable value is self-correction. It is assumed that in the development phases of a new topic the child acquires definite ideas of correct form; models are studied, examples prepared from original work, and principles and rules noted. The child acquires clear ideas of form and uses correct form in practice exercises. Yet in the absorption of original composition lapses occur. These may be due to carelessness or to faulty learning in either the understanding or the practice stage. If errors are due to faulty understanding, the teacher may make note of the fact and set up a separate corrective lesson; if they are due to carelessness or to imperfect mastery, the errors may be corrected incidentally.

Following are samples of a fourth grader's work before and after self-correction:

> In are mural we are showing the Indian huts witch the Indian use for sleeping and storage. I an showing them cooking meat over the fire. A woman is getting water fron the river.

> In our mural we are showing the Indian huts, which the Indians used for sleeping and storage. I am showing a woman cooking meat over the fire. Another woman is getting water from the river.

Proofreading of original compositions should become a well-established habit. Emphasis in the first draft of a composition should be on content, organization of ideas, vividness, and fluency. Research shows that better compositions are produced in this way. Thought is primarily important; but form is important too as a means of observing the conventions and saying just what one wants to say. The composition should be checked, edited, and revised. Chance errors may become habitual if neglected.

As aids to the children in proofreading their own compositions, the teacher may well set up a set of standards, models, or style sheets. Children need such specific aids. The procedure recommended by Pooley for use in the high school is applicable with modification in lower grades. He says: [7]

> A carefully worked out technique of proof-reading can do a great deal to improve standards of written work and correctness in composition. For some reason it is very difficult to get students to reread their own work with a critical and corrective eye. The best procedure is one which is worked out with the group as a whole. When a set of compositions is ready to be handed in, the teacher should follow an accepted procedure of proof-reading. The first step is to check the title of the paper, to make sure that it is correctly placed on the paper, has capital letters where capital letters are required, and that it is correctly punctuated. The next step is to scan the paper for paragraph form. Each paragraph should be properly indented; the first sentence in the paragraph should naturally begin with a capital letter; and there should be some kind of break in the composition to show the changes of thought. The next stage is to check the whole paper for accuracy in spelling and then for accuracy in word usage. Pupils that are dubious of the acceptability of certain phrases, or are unsure of the idiom they have employed should ask help of the teacher before handing the paper in. In some cases it may be advisable to have the papers read over by a fellow-student after the writer has made his corrections as a kind of double check on accuracy. This proof-reading if followed without fail at the time each paper is to be handed in will have a vigorous effect, first in getting pupils to give their own papers a correction before they are handed in and an attitude of respect for correctness and accuracy in all work.

One of the most effective aids to self-correction is the class correction of common errors. The teacher must make a preliminary examination of the compositions or observe difficulties as he supervises the pupils during their writing. Sentences illustrative of common errors are written on the board, and class criticism and correction are invited. After the common errors are treated in this way, the children turn to their own compositions. The teacher naturally helps with individual difficulties.

[7] R. C. Pooley, *Teaching English Usage*, Appleton-Century-Crofts, Inc., New York, 1946, pp. 232–233. Quoted with special permission of the publisher.

If the teacher still feels some compulsion to red-ink children's compositions, he may simply indicate the place where an error occurs, leaving to the child the burden of making the correction.

Recopying probably has little value as a learning exercise. It is usually done mechanically, without thinking. The same amount of time is more profitably spent on original writing. Of course, recopying is justifiable if it has a purpose, such as the preparation of an important letter for mailing.

It is possible that a child plagued with particular types of errors might find a personal stylebook useful.

Evaluation   The major outcomes desired in work in form and mechanics are the attitudes that children gradually develop toward the written product. Whether the product is a story, report, newspaper article, or letter, the major objective is the growing recognition that one's written work very frequently is meant to be read by others. Through the skills of manuscript form and the conventions of punctuation, provisions are made by which written thoughts can be more easily received by others. As the teacher introduces these items, provides examples to dramatize their necessity, and helps children evaluate their progress, the keynote is the development of children's independence in writing through the concept of proofreading. The child's self-awareness through self-checks, individual and group activities to develop needed skills, models and style sheet referents can be steps in the development of self-reliance in the use of the conventions through which the major components of writing are facilitated.

For your consideration

1   Examine several samples of children's written work and evaluate in terms of thought and mechanics. In what ways might improved mechanics enhance the expression of ideas?

2   Using the above samples of work, note the manuscript form and the quality of neatness. Analyze your own attitudes toward the clean and precise and the less neat papers. Do these qualities unduly influence your attitudes toward the content and thought of each paper?

3   Plan a class developmental skill lesson for a new phase of work. Determine the best larger language activity—reporting, letter writing, etc.—into which your developmental skill lesson might fit.

4 Make a list of forms and mechanics that might be appropriate for a particular grade level, considering textbook, course of study, and the needs of pupils.

5 Devise an inventory that might be used as a check sheet for several of the skills you listed in 4.

6 Discuss: Capitalization and punctuation can never give the same clues to written language as voice intonation gives to oral language.

References

ANDERSON, VERNA D., AND OTHERS: *Readings in the Language Arts*, The Macmillan Company, New York, 1964, pp. 258–268.

APPLEGATE, MAUREE: *Easy in English*, Harper & Row, Publishers, Inc., New York, 1963, chap. 11.

DAWSON, MILDRED A., AND G. C. NEWMAN: *Language Teaching in Kindergarten and the Early Primary Grades*, Harcourt, Brace & World, Inc., New York, 1966, chap. 6.

DREWES, RUTH H., AND OTHERS: *Practical Plans for Teaching English in Elementary Schools*, W. C. Brown Company, Publishers, Dubuque, Iowa, 1965.

HATFIELD, W. W.: "Shortest Road to Sentence Sense," vol. 33, *Elementary English*, May, 1956, pp. 270–273.

LAMB, POSE, AND OTHERS: *Guiding Children's Language Learning*, W. C. Brown Company, Publishers, Dubuque, Iowa, 1967, chap. 6.

LYMAN, R. L.: *Summary of Investigations Relating to Grammar, Language, and Composition*, University of Chicago Press, Chicago, Ill., 1929, pp. 82–105.

NIELSEN, WILHELMINA: "Style and Form in Children's Writing," *Elementary English*, vol. 44, March, 1967, pp. 270–272, 286.

PETTY, WALTER T.: *The Language Arts in Elementary Schools*, The Center for Applied Research in Education, Inc., Washington, D.C., 1962, pp. 63–79.

STANLEY, J. C.: *Measurement in Today's Schools*, Prentice-Hall, Inc., Englewood Cliffs, N.J., 1964, chap. 7.

STRICKLAND, RUTH G.: *Guide for Teaching Language in Grades 1 and 2*, D. C. Heath and Company, Boston, 1962, chap. 5.

WOLFE, DON M.: *Language Arts and Life Patterns*, The Odyssey Press, Inc., New York, 1961, chap. 11, pp. 153–167.

16.

SPELLING

Current spelling programs Spelling programs in various schools may range from the extremely informal (in which spelling is incidental to writing and study lists are entirely individualized, made up of words actually needed in pupils' immediate writing activities) to the formal (in which definite lists of words are set up for a class, and all pupils work on a common list). Largely because of the limited amount of actual writing done in the modern school, the entirely incidental handling of spelling would not be defended or used except by the uncompromising idealist; it is generally agreed that the achievement of a desired competency requires that special attention be given to spelling in some definite, systematic manner.[1] Between the extremely incidental, casual handling of spelling and the formal program lies one program which combines features of the incidental and the formal and for which a reasonable case may be made. Spelling in this intermediate program is largely taught in connection with functional activities and the work is largely individualized; but some time is set aside for word study beginning in the middle grades; and a minimum basic list of useful words is set up for the class. This program, which may be designated as a *func-*

[1] Carl Personke and A. H. Yee, "A Model for the Analysis of Spelling Behavior," *Elementary English,* vol. 43, March, 1966, pp. 278–284.

tional-individualized program, is consistent with the basic functional point of view in language teaching. The functional approach, in which skills are related to practical use in purposeful activities, has been maintained up to this point in this book. But a question may be raised as to its general practicability in spelling instruction. Probably the majority of teachers still use, and will continue to use for some time, a predominantly formal program. In this chapter the formal program is presented first in a consideration of the work as most teachers handle it; the functional-individualized program is taken up later in the chapter as a possibly desirable goal for master teachers. The concluding section of the chapter is devoted to a consideration of the contributions of linguistics.

One should hasten to say that the prevailing aim in all modern programs of spelling is to assist the children in writing (a functional point of view). The several programs vary in the means employed to reach this end, involving at times compromises between ideal and realistic learning conditions; but the end sought is the same.

Modern textbooks   In common practice, the program of work in spelling centers in a spelling book. The teacher should acquaint himself with the textbook, critically appraise it, and learn how to use it effectively. Modern textbooks and workbooks include all or some of the following features: (1) a basic vocabulary of words; (2) a grading of words; (3) a grouping of words into units or lessons; (4) provision for the review of hard words; (5) a cycle plan for teaching, study, and testing; (6) a plan for study; (7) study exercises; and (8) tests and possibly norms.

The basic vocabulary provided by the modern speller is likely to include the words used most commonly by children and adults in spontaneous writing, as determined by extensive investigation. Words commonly used are not numerous—about four thousand. James A. Fitzgerald, basing his conclusions largely on his own researches and those of Ernest Horn, concludes:

> Some 3000 well-chosen words and their repetitions comprise 97.6 per cent of the running words, and 4000 commonest words make up about 98.7 per cent of the running writing; the fourth thousand adds less than 1.2 per cent of the running words to be written. These data seem to warrant the assumption that the basic core of spelling words should include between 3000 and 4000, and the mastery of these should be supplemented with careful word study and word usage built upon this core.[2]

[2] J. A. Fitzgerald and P. G. Fitzgerald, *Teaching Reading and the Language Arts*, The Bruce Publishing Company, Milwaukee, Wis., 1965, p. 301.

The grading of words is based primarily on frequency of use by children in the several grades and secondarily on difficulty. Grading is more difficult than preparing total word lists, and the personal opinions of textbook writers are likely to play a more prominent part in grading. The extreme variability of individual children's writing vocabularies, a variability that increases through the grades, is a complicating factor.

Words in a particular lesson or unit may be placed there by chance, following no principle of grouping; they may be grouped according to some principle of word sound, form, or spelling difficulty; or they may be divided according to meaning (topic or context). The pattern of combinations in the textbook should be observed, since each requires adjustments in teaching. Modern practice is moving from chance arrangement to some kind of grouping as a means of facilitating learning. Words may be listed according to similar parts or according to similar spelling difficulties. The practice of grouping by form or spelling difficulty minimizes the factor of meaning and is therefore distasteful to those who take the functional point of view. The functionalists favor grouping by meaning, preferably in context and in connected paragraphs rather than in disconnected sentences. Contextual presentation presumably presents words as they are likely to be used and seems consistent with trends in language teaching.

In a modern speller, provision is made for the systematic, periodic review of words previously studied, and hard words reappear in lists with frequency proportionate to difficulty. In addition, children are encouraged and directed in keeping individual study lists.

Modern practice favors some form of testing procedure as a basis for study. This practice naturally recognizes the extreme variability in the difficulty of words and the variability of individuals in ability to spell the words of a list. The testing procedure reveals to teacher and pupils the hard words and those on which each pupil needs to concentrate. There is considerable variability in the patterns of lessons. In the test-study-test procedure, the preliminary test is a sight test; the children then study the words missed, with or without the direction of the teacher; after study, continuing through several days, the children take a checkup test. In the teach-study-test-study-test procedure, the teacher presents the new list of words to the class; the children study; the midweek test shows

Quoted with special permission of authors and publisher. See also Ernest Horn, "Spelling," *Encyclopedia of Educational Research*, The Macmillan Company, New York, 1960, pp. 1337–1354.

words learned and words needing further attention; time is allowed for further study; and finally the cycle is completed by a checkup test. There are other possible combinations of testing, studying, and teaching. A good case can be made for a test-study procedure on purely theoretical grounds. A disadvantage in the study-test procedure is the amount of time wasted in studying familiar words. The use of the test-study procedure is general in the upper grades. The results are statistically significant. The truth is that the advantages of either procedure can be magnified and the disadvantages minimized by competent teaching.[3]

Since much learning takes place in individual study, the modern text wisely includes a study procedure for the guidance of the students. The process of learning the spelling of a new word has been thoroughly investigated during years of research, and the essential steps of procedure are well formulated and standardized. They are: (1) Look at the word, pronounce it, and think of its meaning. (2) Mentally divide the word into syllables, pronounce it, and look closely at the sound and letter grouping in each syllable. (3) Close your eyes and recall the word by syllables, repeating the letters. (4) Look again to check your visual impression. (5) Write the word from memory; check. (6) Write the word several times. It will be observed that the pupil starts with the whole word—recognition, meaning, pronunciation—then proceeds to the study of parts, and finally returns to the whole word in writing. Visualization and actual writing are important parts of the process. Mature pupils may be trained to perfect the learning procedure by the process of word analysis, recognizing familiar parts and concentrating on difficult parts. Mature pupils also may be encouraged to adopt variations which they actually find helpful. It is not to be assumed that, because a study procedure is outlined in the text or casually referred to by the teacher, the pupils will use it. Pupils must be trained to study till the desired procedure becomes habitual. The approach to spelling is important, not only for the mastery of particular word lists, but also for the handling of new words in school and later life.

Textbooks, and more commonly workbooks, provide study exercises. In a carefully prepared book, these drills are designed to emphasize words confused in meaning, hard words, and difficult parts of words. These exercises should be critically examined and tried. They may be mere busywork, taking time more profitably spent otherwise, or they can be very helpful.

[3] W. T. Petty, "Handwriting and Spelling: Their Current Status," *Elementary English*, vol. 41, December, 1964, pp. 839–844.

Textbooks and workbooks may provide tests, norms, and records of progress. Each word list, usually a week's work, is the basis for week-to-week testing; and records of progress are sometimes kept, possibly in graph form. Tests and records serve as one form of motivation. The former may cover material studied over longer periods, such as six-week periods and terms. If norms are provided, it is possible to compare the achievement of one class with that of the other classes. Test results must be interpreted, of course, in terms of all known facts about the class, including aptitude and previous scholarship.

Adapting word lists   After familiarizing himself with the main provisions of the text, a teacher should proceed to the consideration of how to use the book to get the best results. The mechanical precision of the modern textbook may tempt the teacher to adopt a mechanical program of work, making assignments and testing results. This is a clear evasion of responsibility. No textbook is designed to meet the needs of all classes and of all pupils in the class; a textbook is not sufficient in itself. Authors caution that there must be much *teaching* of spelling by the teacher. One problem is adjusting word lists to meet the needs of the class.

The speller is designed to be used in widely varying areas and is based on a mythical average class. The teacher works with a particular class, usually deviating in various degrees from the average. In the first place, the teacher should examine the word lists to eliminate words that are not useful to the class. The prevailing tendency to include words in children's lists that are used only by adults poses a problem. Time spent on these words has doubtful value; the cold-storage principle is not a valid one. Adult words may be postponed for study in later grades or even left to be acquired as needed in adult life. In the second place, the teacher will face the need of supplementing the basic word lists with words that appear frequently in children's writing but do not appear in conventional lists, such as *pal, chum, gang, pop, bike.* Other words to be added are those that are peculiar to the local community and some that have temporary value. The need for the temporarily used words appears in connection with work in other subjects, particularly in the social studies. Only words of permanent value should be memorized; other words, such as proper names, may be placed on a chart for reference by the children. Spellers commonly contain an alphabetical list of the basic vocabulary to which the teacher may refer in selecting words for memorization.

Any realistic program should make provision, also, for each

child's adding to his study list words peculiar to his needs. It is quite practicable for children to keep an individualized, supplementary list of words that they have occasion to use in writing activities. From the third grade on, an alphabetized notebook can be used for this purpose. In the second grade the word box is usable. It is necessary for the teacher to give some help in preparing the list and in training children in individual study procedures. Such procedures will be described more fully later in the chapter.

Grading spellers   In the teaching of reading, it is recognized that children vary widely in ability, and reading books are selected to meet the needs of children at different levels; it is not assumed that all children should use the same books. Differences are great also in spelling. Research has shown that pupils in grade 3 may range from the first- through the fourth-grade level; pupils in grade 4 may range from the middle of the second grade to the ninth; pupils in grade 5 may range from the third to the tenth; and pupils in grade 6 may range from just below the fourth grade to the senior high school.

A list of twenty words was dictated to a sixth-grade class of thirty-two pupils as a sight test with the results shown in Table 16-1. The number of words spelled correctly varies from 2 to 20, as shown in the distribution in Table 16-2. The significance of the range becomes apparent when the scores of the same pupils on a standard test are considered. The test used was the Morrison-McCall Spelling Scale, list 4.[4] The distribution of the pupils in grade levels is given in Table 16-3. The range is from 2.6 to 8.8.

In spite of everything we know about the range of spelling abilities, we commonly continue to require all children in a grade to use the same book. It would seem logical to adjust books to ability in spelling, as we do in reading. When is a speller properly graded? An end-of-the-term achievement of 90 to 95 percent on a list of words selected at random from the term's work seems reasonable. It would be worthwhile for a teacher to give a preliminary test early in the term of words selected at random from the term's work and to compare scores for individual pupils on the initial test with scores on a similar test given at the end of the term. He may determine what degree of familiarity with the words of a text is required to assure reasonable mastery by the end of the term. As a working hypothesis, the authors suggest that scores

[4] *Morrison-McCall Spelling Scale*, Harcourt, Brace & World, Inc., New York, 1923.

Table 16-1 *Sixth-grade pupils' scores on a sight test (crosses indicate words missed)*

Words	1	2	3	4	5	6	7	8	9	10	11	12	13	14	15	16	17	18	19	20	21	22	23	24	25	26	27	28	29	30	31	32	No. pupils right (each word)
hawk																						×	×			×	×						28
turtle								×		×	×		×			×							×	×		×			×	×	×	×	20
joint									×	×	×		×		×		×							×		×			×	×	×	×	20
trust																					×				×			×	×	×	×	×	25
horrid							×							×	×	×	×	×	×	×	×	×	×	×	×	×	×	×	×	×	×	×	12
swallow																		×	×	×	×	×	×	×	×	×	×	×	×	×	×	×	17
shallow							×	×		×		×		×			×							×			×		×	×	×	×	20
freedom									×								×								×		×		×	×	×	×	24
pretend														×								×		×		×	×		×	×	×	×	23
moment																					×					×	×	×			×	×	26
swamp												×								×					×			×	×	×	×	×	24
leap																		×								×	×	×			×	×	26
eagle																						×	×					×	×	×			27
drain											×									×					×			×	×	×	×	×	24
mere													×			×	×	×	×	×	×	×	×	×	×	×	×	×	×	×	×	×	14
fled																	×	×	×	×	×	×	×	×	×	×	×	×	×	×	×	×	16
harm			×																×							×	×	×				×	26
certain					×										×	×	×	×	×	×	×	×	×	×	×	×	×	×	×	×	×	×	13
deceive				×		×						×	×	×	×	×	×	×	×	×	×	×	×	×	×	×	×	×	×	×	×	×	9
frighten						×												×	×	×	×	×	×	×	×	×	×	×	×	×	×	×	16
No. words right (each pupil)	20	20	19	19	19	18	18	18	18	17	17	17	16	16	16	15	12	12	12	11	11	10	10	9	9	6	6	6	4	4	3	2	

349

Table 16-2   *Distribution of sixth-grade pupils on a sight spelling test (number and percent right)*

Words right	Percent right	Number of pupils
2	10	1
3	15	1
4	20	2
5	25	0
6	30	3
7	35	0
8	40	0
9	45	2
10	50	2
11	55	2
12	60	3
13	65	0
14	70	0
15	75	1
16	80	3
17	85	3
18	90	4
19	95	3
20	100	2

Table 16-3   *Distribution of sixth-grade pupils by grade norms on a Morrison-McCall spelling scale test*

Grade norms	Number of pupils	Grade norms	Number of pupils
2.6–2.7	1	5.8–5.9	1
2.8–2.9	2	6.0–6.1	0
3.0–3.1	0	6.2–6.3	3
3.2–3.3	0	6.4–6.5	3
3.4–3.5	1	6.6–6.7	1
3.6–3.7	1	6.8–6.9	0
3.8–3.9	3	7.0–7.1	0
4.0–4.1	1	7.2–7.3	0
4.2–4.3	0	7.4–7.5	1
4.4–4.5	2	7.6–7.7	1
4.6–4.7	2	7.8–7.9	0
4.8–4.9	3	8.0–8.1	0
5.0–5.1	0	8.2–8.3	0
5.2–5.3	3	8.4–8.5	0
5.4–5.5	1	8.6–8.7	0
5.6–5.7	1	8.8–8.9	1

of 40 to 70 percent right on the preliminary test indicate readiness for the text, that scores of 70 to 90 percent indicate the textbook is too easy and a more advanced book should be tried, and that scores below 40 percent show that the text is too hard and an easier one should be used. There may still remain a pupil or two at either extreme for whom an individualized program of work is advisable. If this criterion were applied to the sixth-grade class reported in Table 16-2, only nine of the children would be properly placed in the sixth-grade book; seven would be placed in lower-grade books; and sixteen would be placed in higher-grade books.

Organization of instruction   If different spellers are used in a class, as suggested in the preceding section, it is obvious that a grouping procedure must be followed. If a single speller is used, the necessity of adjustments to meet individual needs must be equally apparent. In using a single speller a combination of class, group, and/or individual work is in order. Testing may be done with the whole class, and possibly the whole class may profit from a preliminary class study of the word list, as described in a later section. Certainly study must be individualized or organized by groups and directed by the teacher. The superiority of directed study over individual study is established by experiments.

Various procedures for grouping may be used. One is to divide the class into three groups on the basis of the term pretest. The best group—consisting of those pupils who miss not more than four words of a week's list—work by themselves, turning to some other subject when they have completed the study of the words missed on the pretest. The middle group—those who miss four to ten words—receive a minimum of help from the teacher, consisting of assistance in word analysis and suggestions for study. The low group—those who miss more than ten words—work under the close direction of the teacher; a few of the words missed may be selected for each day's study, detailed analysis of words made, difficulties noted, study directed through the several steps, and individual help given.

Presenting a new list of words   This involves teacher-directed study, which precedes individual study or practice in connection with new words. Here the teacher *teaches* spelling, and teaching is distinguished from assigning lessons. The same procedure is followed in presenting a new list to the class as a whole, to groups, and to individuals in so far as the teacher has time to give individual instruction.

The teacher directs the children through the several steps as outlined in the study procedure described above, with emphasis on the various phases as determined by the words and by the needs of the children. He first takes up the pronunciation and meaning of the whole word. Pronunciation and meaning of most words should not present serious difficulties because words commonly used in writing are those commonly used in speaking and reading for many years prior to writing. Exceptions are words that are commonly mispronounced or confused in meaning. Special attention is required for words of the first type, such as *athletic, library, chimney, often, which*. The teacher pronounces the word, calling attention to the difficult part; the children then pronounce it several times. Words commonly confused in meaning are the homonyms, such as *their, there; to, two, too; principal, principle*. These words are best presented and studied in phrases. Time spent on using homonyms and other words in sentences is certainly not wasted.

In the second phase of presentation, sounding-seeing, the word is written on the board and pronounced, and the sound-sight of each syllable or larger phonogrammic unit is noted. The unit of learning is the syllable or larger phonogrammic part, not the letter. The children should note whether the word parts are spelled as they are sounded—phoneme-grapheme correspondence; they should recognize the familiar parts, patterns, and concentrate attention on the unphonetic, hard parts. Certain difficulties will soon stand out: confusing vowel sounds, silent letters, strange consonant combinations.

Sounding-seeing leads immediately to the third phase, visualization. The child says the word to himself with eyes closed or averted and simultaneously tries to "see" it. He checks his visual imagery by again looking at the word.

Fourth step: Now he is ready to write. This important phase strengthens visualization and gives the child the kinetic sense of writing the word. Of course, the first writing should be checked.

As a final, fifth step, writing the word several times fixes the spelling in mind and hand.

The painstaking treatment of new words described in the preceding paragraphs should be saved for those words causing real difficulty. Easy words are disposed of quickly. The teacher checks the pretest for difficulties and records in his textbook for future use hard words and particular parts that cause difficulty.

Rules and generalizations   In the directed study of new words described in the preceding section, occasion will arise for dealing with words that are similar in sound and form, phoneme-grapheme relationships. Comparisons will be made and certain principles will be developed in the form of generalizations. These generalizations have some value in that they help fix in mind the spelling of a new word and provide means of checking spelling. Generalizations take shape gradually and finally reach definite formulation in the upper grades. They are not a very dependable method for learning the spelling of new words, as in a completely phonetic language. The value of a particular rule depends on range of application and variability. Traditional practice limits the number of usable rules to the following:

1   Words ending in final *e* drop the *e* when adding a suffix that begins with a vowel and keep the *e* when adding a suffix that begins with a consonant.
2   Words ending in *y*, preceded by a consonant, change *y* to *i* when adding any suffix except one that begins with *i;* but words ending in *y* preceded by a vowel remain unchanged when adding any suffix.
3   Monosyllables, and words of more than one syllable with the accent on the last syllable, which end in a single consonant preceded by a single vowel, double the final consonant when adding a suffix beginning with a vowel.
4   In diphthongs, *i* comes before *e* except after *c* or when sounded as *a*, as in *neighbor* or *weigh*.

Directing practice   Practice is an important phase of word mastery. It is commonly handled as independent study, to some extent supervised and checked by the teacher, because the instructor feels that his limited time can be spent better on the developmental phases of the work. It should be clear that, in the authors' opinion, practice should be preceded by careful presentation in the form of word analysis and guidance in study. The suggestions of the teacher include sound-spelling relationships, emphasis on the pronunciation of certain words, concentration on hard parts, and comparison of words that are spelled alike. The importance of care in handwriting should be stressed.

Practice commonly takes the form of writing the word a number of times. Possibly second in favor is using the word in sentences. A considerable variety of other exercises is possible. The preparation of practice exercises takes time, and the teacher probably will continue to rely largely on textbooks and workbooks for material. The danger of practice exercises is that they may become mere busywork. If devised by the teacher or selected from commercial material, they should concentrate on the hard words and emphasize the specific sources of difficulty in words. Examples of such exercises are found in spelling workbooks.

Directing reviews   If word lists are well chosen, much practice will be provided in the use of words in spontaneous compositions. However, such functional use cannot be relied on for mastery; periodic reviews seem necessary. The spacing of reviews is determined by the curve of forgetting and varies with the difficulty of words. Textbooks give considerable help both in spacing reviews and in suggesting ways of conducting them. A basic principle is to discover words requiring restudy by testing a selected group. Individual differences are thus recognized, and help can be concentrated where it will do the most good, probably on the slow learners. Causes of difficulty should be noted and suitable steps taken to remove them. Restudy or reteaching will be necessary; practice alone is not sufficient. An abbreviated treatment of the steps in the original presentation is in order, with judiciously chosen emphasis appropriate to each word.[5]

Tests and records   Reference has been made earlier in the chapter to common textbook provisions and to using a pretest in grading spelling books. The pretest serves another purpose—determining accomplishment during the term. Comparisons are made for each pupil between scores on the same test given at the beginning and at the end of the term. The difference in scores shows the amount of improvement the pupil makes; and, of course, the difference between average or median scores shows class accomplishment. The teacher will not be able to interpret the results in comparison with classes in other schools, but comparisons of results achieved by his own classes over several years will provide a basis for interpretation. In the writers' judgment, a final average class score of 95 percent is desirable; 75 percent or less is not satisfactory; and improvement from a score of 40 to 90 percent or from 70 to 95 percent is good.

The informal pretest is prepared by selecting twenty-four to forty words at random from the term's work. The pretest and final test are given under uniform conditions: pronouncing the word, using it in a phrase or sentence, and pronouncing it again. The same rules for scoring are followed in both cases.

Batteries of standardized tests frequently include a section devoted to spelling.[6] Tests such as these make possible the comparison of a class with the age and grade norms derived by the testmakers. To measure the progress of a class throughout the year, however, the utilization of the New Iowa Spelling Scale

[5] David H. Patton, "How to Correct Spelling Errors," in Verna D. Anderson and others, *Readings in the Language Arts,* The Macmillan Company, New York, 1964, pp. 216–219.

[6] See, for example, *Iowa Tests of Basic Skills,* Houghton Mifflin Company, Boston, 1955–1956; *Stanford Achievement Tests,* Harcourt, Brace & World, Inc., New York, 1964; *S.R.A. Achievement Series,* Science Research Associates, Chicago, 1954–1964.

to develop class and group spelling checks is more revealing to the teacher.[7]

Spelling in written work   Word mastery is not accomplished by limiting attention to the spelling of words in special lessons; attention to spelling must be given consistently in all written work. Carelessness is a source of troublesome errors. The pupil should note spelling as part of the proofreading of written work. Words about which he is doubtful should be checked with the teacher or looked up in the vocabulary list or dictionary and should be corrected before a final draft is made.

If attention to spelling seems to interfere with freedom of expression in creative writing, the teacher may permit writing part of a word for identification and later give the pupil the necessary assistance. It is understood that this compromise is made in the interest of free expression and does not absolve the pupil from responsibility for the spelling of words within his normal vocabulary.

Spelling consciousness is strengthened by the occasional exercise of checking all words in a composition. The pupil checks the words that are known to be right, marks with an *x* those known to be wrong, and marks with a question mark those about which he is doubtful. Such checking of judgments should be illuminating to the pupil and the teacher, and may possibly reveal some misspellings that have become habitual.

Beginning spelling   Ordinarily textbook work in spelling is not introduced before the third grade; the teachers in the first two grades are required to improvise a spelling program, possibly using as guides desk copies of textbooks or workbooks. The work in the first two grades is commonly informal and related to purposeful writing. Before beginning work on original compositions the teacher naturally assures herself that the children are ready. Readiness consists of an adequate background of personal experiences and of training in thinking, expressing ideas orally in simple language forms, and reading. The observation of the written forms of words and sentences, such as compositions written on the board by the teacher (possibly at the dictation of the children), is helpful preparation for the children. Early occasions for writing are signing names to papers, writing labels, and copying from the

[7] Harry A. Greene, *The New Iowa Spelling Scale*, Bureau of Educational Research and Service, University of Iowa, Iowa City, 1955, pp. 10–15.

chalkboard simple class compositions such as invitations for mothers to a class party.[8]

In approaching a writing activity, the teacher demonstrates and explains the correct form and conducts a brief practice exercise. The problem is as much a handwriting lesson as a spelling lesson. The letters are identified and named; the forms are learned by the children as they take up the letter groups found in particular words. Instruction and practice on specific letter forms are given as needed.

Gradually, as the child's spelling-writing vocabulary grows through use and confidence in written expression increases, the urge for original work appears. The teacher provides assistance in spelling and other mechanics. A device that has been used successfully is to have each pupil keep an alphabetized vocabulary box with words written on slips of paper about 3 by 8 inches. When a pupil asks for help on a word, the teacher writes the word for him on a slip of paper. The pupil studies it, uses it in his composition, and files it in his box for future use. The children are trained in a learning procedure: watching the teacher write the word, studying, tracing, copying (or, better, writing from memory), checking, and using.

The teacher is warned not to be too critical of spelling errors in the writing of young children. Gertrude Hildreth says: [9]

> Teachers tend too frequently to be oversensitive to spelling errors in the writing of young children, and, as in arithmetic and reading, demand standards of accomplishment too high for young children, forgetting that considerable improvement is the invariable accomplishment of maturity and insight on the part of the child. As Suzzallo suggested, the children are growing in spelling, not grown.
>
> Beginnings in spelling must be recognized even when the spelling is not precisely correct: "movd" for "moved," "aple" for "apple," "dol" for "doll." The child demonstrates that he has made a successful beginning when he can write from memory no more than the correct initial letters of words. This is the first step beyond having no idea whatsover of the spelling of a word. Even such spellings as "gellie" for "jelly," "doler" for "dollar," "frend" for "friend," "mach" for "match," "braslet" for "bracelet" are not far from right, for the number of letters in each word is approximately correct and the syllables are indicated. These errors are not as serious when young children make them as the random spelling of these words would be.
>
> The point is not that the school encourages partially correct spelling or teaches children to spell as they please, but that 100 per cent pre-

[8] Harold G. Shane and others, *Beginning Language Arts Instruction with Children*, Charles E. Merrill Books, Inc., Columbus, Ohio, 1961, pp. 67–73.

[9] Gertrude Hildreth, *Learning the Three R's*, Educational Publishers, Inc., Minneapolis, Minn., 1947, p. 504.

cision is not acquired all at once in spelling anymore than in a child's early efforts to speak. These first partial learnings represent the first stage in the long developmental process of learning to spell correctly. The pupil is closely observed to make sure that he is progressing in spelling right along.

This informal approach to building up a writing vocabulary may be supplemented by a systematic program beginning with the second grade, where either a basic list of words used commonly by children is compiled from the teacher's observations of their needs, or recommended word lists are utilized. There is a definite, well-organized attack, following the general procedures of teaching outlined above for developmental work and for review; and at the same time care is taken to help children acquire useful learning techniques for the mastery of new words.

The emphasis is on the basic words of assured utility—words that children have occasion to use daily. Two new words per day are sufficient, and frequent repetition is desirable. The procedure is essentially a teacher-directed, class or group study procedure.

The functional-individualized program   The compound adjective *functional-individualized* describes a program we shall now discuss. This is frankly a more formal program than individual instruction. It is, perhaps, overconservative and does not present an ideal procedure for the teaching of spelling; but possibly it comes as close to the ideal as the realities of instruction will generally permit.

Hildreth makes a good case for the functional program. Her point of view is well expressed in the following comments: [10]

> In the modern school program, spelling is treated wholly as a practical aid in writing. The pupil is helped to develop correct spelling habits whenever he writes something at school. Ideas to express and a vocabulary of word meanings in which to express them are prerequisites to learning to spell.
>
> Although this position has been advocated for years, it is only recently that many schools have succeeded in organizing spelling work on a functional basis. This aim is achieved through unifying spelling with all the activities in the school day that call for context writing. Spelling is not confined to a "spelling period," but is a skill that is practiced whenever and wherever writing is done. The criterion of spelling success in modern schools is not the percentage of words the child spells correctly in a list for a given grade, or the list of words studied last week or last term, but how he spells whenever he writes.
>
> In the modern school, spelling is taught in connection with projects and activities that give purpose to the writing the children do. The

[10] *Ibid.*, pp. 497–498.

spelling vocabulary is acquired more largely through the study of standard word lists.

According to Hildreth, the modern speller is at fault in containing too many words infrequently used, such as *procrastination, prolong,* and *bona fide;* in arranging words according to difficulty rather than frequency of use; in omitting words peculiar to children's writing; and in including too many words. Hildreth says, "Few words are used very often; a small number, some 3,000 to 4,000 carry the writing burden for the majority of children in the upper grades." [11]

These considerations, together with the fact of extreme variability in individual spelling ability, suggest to Hildreth the need for a *practical* rather than an *academic* program of work. However, the work is not to be entirely individualized. She says: [12]

> Teachers set aside time every day in the week for all pupils who need to study the words in their spelling notebooks, or words checked in their spelling word lists. Periods once or twice a week are not frequent enough for economical learning and retention. In addition to checking spelling accuracy in written work, this daily work includes a short period for the initial study or review of troublesome words. These periods need not be more than ten or fifteen minutes long. Pupils far ahead of the majority of the group would be working on compositions or other activities during the test and study periods. The danger in any predetermined program is that it will become mechanical. The week's work for every child should be individualized so far as his needs require.

Class or group work is presumably used in teaching the basic vocabulary of some 2,000 words. Apparently each child builds up his own spelling list as needs for words arise in writing activities. The particular techniques for handling these individualized word lists are not given by Hildreth; evidently they are left to the teacher. Spelling is not to occupy more than ten or fifteen minutes per day.

The functional-individualized program must be recognized as theoretically sound, although practical difficulty arises with the handling of individual word lists. Certain weaknesses have been pointed out in the formal program; some of these faults can be corrected by the measures suggested. The differences between the two programs—formal and functional-individual—are in large part differences in relative emphasis on class and on individual work. Possibly a sound, practical program could result from combining key features of both programs.

[11] *Ibid.,* p. 493.
[12] *Ibid.,* p. 524.

Chronically bad spellers The chronically bad speller represents the lower extreme of the total distribution. There is no evidence to show that the majority of these poor spellers differ from other children in essential abilities or that they learn spelling in different ways. The instructional procedure is essentially the same as for normal spellers; more intensive work is required, and a slower pace is set. The teacher may probe into the pedagogical history of the child and make a thorough examination of physical and emotional factors to discover contributing causes.[13] A brief summary of steps in diagnosis and treatment is presented here:

1 Give a standard spelling test to discover the amount of deficiency. Compare with achievement in other subjects.
2 Give an intelligence test to discover general mental capacity.
3 Test for defects of hearing and vision.
4 Give reading test.
5 Give test of spelling consciousness to show whether mistakes are due to carelessness or ignorance of the word.
6 Collect misspellings from spelling tests and written work and classify them according to types of errors.
7 Get as much information as possible about the pupil's pedagogical history, especially methods of beginning reading, knowledge of meanings of words, knowledge of phonics, pronunciation and articulation, motor coordination in writing, and emotional attitude toward spelling.
8 From above, assemble probable causes of difficulty in spelling, and adopt appropriate remedial measures such as the following:
    a. Systematic word study; early training may have been inadequate.
    b. Exercises in visualization.
    c. Drill on particular types of spelling errors.
    d. Phonics drills.
    e. Removal of physical defects.
    f. Developing confidence through successful effort.

Contributions of linguistics Linguists, disturbed by the persistent difficulties of children in learning to spell, turn hopefully to the detailed analytical study of the structure of the English language. The approach to spelling is through oral language and the study of sounds (phonology). The Tiedts say:

> The basic concepts of the linguist, that is, the primacy of speech and the changing nature of any language, have a bearing on approaches to spell-

[13] H. A. Greene and W. T. Petty, *Developing Language Skills in the Elementary Schools*, Allyn and Bacon, Boston, 1967, chap. 11. See also Verna D. Anderson and others, *op. cit.*, pp. 209–219.

ing instruction. Greater emphasis is placed, for example, on the teaching of oral language skills as a firm basis for beginning writing and spelling activities, for without knowledge of English words and the sounds of English little progress can be made with spelling English words. Success with spelling is predicated on the ability to hear and distinguish English sounds.[14]

Phonemes-graphemes   Sounds in English are divided into consonants and vowels. There are at least twenty-one consonant sounds, as in the initial sounds of: *bin, pin, tin, din, kin, get, fin, vim, thin, this, sin, zip, shin,* azure, *chin, gin, mint, name, rim, limb, hope.* Eleven vowel sounds are distinguished: *boot, look, coat, bought, cut, hot, cat, let, wait, fit, feet.*[15] But there is little agreement among linguists about the number of phonemes (sounds) in the English language. The number varies from thirty-six to forty-seven, due in part to dialect variations.

Consonant and vowel sounds are not studied in isolation, but in words and even in sentences. The sound of a phoneme is affected by (1) position in the syllable, (2) syllabic stress, and (3) internal constraints.[16]

For use in spelling, of course, sounds of letters and of combinations of letters (phonemes) must be transcribed into written letter forms (graphemes). Unfortunately there is a marked lack of consistency between the sounds and the letter forms. How great and significant is the difference depends on the understanding and prejudice of the author. Some authors claim a 20 percent, others a 90 percent disagreement.[17]

There *is* general agreement that many words in everyday speaking and writing, probably the majority, are spelled phonetically; and that a small number of words, regarded as irregular in spelling, are used frequently and are the major causes of the difficulties in spelling. What shall be done to resolve the difficulties?

Spelling reform   One solution proposed by some linguists is to change English spelling materially. The Initial Teaching Alphabet, now gaining some attention but limited use, is one proposal.

[14] Iris M. Tiedt and S. W. Tiedt, *Contemporary English in the Elementary School,* Prentice-Hall, Inc., Englewood Cliffs, N.J., 1967, p. 168. Quoted with special permission of authors and publishers.

[15] Pose Lamb, *Linguistics in Proper Perspective,* Charles E. Merrill Books, Inc., Columbus, Ohio, 1967, pp. 70 and 72.

[16] Richard E. Hodges and Hugh Rudorf, "Searching Linguistics for Cues for the Teaching of Spelling," *Elementary English,* vol. 42, May, 1965, pp. 527–533.

[17] Lamb, *op. cit.,* p. 62.

It consists of 44 letters, based on incorporating, grouping, and modifying letters of the traditional alphabet of 26 letters.[18] Another proposal is Clarence Hotson's *Ryt Ryting* alphabet, consisting of 43 symbols; this results, it is prophetically claimed, in a 93 percent phonetic correspondence.[19] Attempts to change the patterns of English spelling are not new. The vigorous and well-publicized attempts at spelling reform of George Bernard Shaw, Theodore Roosevelt, and the National Education Association proved futile, and there is little promise for the solution of our spelling difficulties in more recent proposals and movements for spelling reform.

Need for change   Some, perhaps many, professional educators and teachers will sympathize to some extent, if not completely, with Pose Lamb's statement: "Regardless of bias or point of view of the educator, whether expressed in writing or over coffee cups in the teachers lounge, there is general agreement that there is a need for change in the design, nature, structure, and content of our elementary school programs." [20] What change?

Phonetic approach—generalizations   One step in a linguistically oriented program is to organize study around words similar in sound and spelling. Words for study are grouped into patterns, as: (1) *cat, hat; bad, sad; drip, trip*—consonant, vowel, consonant. (2) *save, gave; tone, home*—consonant, vowel, consonant plus *e*. (3) *rain, grain; feed, greed*—consonant, vowel, vowel, consonant. (4) *me, he; my, try*—consonant, vowel. (5) *far, farm; word, bird; clear, fear, dear*.[21] Similarities are noted and applications made to other words similarly pronounced and spelled; then generalizations are made. It is claimed that the use of this approach provides almost limitless possibilities for the expansion of the writing vocabulary.[22]

Recognizing and identifying specific elements in words undoubtedly facilitates learning and does serve as a basic for forming qualified generalizations that will give some help in learning new words. But it may be observed that there is nothing new in this program except perhaps emphasis and extent of use. In the

[18] Tiedt and Tiedt, *op. cit.*, pp. 175–176.
[19] Lamb, *op. cit.*, p. 62.
[20] *Ibid.*, p. 61.
[21] *Ibid.*, pp. 78–85.
[22] Paul R. Hanna and Jean S. Hanna, "Applications of Linguistic and Psychological Cues to the Spelling Course of Study," *Elementary English*, vol. 42, November, 1965, pp. 753–759.

second place, the validity is questionable when words similar in sound but differing in spelling are placed together, as in (5) above. It would seem that whenever there is confusion in sound and spelling, the learner is obliged to check sound against visual appearance. In fact, exceptions of a few words to a pattern group raise uncertainties about all similar words in and out of the pattern group. The learner must have some means of deciding whether a given word is a pattern word or an exception. This must be accomplished by an act of memory, usually based on visual appearance.[23]

The question of the visual versus the auditory presentation of words was investigated thoroughly by a fair number of German scientists toward the end of the last century. After ten years of fruitless debate preceding the studies, the question was resolved by submitting the issue to experimentation in classrooms, by use of scientific methodology of controlled comparison. The results showed conclusively that visual presentation was superior to auditory presentation; but that learning spelling is handled best by a multiple approach of hearing, sounding, seeing, and writing, and that individual preferences have some bearing on learning processes. It seemed that the issue was settled for all time and that teachers had at least one irrefutable principle upon which to base their practice. It seems, now, that the issue of eye versus ear is being raised again. Before teachers are expected to make another about-face, very convincing facts should be brought forth. Conclusions contrary to the visual approach that are based primarily on theoretical grounds, however well fortified by statistical data, should be regarded as hypothetical until supported by objective, controlled investigation in the classroom.

Basic philosophy   It is quite clear that spelling programs devised by linguists hold to a philosophy very different from that of the functionalists represented earlier in the chapter. The linguists select and group words for study according to sound, regardless of meaning and current use. The functionalists select and group words according to content or immediate use. It is a difference between language for a study of structure and language for communication; between the study of words selected for similarity in sound and form leading to generalizations, and the acquisition of a meaningful spelling vocabulary through realistic writing experiences. Both programs include definite word study

[23] Albert H. Yee, "The Generalization Controversy on Spelling Instruction," *Elementary English*, vol. 43, February, 1966, pp. 154–161.

and eventually end in use in actual writing situations. The goal to be reached is the same; the tactics vary. The conflict between the two philosophies is not a new one; an immediate resolution should not be expected.

Interest—motivation The matter of pupils' interest, motivation, is involved. Some linguists refer to customary study as "deadly drill." The hope of the functionalists, of course, is that relating spelling to real writing experiences will provide sufficient incentive for practice. The linguists expect that the intellectual pursuit of the principles of phonology and morphology will relieve systematic word study of some of its tedium. Both schools advocate resorting to extraneous devices, games, from time to time, if and when interest lags.

Synthesis of structural-functional Although controversies about programs, policies, and philosophies persist, teachers must continue to teach and curriculum makers must get on with the business of setting up spelling programs. It is possible that in time conflicts may be resolved by further research of the Hanna-Stanford type and by controlled classroom experimentation. Meanwhile it would seem reasonable for practical teachers to assess the merits of the proposed theories and programs; to synthesize them; and, as far as possible, to set up programs of work in spelling based on elements of agreement, such as the following: [24]

1. The learner's interest—motivation—is important. Interest should be as inherent and as functional as possible. The child should recognize the importance of spelling proficiency and should see the relation of current work—systematic word study, comparison, generalization, repetition—to current and later life needs.
2. The ultimate goal is communication.
3. Children should have many current genuine writing experiences.
4. A basic vocabulary of useful words should be acquired; and techniques for checking spelling and for acquiring the spelling of new words as needed through the use of the dictionary and of individual word study techniques should be developed.
5. Children should keep functional individual word lists to supplement core lists.
6. Practical advantages in the comparative study of word phonology, morphology, history, etc., to identify a few basic patterns and to form applicable generalizations should be utilized.

[24] Lamb, *op. cit.*, pp. 84–89.

7 Spelling should be related to speech, writing, and reading in order to minimize segmented word study.

Evaluation The dynamics of a spelling program require teacher insights into the selection of words to be studied and learned, the processes of spelling teaching, and the provisions for carry-over of spelling learnings to the writing needs of school and later life. Essential for each child is the development of his own spelling consciousness, understanding his responsibility to check words of which he is unsure. By helping children to note their own hard words and providing means for learning, self-checking, and correcting, the teacher assists growing independence in writing. Carelessness in spelling, detected by senior high school teachers, college instructors, and employers, penalizes young adults who may have good contributions but negate their writing by being unaware of the convention of spelling.

For your consideration

1 Analyze several spelling books of different series, noticing: (*a*) statements by the authors as to their criteria for the selection of words; (*b*) provisions for the sequence of spelling learning through the grades; (*c*) suggestions for lesson planning, for motivation of children, for provisions for retention and review; (*d*) evidences of handwriting and spelling relationships.
2 Sample every tenth word in a master list of a spelling book for a specific grade level. Analyze these words, using the New Iowa Spelling Scale.
3 Give a pretest covering a semester's work to one class. Interpret the results and suggest an appropriate plan for the organization of instruction.
4 Work out a procedure for introducing a new group of words to a group or class.

References

ANDERSON, PAUL S., *Language Skills in Elementary Education*, The Macmillan Company, New York, 1966, chap. 5.
DALLMAN, MARTHA: *Teaching the Language Arts in the Elementary School*, W. C. Brown Company, Publishers, Dubuque, Iowa, 1966, chap. 8.

DAWSON, MILDRED A., AND FRIEDA H. DINGEE: *Children Learn the Language Arts*, Burgess Publishing Company, Minneapolis, Minn., 1966, chap. 7.

———, M. ZOLLINGER, AND A. ELWELL: *Guiding Language Learning*, Harcourt, Brace & World, Inc., New York, 1963, chap. 18.

FITZGERALD, J. A.: "An Integrating Basic Communication Vocabulary," *Elementary English*, vol. 40, March, 1963, pp. 283–289.

FRIES, C. G.: *Linguistics and Reading*, Holt, Rinehart and Winston, Inc., New York, 1964.

GLEASON, H. A.: *Linguistics and English Grammar*, Holt, Rinehart and Winston, Inc., New York, 1965.

GROFF, PATRICK: "Visual and Auditory Perception Training and Spelling Achievement," *Elementary English*, vol. 42, February, 1965, pp. 163–164, 168.

HALL, R. A.: *Sound and Spelling in English*, Chilton Company, Philadelphia, 1964.

HANNA, PAUL R., AND JEAN S. HANNA: "The Teaching of Spelling," in Iris M. Tiedt and S. W. Tiedt: *Readings on Contemporary English in the Elementary School*, Prentice-Hall, Inc., Englewood Cliffs, N. J., 1967, pp. 181–197.

———: "Needed Research in Spelling," *Elementary English*, vol. 43, January, 1966, pp. 60–66, 89.

HILDRETH, GERTRUDE: *Teaching Spelling: A Guide to Basic Principles and Practices*, Holt, Rinehart and Winston, Inc., New York, 1955.

LEE, J. MURRAY, AND DORRIS M. LEE: *The Child and His Curriculum*, Appleton-Century-Crofts, Inc., New York, 1960, pp. 346–349.

LEFEVRE, C. A.: *Linguistics and the Teaching of Reading*, McGraw-Hill Book Company, New York, 1964, chap. 8.

LEONARD, EDITH M., AND OTHERS: *Basic Learning in the Language Arts*, Scott, Foresman and Company, Chicago, 1965, part 6.

MC KEE, PAUL: *Language in the Elementary School*, Houghton Mifflin Company, Boston, 1939, chaps. 6–9.

PETTY, WALTER T.: "Handwriting and Spelling: Their Current Status," *Elementary English*, vol. 41, December, 1964, pp. 839–844.

RUSSELL, DAVID H., AND OTHERS: *Child Development and the Language Arts*, National Council of Teachers of English, Champaign, Ill., 1953, pp. 20–22.

SMITH, JAMES A.: *Creative Teaching of the Language Arts in the Elementary School*, Allyn and Bacon, Inc., 1967, chap. 9.

STRICKLAND, RUTH G.: "The Contributions of Structural Linguistics to the Teaching of Reading, Writing, and Grammar in the Elementary School," *Bulletin of the School of Education*, Indiana University, vol. 40, no. 1, January, 1964, Bloomington, Ind.

TRAUGER, W. K.: *Language Arts in Elementary Schools*, McGraw-Hill Book Company, New York, 1963, pp. 93–156.

17.

HANDWRITING

The teaching of handwriting early in the twentieth century was dominated by principles and procedures promoted by specialists whose interests seemed to be in handwriting for its own sake. There has been a succession of systems—Spencerian, vertical, Palmer—varying in style but alike in basic principles: (1) setting rigid patterns of letter form and slant, (2) emphasizing formal drill exercises, (3) prescribing movement, and (4) requiring the use of certain materials. The purpose, apparently, was to make a fancy calligrapher of every child.

Traditional formalism was attacked by educators and teachers on several grounds: (1) The methods used—posture, copy, and drill exercises—were inappropriate for children. (2) The results were artificial and there was little carry-over into actual writing in school and in life. (3) Some scripts, in spite of pleasing appearance, were difficult to read. (4) Learning to write was unnecessarily complicated. (5) The extreme emphasis on drill took all the joy out of learning to write. (6) Emphasis on formal drill disregarded the natural stages of neuromuscular development of children. (7) Individuality of style was unnecessarily sacrificed to the fetish of uniformity. (8) In spite of years of training, children failed to acquire a free, easy handwriting movement.

Some remains of traditional practices still persist in the classroom. Some of today's teachers were trained in the old methods, or not at all, and the charges are made by qualified observers that handwriting is still taught by pointless drill methods and that the skill is often poorly taught.[1]

The present trend is toward a functional program that (1) defines competency in terms of standards acceptable in the social and business correspondence of adults; (2) encourages individuality of style; (3) emphasizes legibility, appearance, and ease of writing; (4) minimizes formal practice; (5) relates handwriting to written composition; (6) favors a natural arm-hand-finger movement, adapted to age and maturity; and (7) permits the use of handwriting materials commonly used at home and in the business world.

Penmanship is not isolated from work in other subjects. From the very beginning, a child has something to write and a reason for writing it. He composes real messages, reports, notes, summaries, outlines, lists, and booklets. These experiences provide both motivation and some practice. The writing program is a functional program.

The functional approach is not to be confused with the purely incidental treatment of handwriting; systematic instruction and practice are provided. The amount of writing in school does not assure mastery and for a time the child will need to turn aside from writing messages and memoranda to practicing handwriting. But this practice is closely related to the purpose it serves, and the amount of practice is determined by the end served.[2]

The functional program, then, is a combination of purposeful writing experiences and systematic training. The precise combination is the teacher's practical problem and the burden of the remainder of this chapter.

Can handwriting be taught?   Before the development of a practical program is discussed, a pertinent question may be considered: Can handwriting be taught? The unsatisfactory results of traditional teaching and of the haphazard measures that teachers have

[1] Theodore Irwin, "Why Our Kids Can't Write," in Verna D. Anderson and Others, *Readings in the Language Arts*, The Macmillan Company, New York, 1964, pp. 144–153. See also Walter T. Petty, "Handwriting and Spelling: Their Current Status," *Elementary English*, vol. 41, December, 1964, pp. 839–844.

[2] Paul C. Burns, *Improving Handwriting Instruction in Elementary Schools*, Burgess Publishing Company, Minneapolis, Minn., 1963, chap. 1.

sometimes resorted to in an effort to adjust traditional teaching to modern points of view may give rise to a feeling of hopelessness and helplessness. That handwriting can be taught was revealed clearly in the early, classic studies of Cole and of Pressey and Lehman. Cole devoted ten years to developing and trying out a system of diagnostic instruction. Results were obtained in progress made by 398 high–third-grade and low–fourth-grade children, and comparisons were made with 388 children in the same grades and schools taught by conventional methods. Pupils using the two methods were not selected, an attempt was made to equate teachers and time, and the results were scored by disinterested persons. Speed was about the same for both groups, but results in quality were markedly different. The improvement in median quality score for the conventional group was 34 to 35; for the diagnostic group, 35 to 47 (Ayres scale). The difference in improvement is more striking when viewed graphically in one-tenth steps on the Ayres scale.

These are samples of a child's writing that show average improvement during four months of diagnostic teaching:

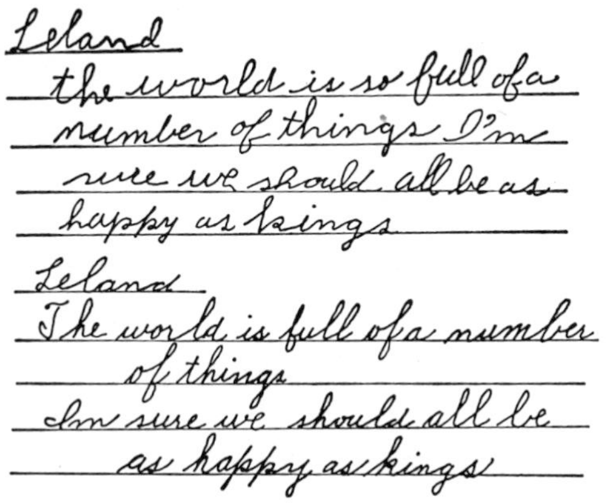

Figure 17-1. Samples showing average progress in four months of diagnostic instruction.

According to Cole, the conventional groups improved very little, but the diagnostic groups, in less than four months, made an average improvement equal to three years at the normal rate.[3]

[3] Jess S. Hudson and others, *Language Arts in the Elementary School,* Twentieth Yearbook, National Education Association, Department of Elementary School Principals, Washington, 1941, p. 466.

Similar results were obtained in experiments carried on by Guiler and by Pressey and Lehman: [4]

Guiler analyzed the handwriting of fourteen pupils from grade VII with Ayres Handwriting Scale. He then analyzed the individual's needs by means of Pressey's Chart for Diagnosis of Illegibilities, West's Chart for Diagnosing Elements of Handwriting, and Gray's Standard Score Card. A table was made of the difficulties in the formation of each letter. This was followed by individualized group instruction which had for its goal the correction of each individual's difficulties. During the year the class improved in quality from an average of 43.6 on the Ayres scale to an average of 56.8, and in rate from an average of 75.4 to an average of 84.6 letters a minute. This was the equivalent of a normal gain for three years. In the experiment of Pressey and Lehman a similar procedure was used. They worked with twenty-three pupils from grade IV B and used both an experimental and a control group. The two were taught by the same teacher twice a week for thirty minutes for 9.5 weeks. The experimental class increased its average score in quality from 32 to 46 on the Ayres scale, and its rate from 51 to 69. The corresponding changes for the control class were 31 to 34 in quality and from 46 to 50 in rate. Both experiments establish the fact that corrective practice applied at the point of error is effective.

Unfortunately these early studies have not attracted much attention nor materially affected current practices. Their significance and promise are sufficiently startling and constructive to justify further investigation.[5]

Stages in handwriting   For the purpose of this presentation, training in handwriting may be divided into two stages. The first stage comprises the work of the first two and one-half or three grades, in which the letter forms are taught and habits of position and of use of writing materials are initiated. In the second stage, from the fourth or upper third grade, when familiar letter forms and habits are set, the teacher is concerned with improving skill and ease of writing. The second stage extends through the upper elementary grades and on into junior and senior high schools. It will be considered first in this chapter.

Relating handwriting to purposeful experiences   The heart of the functional program is purposeful experiences. This means, primarily, that children must have abundant opportunities to use

[4] H. B. Reed, *Psychology of Elementary School Subjects*, Ginn and Company, Boston, 1938, pp. 280–281. See also Hilda Lehman and Luella C. Pressey, "Teaching Handwriting Diagnostically," in C. W. Hunnicutt, and W. J. Iverson, *Research in the Three R's*, Harper & Row, Publishers, Inc., New York, 1958, pp. 283–285.

[5] Dan W. Andersen, "Handwriting Research: Style and Practice," *Elementary English*, vol. 42, February, 1965, pp. 115–125.

handwriting in real situations. Typical experiences are writing business letters to request illustrative material in the social studies, writing friendly letters to sick classmates, making outlines and records of work accomplished, writing announcements and advertisements, writing plays, contributing to a newspaper or magazine, writing stories and original poetry, and preparing minutes of meetings. Most of these experiences constitute a normal part of schoolwork, curricular and extracurricular; but some are devised by the teacher to provide special opportunities for training in useful language experiences, of which handwriting is a part.

The use of writing experiences as a part of a functional program in handwriting provides purposeful situations, which in turn provide immediate motivation for good handwriting. Adequate standards are set, work is judged, careful attention is given to the use of good handwriting and to the practice of good form, difficulties are noticed, and incidental instruction and practice are given. Properly handled, much progress toward desired handwriting goals may be made in purposeful writing experiences.

Measuring initial achievements   Incidental instruction and practice in penmanship during purposeful activities generally are not sufficient to develop desired competency in handwriting. A supplementary training program is required. The amount of training needed varies widely with individuals, and the teacher's first problem is to determine who needs the training.

A rough evaluation may be made by examining samples of children's purposeful writing and comparing the writing with acceptable standards for the grade. Or the teacher may give a standard test, such as the Ayres handwriting scale, which gives scores in quality and speed.[6] The scores should be recorded on a scatter diagram, with identifying letters, as shown in Table 17-1. Norm lines should be drawn for the grade, showing standards given on the scale. To aid further in the interpretation of results, the teacher may note on the diagram the norms for grades above and below his grade. A glance at the results gives a picture of the distribution of ability in the class and serves as a general diagnosis of needs. It will be observed that the median lines separate the class into several groups with reference to quality and speed. Each letter represents an individual child.

Organization of instruction   The preliminary measurement of achievements gives at least a tentative basis for the organization

[6] Cooperative Test Division, Educational Testing Service, Princeton, N.J.

of instruction. Three groups may be distinguished for instructional purposes: (1) norm or above, (2) near but below norm, and (3) seriously deficient. The children who are at or above the grade norm in quality and speed may be excused from systematic training

Table 17-1.   *Handwriting scores, third-grade class*

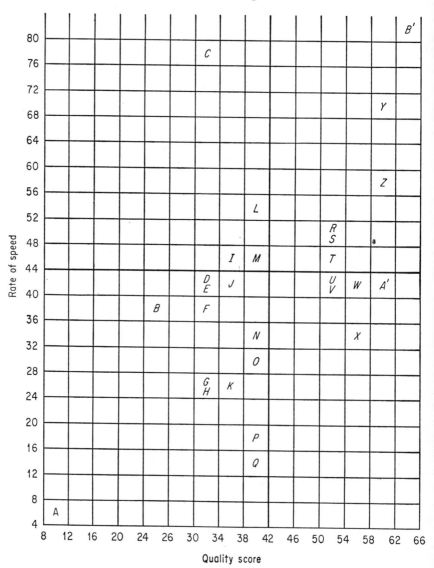

as long as they maintain proper standards in written work, or further training may be made optional. The remaining pupils need some help; the amount and kind varies with the children. The children near the goal may be brought to the grade norm with a little carefully planned training, which should be given early in order to free the teacher for the detailed, laborious work required by those with serious handwriting deficiencies. It is possible that those near the grade norm may be brought quickly to standard by providing them with adequate motivation; giving attention to a few letter forms and combinations of letters that cause difficulty; improving appearance of writing by suggestions about slant and alignment; checking basic mechanics of posture, position of paper, and pen holding; and making pupils conscious of writing deficiencies. The particular help given will be dictated by an analysis of samples of the pupils' handwriting and by observation of pupils as they write. The teacher will notice general, key difficulties in products and habits and will try to eradicate them. It is possible that this general training will be helpful for the lowest as well as middle group, so that for a time both groups can be taught together.

Locating specific difficulties   There remains the third group, those children who have serious handwriting difficulties. There is no satisfactory alternative to intensive individual diagnosis and treatment. The primary attack is on letter forms. Secondary emphasis is given to speed and ease, general qualities of slant, alignment, and spacing, and the factors of attitude, form, and mechanics that condition performance.[7]

In the attack on letter forms it is necessary to give consideration to each letter. The children should have a set of acceptable forms for the grade to serve as models. These may be found in the textbook or writing manual, or the teacher may profitably prepare such a list. It is better to set up as models good handwriting that is characteristic of the pupils of the grade rather than perfect copybook specimens. The teacher-prepared set of models may be duplicated and given to the children as a checklist or work sheet; or commercial material may be secured.

The next step is to secure a letter-by-letter analysis of the children's writing made by the children themselves and checked

[7] Ernest Horn, "Questions for Research in Handwriting," *Elementary School Journal*, vol. 62, March, 1962, pp. 305–312. See also Burns, *op. cit.*, chap. 7.

by the teacher. On his checklist, the child may note each letter he makes satisfactorily; blanks remaining indicate the letters on which additional work is needed.

Finding the cause of difficulties   Now the diagnosis proceeds with the determination of the exact nature and causes of the difficulties. The child should study his letter forms to determine the nature of illegibilities and variations from the model letters. Common faults will gradually become apparent. The most difficult letters are *a, e, r,* and *t;* the most difficult numerals are 5, 6, and 7. Fourteen forms of illegibility account for nearly one-half of the total illegibilities: *a* like *ci, a* like *o, a* like *u, b* like *li, d* like *cl, e* closed, *h* like *li, i* with no dot, *n* like *u, o* like *a, r* like *i, r* like half *n, t* like *l, t* with cross above. Diagnostic sheets for each letter may be selected or made, indicating defects in formation; or commercial material may be secured for the use of teacher and children.

Treatment of errors   The exact definition of the nature of the difficulty often suggests the proper remedy, such as closing the *d,* straightening the back of the *b,* or opening the *e.* However, in the matter of treatment too, proper commercial material can help by giving specific suggestions on how to correct particular errors.

In the study-practice of a letter form the child should note the nature and cause of the difficulty, study the correct form, write words containing the letter, use the word in a sentence, use the correct form in original writing until it becomes habitual, and review as needed for maintenance of correct habits.[8]

Keeping records of progress in mastering letter forms serves as a powerful incentive for improving handwriting.

Handling corrective work   Corrective work will be handled on an individual or small group basis. On individual work, Dan W. Andersen says: [9]

> Evidence would seem to indicate that there is little being done in the individualization of handwriting instruction. Yet those studies that have been concerned with the effects of individualized techniques show excellent results. [As reported by Cole and Pressey, earlier in the chapter.] The fact that only 7 per cent of those schools surveyed indicated a planned program for diagnosis and remediation of handwriting difficulties raises some real questions. There is a need to consider the nature of the developmental and diagnostic help given to children to improve

[8] F. N. Freeman, *Handwriting Faults and How to Correct Them,* The Zaner-Bloser Company, Columbus, Ohio, 1958.

[9] Andersen, *op. cit.,* p. 123. Quoted with special permission of the National Council of Teachers of English.

their handwriting if a formal program of skill training desires to help children assume major responsibility for the maintenance and development of their own writing skills.

If the corrective work is teacher-directed, the children who have similar difficulties are taught simultaneously or individually. Both procedures have been used successfully. The choice may be dictated by the commonness of the difficulties, the availability of instructional material, and the maturity of the pupils. The authors personally favor the grouping procedure because they feel that children generally need the stimulation of companions and expert guidance of the teacher. To the authors' knowledge, satisfactory material for a completely individualized program is not generally available. Of course, extreme deviations and errors will require individual work on the part of teacher and pupil.[10]

Improving speed and quality Although the primary analysis and concentration of effort is on letter forms, some attention may be given profitably to speed; to qualities other than letter formation, such as alignment, spacing of words and letters, slant, and neatness; and to techniques, such as placing of the paper, position and movement of the arm and hand. These elements may be handled incidentally in connection with purposeful writing and practice work on letter forms. Speed develops naturally with age and practice. Improvement in other qualities may be expected, incidental to practice on letter forms.[11]

Instruction may be given directly by the teacher; suitable commerical materials may be utilized for diagnosis and remedial suggestions; or self-help devices in the form of diagnostic work sheets may be introduced, such as the following:

Diagnostic and Remedial Chart for Handwriting

FAULT	REMEDY
1. Line color:	
a. Too light	Hold pen nearer the point.
	Lessen angle of pen to paper.
	Hold pen with eye of pen facing paper.
b. Too heavy	Hold pen further from the point.
c. Shaded curves	Hold pen with eye of pen facing paper.
d. Heavy downstrokes	Lessen pressure of forefinger on pen.

[10] E. A. Enstrom, "Individualize Your Group Teaching of Handwriting," *Grade Teacher*, May, 1962, pp. 48ff.

[11] Burns, *op. cit.*, chap. 6.

Diagnostic and Remedial Chart for Handwriting (cont'd)

FAULT	REMEDY
2. Size:	
a. Irregular	Bend thumb in writing.
b. Too large	Use combination of finger and arm movement, holding pen nearer the point.
c. Too small	Combine arm with finger movement, holding pen further from the point.
3. Slant:	
a. Irregular	Shift paper to left, keeping writing directly in line with eye.
	Direct writing movement toward the center of the body.
b. Too slanting	Lessen slant of paper.
c. Lacking slant	Increase slant of paper.
4. Letter spacing:	
a. Irregular	Regulate slant of letters.
b. Crowded	Lessen slant of letters.
c. Scattered	Increase slant of letters.
5. Beginning and ending strokes:	
a. Irregular	Regulate letter size.
b. Too long	Make smaller letters.
	Lessen slant of letters.
c. Too short	Increase size of letters.
	Increase slant of letters.
6. Word spacing:	
a. Irregular	Make beginning and ending strokes uniform.
b. Crowded	Shorten beginning and ending strokes.
c. Scattered	Lengthen beginning and ending strokes.
7. Alignment:	
a. Irregular	Shift paper to left oftener, keeping writing directly in line with eyes.
b. Under line	Lessen slant of paper.
c. Over line	Increase slant of paper.

Planning practice units of work   The plan of work implicit in the preceding discussion is an attack on separate letters in a more or less chance order. In this plan, as used by Cole, the individual letter constitutes a unit. It is possible to group letters in some fashion such as by similarity of movement. This combination may contribute to the child's understanding of basic letter forms and may facilitate mastery of letters. Possibly investigation may show that if a child has difficulty with one letter of a group he has difficulty with others, such as *n* and *m*, *o* and *a*. Then grouping by form would have a logical and practical justification. It would simplify somewhat both diagnosis and remedial treatment. Types of movement are overcurved, undercurved, and mixed; they suggest an order of treatment. Handwriting courses and workbooks commonly use such grouping. The following combinations have been proposed: (1) *e, i, u, w;* (2) *s, c, r;* (3) *c, o, a;* (4) *m, n, v, x;* (5) *t, d, p;* (6) *l, b, f, h, k;* (7) *j, g, y, z, q.*[12]

Using handwriting workbooks   Handwriting workbooks are commonly designed for class procedure; the children progress through the course together, although some incidental provisions are made for discovering and working on individual difficulties. The course usually outlines a systematic program of work in all phases; it follows the unit plan of grouping letters; and it contains provisions for presentation, diagnosis, practice, and testing, with model letters and words for practice. To the inexperienced or imperfectly trained teacher this comprehensive and ready-made program of the workbook may be extremely useful. The workbook is also useful to the teacher who attempts to carry on work at several levels simultaneously. The new word or letter form should be presented to the group in brief instructional periods. However, it must be recognized that such formal handling of writing instruction may not meet requirements of a functional-diagnostic program as described above.

Until instructional material suitable to such a program is made available, the teacher is obliged to adapt material designed primarily for formal, whole-class work to an individualized group program. Following the inventory of individual difficulties suggested above, the teacher may select and use parts of the workbook material that provide instruction and practice on particular difficulties. Even more practical is making an analysis of difficulties, with the units (letter groups) of the workbook as a basis. A work sheet may be prepared, containing goals, an index of the material of the workbook by letter groups, and provision for noting results of inventory tests and records of improvement. The example shown in Table 17-2 of such a work sheet (for grade 6 in the New Laurel Handwriting Series) may prove suggestive.[13] In this work sheet, letter groups are the groupings found in the pupil's workbook,

[12] Verna D. Anderson and others, *Readings in the Language Arts,* The Macmillan Company, New York, 1964, pp. 173–193.
[13] Modified from J. C. Almack and others, *New Laurel Handwriting Series, Grade Six,* Laurel Publishers, Scranton, Pa.

and the numbers in the second column refer to pages in the workbook on which practice exercises are provided; spaces are provided under "Results of inventory tests" to record the results of the initial inventory tests; spaces under "Improvement record" are used to record progress from test to test, culminating in achievements at grade level or above it. It will be noted that, in addition to records of letter forms, places are provided for other aspects of handwriting, such as joining letters and spacing, and for general skills contributing to the handwriting product, such as posture, and pen holding.

A point much stressed in workbooks is the presentation of letters and combinations of letters in contextual material, commonly taken from the several curriculum areas. The purpose is to maintain a functional point of view in writing. This approach, well advised in a formal program, loses its force in a functional program. When practice in handwriting grows out of current writing experiences, no further emphasis need be given to contextual presentation.

All the other helps given in the workbook should be used: identification of difficulties, causes of errors, remedial procedures, practice exercises, and tests.

Teaching a practice unit of work   This section considers the handling of an instructional unit for a class, group, or individual. Difficulties are presumably discovered in some writing experience in a functional program or in a copy-test exercise in a formal program. The teacher's task is to direct the children's work on the difficulty and bring practice of the correct form to the point of ready use in connected writing. The major steps of development are those outlined above in the section on Treatment of Errors. (1) The first step is observing the correct form and noting deviations from the standard. After the teacher has asked the children about the difficulty, or pointed it out, he notes the cause and gives corrective measures. (2) The teacher demonstrates the writing of the correct form on the chalkboard or on a transparency projected by an overhead projector. As he writes he calls attention to significant features, including the point of beginning, the direction of stroke, and the height of the letter. Several rewritings may be necessary for emphasis. (3) The teacher erases the letter, letter combination, or word, and the children write the whole word or letter from memory; they do not copy or draw. (4) The children then compare their work with the correct form rewritten on the board and consider faults, if any. Reteaching as well as retrial may be necessary. This procedure is continued until the children

Table 17-2 *Handwriting work sheet, grade 6*

Pupil _____

	Practice pages	Results of inventory tests			Improvement record			
		Below grade	Grade level	Above grade	Test result	Test result	Grade level	Above grade
Overall quality score	48							
Overall rate score								
Letter groups: i, u, w	6–7							
e, r, s	8–9							
O, A, o, a	10–11							
m, n, v, c	14–15							
x, t, d, p	16–17							
D, E, l, k, h	18–19							
Numbers, signs	22–23							
T, F, b, f	26–27							
M, N	28–29							
g, q, y	30–31							
G, S, L	34–35							
W	36–37							
P, B, R	38–39							
I, J	40–41							
C	42–43							
H, K, M	46–47							
N, U, V	46–47							
W, X, Y	46–47							
Q. Z	46–47							
Joining letters	13, 32							
Word spacing	25							
Slant	21							
Alignment								
Uniformity of heaviness	20							
General skills: Posture	3							
Pen holding	3							
Position of paper	3							
Movement								
Rhythm								
Speed	33							

can produce a reasonably satisfactory letter or word. (5) The letter is then rewritten a number of times and finally combined with other letters to form words and is then used in phrases and sentences. (6) The final work is evaluated; if satisfactory, it is checked on the record sheet as provisionally mastered. As a follow-up the child may check his writing in purposeful compositions, restudying and repracticing as necessary. Sometimes during practice, children's writing becomes worse as attention shifts; a good procedure to combat this tendency is to have the child mark the best letter form in each line before proceeding to write the next set.

While directing practice on particular letter forms, the teacher calls attention to such general matters as are needed by the children: alignment, spacing, color, slant, grasp on pencil or pen, position of arm, hand, and body, position of paper, relaxation, speed, and rhythm. During directed practice the cause of a particular difficulty may be traced to weakness in one of the general factors. If the defect seems sufficiently crucial in the handwriting of a particular child, improvement in the general factor may be set up as a specific, immediate goal. However, satisfactory performance in general factors is best treated as a means to producing easy, legible, economical writing, not as an end in itself.

Individual work   A certain amount of practice, following the instruction of the teacher, can be carried on independently with general direction and checks. If instruction as well as practice is handled on an individual basis, it is necessary either to develop general study procedures which the children can follow independently or to use self-help materials providing the instructional aids that the teacher normally supplies; such aids include diagnosis, remedial procedures, practice, and evaluation. Developing general habits of study is difficult but not impossible.

Standards   Standards are set by the demands of good social usage and vary with occupational and social needs. Grade norms as set by standard scales are not high; they should be reached and maintained by most children in any class with a minimum of time and effort. Individuality of style is permitted and encouraged within the limits of legibility and ease of writing.

Motivation   The primary motivation is found in purposeful writing wherein accuracy and legibility are regarded as a courtesy to the reader. In school many occasions arise where the necessity for good handwriting is immediately felt. Specific motivation for improvement is found in measuring achievement, locating specific deficiencies, and checking and recording progress. One device that has been used successfully is a class goal-filing chart. On a large piece of cardboard, samples of the children's writing are arranged in three columns, forming a crude scale: unsatisfactory for the grade, satisfactory, and better than satisfactory. Pockets are placed below each sample. Children file their compositions from time to time in what they consider the proper pocket. The teacher checks and, if he agrees, leaves the compositions where he finds them. If the teacher feels that a child's judgment is in error, he takes the matter up with the child and they agree upon a proper disposition of the composition.

Following are some typical samples.

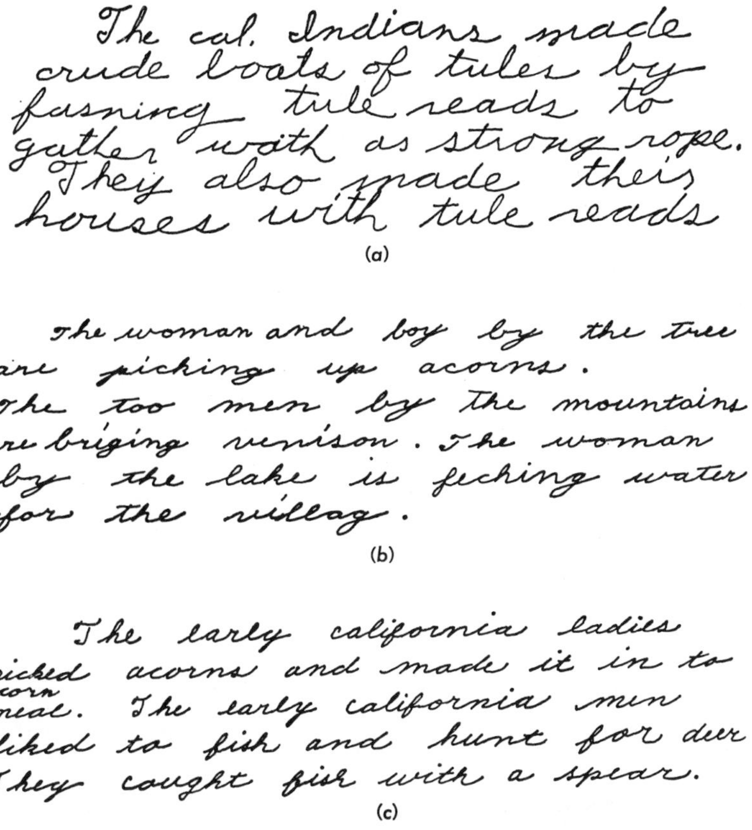

> The cal. Indians made crude boats of tules by fasning tule reads to gather with as strong rope. They also made their houses with tule reads

(a)

> The woman and boy by the tree are picking up acorns.
> The too men by the mountains are briging venison. The woman by the lake is feching water for the villag.

(b)

> The early california ladies picked acorns and made it in to meal. The early california men liked to fish and hunt for deer They caught fish with a spear.

(c)

Figure 17-2. Samples of fourth-grade children's handwriting regarded by the teacher as (a) unsatisfactory, (b) satisfactory, and (c) better than satisfactory.

Another good device for motivation and measurement of progress is the collecting of samples of children's handwriting at the beginning of the year and occasionally throughout the year. Samples filed in individual folders show progress. Pairs of samples showing marked progress may be displayed on the bulletin board. They serve also as publicity material for parents and for the public on school visiting days.

Checking handwriting in written work   It is necessary at this point to stress again the importance of checking handwriting in all written work. The gains in skill resulting from directed practice work will be maintained only if children give deliberate attention to using good handwriting and to habitually checking results. Particular attention should be given to the specific skills and abilities on which the children are working at the time.

Beginning handwriting   We turn now to the first stage, work in beginning handwriting. Beginning work is like later training in point of view, procedures, problems of individualization, organization of instruction, and basic mechanics. The fundamental principles and procedures are the same; the differences lie in the adaptation of work to a lower-grade maturity level.

The functional point of view operates in beginning as in later writing. It is especially important that children acquire early an understanding of handwriting as a means of communication; therefore, the child's first writing should have meaning and purpose by being related to immediate activities. These are found in having the child write his own name and address, thank-you notes, signs, notes to parents, friends, and sick classmates, invitations, greeting cards, announcements, lists of games, activities, songs, tools and materials for room activities, library books read by pupils, records of experiences, names of characters in stories, riddles and rhymes, original stories, posters, notices, programs, slogans, records of birthdays and ages, charts, captions.[14]

Readiness and preparation for writing   Writing is a complex skill requiring a degree of maturity in mental and physical processes. Instead of abruptly precipitating a class or individual into writing experiences, the teacher does well to check readiness and to

[14] Pose Lamb, *Guiding Children's Language Learning*, W. C. Brown Company, Publishers, Dubuque, Iowa, 1967, pp. 184–200. See also Harold G. Shane and others, *Improving Language Arts Instruction in the Elementary School*, Charles E. Merrill Books, Inc., Columbus, Ohio, 1962, pp. 363–378.

provide preliminary experiences. The ability to organize and express ideas orally is indicative of mental readiness. The necessary manual skills may be inferred from performance in games, drawing at the chalkboard, making clay figures, cutting and coloring paper, constructing toys from wood, and rhythmic responses to music.

Pupils get specific preparation watching the teacher write at the board. They gain some understanding of sentences, words, letter forms, the writing process, and the left-to-right direction as the teacher writes records, directions, and notes on the board at the dictation of the children.

The teacher should watch for spontaneous efforts at copying or original writing. One kindergarten teacher says that when her children show an inclination to begin writing she sends home to the parents a pattern sheet for children's letters, to avoid the necessity of learning new patterns when the childen go to the first grade.

cursive - connected

Manuscript writing   An early decision as to style of writing and the selection of letter forms is necessary. The chief question is whether to use manuscript or cursive writing. The marked trend toward manuscript writing in beginning work seems justified on both theoretical and practical grounds. The chief arguments for its use are that (1) it is better adapted than cursive to the muscular development of children, requiring less fine coordination and less sustained effort; (2) the child can begin meaningful writing sooner; (3) it is similar to the form the teacher uses in making charts and is comparable to the printed letter forms.[15]

A transition to cursive writing is commonly made in the high second or low third grade. The selection of letter forms that are similar in cursive and manuscript facilitates the change; the problem of transition is then simply that of writing the word in one continuous movement with the connecting strokes. The letters that represent different forms in cursive writing require careful teaching—*b, e, f, k, m, n, r, s, z*. The capital letters in cursive writing represent even greater divergency when compared with the capital letters of manuscript writing. It is an oversimplification to consider cursive writing as connected manuscript writing.

Another consideration in the transition to cursive writing is the moderate use of cursive writing by the teacher prior to giving

[15] Verna D. Anderson and others, *op. cit.*, pp. 153–171. See also J. K. Noble, "Handwriting Programs in Today's Schools," *Elementary English,* vol. 40, May, 1963, pp. 506–512.

reading instruction to the children, using a procedure such as the following: "When we started to school, boys and girls, we learned manuscript writing because that seemed easiest for us. That is *one* kind of writing. There is another kind of writing, which most of your mothers and fathers use. Suppose I start using *grown-up* writing—cursive writing—on the board for you to start reading. Later on, we'll all start learning to write this way. On the board we have our sentences that tell the date. The sentences say: *Today is May 29. It is Wednesday.* This is how our sentences look in cursive writing." The teacher writes each sentence in cursive writing directly below the manuscript sentence. Each following day, the process of writing the date sentences in manuscript and cursive writing is continued. Gradually simple directions are written on the chalkboard for further practice in reading "grown-up" writing. The teacher might prepare name cards for each of the children in the room. These can be filed in a pocket chart for recognition games, and can be used as a beginning for instruction in cursive writing. By working with individuals, the teacher can help each child learn to write his name. Spelling textbooks and language arts courses of study frequently combine handwriting and spelling teaching, and the teacher needs to be aware of the interrelationship between these two writing factors.[16]

Children like to make words with the new letters as learned; they sometimes make a game of it, coming from home with lists of words which they have worked out. The capitals must be taken up separately, but they can be taught in much the same manner.

Mechanics and materials   The functional program places less emphasis on mechanics than does the traditional, formal program. In the former, mechanics are considered in relation to quality, ease of writing, physical well-being, and the conditions under which writing normally takes place.

Beginning practice at the chalkboard or on large sheets of unruled paper seems to be a wise procedure. It favors the use of large muscles, children like it, and the teacher can supervise the work easily. The pupils should, of course, assume the correct position, hold the chalk or pencil properly, and write in a large script. The transition from chalkboard to paper writing may be made as soon as competency in chalkboard work is achieved.

[16] Virgil E. Herrick and others, *New Horizons for Research in Handwriting,* University of Wisconsin Press, Madison, Wis., 1963, pp. 20, 37.

Some pupils may write at the board while others work at their seats.

Large soft pencils may be used at first. Practice is begun on unruled paper. Many teachers use 12- by 18-inch pieces of unlined newsprint, folded into eighths, when children begin to practice separate letters; the areas marked by the folds tend to give a definite space for the writing of each letter. Newsprint of this size can be folded lengthwise into fourths, providing space for writing short sentences. Ruled paper is introduced later. In general, standard ruling is 1 inch in the first grade, ¾ inch in the second grade, ½ inch in the third, and ⅜ inch in the upper grades. Often in the first and second grades, faint dotted lines (slotted faints) divide the solid lines on the 1-inch paper, assisting children in determining the height of half-size letters, the proportions of letters made up of part circle and stroke, and capital letters. Later, in writing with a pen, a good quality of paper is desirable. Ballpoint pens and fountain pens are used.

In learning manuscript writing, the paper is placed directly before the child, aligned with his desk. Later, in cursive writing, placing the paper at a slant is an important factor in letter alignment and slant. Erectness and the proper position of the arms provide a free, comfortable writing posture conducive to good physical condition. A firm but relaxed manner of holding the pencil or pen contributes to quality of line and ease of writing. The movement is a combination of arm and finger motion; the arm is used in making the longer strokes and in carrying the hand across the page, and the fingers are used in executing the details of letters. Good writing becomes a rhythmical combination of irregular movements, of stresses and pauses. Rhythm is a result of maturity and training.

Practice-unit organization and sequence In the informal functional handling of writing in the primary grades, especially in beginning work, the organization is around writing experiences that have high interest because of immediate purpose. For example, in beginning work the children have occasion to sign their names; later, they write individual notes to parents, inviting them to a class party. In such an informal program, words and letter forms appear in a chance order. New words and letters are learned as required. Instruction consists mainly of showing and copying and is incidental to the experience. Repetition comes through use.

Handwriting books offer a more systematic type of work

organization. Words are selected that rank high in frequency of use in children's vocabularies, and some attention is given to emphasis on the most frequently used letters first, to sequence, and to a maintenance program of reviews.

Handling a practice instructional unit   Generally, the procedures used in handling an instructional unit in later work apply here; learning is the same on both levels. The experience provides the point of attack and the basis of instruction. After explaining the need, the teacher demonstrates by writing the word, phrase, or sentence required. Oral instructions accompany the demonstration, calling attention to forms of letters, beginning point, direction of movement, spacing, etc. New or difficult letters receive special emphasis and may be isolated for a short training exercise. The word is the basis for writing, not the letter; and children write the whole word from memory. Work is checked with the teacher's copy for correctness; then practice follows. Individual difficulties are noted, and corrective work given. Training in position, holding the pencil, movement, and placing the paper are given incidentally. Work is compared with previous production to show progress.

Individual differences   Individual differences are evident in the early as well as the later grades. Not all children are equally ready to begin writing, and as training progresses different levels of competency are apparent. Resourceful teachers distinguish degrees of maturity and competency, group children with similar needs, and provide a differentiated program of work suited to group needs.

Left-handedness is a problem mainly for the primary teacher. The degree of dominance of the left or right hand should be established when writing is begun, and appropriate habits should be formed. Presumably, left-handedness is well established before the child enters school, and it is unwise to attempt a change. If there is doubt about the preference of hands, simple exercises may be used as checks.[17]

At this point it is emphasized that the left-handed child needs understanding and sympathetic handling. Practically every instrument, tool, and gadget that he is called on to handle all through life is made for a right-handed person: scissors, jackknife, pencil sharpener, broad-armed chair in college classrooms, and even the lowly can opener—all are "opposite" for him, and he is constantly

[17] Verna D. Anderson and others, *op. cit.*, pp. 171–173. See also Virgil E. Herrick and others, *op. cit.*, pp. 25–26.

adapting himself to awkward positions. It has been suggested that in the case of cutting, the best solution for the young left-handed child might be that of learning to shift to the right hand; hence, these children may learn to write and draw with the left hand, if they show a strong degree of preference, while learning to perform other tasks with the right hand.[18]

In studying the writing habits of left-handed children, who number 11 percent of the population, Enstrom found three techniques being used to produce efficient quality and rate, nonsmeared papers, and healthful posture. These techniques were being used by children who had learned to keep the writing hand below the writing line and who slanted their papers in the opposite direction. In each of these desirable techniques, the angle of slant of the paper varied. Children who had learned to write by hooking the hand to approach the writing line from above are penalized by not having the hand move freely across the page and by smearing their writing. In the case of the "hookers," Enstrom suggests that very few "hookers" can be changed beyond grade 4 and that these children should be given techniques to achieve the best writing possible for them. The researcher makes a strong plea for adequate understanding of the teaching of handwriting to the left-handed primary-grade child, in order to facilitate a research-based developmental program.[19]

Evaluation The functional approach to handwriting seeks to provide attitudes toward legibility and the supporting skills needed to produce the legibly written product with ease of performance at an adequate rate of speed. The program implementation presents handwriting as an essential tool for communication but provides specific times for initiation, practice, and maintenance of the skills of penmanship. Studied consideration of the initial phases of teaching manuscript and cursive writing is necessary to provide children with a basic framework of letter formation, spacing, and alignment. As children progress through the grades, handwriting, recognized as the medium by which thoughts are written, is duly considered when preparing the final report, letter, or story—

[18] E. A. Enstrom and Edna H. Crittenden, "Scissors and the Lefty," *The Educational Forum*, vol. 32, January, 1968, pp. 217–220.

[19] E. A. Enstrom, "The Extent of the Use of the Left Hand in Handwriting and the Determination of the Relative Efficiency of the Various Hand-Wrist-Arm Paper Adjustments," doctoral dissertation, University of Pittsburgh, 1957, *Dissertation Abstracts*, vol. 17, 1957. See also E. A. Enstrom, "Research in Teaching the Left-handed," *The Instructor*, vol. 74, October, 1964, pp. 44–46, 104.

for the point must be made that often the rough-draft letter little resembles the finished product, particularly when many ideas are emerging in considering a problem or a topic. In dealing with the handwriting plight of many upper-grade children, the teacher might well bear in mind the sometimes overwhelming amount of written work assigned daily and weekly to these children.

For your consideration

1   Plan a lesson for the introduction of a new handwriting skill for a grade level in which you are interested.
2   If possible, observe in a primary-grade classroom during a handwriting activity. Notice how individuals differ in (*a*) approach to the writing task, (*b*) maintenance of interest, (*c*) handling of paper and use of pencil, (*d*) rate and ease of writing, and (*e*) the quality of the finished product.
3   Collect papers from a class of fourth, fifth, or sixth graders. Analyze group needs in the following areas: single letter formations; problems concerning specific letter combinations; alignment; and spacing.
4   Using your observations in 2 or your analyses in 3, plan a series of lessons designed to reteach or to extend specific handwriting skills.

References

ANDERSEN, DAN: "Handwriting Research: Movement and Quality," *Elementary English*, vol. 42, January, 1965, pp. 45–53.

———: "Handwriting Research: Style and Practice," *Elementary English*, vol. 42, February, 1965, pp. 115–125.

ANDERSON, PAUL S.: *Language Skills in Elementary Education*, The Macmillan Company, New York, 1966, chap. 3.

DALLMAN, MARTHA: *Teaching the Language Arts in the Elementary School*, W. C. Brown Company, Publishers, Dubuque, Iowa, 1966, chap. 7.

DAWSON, MILDRED A., AND FRIEDA H. DINGEE: *Children Learn the Language Arts*, Burgess Publishing Company, Minneapolis, Minn., 1966, chap. 8.

———, M. ZOLLINGER, AND A. ELWELL: *Guiding Language Learning*, Harcourt, Brace & World, Inc., New York, 1963, chap. 17.

FREEMAN, FRANK N.: *Guiding Growth in Handwriting*, The Zaner-Bloser Company, Columbus, Ohio, 1965.

——— AND THE ZANER-BLOSER STAFF: *Handwriting Faults and How to Correct them*, The Zaner-Bloser Company, Columbus, Ohio, 1958.

GREENE, H. A., AND W. T. PETTY: *Developing Language Skills in the Elementary Schools*, Allyn and Bacon, Inc., Boston, 1963, pp. 524–535.

HERRICK, VIRGIL E.: *New Horizons for Research in Handwriting,* University of Wisconsin Press, Madison, Wis., 1963.

LAMB, POSE: *Guiding Children's Language Learning,* W. C. Brown Company, Publishers, Dubuque, Iowa, 1967, p. 198.

LEE, J. MURRAY, AND DORRIS M. LEE: *The Child and His Curriculum,* Appleton-Century-Crofts, Inc., New York, 1960, pp. 340–351.

LEONARD, EDITH M., AND OTHERS: *Basic Learning in the Language Arts,* Scott, Foresman and Company, Chicago, 1965, part 5.

MC KEE, PAUL: *Language in the Elementary School,* Houghton Mifflin Company, Boston, 1939, chap. 10.

MYERS, EMMA H.: *The Whys and Hows of Teaching Handwriting,* The Zaner-Bloser Company, Columbus, Ohio, 1963.

NATIONAL COUNCIL OF TEACHERS OF ENGLISH, *Language Arts for Today's Children,* Appleton-Century-Crofts, Inc., New York, 1954, pp. 219–225, 248–257, 335.

———: *Research on Handwriting and Spelling,* Champaign, Ill., 1966.

NOBLE, J. K.: "Handwriting Programs in Today's Schools," *Elementary English,* vol. 40, May, 1963, pp. 506–512.

RUSSELL, DAVID H., AND OTHERS: *Child Development and the Language Arts,* National Council of Teachers of English, Champaign, Ill., 1953, pp. 20–22.

SOLTIS, ROSEMARY: "Handwriting: The Middle R," *Elementary English,* vol. 40, October, 1963, pp. 605–607.

WEST, PAUL V.: *The American Handwriting Scale,* A. N. Palmer Company, New York, 1957.

PART 4

PLANNING
A
LANGUAGE
ARTS
PROGRAM

18.

CURRICULUM: GOALS AND SEQUENCES

It is necessary in setting up a language program to plot the course that language development is to take and to clarify as clearly as possible the levels of growth that may be expected for each grade. This overall planning is primarily the responsibility of curriculum makers, but it is a task so complicated by details and by variabilities in classes that curriculum makers can never hope to give more than general direction. The teacher's concern in the overall program of work is twofold: (1) to preserve continuity from grade to grade in the language development of pupils and (2) to meet the needs of particular groups of pupils whose abilities actually spread over many grades.

Numerous references to grade goals and sequences have been made throughout this text, both in expository form and in examples. We now come to grips with the matter in summary form.

Difficulties The task described above is easily stated in general terms, but the actual setting up of defensible goals for a particular school or class presents difficulties that should be recognized and faced candidly from the outset. The first difficulty is occasioned by the varying social needs of pupils in various schools. Schools generally are located in neighborhood areas in which the school population is relatively homogeneous; but the school populations of different areas vary widely in socioeconomic status, culture, and language background. Some schools draw largely from business- and professional-class families that maintain a high level of spoken language in the home; the language here heard from infancy is the language of educated people, and social pressure favors the use of good English. Other schools draw largely from quite different populations—from people in low-income brackets, unskilled la- borers, and groups in which any one of several foreign languages is spoken in the home. It is a basic principle that language training and standards of acceptability should conform to the cultural needs of the population that the school serves. No one program or pattern can be devised that will meet the needs of all communities. This means, of course, that much of the responsibility for planning the language program will be borne by the local school staff and by individual teachers in the school. A curriculum-research depart- ment or committee in a state, city, or country system may set up a philosophy and sketch the general features of the language pro- gram, and it may state in general terms the kind of adaptations to local schools that need to be made; but local school staffs and individual teachers must expect to adapt the general program to their specific needs.[1]

A second difficulty in the problems now being considered arises from the nature of language and from the complexity of growth in language, as shown in Chapter 1. Language serves many specific purposes and takes many forms, such as telling stories, giving reports, outlining, summarizing, and engaging in discus- sions. Training in one kind of experience carries over to others to some extent; but the identity of each must be recognized by the speaker, and suitable adaptations in techniques must be made. Growth in language means growth simultaneously in many inter- related but separate experiences. Moreover, growth in any ex- perience means growth in a number of specific attitudes, abilities, and skills of which the experience is composed. An experience cannot be isolated and taught entirely separately from other ex- periences; nor can attitudes, abilities, and skills be entirely isolated from experiences and from each other, and developed separately.

A third difficulty arises from dealing with extreme variations in language abilities represented by members of any class, as was noted in Chapter 3. If all the children of a class were equally mature in language, teaching would be simpler, although not

[1] Joe L. Frost and G. R. Hawkes, *The Disadvantaged Child,* Houghton Mifflin Company, Boston, 1966, pp. 1–12.

simple. But children are not equally mature. Statistically stated, the range in variability of the members of one class may be as much as six to eight grades.

Objective data are impressive enough, but even they do not reveal the problem in all its complexity. It might be assumed, for example, that children who are low in average performance are low in every experience and in every ability and skill that contributes to average performance. This is not the case. A low-average child often rates high in some specific phases of the work. For example, one child wants to recite all the time, while another child voluntarily participates seldom or not at all; one child defends his position to the bitter end, while another gives in without a protest; one child responds favorably to criticism, while another is extremely sensitive and easily hurt; one child thinks clearly and sticks logically to the point under discussion, while another child wanders aimlessly. The true and complete picture of individual differences is revealed to the teacher only as he systematically studied his pupils' work and behavior from day to day. The unevenness of development makes it difficult to set rigid class and individual goals.

The following are two poems written by two third-grade boys during a story-writing period when the teacher had imposed no restrictions. The children were free to write about anything in prose or in free-verse poetry. Most of the children wrote in prose, but for reasons of their own these boys chose poetry as their medium. Nothing has been changed in either poem except spelling.

THE LITTLE TREE
    (John's story)

Once there was a little tree
Just as pretty as could be
But then one day a little bee
Made a nest in that little tree.

NIGHT
    (Jim's story)

The sun was dying
The moon was slowly being born
The stars were being christened
For on was coming night.
Pure twilight now was present.
Now the light is dim

Ah! now all is darkness
Night is here again.

Between these two poems there is an almost inestimable span of maturity. How many adults could so well describe a sunset? One wonders what would prompt an eight-year-old to express himself in such phrases as "stars were being christened" and "on was coming night." Yet there is no doubt that, as he wrote, Jim was actually experiencing a twilight. Such widely differing abilities of expression are sometimes hard to explain, yet they are present to some extent in every grade. The teacher accordingly must cope with these differences in such a way that the immature child will be stimulated and the mature child guided. No two children are alike nor can they be handled in exactly the same way. Every teacher must cope with the personalities involved; and while he must provide for the Jims and Johns, he must organize his work in the main around the group as a whole—its needs, its capacities, its maturity.

A fourth and final difficulty is the inadequacy at the present time of research in the field of specific planning. The consequence of this weakness is seen in wide disparities in teaching practices—not entirely explained by varying philosophies and by adaptations to local needs—and in the lack of authoritative information on which may be based a program of setting grade goals.[2]

Some data bearing on the objective phases of language—punctuation, capitalization, usage, and sentence structure—are available, but the study of the more basic matters of the specific social uses of various language experiences as well as the study of the nature, development, and interrelationships of the important general abilities has barely gotten under way. Setting grade goals, then, is still in the hypothetical stage to a large extent. Teachers naturally will use such research material as is available and will use the opinions of experts where dependable factual information is lacking; but they will face the necessity of doing a good bit of guessing.

Principles   A positive step in setting up a sequence of grade goals is to establish basic principles that can be applied to various phases of the language program. The first basic principle is that of current need. This is determined by use in all parts of schoolwork and

[2] Arno Jewett and others, *Improving English Skills of Culturally Different Youth in Large Cities*, U.S. Office of Education, Washington, D.C., 1964, pp. 35–79.

outside the school. The principle of current need has wide applicability: to the kinds of language experiences included, to general abilities, and to specific skills. The implication, of course, concerns the needs of particular classes. In considering current need, weight will be given to the frequency with which the experience, ability, or skill is required in use and to the crucial importance of the experience or of the ability or skill as a factor in carrying on the experience. The question of priority comes up inevitably. Teachers cannot profitably attempt to meet all the current needs of children. Which are the most important? For example, in speaking, is correct usage more important than freedom of expression? Teachers must set reasonable limits to their programs. Exact, detailed directions about what to do in every situation cannot be given, but teachers can consider the matter and use their best judgment to formulate general policies.

Determining needs and setting up goals A comparatively simple and practical approach is to make an analysis of a basic textbook or course of study. The textbook, if reasonably satisfactory, provides in convenient form the results of extended study and research of competent persons. The work is necessarily detailed, providing a complete series of grade goals designed to meet the developmental needs of children. The book will give a program of work for grades and planned sequences among the grades. It will show the basic experiences that the authors regard as essential and also the work in related abilities and skills. The course of study is usually more general in character, leaving out many essential details. The summary at the end of the chapter will show the kind of material gained from a course-of-study analysis and will be useful for comparison with other sources and for the study of particular problems of grading and sequence. Attention may profitably be given to the specific items—experiences, abilities, and skills—assigned to the several grades and to sequences from grade to grade.

It is unlikely that a program of work outlined in a course of study or textbook, such as that at the end of the chapter, will meet exactly the needs of a particular school or class, but it will show the general nature of curriculum content, and it may serve as a point of departure in setting up a particular program.

Surveys of local needs The adaptation to local needs of the basic program as outlined in a course of study or textbook is best based on thorough surveys of such needs. The accumulated experience of teachers working in a particular school will contribute much useful information. Teachers as a group may profitably organize surveys to show what kinds of language experiences are carried on by children in the home and in the community; what patterns of language expression prevail; what standards of usage are acceptable; what specific difficulties of construction, usage, and speech, particularly pronunciation and enunciation, are common; and what resources in personal experiences may be used to provide content.

Absolute grading versus a flexible plan   Another positive attack on the problem of grading is to decide on a basic pattern for organizing the overall program. Two choices are possible: organizing goals by grades or indicating sequences of goals regardless of grades. Organization by grades is the traditional and still the common plan in courses of study and in textbooks. From the point of view of the teacher, it is definite and specific; it shows exactly what should be accomplished in a particular grade. It assumes that language work can be broken down into specific stages of development, that these stages can be allocated to particular grades, and that the goals are reasonably satisfactory for the grade and for all the pupils of the grade. Sequences are implied but not shown; to determine sequences the teacher must consult the specifications of preceding and following grades.

Although the absolute grading plan is almost universally followed in courses of study and in textbooks, its limitations are apparent to theorists and teachers. Language development cannot be broken down into a fixed set of discrete steps, and the variabilities of individuals within classes are so great that fixed goals are quite meaningless for many individuals. Everyone agrees that grade goals should be flexible, adaptable to various classes and to individuals within classes, and that learning should be continuous.

A possible alternative to fixed grading is to block out desirable sequences, enabling the teacher to determine with reasonable exactness just what stage a class, and each individual in a class, has reached. This plan is favored by an impressive number of competent authorities. For example, Nila B. Smith says, "It is quite possible that, for the sake of practical curriculum making, *moments of initial attack* upon specific problems may be worked out for individual school systems, but obviously *no set standards of mastery can be imposed upon children at any specific grade level.*" The analysis of outcomes in conversation and in discussion "indicate clearly that it is possible to map the *direction of growth* in each of the areas." [3] And the Commission on the English Curriculum says, "Instead of arbitrary standards for the various grade levels . . . teachers need descriptions of systematic sequences in language learning which apply to all pupils." [4] And adds, "They [teachers] do not think primarily of grade placement of materials . . . but think rather of next steps in the development of each child in language power." [5]

Sequences should be planned for important lines of growth, in both experiences and in abilities and skills. Sequences in conversation, telephoning, discussion and planning, telling stories, dramatizing, and reporting are described by Hatfield.[6] Sequences in abilities and skills have been worked out in several courses of study.[7]

The flexible plan emphasizes the important principle of continuity of learning and provides flexibility in adapting work to the needs of a particular class and to individuals. The teacher is encouraged to study the levels of development of his pupils and to begin instruction where they are. He may be relieved of the necessity of doing prescribed work regardless of the needs of his pupils, and he does not feel compelled to reach fixed goals.

The grading of experiences From a consideration of the general problems and points of attack in laying out a program of work by grades, we turn to the specific problems involved in the grading of specific parts of the language program: experiences, attitudes, abilities, and skills. The grading of experiences logically requires first consideration.

When one analyzes the experiences allocated to the several grades by various courses of study and textbooks, one gets some interesting results. The striking fact is that the same general

[3] M. R. Trabue and others, *Teaching Language in the Elementary School,* Forty-third Yearbook, National Society for the Study of Education, University of Chicago Press, Chicago, 1944, part 2, pp. 92–93.

[4] National Council of Teachers of English, *The English Language Arts,* Appleton-Century-Crofts, Inc., New York, 1952, p. 189.

[5] National Council of Teachers of English, *Language Arts for Today's Children,* Appleton-Century-Crofts, Inc., New York, 1954, p. 54.

[6] W. W. Hatfield, *An Experience Curriculum in English,* Appleton-Century-Crofts, Inc., New York, 1935, chap. 13.

[7] Los Angeles County, *A Guide to Curriculum Development and Course of Study,* Elementary Schools of Los Angeles County, Calif., 1965. See also Castro Valley Elementary School District, *Language Arts Guides: Grades K–3, 4–6, 7–8,* Elementary Schools of Castro Valley, Calif., 1960. Kansas City, Missouri, *Teaching English in the Elementary School: A Resource Guide,* Kansas City, Mo., Public Schools, 1961. San Diego Unified School District, *Curriculum Guide,* San Diego (City) Unified School District, Calif., 1961.

types of experience appear in practically every grade. For example, oral communication, conversation, discussion, and asking and answering questions appear in the kindergarten and continue through the eighth grade; telephoning begins in about the second grade, and meetings in about the fifth. Generally oral forms appear early, indicating the dominance of oral experiences in the early grades. Certain written forms, such as friendly letters and invitations, appear early also, and they are used throughout the grades. The more complex written forms, such as outlines and summaries, begin in the intermediate grades. In the judgment of authors and of curriculum makers children carry on about the same experiences at various grade levels and they need continued instruction and practice. The appearance of a number of experiences in a grade does not signify that all of them receive the same emphasis; for example, in one fourth-grade book, conversation appears in every unit, and invitations in only one. Nor should one assume that the same elements in experiences are taught in all grades; there is a progression of elements within the experiences.

The principle of immediate need operates in the grading of experiences and in relative emphasis on experiences. Work on speaking and writing experiences is begun in the grades in which the children normally begin to use these experiences extensively. When the experience is too difficult for the children alone to handle, the teacher helps, as in letter writing at the second-grade level.

Sequences within experiences   Since the same experiences spread over many grades, it is obvious that the major grade differentiation does not occur in kinds of experiences. The same experiences are carried on at increasingly higher levels of performance. Hatfield offers such a breakdown of the various experiences, "experience strands," into steps of increasing social complexity. For example, in conversation: [8]

1   To talk with a familiar small group about home experiences.
2   To talk with a familiar small group about shared experiences.
3   To be a good host to visitors from another room or from outside the school.
4   To be a satisfactory guest.
5   To converse interestingly and pleasantly with mere acquaintances.

[8] Hatfield, *op. cit.*, pp. 138–141.

6 To converse during "refreshments" served at a table, to not more than eight persons at once.

7 To meet strange children gracefully and graciously.

Letter writing may be used as another example of the graduation of work to meet increasing difficulty and the maturity of the pupils. In the beginning, the letter takes the form of a simple communication dictated to the teacher by the pupils. The pupils help plan the content, sentences, and organization; the teacher provides the heading and salutation. The class letter may be copied by the pupils. Gradually the pupils take over more responsibility for various parts of the letter; first, a simple salutation and close; later, the heading, varied forms of close, and addressing the envelope. Classwork gradually gives way to individual composition at the later third- or fourth-grade level; and with a minimum of guidance from the teacher, the pupils assume full, individual responsibility.

In sum, each major experience of the language curriculum is broken down into steps of difficulty, a desired sequence is indicated, and goals are set for classes and individuals in terms of maturity and capacity. The exact definition of these goals is one of the major tasks of curriculum makers and teachers, and is a practical and very necessary piece of work. Courses of study and textbooks give some help.

Grading and sequences of attitudes, abilities, and skills We face the same problems in grading attitudes, abilities, and skills that we face in dealing with experiences: What emphasis should be given to each at the several grade levels? What is the order of importance, or the sequence?

The primary weaknesses of the traditional program are that it fails to give proper attention to lifelike experiences and that it attaches too much importance to mechanical performance, such as usage and punctuation, to the neglect of other, more important factors. The emphasis placed on attitudes, abilities, and skills largely determines the quality of language work.

There is some authority for the following listing of factors in order of emphasis and of importance for language development:

1 Attitudes:
Be willing to participate.
Desire to improve.
Discover and correct own errors.

2   Courtesies:
Listen attentively.
Give and take criticisms pleasantly.
Behave amiably.

3   Content:
Select topics that are good, limited, and appropriate to situation.
Choose interesting details.
Express thought completely.
Express own thoughts and feelings.
Distinguish between real and make-believe.

4   Organization:
Stick to the point.
Follow good sequence.
Use good beginning and ending sentences.
Paragraph properly.

5   Vocabulary:
Use vivid, apt words and phrases.
Avoid trite words and phrases.

6   Sentences:
Express complete thought.
Avoid gross crudities.
Use variety.

7   Speech:
Speak audibly.
Speak distinctly.
Use correct pronunciation.
Use pleasing voice.
Deliver speech effectively.

8   Usage:
Use verbs appropriate to the situation.
Use pronouns correctly.
Use adverbs and adjectives correctly.
Avoid redundancies.

9   Written mechanics:
Use correct capitalization and punctuation.
Use proper manuscript form.
Be neat.

There is one point in the grading of abilities and skills on which there is general agreement, namely, that developing proper attitudes should receive first consideration. This priority is true, not only in the earliest grade in which language is taught, but also in every grade. Until a teacher secures free and voluntary willingness to participate, he cannot hope to take steps in the direction of improving ability in the technical aspects of language.

The problem first appears in oral work. Fundamental factors of personality are involved. Desire to improve and willingness and ability to discover and correct one's own deficiencies come later, but they are equally fundamental factors.

Courtesies are placed high on the list because they are closely related to willingness to participate. Particularly important is friendly, appreciative listening. To John, who has so much to say that he frequently interrupts, the teacher may need to comment, "You remember, John, Mary listened when you told your story. Now she wants to tell *her* story. Wouldn't it be polite if you would listen?"

There is little room for disagreement about the high ranking of content. It is both logical and practical in a functional program of language instruction to emphasize the importance of the material that is communicated. On this point we must make a sharp break with traditional practice. How much overemphasis in the past was placed on minor matters of form, while important problems of content were neglected! If the present-day teacher can secure a willingness to participate and can assure the child that he has something worth saying, that teacher has the leverage with which to deal with the more advanced refinements of thinking and expression. Naturally, not all the specific abilities in content should be stressed at one time. The ability to make worthy contributions, for example, is a gradual growth. The teacher will begin with training in the selection of topics suitable to an occasion and will later take up other specific abilities in their proper order in the developmental sequence.

Organization is closely related to subject-matter content, and certain phases, such as a simple time sequence, can be treated early. There is need here, also, to distinguish essentials from nonessentials and to put first things first. For example, instruction in composing good beginning and good ending sentences is a refinement that should follow mastery of sticking to the point and of securing a clear, logical sequence of ideas; emphasis on beginning and ending sentences has commonly been begun too early.

Vocabulary and sentence structure are closely related to clear, apt, vivid expression. Some work on these factors of effective expression may begin in the early grades. Questions concerning how much emphasis should be given to vocabulary and sentence structure involve questions concerning the general type of language program being taught.

Usage and the mechanics of speaking and writing are placed relatively low on the list, not to minimize their importance, but to put them in their proper relation to matters of attitude, content, and organization. There is involved, also, the problem of simplifying the learning task for the child by not setting too many goals for simultaneous attack. Still, there is room for the exercise of judgment in introducing these elements. For example, certain types of speech difficulties, such as baby talk, should be recognized and dealt with early. Or, the teacher may have to say on occasion, "I'm sure your story is very interesting, Nancy. Could you speak a little louder so that Betty and I can hear every word? We don't want to miss any of it." Attention to many items of less importance, such as undue emphasis on posture and mannerisms, can, however, be safely postponed.

An analysis of the provisions of textbooks and courses of study shows that the same factors are stressed in many grades. Obviously, attitudes, abilities, and skills are not mastered once for all in any grade; rather, there is a gradual growth and a need for reteaching in several grades. As in the case of experiences, grading is not based on the kind of factor but on sequence of growth within each factor.

Grading particular elements of composition, mainly written In preceding sections we have been concerned with certain general qualities of language work, oral and written, and with certain general abilities and skills related to those qualities. It is recognized that these general qualities and abilities are fundamental and vital and that they deserve the chief emphasis in teaching. But they are intangibles involving elements of thought, feeling, and judgment, which makes it necessary to deal with them in broad terms. There are certain other elements of language, mainly matters of form, that can be treated more objectively and specifically; and some of these are now considered: sentence structure, capitalization, punctuation, and usage. To a great extent, these matters of mechanics are controlled by rigid conventions; but standards are constantly changing, and personal preference is permitted to some degree.

In terms of averages, the sentences of children in the primary grades are largely simple in kind; complex, compound, and complex-compound sentences increase through the grades in the order named. This fact suggests a general order of natural development and emphasis. However, even more striking than the general progression is the fact that all kinds of sentences are used at all grade levels, at least above the second. The kinds of sentences used are largely affected by experiences, by the language heard in the home, and by the character of the teaching; if given opportunity and encouragement, some children in the primary grades will use complex forms of sentence structure, such as dependent clauses in an inverted order. The implications for teaching, therefore, are that the general emphasis in instruction should follow the general order of development of thinking, but that individual children should be encouraged and helped to use types of sentence structure suited to their capacities and maturity.

Capitalization and punctuation are the most nearly mechanical elements of composition. Considerable evidence has been accumulated concerning needs at various grade levels (determined by use in spontaneous writing), the proper order of treatment, and various levels of difficulty. Textbooks and courses of study are usually quite definite in listing grade requirements in these areas.

Usage is largely affected by local language patterns, and local surveys are necessary in setting up a usage program. However, the peculiarities of the English language and language patterns affecting large areas are such that certain basic crudities are widespread. These common crudities are well known, and their grading is commonly indicated in detail in courses of study and in textbooks.

Many of the specific points in the grading and sequence of the materials of a language arts program, including activities and attitudes, abilities, and skills, are found in the analysis of the contents of textbooks from the McKee and others *English for Meaning* series that follows.[9] Items are listed in grades where they first occur.

EXAMPLE OF GRADING IN A TEXTBOOK

Second Grade
Language Activities
Taking part in conversations and discussions   *Taking your turn to tell things. Talking so that all can hear you. Talking when no one else is talking. Listening carefully. Greeting callers. Making introductions. Using the telephone correctly. Telling who is talking. Being courteous in using telephones. Knowing what to say when another person is wanted. Placing a call. What to say when getting a wrong number. Speaking clearly. Keeping the conversation brief. Asking questions when you do not understand others.*

Making reports   *What to include in a report. Telling enough about the subject. Telling things in the right order. Telling only what will interest others. Writing an original report.*

[9] Paul McKee and others, *English for Meaning, Grades One through Eight*, Houghton Mifflin Company, Boston, 1968; selected and adapted from the Skills Taught Chart. Quoted with special permission of author and publisher.

Writing letters   *Deciding on topics of interest to your corresepondent. Three parts of a letter. Being polite. What to include in a thank-you letter. What to include in an invitation. Answering questions in letters. Working with different kinds of letters.*

Telling stories   *Tell the whole story. Telling a story from pictures. Telling things in the right order. Listening to stories. Choosing good endings.*

Giving descriptions, explanations, and definitions   *Deciding what to say. Saying exactly what you mean. Writing things in the correct order.*

Giving reviews   *What to tell in a book review. Giving a book review orally. Writing a book review.*

Language Mechanics

Sentence sense   *Distinguishing between sentences and groups of words which are not sentences. Keeping sentences apart. Separating run-together sentences. Adding words to a sentence if it does not tell enough. Distinguishing between a statement and a question. Writing original sentences.*

Word study   *Selecting the word which best fits a given meaning. Learning new meanings and words. Choosing words that say exactly what you mean. Using pictures to learn word meanings. Finding opposites.*

Letter and manuscript form   *Knowing three parts of a letter. Placing three parts of a letter on paper. Arranging a poem on paper. Arranging a book review on paper. Arranging a story on paper. Arranging a report on paper.*

Speech habits   *Keeping words apart. Sounding the endings of words. Sounding vowels correctly. Pronouncing* th *and* thr *correctly. Pronouncing words clearly and correctly.*

Capitalization   *The word "I." First word in a sentence. First word in the greeting of a letter. First word in each line of poetry. Names of persons and pets. Names of school, towns, cities and streets. Mr., Mrs., Miss. Names of days and months. Signature of a letter.*
Period   *At end of a statement. After Mr. and Mrs.*
Comma   *After greeting in a letter. Between day of month and year.*
Question mark   *At end of question.*
Apostrophe   *In contractions.*
Underlining   *Titles of books.*

Usage
Am—am not; aren't—isn't; came—come; did—done; is—are; saw —seen; went—gone; any—no.

Grammar
Making verbs agree with their subjects.

Fourth Grade

Language Activities
Taking part in conversations and discussions   *Using the telephone to get help. Using the telephone directory. Giving and answering invitations.*

Making reports   *Telling things in the correct order. Making each sentence tell something new.*

Writing letters   *Answering an invitation. Distinguishing between a friendly and a business letter. Telling all that is needed in business letters. Ordering something by mail. Asking and answering questions.*

Telling stories   *Using direct quotations. Hinting at what is going to happen. Telling only things related to the point of the story. Making others wonder what finally happened. Telling how things turned out.*

Giving descriptions, explanations, and definitions   *Telling directions in correct order. Giving all the information needed. Evaluating directions.*

Giving reviews   *What to tell in reviewing a movie. Giving a review of a movie. Evaluating reviews of movies. Reviewing a radio or television program. Evaluating reviews.*

Making announcements   *Telling all the important facts. Writing an announcement. Evaluating announcements.*

Language Mechanics

Sentence sense   *Learning when it is permissible to use a group of words which is not a sentence. Combining short, choppy sentences to make a longer sentence. Recognizing statements, questions, and exclamations. Beginning sentences in various ways.*

Paragraph sense   *Beginning a new paragraph. Using new paragraphs in writing conversation.*

Word study   *Using content to learn word meanings. Learning to use the dictionary. Finding in the dictionary the most suitable meaning for a word.*

Letter and manuscript form   *Knowing the parts of a business letter.*

Speech habits   *Learning to correctly pronounce words commonly mispronounced.*

Capitalization   *Titles with names of persons. Initials in persons' names.*
Period   *After initials in persons' names.*
Comma   *After closing in a business letter. In a series. In direct quotations, to separate words being quoted from other words, unless a question mark or exclamation mark is needed. After* Yes *and* No.
Exclamation point   *At end of exclamation.*
Apostrophe   *In forming possessive nouns.*
Colon   *After greeting in a business letter.*
Quotation marks   *To set off words being quoted in direct quotations.*

Usage   *Standard English defined; doesn't—don't; good—well; let—leave; there—their; indefinite they—he; I—me; to—too—two; took—taken.*

Grammar   *Recognizing nouns (common, proper, possessive, singular, plural). Recognizing verbs (action, state-of-being). Using pronouns only when reference is clear. Using pronouns correctly (in compound subjects, and after action verbs and prepositions).*

Sixth Grade
Language Activities

Taking part in conversations and discussions   *Welcoming others to a group engaged in conversation. Helping the group to make a decision. Summarizing a discussion. Changing the subject to avoid hurting the feelings of others.*

Welcoming a newcomer. Telephoning at convenient times. Being courteous to older persons.

Making reports   *Reporting information accurately. Making and using a bibliography. Using a table of contents.*

Writing letters   *Writing letters of congratulation. Distinguishing among different kinds of social letters. Ordering several things in a letter. Using mail order forms.*

Telling stories   *Making each sentence tell something which has not already been told.*

Giving descriptions, explanations, and definitions   *Distinguishing between a description and a definition. Classifying what is being defined. Telling how what is being defined differs from others in its class. Telling what a thing being defined does or is for. Not telling more than is needed in a definition. Giving reasons for one's opinion. Distinguishing between directions, explanations, and reasons. Telling explanations in correct order. Evaluating definitions, explanations, and reasons.*

Language Mechanics

Sentence sense   *Identifying simple subjects and complete subjects. Identifying simple predicates and complete predicates. Recognizing subjects and predicates in questions, exclamations, and commands.*

Paragraph sense   *Making each paragraph topic a part of the subject. Making a preparatory outline of paragraph topics. Making each sentence in a paragraph tell something not already told.*

Word study   *Learning to use prefixes. Learning words that can be used in place of "said." Using a single word to say what could otherwise be said only by using a group of words. Using colorful action words.*

Letter and manuscript form   *Arranging a bibliography on paper. Using a mail order form. Arranging a list of items when ordering several articles by mail.*

Period   *Before the second part of a divided quotation when it begins with a new sentence.*

Comma   *Before the second part of a divided quotation when it does not begin with a new sentence. Between the names of day and month. Before certain connecting words when used to connect what would otherwise be separate sentences. To set off words in apposition. Between last name and first name or initials of person when last name is given first. Between page numbers in indexes and bibliographies.*

Question mark   *Following any question being quoted in direct quotation.*

Exclamation point   *Following any exclamation being quoted in direct quotation.*

Dash   *Between page numbers in a bibliography.*

Usage   *Between—among; blew—blown; chose—chosen; do—does; drew—drawn; flew—flown; froze—frozen; has—have; hasn't—haven't; in—into; lie—lay; misuse of adjectives and adverbs; rode—ridden; spoke—spoken; stole—stolen; swam—swum; teach—learn; to—at.*

Grammar   *Recognizing connecting words. Using connecting words to combine ideas and to connect sentences. Learning about principal parts of regular and irregular verbs. Recognizing intensifiers and qualifiers. Using adjectives and adverbs correctly (to tell or ask how, and in making comparisons). Recognizing prepositions and prepositional phrases. Using prepositions correctly.*

Eighth Grade
Language Activities
Taking part in conversations and discussions   *Conducting informal interviews. Giving good reasons for opinions. Leading a discussion. Preparing for club meetings.*

Making reports   *Obtaining accurate information. Using direct quotations. Writing for the school newspaper. Writing a news story. Choosing a subject of general interest. Writing impartially. Presenting facts in order of importance. Writing headlines. Writing editorials. Evaluating news writing.*

Writing letters   *Enclosing a check or money order. Writing post cards. Making adjustments by letter. Writing letters of application.*

Telling stories   *Bringing the story to a quick close as soon as the outcome is revealed. Using enough conversation to make the story lively. Making the climax give the reader a definite feeling (e.g., amusement, excitement, sorrow, etc.). Solving the main character's problem in a way that leaves the reader feeling satisfied.*

Giving descriptions, explanations, and definitions   *Making a habit of observation. Describing for identification. Telling enough so that the description will fit only the person or thing being described. Making the main parts of an explanation separate and clear.*

Giving reviews   *Comparing reviews found in newspapers and magazines.*

Making announcements   *Making an oral announcement.*

Language Mechanics
Sentence sense   *Recognizing and using clauses. Recognizing and using dependent and independent clauses. Diagraming clauses. Recognizing and using phrases. Diagraming phrases. Identifying and using complex sentences.*

Paragraph sense   *Using transition words when writing a composition of more than one paragraph.*

Word study   *Learning about signs, symbols, and words. Learning about the need for good communication. Distinguishing between factual and emotional language. Distinguishing between casual and formal English. Using sound and context to determine words unfamiliar in print. Using concise words and expressions. Recognizing words used by poets to complete the images and fit the rhythm of poems. Using synonyms and antonyms to express shades of meaning. Learning to add to one's vocabulary.*

Letter and manuscript form   *Writing a post card correctly. Writing checks and money orders correctly. Endorsing a check correctly. Learning the form of a news story.*

Speech habits   *When reading poetry aloud, letting the voice bring out rhythm and word sounds without overemphasizing them. Pausing only where there is punctuation when reading poetry aloud. When reading poetry aloud, bringing out meaning by varying tone and stressing only words that should be stressed. Speaking into a microphone at the best distance for effective pickup. Speaking directly into a microphone. Speaking naturally, distinctly, and at a moderate rate when using a microphone.*

Capitalization   *The interjection "O."*

Comma   *After introductory phrase, when it is needed to make the meaning clear. Between a person's name and a title following. After a participial phrase that begins a new sentence. After an introductory adverbial clause. To set off a relative clause that is not needed to identify the word it modifies.*

Colon   *After the name of the speaker in writing dialogue.*

Semicolon   *In compound sentences.*

Usage   *Become—became; draw—drew—drawn; forget—forgot—forgotten; hisn—hern, avoiding use of; play—played—played; set—set—set; shrink—shrank—shrunk; spring—sprang—sprung; swear—swore—sworn; titles and names.*

Grammar   *Recognizing intensive and reflexive pronouns. Using indefinite pronouns as subjects. Using collective nouns. Agreement of verbs with certain nouns ending in "s." Using verbals as adjectives, adverbs, and nouns. Recognizing participles and participial phrases. Recognizing gerunds and gerund phrases. Recognizing infinitives and infinitive phrases. Using coordinating conjunctions. Recognizing clauses, independent and dependent. Using correlative conjunctions. Recognizing complex sentences. Using dependent clauses as adverbs and adjectives. Recognizing relative pronouns. Recognizing relative adverbs. Recognizing relative clauses. Recognizing restrictive and nonrestrictive clauses. Recognizing subordinating conjunctions. Using noun clauses.*

For your consideration

1 In one experience, such as taking part in a discussion, trace sequences through several grades in a course of study or teacher's guide. You might want to concentrate on one or two aspects, such as: sticking to the point, asking others for clarification of a statement, or giving others a chance to participate.

2 List the language experiences for a particular grade found in a textbook or the language arts guide for a particular district. Compare with work in preceding and following grades.

3 List specific attitudes, abilities, and skills found in a course of study or a textbook for a particular grade. Compare with work in other grades.

4 Collect samples of children's work from several grade levels. Note development. Check various aspects of the work samples with the suggested grade goals for written work found in language arts textbooks.

References

BLOOM, BENJAMIN: *Taxonomy of Educational Objectives*, Longmans, Green and Company, New York, 1956.

BROENING, ANGELA, AND OTHERS: *Conducting Experiences in English,* Appleton-Century-Crofts, Inc., New York, 1939, chap. 16.

BRUNER, JEROME S.: *The Process of Education,* Harvard University Press, Cambridge, Mass., 1960.

CROSBY, MURIEL: "Of the Times and the Language," *Elementary English,* vol. 44, February, 1967, pp. 106–113, 147.

DALLMAN, MARTHA: *Teaching the Language Arts in the Elementary School,* W. C. Brown Company, Publishers, Dubuque, Iowa, 1966, chap. 3.

DAWSON, MILDRED A., M. ZOLLINGER, AND A. ELWELL: *Guiding Language Learning,* Harcourt, Brace & World, Inc., New York, 1963, chap. 3.

EDUCATIONAL POLICIES COMMISSION: *The Central Purpose of American Education,* National Education Association, Washington, D.C., 1961.

FOWLER, MARY E.: *Teaching Language, Composition, and Literature,* McGraw-Hill Book Company, New York, 1965, pp. 65–68.

GOLDSTEIN, M. B.: *The Teaching of Language in Our Schools,* The Macmillan Company, New York, 1966, chap. 18.

HATFIELD, W. W.: *An Experience Curriculum in English,* Appleton-Century-Crofts, Inc., New York, 1935, chaps. 11, 13–17, pp. vi–viii, 247–256.

LEFEVRE, CARL A.: "Language and Self: Fulfillment or Trauma," parts 1 and 2, *Elementary English,* vol. 43, Feb.–March, 1966, pp. 124–128, 230–234, 284.

LYMAN, R. L.: *Summary of Investigations Relating to Grammar, Language, and Composition,* University of Chicago Press, Chicago, Ill., 1929, pp. 58–64, 184–186.

MC CARTHY, DOROTHEA, AND OTHERS: *Factors That Influence Language Growth,* National Council of Teachers of English, Champaign, Ill., 1953, pp. 3–5.

MC KEE, PAUL: *Language in the Elementary School,* Houghton Mifflin Company, Boston, 1939, pp. 61–69, 490.

MICHAELIS, JOHN U., AND OTHERS: *New Designs for the Elementary School Curriculum,* McGraw-Hill Book Company, New York, 1967, pp. 75–86.

NATIONAL COUNCIL OF TEACHERS OF ENGLISH: *The English Language Arts,* Appleton-Century-Crofts, Inc., New York, 1952, chap. 4, pp. 13, 15, 34–40, 188–190, 248–249, 297–298.

——: *Language Arts for Today's Children,* Appleton-Century-Crofts, Inc., New York, 1954, chap. 3.

RUSSELL, DAVID H., AND OTHERS: *Child Development and the Language Arts,* National Council of Teachers of English, Champaign, Ill., 1953, pp. 17–22, 42, 44.

SHANE, HAROLD G., AND OTHERS: *Improving Language Arts Instruction in the Elementary School,* Charles E. Merrill Books, Inc., Columbus, Ohio, 1964, chap. 4.

STRICKLAND, RUTH G.: *The Language Arts in the Elementary School,* D. C. Heath and Company, Boston, 1957, pp. 329–330.

TABA, HILDA: *Curriculum Development: Theory and Practice,* Harcourt, Brace & World, Inc., New York, 1962, chap. 1.

TIEDT, IRIS M., AND S. W. TIEDT: *Contemporary English in the Elementary School,* Prentice-Hall, Inc., Englewood Cliffs, N.J., 1967, chap. 1.

TRABUE, M. R., AND OTHERS: *Teaching Language in the Elementary School,* National Society for the Study of Education, University of Chicago Press, Chicago, 1944, part 2, pp. 22–26, 99, 113–114, 166.

19.

PLANNING

A

PROGRAM

OF

WORK

FOR

A

CLASS

Some planning can be done before school begins by gaining knowledge of the community; by studying teacher's guides, courses of study, and textbooks; by looking up school records; and by conferring with the principal and other teachers. Early in the term the teacher, as he comes face to face with the children, will reconsider his original plans by studying the accomplishments, capabilities, and needs of his pupils. Within a few weeks or a few months the teacher should know his pupils and be able to complete his preliminary plans for the year's work. All teachers need to make some preliminary plans. The need is more urgent for beginning teachers and for teachers taking up a position in a new school. We consider preliminary planning primarily from the point of view of the beginning teacher, who faces the problems for the first time. Consideration of the total curriculum pattern, as treated in Chapter 18, should be helpful here.

Setting tentative goals   The first task naturally is setting up goals for the class, defining as clearly and as accurately as possible just what should be accomplished during the term. The teacher should examine his local course of study or teacher's guide and make note of any help given in defining goals for the grade. If

413

the course is complete, he may find there a comprehensive listing of goals; if not, he must look elsewhere, in textbooks or in supplementary books for grades in which no official textbook is provided. Probably the textbook will be used generally. The contents of the book in terms of specific objectives may be found listed in the table of contents, index, or manual, but probably it will be necessary for the teacher to examine the introduction and to go through the book page by page to make his own analysis and listing. The teacher may find certain textbooks, such as McKee's *The English for Meaning Series,* which lend themselves to specific analysis of goals for the total program as well as for specific grade goals: [1]

MAJOR LANGUAGE JOBS
1. Taking part in conversations and discussions (including the making of introductions and the use of the telephone)
2. Making reports (oral and written)
3. Writing letters
4. Telling stories (oral and written)
5. Giving descriptions, explanations, directions, and definitions (oral and written)
6. Giving reviews (oral and written)
7. Making announcements
8. Learning about poetry—writing creatively

LANGUAGE MECHANICS
1. Sentence sense
2. Paragraph sense
3. Word study
4. Letter and manuscript form
5. Speech habits
6. Capitalization
7. Punctuation
8. Grammar
9. Usage
10. Revision and proofreading

In using the scope and sequence outline in the *English Skills Chart,* the teacher can note review learnings in the major language jobs and the new abilities, attitudes, and skills that will be presented in his own grade level.

It will be observed that the contents of the language program are classified into the major objectives of experiences, abilities, and skills.

[1] Paul McKee and others, *English for Meaning, Grades One through Eight,* Houghton Mifflin Company, Boston, 1968. See also *English Skills Chart: English for Meaning Series,* Houghton Mifflin Company. Quoted with special permission of authors and publisher.

Checking tentative objectives against pupil and community needs
The textbook analysis gives the teacher some idea of normal expectancy; it may or may not provide an appropriate set of goals for
his particular class. To make this adjustment the teacher necessarily gives some attention to the socioeconomic status of his pupils,
to language patterns and standards of acceptability prevailing in
the community, and to the kinds of language experiences likely to
be engaged in by his pupils.

*Preliminary evaluation of performance and diagnosis of specific
needs* Soon the teacher should begin a systematic evaluation of
the children's performance in language and in time make a more
complete diagnosis of specific individual needs. By simply listening
to children tell stories, make reports, and engage in discussions,
and by examining typical sets of compositions, the teacher will be
able to make some estimate of the general language ability of the
class, identify exceptional children, and possibly locate some
specific areas of weakness. This informal, casual, sketchy type of
evaluation, which it is assumed any teacher will make, is valuable
as far as it goes, and it may be adequate for some teachers. Others
will want to supplement informal general evaluation by a more
detailed, systematic kind of evaluation in order to bring into view
all important phases of the language program and to reveal specific individual needs by means of checklists and tests. Evaluation
may be broken down profitably into the chief categories of objectives and approached in order of relative importance: (1) experiences and (2) abilities and skills.

Preliminary evaluation of experiences It is well to begin a language survey with an evaluation of performances in the chief
kinds of language experiences with which the class is concerned:
conversation, discussion, storytelling, letter writing, and the like.
The procedure of evaluation is simply that of providing opportunities for the children to participate in the experiences, estimating
the quality of performance, and keeping records. The instrument
of evaluation is the teacher's judgment, for which there is no
alternative at present in the oral as well as written phases of work.
Recordings are very helpful as an aid to evaluation of oral performance. Although standard scales for measuring written work
have been devised, they fail in the main to add either to reliability
or to the ease of making judgments.

Keeping records is an important step in the diagnostic procedure. A record form is made by listing the experiences on the

left-hand side of a sheet of cross-section paper and writing the names of the pupils across the top, as in Table 19-1. As the children participate, the teacher records his evaluations of individual performances, using a simple system of marks such as a check for *satisfactory*, a plus sign for *better than satisfactory*, and a minus sign for *unsatisfactory*. The record will be cumulative, and in time it will provide a fairly complete record of the performance of each child in each experience. It is to be noticed that the record form indicated in Table 19-1 does not provide preliminary assessment of the various experiences and skills involved in the processes of reading. The teacher is advised that specificity in determining the progress of reading skills and abilities is necessary before an adequate program of reading instruction is begun. Similar inventories that analyze the necessary prerequisites for reading should be utilized by the teacher.

In evaluating performances in experiences it is probably well to begin with the major areas and then make the analysis more detailed as need arises. Thus, the teacher may begin his survey with oral communication, written communication, and study and research. As needed and when practicable, the teacher can extend the survey to include specific types of oral communication— conversation, discussion, storytelling, asking and answering questions—and to specific items in other categories.

The survey shows to the teacher the main areas of strength and weakness and, with his judgment of the social values of the experiences for his particular pupils, provides a basis for selecting and emphasizing types of experiences throughout the term.

In the preceding discussion nothing was said about the reliability of the teacher's judgment or about means of increasing that reliability. We shall assume, however, that since the teacher's judgment is considered in the training of teachers, it is to some extent reliable. Furthermore, the reliability of judgment of mentally alert teachers increases rapidly with experience. As he works with children, especially with pupils of a particular class or grade, the teacher arrives at the point where he recognizes strengths and weaknesses. He can improve reliability of judgment still more by deliberately setting his mind to the task, by collecting and studying samples of his pupils' work and the work of others on the same grade level, and by basing his evaluation on specific points of merit—so-called "standards." Much of the work in the preceding chapters should contribute to an understanding of what may reasonably be expected of children in various kinds of experiences at various grade levels.

Table 19-1   *Chart for recording pupils' performances in language experiences*

Language experiences	Names of pupils
Oral communication	
Conversation	
Discussion	
Telephoning	
Questions	
Written communication	
Friendly letters	
Business letters	
Invitations	
Diaries	
Notes	
Dramatization	
Choral speaking	
Creative	
Stories	
Verse	
Plays	
Observations and descriptions	
Giving information	
Talks and reports	
Announcements, explanations, and directions	
Introductions	
Interviews	
Forms	
Study and research	
Records	
Written reports	
Outlines	
Summaries	
Bibliography	
Dictionary	
Index	

Preliminary evaluation of abilities and skills   The basic step in the evaluation of abilities and skills is obviously to determine which are most needed in carrying on experiences effectively. Analysis will reveal much overlapping; that is, the same abilities and skills operate to some extent in many experiences. Thus, having something to say, sticking to the point, organizing logically, and using appropriate words and sentences apply to conversation, discussion, storytelling, letter writing, and creative composition. The importance of the different factors naturally varies somewhat with the experience. The business letter, for example, introduces a new use of the colon; outlining, a new use of capitals. The practical problem of the teacher is to think through and set up the specific abilities, skills, and attitudes required for mastery of particular language experiences.

As a practical procedure in setting up the proper objectives, the teacher may list specific abilities and skills separately for each language experience. This plan emphasizes the close functional relationship between experiences and abilities and skills; but it results in the preparation of a considerable number of checklists—as many lists, in fact, as there are experience units. There would be much overlapping in the several checklists, of course. An alternative is to use a master checklist of abilities and skills, as in Table 19-2. In planning work on an experience unit, the teacher could go over the master list and note the particular abilities and skills that should be stressed in the unit, omitting irrelevant and nonessential items. Thus, in a unit on conversation, the teacher could include such items as free participation, having something to say, sticking to the point, and appreciative listening. This alternative procedure emphasizes the common need of certain abilities and skills in various experiences and serves to promote continuity and consistency of attack. For the teacher's own information, and possibly for the use of pupils, it would be profitable to complete an ability-skill analysis record of all experiences. There is an advantage in putting the results into a single chart, as suggested in Table 19-2. The teacher, of course, should include in the chart and analysis only those items important for his grade and class.

For evaluating all oral phases of work the teacher must make spot judgments, paying attention to attitudes, as pupils recite; to qualities of speech; and to such general abilities as content, sticking to the point, usage, and sentence structure. It is good procedure in evaluation, however, to concentrate on one or two particular items at a time.

Written work may be examined at leisure more objectively.

Table 19-2   *Abilities and skills in language experiences*

Abilities and skills	Conversation	Discussion	Telephone	Questions	Letters (friendly)	Letters (business)	Invitations	Diaries	Notes	Drama	Choral speaking	Stories	Verse			
Attitudes:																
Free participation																
Improvement																
Self-correction																
Courtesies:																
Listening																
Criticisms																
Amiability																
Content:																
Topics																
Details																
Completeness																
Originality																
Organization:																
Pointedness																
Sequence																
Sentences																
Paragraphing																
Vocabulary:																
Vivid, apt																
Not trite																
Sentences:																
Completeness																
Accuracy																
Variety																
Speech:																
Audibility																
Distinctness																
Pronunciation																
Voice																
Delivery																
Usage																
Written mechanics:																
Capitalization																
Punctuation																
Manuscript form																
Neatness																

In evaluating general qualities of content, organization, vocabulary, and the like, the teacher will still necessarily rely on his judgment. In written mechanics and usage, however, it is possible to use objective tests, either informal ones made by the teacher or appropriate standard tests. Generally speaking, teacher-made, informal objective tests are more easily adapted to the work of a particular grade. Patterns for suitable tests may be found in textbooks, workbooks, and standardized tests.

In individual and class diagnosis lies the basis for the whole instructional program. It is generally agreed that conditions of good learning require specific language goals, recognizable and known to the pupils as well as to the teacher. Purposeful effort is motivated by a consciousness of need and concrete evidence of progress.

Blocking out large units of work   At this point the teacher is ready to make a tentative layout of the term's work, involving a basic pattern of unit organization and a plan for a sequence of units. Units should be organized in terms of experiences. The teacher decides what experiences should be included in the language program and how much emphasis each should receive. The sequence should be flexible. It is usually desirable to continue work on one experience until demonstrable progress is made. The selection and timing of the experiences may be profitably determined by the current situations arising in curricular and school-life activities. For example, early in the term when new children are arriving and when parents are visiting the school in considerable numbers, it is appropriate to have a unit on making introductions; and when the pupils are beginning a new unit in the social studies, attention in language may be given to discussions and making reports.

As important as the sequence of experiences is the emphasis on particular abilities and skills within experiences. Growth in the basic abilities and skills is the essence of growth in language power, and emphasis on the basic abilities should follow consistently through all experiences and should be adjusted to the level of language maturity of the class. For example, at the lowest level of pupil maturity the teacher faces the problem of securing voluntary participation. This problem should be faced and met whenever the children are engaged in storytelling, discussion, or dramatization.

In sum, then, the teacher plans the work in terms of the major experiences taken up as current needs of the class dictate; and in each experience he stresses consistently the abilities and skills common to all language work and those required by the particular experience. The experience and its component abilities and skills constitute the working unit.

Selection of subject matter for units   The textbook provides a program of experiences and of abilities and skills; of necessity the book provides subject matter as well. The program of subject-matter content is suggestive and illustrative; it is not prescriptive. In fact, content—what children speak and write about—may often be better derived from the experiences and current interests of children. The teacher will add considerable vitality to the language program by encouraging pupils to make use of their experiences at home, on the playground, on vacation, with pets and hobbies, in assembly programs, in school organization, and especially in work in other curricular areas.

Instructional organization   After blocking out the instructional program and making a tentative plan for sequence, the teacher is ready to give consideration to the organization of pupils. He must at this point take into consideration the nature of learning in a particular phase of work and set up conditions that will provide for maximum individual growth.

Whole-class work   One phase of the program is the carrying on of purposeful language experiences, such as conversation, story-telling, and dramatization. This phase can be handled well by whole-class work. The class provides the stimulus for the experience and a social situation; clarification of ideas develops from class discussion; a pressure for maintaining high standards results from an interchange of friendly constructive criticism. While the class is engaged in the common experience, individual needs, of course, should not be neglected. For example, seven-year-old Susan is led to realize that John, at the other side of the room, does not listen to her story because she does not make him hear. Because Jack is not chosen for the main part in a marionette show, he is finally convinced that his baby habit of sounding *w* instead of *l* (*wook* instead of *look*) is no longer an asset. Mary discovers that if she wants to contribute to the conversation period, she must cultivate a more pleasing voice and speak in sentences; and thirteen-year-old Tony finds that he can never be the announcer in the class radio show unless he enunciates more clearly.

Goals and standards of performance vary according to the individual; each is judged in terms of his own capacities and is encouraged to strive constantly for improvement. During a whole-class poetry-writing period one child wrote:

> *I had a cat*
> *And she was black*
> *She went for a walk*
> *And she never came back.*

Another child produced during the same period:

> *Little Brook*
> *Why do you bubble all the way*
> *As you go*
> *Through forests and fields*
> *And cities and towns?*

The first child must be commended for his effort and his rhythm, while at the same time he is led to realize that what he has written is a nonsense rhyme rather than a true poem. Jingles are fun and may be enjoyed as such, but they should not be confused with poetry. A specific goal for the first child would be familiarity with more poems and the realization that a real poem not only presents a sound picture but also tells something. He probably lacks words with which to express himself and needs further vocabulary work. He also needs opportunity and encouragement to express himself imaginatively, probably in prose. Even one good sentence submitted by this boy would call for commendation. The second author, on the other hand, has given a beautiful picture of the happy little brook, and one feels that she has had ample experience in free expression, although she needs help in punctuation and capitalization.

Individual work   The carrying on of experiences provides practice in the development of attitudes, abilities, and skills. This practice, incidental in nature, may not be sufficient to provide satisfactory mastery of all language elements; and to the extent that it is not sufficient, the teacher must provide directed training lessons on the essential language elements for those children who need them. In this phase of the work, the whole-class procedure is not usable except in the rare situations where all, or a great majority, of the pupils need the same specific training. Instead of teaching the class as a whole, the teacher must either break it up into small groups needing the same remedial work or use an individualized procedure.

A guide for the group or individualized program is provided by the analysis and checklist record of abilities and skills. In the grouping procedure, the children who need the same training lessons are taught as a unit. Grouping reduces the number of instructional groups to practical limits and makes it possible for the teacher to do some pointed teaching. In the individualized plan, each pupil works on his own particular difficulties. Much reliance must be placed on self-help instructional material. This material should be broken down into specific topics, should be readily available to the pupils, and should be self-instructional and self-corrective. The advent of programmed instruction provides the long-awaited breakthrough in self-help materials and techniques.

In sum, the proper organization of instruction in language provides two basic types of work: (1) classwork for experiences, with incidental practice on specific abilities and skills and (2) special-training exercises or lessons on specific abilities and skills, largely group and individual, to the extent that special training is necessary to secure desired growth. The two types of work are complementary.

Multiple-grade situation   In the single-grade situation children vary widely in language maturity, especially in abilities and skills; and an effective plan of pupil organization must be devised to meet these differences. In the multiple-grade situation, also, individual differences are great, but possibly not much greater. This situation differs from the former in that children vary in age and grade as well as in ability. The plan of pupil organization in the single-grade situation also serves very well for several grades. At times language experiences are carried on simultaneously in all grades, as in conversation and discussion; and within each experience there is incidental concentration on specific goals according to individual maturity and needs. At other times the children will be engaged in a common project or unit, as preparing a play to celebrate Thanksgiving. In this unit work there are different tasks for children of different levels of maturity. All may participate in planning and in evaluating. Mature children do most of the research work and the writing of the script, while the younger children perform assigned tasks and participate as actors. The techniques of attitude-ability-skill analysis are usable. Special-training exercises on specific skills and abilities, oral and written, are handled as group or individual work. Possibly more use must be made of individual work; and for this purpose suitable self-

instructional material in the form of workbooks and other instruc-
tional-practice devices is of greater importance.

Materials   An essential part of planning and implementing a
program for a class consists of locating, selecting, and gathering
the necessary instructional materials, including those essential for
stimulation (such as sources of content in other subjects), instruction (such as sample letters useful in building understanding of
content and form), diagnosing individual and class needs, testing
accomplishments, and practice on specific abilities and skills.

Contents of textbooks   A good textbook meets these needs in part.
In the first place, a textbook provides a basic program of unit work
in experiences and in related abilities and skills generally appropriate to the grade, and it gives emphasis to the several experiences
according to their importance. The sequence is timed—in part,
at least—to meet the progressive needs of children throughout the
year. Instruction and drill in specific abilities and skills are introduced as needed to carry on the various experiences. The textbook
is the product of the study and thinking of specialists who are
qualified by research and experience to write in their fields. In
using the textbook, the teacher is taking advantage of this specialized, technical knowledge and competence.

In addition to a general plan of organization, the textbook
offers certain other resources, such as samples of stories, reports,
outlines, and the like. If wisely chosen, they suggest reasonable
goals. However, for any particular class, such goals may be too
high or too low. The teacher, therefore, should collect from time
to time samples of his pupils' work to serve as supplementary
models. In addition to their easier adaptability to a particular class,
the local samples are more interesting than textbook models.

Another common feature of textbooks is lists of key points—
standards—for particular experiences. Any such list may be well
devised; the important question, however, is, What use should
be made of it? In the authors' opinion, it is better to let children
derive their standards from a study of samples and to use the
textbook lists mainly for checking their own items than to have
them begin by studying the standards of the textbook. The textbook lists of standards usually contain many items, and the implication here is that all children are to work on all of them simultaneously. Again, in the authors' judgment, such a procedure
presents an impossible task to the children; if a long list is used,

and it should be, each child should select one or two items for emphasis in giving a story or report. Such selection and concentration provide opportunities for individualizing work within a common experience.

Textbooks also provide practice and remedial exercises. Usually in this connection some kind of pretest or diagnostic test is suggested so that only the children who need the practice get it. This is a common-sense procedure. It is possible that some of the exercises will not be needed by any child. It is also likely that common difficulties will be found that are not covered in the test and practice exercises. In this case the teacher should devise tests suited to the particular needs of the children, possibly using the textbook exercises as models.

It may be found that the practice exercises in textbooks are largely devoted to the mechanics of speaking, writing, and usage. Little provision is commonly made for exercises in the development of ability to select suitable topics, to limit the scope of topics, to stick to the point, to follow a clear sequence of ideas, and to introduce interesting details and apt illustrations. Yet these language abilities are regarded as primarily important in the language program. If training exercises in this latter group of abilities are needed, as they may well be, the teacher will be obliged to supply them.

A further common textbook provision is the statement of principles and rules relating to concepts, usages, and mechanics. Rules and principles, it is generally agreed, should not be memorized from the textbook but should be arrived at inductively by pupils through a study of live examples. The textbook statements can then serve as checks on the children's own generalizations.

There are several general ways in which a book can be used. One is, obviously, to follow it chapter by chapter and exercise by exercise. It is unlikely, however, that a textbook prepared for use in different sections of the country and for different types of schools will be found perfectly adapted to the needs of a particular class. Such use is tolerable only in the hands of a teacher who lacks confidence or thorough training.

At the other extreme, the textbook is used only as a reference-exercise source. In this case, the basic program is developed from purposeful experiences, largely arising in connection with other curricular and extracurricular activities, and units and exercises are selected from the textbook as they are needed for training in particular abilities and skills. Mature, well-trained, progressive teachers are inclined to favor such use of the textbook because in this method the functional concept of language work is emphasized. The textbook work is also made vital and purposeful. However, this procedure may lose the planned continuity and sequence of training in essential skills which the textbook provides, and the teacher thus undertakes the responsible task of not only selecting the experiences but also working out a systematic, sequential, developmental program. This is certainly not impossible to do, but the teacher must recognize his responsibility and accept the amount of work involved.

There is a third plan, which combines adjustment to present needs and the systematic treatment of technical content. The teacher follows the order of experiences set by the textbook, but instead of using the exact topics for oral and written work given in the text, he draws them from the current lives of children. This procedure is thoroughly consistent with the purpose and specific recommendations of many textbook authors. For example, as the basis of learning how to obtain information from books, one textbook presents a section entitled, "Using Study Helps." Through a brief study of birds, the attention of the child is directed to an example of a contents page and to an index page. Material on the use of a dictionary and an encyclopedia in obtaining information about birds is given. The section terminates with ideas and practice relating to finding many ideas in paragraphs and to outlining procedures, with children engaging in the development of an outline from a selection describing different kinds of birds' nests.[2] It is doubtful that a particular class will be studying birds at the particular time this language unit is taken up in the text; however, work in social studies and science units provides topics, problems, and materials that need these research techniques.

The textbook, then, may serve as a general guide and model in programming language experiences and in using other curricular activities for developing language abilities; its particular subject-matter content need not be followed slavishly. The exercises for developing technical skills may be used, if needed, or similar exercises may be devised by the teacher to provide specific training. This third plan conserves the general plan of organization and the systematic program for the development and maintenance of technical aspects of language training as provided by the textbook, but it makes the work functional and relates it to current needs.

[2] Harry W. Sartain and others, *English Is Our Language: Book 4*, D. C. Heath and Company, Boston, 1966, chap. 7, pp. 160–183.

Planning without a textbook   In those situations for which a textbook is not reasonably adequate or for which published materials are not directly usable, as in the case of teaching non-English-speaking children, the teacher must develop and accumulate a supply of instructional materials adapted to his particular program of work.[3] Copies of textbooks and workbooks will be useful in suggesting a basic program in experience, ability, and skill areas, and in devising usable class, group, and individual assignments. Such books are McKee's *We Talk and Listen* for grade 1; and *Let's Talk* and the worktext *Let's Write* for grade 2.[4] For example, the books designed for the second grade provide a program of work that includes:

> *Talking and writing experiences:* talking and listening (conversation, discussion, telephoning, making introductions), making stories and enjoying poems, planning letters together, telling things you know, telling others about books, telling what things are like.

> *Specific abilities:* deciding what subject to talk or write about and selecting ideas to be expressed on that subject; talking and writing simply, clearly, and exactly enough so that others can understand what is meant; learning items essential to talking and writing correctly (using and pronouncing words correctly, capitalizing when necessary, using commas correctly in a letter and learning three uses of a period); learning items that are essential to the amenities attached to communicating with others, indicating consideration for the rights and feelings of listeners and readers.

In addition to suggesting content, these books give useful helps in teaching procedures and in the development of materials and units of work that will provide a framework for language arts instruction in the primary grades.

Supplementary practice material   Teachers often feel a need for more and different types of practice material than are provided in the text. Authors commonly provide supplementary practice exercises in workbooks designed to accompany and parallel work in the texts. Workbooks provide a source of supplementary practice material. If selected to meet the needs of children and chosen for their excellence in reinforcing learning, workbooks can augment

[3] Louise Lancaster, *Introducing English: An Oral Prereading Program for Spanish Speaking Primary Pupils*, Houghton Mifflin Company, Boston, 1966.
[4] Paul McKee and others, *We Talk and Listen, Let's Talk,* and *Let's Write,* Houghton Mifflin Company, Boston, 1966. Quoted with special permission of author and publisher.

a language program; however, slavish adherence to a page-by-page approach often takes time from many children that could be used to better advantage. The teacher can devise a reasonably satisfactory supply of permanent practice material by securing several copies of workbooks. Mounted on stiff paper, selected exercises may be used repeatedly if covered with transparent material, such as x-ray film, on which answers can be written with a greased pencil. The material is filed in a convenient place, accessible to pupils, possibly in a standard vertical file. The topics for filing are the particular abilities and skills, mainly written, for which practice material is needed, for example, content and organization, usage, capitalization, and punctuation. The teacher naturally selects the exercises that serve his purposes in meeting the needs of a particular group of pupils. This material cannot be used for whole-class assignments, but it serves very well for individual and small-group assignments.

Supplementary practice work should be individualized—directed at the point of difficulty. It is inevitable that children will be working on many difficulties at one time. The teacher will have little time for making assignments, giving oral explanations, and checking. It follows that the material—described above—should be housed so that the children can get it with a minimum of teacher effort and that it should be self-instructional and self-checking. The answer key may be placed on the back of the practice exercise.

The criteria for selecting various forms of instructional media parallel those for selecting textbooks and workbooks. The main issue to be resolved is met by the question, How will a particular aid, several devices, or a set of practice materials developed or purchased for one or several classrooms augment the total language program? The selection of machines and accompanying filmstrips, film loops, records, tapes, and tachistoscope devices needs to be considered in terms of instructional goals and the scope and sequence of learnings in the language arts program. Programmed instruction and the tools for individual learning should be analyzed as to their usefulness in developing, maintaining, or reinforcing specific skill elements of the language arts.[5]

[5] John Jarolimek, *Social Studies in Elementary Education*, The Macmillan Company, New York, 1967, chaps. 4–5; Nila B. Smith, *Reading Instruction for Today's Children*, Prentice-Hall, Inc., Englewood Cliffs, N.J., 1963, pp. 82–88; Ruth Ann Sponberg, "You and Computer-assisted Instruction—1," *The Instructor*, vol. 77, August–September, 1967, pp. 170–171.

Schedule   In the completely integrated program, language does not appear on the schedule as a separate subject, and may be part of a larger block of work—in connection with social studies, for example. Extra time should be allowed for work in language when it appears with another subject. If social studies alone is allotted one hour, social studies plus language should be allotted at least one and one-half hours. If language is assigned a separate period on the schedule, it should be placed close to the subjects with which it is closely related, probably social studies, science, and health. Language work derives a large part of its content from the closely related subjects. The needs for particular abilities and skills, and their practice, are provided incidentally in the related subjects. As a separate period, language should occupy about one-half hour a day; when combined with handwriting and spelling, about one hour. These three language arts are sometimes grouped to provide for integration of related phases and for economy of time in handling writing material.

Determining accomplishments and progress   A final step in laying out a program of work for a class is to make plans for determining accomplishments and progress during and at the end of the term. Starting points for evaluation are found in the preliminary survey records consisting of samples, checklists, and tests that were made at the beginning of the term.

Progress in carrying on oral experiences is measured by the teacher's judgment of daily work and test exercises. Marking component abilities and skills used in carrying on the oral experiences helps to increase the reliability of the judgment of the total experience and serves as a continuing diagnosis. Original checklists can be used to record progress and accomplishment.

In the preliminary survey, samples of written work are taken. Samples taken later, during and at the end of the term, serve to show progress. If the children keep individual folders into which group stories and poems as well as their own individual stories are slipped, they will be able to note their own progress from time to time. Children of all ages like these collections, which can be bound into a booklet to take home at the end of the year. Illustrations of some of the stories and even simple songs can be included. As in evaluating oral work, listing key qualities of written work and checking each separately adds to the reliability of the teacher's judgment and serves for continuing diagnosis. If an informal, objective scale comprised of representative samples of pupils' work is constructed, it can be used as an evaluation instrument.

Some standard scales are available, of course, but the value of these for practical local use is doubtful.[6]

The skills and general abilities of written expression—sentences, usage, punctuation, capitalization, manuscript form—can be measured by checking childen's compositions from time to time, by using test exercises provided by textbooks, by preparing informal objective tests covering specific items, or by standard tests. Standard tests, of course, make possible the comparison of the class with other classes and grades, although the value of the comparison may be lost if the content of the test does not correspond fairly well to the content of the textbook or course of study. It is often advisable to construct informal objective tests that include the specific language elements of the grade and to give them at the beginning of the term and again at the end in order to measure and stimulate progress. Such a test may be closely adapted to the textbook and course of study, but it will not necessarily provide a means of comparison with the work of other classes.

For your consideration

1   Study and report the general plan for the organization and sequence of work in one grade, using a language arts textbook or a school district's course of study.

2   List the goals for one grade from a textbook and a course of study in terms of (*a*) experience and (*b*) attitudes, abilities, and skills.

3   Using information in 2, develop usable checklists and class individual record forms.

4   Develop criteria for the selection of any of the following materials useful in the teaching of the language arts: (*a*) textbooks and workbooks; (*b*) records, motion pictures, filmstrips, film loops; (*c*) programmed instructional materials.

References

BAUERFEIND, R. H.: *Building a School Testing Program*, Houghton Mifflin Company, Boston, 1963, chap. 8.

BECK, J. M., AND R. W. SAXE: *Teaching the Culturally Disadvantaged Pupil*, Charles C Thomas, Springfield, Ill., 1965, chap. 6.

[6] H. A. Greene and W. T. Petty, *Developing Language Skills in Elementary Schools*, Allyn and Bacon, Inc., Boston, 1963, pp. 514–519.

BROWN, DOROTHY L., AND MARGUERITE BUTTERFIELD: *The Teaching of Language in the Primary Grades*, The Macmillan Company, New York, 1941, chap. 9.

CORBIN, RICHARD, AND MURIEL CROSBY: *Language Programs for the Disadvantaged*, National Council of Teachers of English, Champaign, Ill., 1965, pp. 39–98.

DALLMAN, MARTHA: *Teaching the Language Arts in the Elementary School*, W. C. Brown Company, Publishers, Dubuque, Iowa, 1966, chap. 3, pp. 331–333.

DAWSON, MILDRED A., AND OTHERS: *Guiding Language Learning*, Harcourt, Brace & World, Inc., New York, 1963, chap. 3.

EBEL, R. L.: *Measuring Educational Achievement*, Prentice-Hall, Inc., Englewood Cliffs, N.J., 1965.

FOWLER, MARY E.: *Teaching Language, Composition, and Literature*, McGraw-Hill Book Company, New York, 1965, chap. 16.

FROST, J. L., AND G. R. HAWKINS: *The Disadvantaged Child*, Houghton Mifflin Company, Boston, 1966, chap. 21, pp. 175–182.

GREENE, H. A., AND W. T. PETTY: *Developing Language Skills in the Elementary Schools*, Allyn and Bacon, Inc., Boston, 1967, chap. 17.

GRONLUND, NORMAN E.: *Measurement and Evaluation in Teaching*, The Macmillan Company, New York, 1965, chaps. 12–14.

HERRICK, VIRGIL E., AND LELAND B. JACOBS: *Children and the Language Arts*, Prentice-Hall, Inc., Englewood Cliffs, N.J., 1955, chap. 17.

LAMB, POSE, AND OTHERS: *Guiding Children's Language Learning*, W. C. Brown Company, Publishers, Dubuque, Iowa, 1967, pp. 50–57.

LEE, J. MURRAY, AND DORRIS M. LEE: *The Child and His Curriculum*, Appleton-Century-Crofts, Inc., New York, 1960, pp. 351–359.

LYMAN, R. L.: *Summary of Investigations Relating to Grammar, Language, and Composition*, University of Chicago Press, Chicago, Ill., 1929, pp. 198–211.

NEBRASKA CURRICULUM DEVELOPMENT CENTER: *A Curriculum for English: Grades 1–6*, National Council of Teachers of English, Champaign, Ill., 1966.

POOLEY, R. C.: *Teaching English Usage*, Appleton-Century-Crofts, Inc., New York, 1946, chaps. 9–10.

SHANE, HAROLD G., AND OTHERS: *Improving Language Arts Instruction in the Elementary School*, Charles E. Merrill Books, Inc., Columbus, Ohio, 1964, chap. 4.

STANLEY, JULIAN C.: *Measurement in Today's Schools*, Prentice-Hall, Inc., Englewood Cliffs, N.J., 1964, chaps. 7 and 10.

STRICKLAND, RUTH: "Evaluating Children's Composition," in J. C. MacCampbell, *Readings in the Language Arts in the Elementary School*, D. C. Heath and Company, Boston, 1964, pp. 263–278.

TRABUE, M. R., AND OTHERS: *Teaching Language in the Elementary School*, Forty-third Yearbook, National Society for the Study of Education, University of Chicago Press, Chicago, 1944, part II, chaps. 5–8.

WOLFE, DON M: *Language Arts and Life Patterns*, The Odyssey Press, Inc., New York, 1961, appendix 9, pp. 571–582.

20.

LANGUAGE
IN
AN
INTEGRATED
PROGRAM

During the second half of the twentieth century, the teaching of the language arts has been under close scrutiny. In particular, the structure of the English language—including the sound system and the grammar structure—has been incorporated into and emphasized in teacher preparation programs and in teacher inservice programs. Emphasis on the teaching of the structure of language has resulted in the development of instructional programs in English from the elementary school through the senior high school. Shane has described the changes that are occurring as the "quiet English reformation." [1] This era is one in which the teacher of the language arts is required to read, study, investigate, adapt, and evaluate as curriculum objectives, procedures, materials, and methods vary and change.

The variety of elementary and junior high school organizational patterns, such as team-teaching patterns, departmentalization, and cross-grade grouping, affect the instructional program in the teaching of the language arts. It does not seem unreason-

[1] Harold G. Shane, *Linguistics and the Classroom Teacher: Some Implications for Instruction in the Mother Tongue*, Association for Supervision and Curriculum Development, National Education Association, Washington, D.C., 1967, p. 1.

able to assume that, regardless of the organizational pattern, each teacher should be concerned with the teaching of the language arts. For the elementary school teacher, it has been suggested that he spend 40 to 60 percent of his time teaching English and related skills.[2] Within the setting of any school or classroom pattern, the teacher of the five- to fourteen-year-old child—be he the teacher of one section of the nongraded primary, the social studies teacher, the reading teacher, the science teacher, coordinator of large-group instruction in a particular subject or cross-subject field, or teacher in a self-contained classroom—needs to consider the sequential development of the components of the language arts.

These brief comments have been made as an introduction to this final chapter. To the preservice teacher, the descriptions of the integrated program are presented to illustrate successful interpretations of this concept. To the inservice teacher who may be teaching in any one of the possible organizational patterns, this chapter may be read to elicit some thoughts as to the place of the English language arts in any subject-matter field or content area in the schools of today.

Two basic types of programs are recognized as adequately providing for the growth and development of children in language. One, designated as the *functional* program, provides for closely relating language to work in other areas of study but sets aside some particular periods for systematic work in language. The other type is an *integrated* program; language work does not appear as a separate subject, but is very closely tied into other areas of study. The two programs are recognized, in a sense, as both functional and integrated: functional in that they center in real language experiences, designed to meet the needs of everyday living; integrated in that what children talk and write about is derived largely from work in other study areas, which provide motivation for and practice in language abilities and skills. The difference between the two programs lies in the degree of integration—a variable depending on the skill of the teacher—and is primarily a matter of scheduling. There is little difference in philosophy and in actual teaching techniques.

The program may be completely integrated around a single area, as shown in the first example that follows; or partially integrated around short units of work, as shown in the second

[2] William P. Viall, "English Teacher Preparation Study," *Elementary English*, vol. 44, October, 1967, p. 641.

example. The functional program, or some other type of systematic program, is familiar to most students from personal experience. It may be observed that the functional point of view has prevailed in the treatment of various phases of the language program to this point in the book. The completely integrated program may not be so well known. The completely integrated program demands teaching ability of a high order. Before bringing the presentation to a close, it may be helpful to get a final, close-up view of the integrated programs.

Nature study: plants, third grade

The following description of a completely integrated program is based on work carried on by Miss Butterfield, one of the authors of this book, in the third grade of the Potsdam Campus School. It shows how closely interwoven are the different school subjects and how many vicarious experiences may radiate from one basic theme. A center of interest—in this case nature study—will, if granted freedom, reach out and enter almost every phase of the school curriculum. By bringing together the various skills, knowledges, and appreciations of these different areas, both pupils and teacher may increase their understanding of the function of language.

In the present account of procedures and in the accompanying samples of children's work, the reader will find concrete illustrations of many points made elsewhere in this volume.

How the study originated At the beginning of the fall school term when the children were asked what they would like to study about, flowers was one of the topics mentioned. The teacher felt that this was probably suggested by the time of year and by the fact that many garden flowers were in their prime just then. She doubted that the subject would be of long-term interest.

Plants for the schoolroom The first objective seemed to be to make the schoolroom attractive, and to this end many fall flowers were brought and arranged by the children. Simple rules regarding color and arrangement were discussed. It was decided that the flowers should be of different heights, of an uneven number, and so grouped that there should be balance and color variation. Holders and vases appropriate for particular flowers were selected.

A library book containing illustrations of flowers and of simple flower arrangements was located, and the children tried to imitate the suggestions and examples.

Names of common flowers—zinnia, bachelor's-button, aster, cosmos, etc.—were mentioned and listed on the board. The children took pride in their ability to recognize these flowers, to pronounce their names, and to spell them correctly.

As the supply of garden flowers dwindled, wild flowers were gathered. Children brought goldenrod, wild asters, and Queen Anne's lace, and they arranged their bouquets attractively. One section of the chalkboard was reserved for names of new flowers. If any child thought of an unusually vivid descriptive word, he wrote it opposite the flower name on the board. These words invited class criticism, both favorable and adverse; and some children developed remarkably in their ability to describe accurately the appearance, color, and other qualities of certain flowers.

An interest in wild flowers led naturally to the study of seed dispersal; a chart was made, picturing different methods of dispersal and showing samples of each kind of seed. This project entailed considerable organization, labeling, lettering, and measuring. Words involved were listed and used in spelling lessons:

dispersal	winged	traveler
carrier	pods	sticktight

A trip to get plants   Plans were next made for supplying the schoolroom with winter plants. A retired teacher offered the contents of her large and lovely window box and garden. The children went one fine autumn afternoon just before the first frost to the home of Miss F, where they saw so many beautiful plants that they scarcely knew which they liked best. In anticipation of this dilemma, there had been a discussion among the pupils before they left school; they had selected spots in the room which needed or could accommodate plants and had accordingly taken just enough pots. At last all agreed upon a large begonia full of bloom, a coleus, and a pink ruffled petunia, which one little boy simply could not give up.

The children put bits of stone over the drainage hole in each pot and added sand, fertilizer, and loam from a bed; then the plants were lifted tenderly so as not to disturb the roots. More good soil was added and firmed about the plants. They were then watered and placed in Miss F's garage to become accustomed gradually to being indoors. The children understood that, if brought suddenly into a warm room, a plant might wither and lose some of its leaves.

Since Miss F had not been at home when the children made their visit, some doubts were expressed as to whether or not she would understand where the plants in her garage had come from. Reassured, the children suggested that they thank her for the plants, and the following letter was written:

> Potsdam, N.Y.
> September 17, ———

Dear Miss F,
> We want to thank you for letting us dig up your plants and for leaving trowels and fertilizer for us to use. We enjoyed digging the plants and potting them, and we are anxious now to get them in our room.
> > Sincerely yours,
> > Grade Three
> > Room 15

This letter was composed by the group and copied from the board by three children who considered themselves good penmen; then a committee chose the letter they considered the best of the three written. The class elected a messenger who, on his way home from school, delivered the letter to Miss F's door.

Water plants   About this time a child brought a small goldfish to school, and suitable accommodations had to be provided for it. By referring to library materials the class learned that plants should be grown in the water in order to keep it in good condition for fish. Pondweed was obtained, and the pupils learned that while some plants grow only in dirt, others grow only in water. The pondweed was planted in sand in the aquarium, and the children enjoyed watching it grow. Snails were brought to keep the aquarium clean. Other varieties of local water plants were discussed, and common names listed.

Slips   In a short time, it was noted that the branches of ivy had some tiny roots, and the term *slip* was introduced. The children learned that some plants could be started from slips, while others grow from seeds, roots, or bulbs; lists were made of plants reproduced in each manner.

About this time the children had fun playing a game of flower riddles, which they made up and asked each other. There was, naturally, wide variation in quality, but all the children seemed anxious to include as many good descriptive words as possible without telling what their plant or flower was. The following are samples:

> I grow in the ground.
> I have stems.
> I am red or blue.
> Who am I?

> The old-fashioned ladies
> Are trooping to town
> With their bright yellow dresses
> All trimmed with down

> I grow from seeds.
> My stems are slender, tall,
> And sway in the breeze.
> My graceful flowers are pink,
> White, or sometimes almost red.
> But my delicate leaves
> Are always green.

After two or three weeks it was time to bring the plants from the garage. A committee was appointed to go with the teacher in her car to get them.

The children were delighted to find their plants so large and beautiful. Since Miss F had given the pupils permission to take any other plants in the garage, they decided to take a geranium, which had a pink blossom, and a large shamrock plant. With a car full of plants, pupils and teacher went back to the school.

Several children brought plants from home, and in order to make space for them all, two bookstands were put together to make a corner around the reading table. On top of these low cases the plants seemed to thrive. Children took turns watering and caring for them.

Winter bouquets   When, at last, the garden flowers were frozen and withered, the class talked of seed pod bouquets for the winter, and one warm morning late in autumn the class took a walk to see what could be found that might be useful. Along a hedge, at the edge of a garden, and in a vacant lot were found many stalks of weed seed pods, which were carried back to the school. The children quickly became conscious of the variety of size, color, and shape of seed pods; and the collection continued to grow as children found leaves, stalks, grasses, and berries in their own or neighbors' back yards and along the way to school.

A wall vase was filled with bright bittersweet berries attractively arranged. Milkweed pods, brown sorrel stalks, Queen Anne's lace (much dried but still delicate), and other grasses were arranged in a tall black vase by a group of children and placed on a low filing cabinet in a shadowed corner of the room because these plants did not need light.

Some of the weeds were carefully packed in a carton and stored in the school basement. At Christmas time, when the question of gifts for parents arose, the pupils thought of several uses for these dried weeds. Some of the delicate grasses furnished designs for spatterwork. Some children made small, flat, clay flower bowls, which were painted and fired in the school kiln. With a clay frog in the center and an arrangement of dried weed pods, these bowls made individualized gifts. Some children experimented with coloring the weeds. Painted milkweed pods were considered especially attractive.

Plant care   During the winter, the plants were routinely cared for, and they also occasioned sporadic outbursts of conversation and discussion. The Wandering Jew in the hanging basket grew so long that it was dangerously near the radiator. Therefore, after pupil consultation, a bit was pinched off, rooted, and stuck back into the container. When, along in January, all the plants looked a bit sickly, liquid fertilizer was mixed and administered. The coleus grew so tall that some branches had to be snipped off and rooted in water. Various new plants were started from slips. One especially vigorous plant was potted and sent to a sick member of the class with the following letter:

> Dear Gail,
>   We thought you might like to see some of the coleus you helped pot last fall. The plant grew so big we had to break some off. We put the piece in water and made a little plant for you from the slip. We hope you will like it.
>   The plants have all grown so you wouldn't know them. Pat is watering them this week.
>   Come back soon.
>
>   With love,
>   Grade Three

Planning the year's work   During the developments just described it had become apparent to the teacher that the study of flowers had progressed into a study of plants and that the whole subject had become one of more than passing interest. She discussed with the children the many different kinds of plants and their uses for other than decorative purposes. Working together, teacher and children listed four large major topics they wanted to explore during the year:

Plants for the Schoolroom
Plants for Food
Plants We Wear
Other Plants We Use

These questions were listed on the chalkboard:

1   Why do different plants live in different parts of the country?
2   Where do fresh vegetables come from in the winter?
3   What is fertilizer made from?
4   What do plants need for growth besides water?
5   How are different colors of the same flower secured?
6   How are different varieties of apples, fruit, etc., produced?
7   What makes different kinds of soil?
8   How is enough flour for all the bread obtained?

Since there had to be some order to the study, it was decided to begin with the unit on "Plants for Food," topic 2, as early in the autumn as possible and allow it to run simultaneously with topic 1.

Familiar vegetables and fruits were listed separately on the board; the children brought samples; and finally there was a large exhibit. Each article was labeled, a poster was made, and the following invitation was issued to the children of another grade:

We would like to have you come to see our Harvest Collection of fruits and vegetables Tuesday between 2 and 3 o'clock.

Grade Three
Room 15

Ways of cooking the various vegetables were discussed. Children brought recipes from home. Measurements and simple abbreviations, such as tsp., tbs., c., pt., qt., ½, and ¼, were discussed, and rules of cooking to preserve all the good food values were pointed out. There were many conversations about favorite dishes and such remarks as "I like potatoes creamed better than fried" and "This noon my mother cooked some carrots with meat. I like them that way." Several children reported having sampled a vegetable hitherto untasted: "Last night we had parsnips and I ate some. Boy! They're good." Several mothers expressed delight over their children's willingness to try new foods. Dates, figs, and dried apricots were sampled at school and described as seedy, sticky, sweet, tart, etc. Some children had never before heard of these fruits.

Methods of preserving were also studied—canning, pickling, drying, and quick freezing; and many new words were thus added to vocabularies. The library was a constant source of information; and in connection with the harvesting and preserving of fruits and vegetables, considerable interest was generated about Indians and other primitive peoples, as well as about pioneer methods of preparing for the winter.

In October the children were asked to find out from their mothers' grocers where the fruits and vegetables in their stores had been grown. From these reports a chart was made, and it was quickly noticed that the majority of the green goods in the stores at that time of year had been grown locally, or at least in the state.

Just before Christmas another canvass of the grocery stores revealed the fact that, while cabbage, apples, potatoes, squash, and a few other items were state-grown, most of the fresh foods were by now coming to us from a distance. This entailed simple map study. California, Florida, Texas, and Arizona were located. Tie tags from bunches of carrots, broccoli, etc., were collected and brought to school, and the children took great interest in locating Phoenix, Arizona, and Salinas, California, on a map and noting the distance traveled by lettuce and other vegetables. A world map became of interest when someone reported finding grapes from Chile. Two other entries were made on the chart, one in March and one in June. Each time new states were located; and when it was understood that all the lettuce, celery, and carrots in the stores had to travel hundreds of miles to reach us, it made quite an impression.

Slides and films were shown depicting citrus groves, market gardens, and packing houses in distant parts of the country. Methods of transportation were investigated, and many new words added to the pupils' vocabularies:

budding	transportation	cultivation
soil	labor	rotation (of crops)
irrigation	graft	marketing
pollination	harvest	grading
drainage	select	pest

Distances and the amount of required handling were roughly estimated; and thus the children came to some little realization of the amount of work necessary and the number of people involved in getting a head of fresh lettuce from California to New York. The effect of climate on crops, people, and customs was also discussed.

At school, a potato placed in a warm cupboard soon showed sprouts coming from its eyes, and it was learned that potato growers plant pieces of potatoes instead of seeds. The terms *sprout* and *eyes* were thus learned. A bushel of potatoes was traced from a nearby farm to New York City, and an estimate was made of the number of people who handled it—each person earning his living by his work. The children understood why potatoes must increase in price between the farm and the home. One child wrote a letter to his cousin in New York City to ascertain just how much was being paid for potatoes there, and the class was much interested in the reply.

Class letters asking for information were also written to the Farm Bureau and the Potato Growers' Association. Several children were taken by their parents to visit large potato farms in the vicinity, and these visits were reported to the class. Machines, such as potato planters, potato diggers, and spraying machines, were pictured. Words such as *insect, insecticide,* and *poison* were added to the pupils' vocabularies.

A carrot in water sprouted green leaves, and a tomato ball (moss implanted with tomato seeds) placed in a dish of water soon had tiny plants protruding from it. Beans resting on damp cotton further illustrated the sprouting process. There were also simple experiments to show the effect of moisture and different kinds of soil and fertilizer on plant growth. All these activities entailed record keeping, discussion, reporting, writing of dates, spelling, reading for information, illustrating, and vocabulary growth. The child who attempted to report without knowing what he was going to say was soon "shushed" by the class; but because there was such a wide variety of activities, everyone had a deep interest in something or other, and even the poorest members of the group had their innings.

In February a child brought some pussy willow branches to school. They were arranged in water, and the children watched the buds come out and change to hairy green catkins. Pictures were drawn of them, designs were made using the pussy willow motif, and descriptive words were listed: *fuzzy, dangling, hairy, soft, furry.* Several children wrote individual poems about pussy willows.

Gardening Sometime in February a child reported that his father was ordering garden seeds. The class discussed the need for seeds and the reason why most people did not have seeds but preferred to buy tested ones. The words *pollination* and *hybrid* were mentioned. Variety in fruits and vegetables was recalled, and the children described different strains of apples, with their characteristic appearances and flavors. McIntosh Red, Greening, Snow, Tollman Sweet, Early Harvest, and Northern Spy were listed. It was also learned that, by cross pollinating and grafting, new varieties of fruits, vegetables, and flowers were created.

Some of the children wanted to make a garden and raise something. An old window box was brought from the school basement, painted, and placed near a window. The following letter was written to two seed companies:

> Campus School
> Potsdam, N.Y.
> February 23, _____
>
> Gentlemen:
> Please send us your catalogue of flower and vegetable seeds.
> Thank you.
>
> Yours truly,
> Grade Three
> Room 15

Garden helpers   Someone reported that bees are helpful in pollination and, in many cases, necessary. A committee was appointed to find out everything possible about bees and their work. A classroom bee house was found, but to the children's disappointment no live bees were obtainable.

From reading it was learned that insects are influential in plant life, and some were listed:

GARDEN FRIENDS	GARDEN PESTS	CONTROL
toads	potato bugs	spray
birds	grasshoppers	dust
ants	bean beetles	pull stubble
earthworms	tomato worms	
bees	moles, mice, rats	
ladybugs	corn borers	

An ant house was obtained and stocked. For weeks these interesting creatures were watched, cared for, and fed honey and water. The queen, easily recognized by her size, was a never-failing source of interest. When the children came to school in the morning, they gathered immediately around the ant house to see where the tiny busybodies were and what they were doing. The children watched the ants moving gravel bit by bit from one room to another; and they saw them stroke and care for their queen and carry food to the nest. From this observation it was easy to understand how, by their industry, the ants helped keep the soil porous beneath plants.

Many pictures were drawn at different times illustrating the ants, their work, their home, and their habits. These pictures were the result of individual interests and were quite spontaneous. Whenever a child saw something interesting which he wanted to illustrate, he did so and placed his picture, when finished, on the chalk tray, where it usually occasioned criticism, either favorable or unfavorable, and sometimes downright challenge if he had misrepresented some phase of ant life. A magnifying glass, which aided in the study of ants, proved valuable in examining other objects about the room.

Many new words and meanings were added to the pupils' vocabularies. Praise was given to children who used new words often and naturally, and the children themselves registered displeasure and quickly supplied the needed word when someone spoke of a "thing" or a "jigger."

A daffodil bulb   Early in the winter a daffodil bulb was planted in peat moss, and the pot was anxiously watched for signs of the plant's growth. When the first pale-looking shoot became visible there was great excitement and the best of care was tendered the young plant. During the day the pot was placed in a sunny spot near a window, but not on the sill since that was too near a radiator. At night it was placed well away from the window lest it become chilled. When the blossom finally appeared and broke from its covering, everyone thought it lovely and marveled that such a large bloom could have been hidden in such a small, drab, hard bulb.

Words were listed which accurately described the blossom:

creamy white	soft lemon yellow	pale green
trumpetlike	graceful	beautiful
lovely	sweet-scented	fragile

Some children wanted to write stories or poems about the flower, but felt handicapped by spelling difficulties. A spelling lesson was accordingly made up of the most commonly needed words, while other words probably needed were written on a side board and left there for reference. The children were told to write their stories, spelling as best they could. Spelling "wouldn't count"; *good* stories were wanted, and spelling could be corrected later.

Five stories or poems follow, each one written individually. Often words were so poorly spelled that the teacher could not read them; but with the children to interpret, the stories were soon corrected:

> *I am a daffodil in the ground, and they call me brown.*
> *I am a daffodil sitting on a hill.*

> *I am a flower.*
> *I'm pretty as can be*
> *And a woman picks me off my "feet."*

Once I had a sleepy little bulb which I thought would never wake up. But at last, one day, up popped a tiny hand and then another and another. Last of all up popped the head, and there was a trumpet daffodil.

THE LONELY LITTLE BULB
Once upon a time there was a little bulb. He was very lonely in the ground until one day the sun came out very bright and he said, "I'd better grow now, or they'll be worrying about me." So every day he grew an inch. And one day he had four great big leaves on him. He said, "It's about time I poke my head out." Then he had more things to see in the whole world than in the dark ground, and he lived happily ever after.

There was a little bulb in the ground. One day the sun came out. The bulb popped its head up and looked all around. He looked at trees and then he looked to see where he was growing. He didn't know his name, but he was sure he must be very beautiful.

Finally a lady picked him and took him into the house. How happy and proud he felt!

After the blossom had withered, the bulb was taken out of the moss, the mass of roots was examined, and the bulb was laid on the window sill to dry. Later a child took it home to plant in the garden, where it would bloom again the next year.

The talk about bulbs spending the winter under the ground led to pictures depicting gardens of spring flowers and to some pictures representing bulbs beneath the earth—the bulbs having "baby faces" smiling as the sun shone from above.

One day in March after one of the heaviest snowfalls of the season, someone mentioned the brown bulbs awaiting the coming of spring and the warmth of the sunshine. Looking out of the window, one child said he had the beginning sentence for a poem, and he repeated slowly:

> *On top of the ground*
> *The snow lay deep.*

To this another child almost immediately added:

> *Down under the ground*
> *Brown bulbs were asleep.*

Then, working together, the group soon had the following lines:

> *Then came the spring*
> *With rain and sun.*
> *Whispered a bulb,*
> *"Our work has begun.*
> *Come, stretch up your leaves,*
> *And send out buds*
> *For springtime has come*
> *And the garden is ours."*

After the poem had been repeated a few times, a child suggested that, since we had used the word *spring* earlier in the poem, it might be better if we changed the next to the last sentence to read, *For winter has gone.* Then *ground* in the third line was changed to *earth*, *buds* in the third from the last line was changed to *flow'rs*, and the poem now read:

> *On top of the ground*
> *The snow lay deep.*
> *Down under the earth*
> *Brown bulbs were asleep.*
> *Then came the spring*
> *With rain and sun.*
> *Whispered a bulb,*
> *"Our work has begun.*
> *Come, stretch up your leaves*
> *And send out flow'rs,*
> *For winter has gone*
> *And the garden is ours."*

So much satisfaction was expressed in the finished product that each child wanted a copy of the poem to keep. It was pointed out to the children that authors and poets wrote and rewrote their stories many times before they were finally published and that the rearranging of words showed that the class was improving and growing.

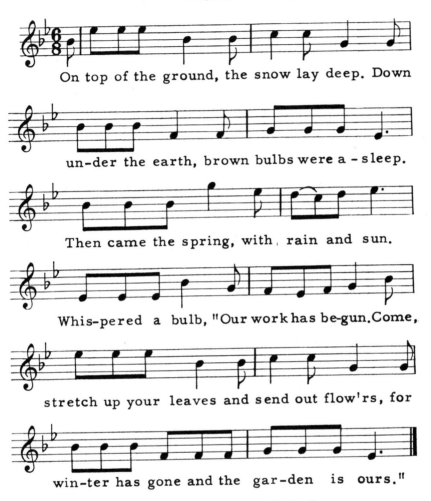

On top of the ground, the snow lay deep. Down

un-der the earth, brown bulbs were a - sleep.

Then came the spring, with rain and sun.

Whis-pered a bulb, "Our work has be-gun.Come,

stretch up your leaves and send out flow'rs, for

win-ter has gone and the gar-den is ours."

Figure 20-1. Creative song, "Spring."

The poem was given as a choral speaking piece, with a small group as the second voice doing the part said by the bulb. Before long, someone suggested writing a tune for the poem, and so music was composed for it by the group.

A window-box garden The arrival of the seed catalogues occasioned great interest and much conversation. The pictures were studied, and hard words were sounded. In a few days the catalogues had been worn to a pulp as the children pored over them trying to decide what they wanted. Abbreviations such as *pkt., oz., lb., ft.,* and *in.,* and words such as *dwarf, giant,* and *mixture,* especially as applied to seeds, were studied. Prices were noted and compared.

After much discussion it was decided that some of everything listed in the catalogues really could not be planted, that probably dwarf varieties would be more suitable than giant, and that varieties which matured early were desirable for results before school closed in June.

It was finally voted to plant lettuce, radishes, and petunias; and a committee was appointed to choose the seed and fill out the order blank. According to the catalogue, head lettuce took much longer to mature than the leaf variety, so the latter was ordered. One little boy held out for Giant White radishes, but he was outvoted in favor of a variety called Cherry-Belle, which looked especially attractive in the picture and was said to be a quick grower. A package of dwarf petunias—mixed colors—was also chosen. The total cost and the amount each child had to contribute were computed, and the order was mailed.

Now the window box was measured, and the terms *length, width,* and *depth* were learned in connection with the problem of determining the amount of soil needed to fill the box. Since there was still frost in the ground and good earth would be hard to get, the teacher bought two large bags of well-fertilized soil at a nearby agricultural college. Children lugged sizable rocks to school to provide drainage in the bottom of the box. The soil was added and patted into place. Though the pupils had been reared in a small village where everyone had plenty of out-of-door experience, this soft soil seemed to have a peculiar fascination for the children, and in odd moments there was always a child or two standing beside the box, just letting dirt trickle through his fingers.

When the seeds arrived there was more excitement. As planned, lettuce was to be planted in one end of the box, radishes in the other end, and the petunias as a border around the edge. The seeds were examined and the differences noted. Each child had some seeds to sow. Water was sprinkled over all. Great satisfaction was expressed by all the pupils.

Never were seeds more carefully tended nor more closely watched than those in the window box. A few radish seeds had not been completely covered, and one of these produced a sprout sometime between 11:20 A.M. and 12:45 P.M. The sprout was the cause of wild excitement when noticed by the first child to enter the room after lunch.

Other spring activities   With the coming of spring it could be seen that the winter's study of plants had been truly effective.

Never in her long experience had the teacher known a group of children so observing and so interested in all growing things. The earliest swelling of tree buds was noted and watched. Crocus, daffodil, and tulip plants were reported as soon as they showed a spear.

Early in March a section of the board was given over to "Signs of Spring," and some of the entries were as follows:

March 8. Jimmy saw crows.
March 8. Eddie thought he saw two robins.
March 9. Ice on the river is thawing—David says.
March 9. Tulip sprouts at Susan's house.
March 11. Alice's' mother tapped trees.
March 13. Dorothy brought pussy willows.
March 20. Pat got stuck in the mud.
March 22. Ronnie's dog is shedding hair. He's very itchy.

The Easter season occasioned the writing of numerous individual stories and poems in which the flowers vied with the Easter Bunny as themes.

An Easter basket was packed for a sick classmate; in addition to the jellies, fruit, puzzles, and games in the basket, each child made a picture, wrote a note, or sent an Easter message.

All winter it had been noted at the regular weekly meeting of the Book Club that an unusually large number of the books reported by the children had been informational books—books read to "find out something."

Now wild flowers and bird guides were in constant demand. Names of spring flowers were listed on the board and used in spelling. Small bouquets were soon gathered and brought to school, and the conservation of these wild plants was discussed. Careless pulling of plants was condemned.

On a walk one spring morning, the class saw various kinds of fruit trees in bloom or just leafing out. Peach, plum, pear, and apple trees were noticed, the shape and size of trees were compared, and their leaves and flowers were examined and described.

Large sprays of apple trees were brought into the classroom while still in bud, and the beauty of the opening flowers appreciated. The community's one and only magnolia was visited, and it served to emphasize the fact that people in other parts of our country have, due to climate, different plants. Pictures of fruit orchards in bloom, azalea gardens, and hibiscus hedges were brought by the children, and slides and films helped give an idea of flowers grown in other climates.

Spring stories and poems were written by the children and left on the teacher's desk for reading. Some stories were read in the original, while some were worked over by the children; but each child had a chance to read his work to the class:

SPRING

The flowers are blooming,
And the birds are coming back.
The grass blades are all peeping
From their long winter's nap.

The squirrels are running up the tree
And having lots of fun.
I'll tell you a little secret—
Spring has come.

IN SPRING

My mother bought me a pair of roller skates one spring day, so I went skating. I saw a robin singing in a tree and a woodpecker. There were lots of buds on the tree. The boys and girls were playing hop-scotch, picking pussy willows and flowers. Some were playing baseball or jumping rope. They were all glad spring had come at last.

MICKEY

I have a cat. He has a little house in the rose bushes. He and the other cats go in to get away from the dogs, sometimes to get out of the rain and sometimes just to play in it.

One warm, lovely morning in May the group working together wrote a poem which seemed to describe what they had seen and felt as they came to school:

SPRING MORNING

I like to see the sun
Shine on houses
On a spring morning
And the dancing shadows
Of leaves.
Birds sing gay songs,
Sweet scents fill the air,
Bright flowers bloom in the garden,
And everything
Is fresh and beautiful.

During odd moments in school and without help or suggestion, a little girl wrote a story which she called "Wind and Fairies." When the story was completed she read it to the class and was complimented:

WIND AND FAIRIES

The fairies live in a little yellow buttercup near the meadow. They work hard all day.

In early morning some spread dew while others open the flowers. They dance on the little yellow dandelions in the afternoon, and at night they close the flowers. After their work is done they dance by the light of the fireflies.

One day, while they were playing in the meadow, a big wind came and blew down all the buttercups, even their house. The fairies started to cry because it was such a nice house.

"Where can we find a new house?" said one of the fairies.

"In the woods would be a good place," said another fairy.

So they started out to the deep woods. They walked and walked until they came to a gurgling stream where they saw a beautiful white water lily. Here would be a good place to live. They could get water easily and also go swimming.

"Oh! We will have lots of room in here."

"It will be strange living in a bigger house. We lived in such a little one before!"

"What beautiful white walls."

Then they all decided to go swimming. They splashed water on each other and got their curly hair all wet.

"But what will happen to us when the water lily dies," said the oldest and smartest fairy.

"Oh! Gosh, I never thought of that," said the tiniest fairy.

"We will surely get seasick if we stay here too long. I wonder if there are any fairy hospitals near here."

"In the winter we can live in a bird's nest and go back to our buttercup in the spring. By that time it should be grown up."

In the spring they returned to their old home and lived happily ever after.

Judged by adult standards the above story leaves much to be desired. The young author seems to have run out of plot about midway in the story. Her beginning is good, however; and by taking the fairies back home again, she provides a satisfactory ending. The children liked the tale, and there was a sort of mass pride in the fact that a member of the group had written such a long story unaided.

Spurred by these individual stories, someone suggested that the class write a story. Beginning sentences were submitted, and Dorothy's was voted the best:

One warm moonlight night all the fairies gathered together and made a little brown bulb which they planted in Jeanie's garden.

For several days the story was worked on. Sometimes there were so many ideas for words or phrases that a vote had to be taken; and much rearranging was done, including the adding of descriptive words and the improvement of sentences. Finally the story was completed, copied by each child, and included in the individual story booklets:

THE FAIRY FLOWER

One warm moonlight night all the fairies gathered together and made a little brown bulb which they planted in Jeanie's garden.

"Next spring we will have a beautiful flower," said the Queen. "It will be different from any other flower in the garden."

Winter came. Cold winds howled. The flowers in Jeanie's garden withered and turned brown. Soft white snow fell and covered all the land with a fleecy white blanket.

But down under the earth while all this was happening, the little brown bulb was sound asleep. While it took its long winter rest, something was forming inside its shiny jacket which would make a lovely flower by and by.

At last winter passed. Bright sun melted the snow and warmed the earth. South wind blew and warm rain pattered down on the ground.

In its dark bed the little bulb began to feel restless.

"Oh, hum!" it sighed sleepily. "My jacket is getting tight. I must be pushing up."

Meanwhile, above the earth, the fairies were watching closely for the first sign of their bulb.

Lightwing, the tiniest fairy of all, saw the wee tip of green sprout first and flew excitedly to the Queen.

"Your Highness!" she gasped. "Our flower! It is growing! I saw it."

Off fluttered the fairies after Lightwing, and in no time at all they were grouped around their wee plant, pointing and all talking at once.

The Queen Starbright spoke. "We must care for our plant and protect it from danger. We must keep the dirt loose around it and see that it gets water."

Days went by. The plant grew and grew. First came two dainty green leaves. Then, one warm sunny afternoon, Twinkletoes spied a chubby green bud just peeping up between the leaves.

There was great excitement when the fairies gathered around. "Oh!" they chorused, "It will be a lovely blossom."

"I hope it will be pure white," said Queen Starbright.

Several days went by. The fairies never left their bud alone for a minute. In the daytime they danced and played happily about it. At night Twinkletoes slept under a nearby clover leaf so that if the bud should open, she could hurry to tell the Queen.

One night, when Twinkletoes was just ready to drop off to sleep, she heard a faint "pop." Looking up she saw the bud gradually opening.

Off raced Twinkletoes to tell the other fairies the good news. Soon all were gathered around in a circle watching breathlessly as their bud slowly, very slowly opened into a beautiful pure white flower.

Its delicate drooping petals were as soft as velvet and it swayed gracefully on a long slender stem.

"Oh," gasped the fairies. "Oh, isn't it beautiful?"

For a moment they gazed silently at the wonder blossom. Then Lightwing spoke. "Your Majesty! You must have your palace here," she said.

"If it will please you, my subjects, I will be glad to live here in our flower," replied Queen Starbright.

The fairies were very happy as they danced and sang around their flower.

"At last our Queen has found a palace lovelier than any dream," they said.

Not content with having written a story, the children wanted to do something with it; so it was decided to try to give it as a play. A song was composed as a finale:

All day we dance around our flower.
At last our queen has found her bower.
Tra la la la la la la la.
Our queen has found her bower.

Since there was little conversation in the story, it was decided to have a reader, with the various characters speaking only occasionally. Additional conversation was ad-libbed; but the reader carried most of the part, pausing to allow time for dances. To provide a part for the boys, a group of elves was introduced. They danced and sang with the fairies.

Simple crepe-paper costumes consisting of skirts for the main characters, capes for the fairies, caps for the elves, and green mitts plus five white petals for the bulb served to make the children feel important and took little time to construct. The bulb slept under a brown paper-covered carton and rose therefrom at the proper moment.

For a background, the children cut large, conventionalized flower shapes, which they colored brightly with chalk. These and a few large paper leaves were taped to the wall at the back of the stage. A large, paper clover leaf mounted on a piece of wallboard, which was leaned against the wall, provided a place for Twinkletoes to sleep. Everything was kept extremely simple, and there was only one reherasal in the auditorium. It was the children's story. They had chosen the characters and done the planning. Every child had a part and a bit of costume, and his name was on the program, which was read by the announcer. To the list of characters the announcer added a brief explanation of the story and study:

> This year we've been studying about plants and flowers. During the winter we had a bulb which blossomed. The blossom was so pretty that we wrote a story about it. Then we decided to make a play of the story. This is what you will see. We made a song for it too.

The play was given at the regular assembly period. Individual invitations had been taken to mothers, and several group invitations had been written and delivered to other grades. The play was well attended, and both actors and audience seemed to enjoy the performance and feel that it was worthwhile.

A picnic   A few days before the end of school, a visit to Miss F was arranged. One pleasant morning each child, carrying a plant, a rooted slip, a marigold plant raised from seed, a bulb, or a vine, walked the short distance to Miss F's house.

She welcomed the class warmly with exclamations of "Oh!" and "Ah!" for the beauty of the plants, was duly appreciative of the slips all ready for her to put into her window box, and made the children feel that they had a real part in her garden. Fresh, fat molasses cookies with plump raisins in their centers were served from an old-fashioned earthenware cooky jar, and all the children were happy. They thanked Miss F and told her how much they had enjoyed the plants during the winter.

Instead of the customary end-of-year picnic, the children suggested a vegetable lunch in the room at school. The radishes had grown lustily but had failed to "radish"; they were all tops. Not to be cheated, however, the children brought radishes from home gardens, as well as cucumbers, lettuce, carrots, and tomatoes. Desks were arranged to form a long table, and individual salads were made on paper plates. Each child brought his own sandwiches. A cool fruit drink was made, two or three children brought homemade cookies, and one farm boy brought fresh strawberries. To the children this lunch seemed replete, and the teacher was gratified to find so much satisfaction in the simple fare.

Social studies: America in song and story, fifth grade

The following is a short description of a year-long unit of work in which language plays an integral part. It was taught by Mrs. Ragnhild Stillman, fifth-grade teacher in the Campus School,

State University Teachers College, Potsdam, New York. Because the teacher was a trained musician, the study was rich in music and folklore. However, other areas were not neglected. It is of necessity presented in brief summary.

Mrs. Stillman believed that her fifth-grade children should have a knowledge of the beginnings of their country. They should understand what is meant by a republican form of government, its origins and composition. They should know how the myriad nationalities, religions, ideologies, racial backgrounds, languages, customs, and political divisions have melded together to form a wonderful nation. They should know that such a melding must of necessity be slow, that errors of judgment are bound to occur, and that only by the honest and constant watchfulness of all citizens can errors be avoided. With these lofty aims in mind, Mrs. Stillman developed the program with the children.

The United States was divided into five areas for study: New England, Middle Atlantic states, Southeastern states, Middle West including Southwest, and Western and Mountain states.

Beginning with New England, committees of children began research on the historical background and settlement of the country. Questions were asked and topics noted for study, such as the background of the Pilgrims and reasons for coming to America, treatment of the Indians, form of government, development of the town meeting, religion, growth of the colony and the area, witchcraft, development of seafaring, whaling and fishing industries, sea chanteys, folk songs and dances, effects of topography on New England life, legendary characters and heroes, hero literature, language of the people, products and industries, modern cities and population, rivers, and present-day New England.

Finding information on these topics required endless reading and research by individuals and committees. Letters were written to chambers of commerce, government agencies, travel bureaus, and individuals asking for information and conveying appreciation for favors received. Information was checked and rechecked for accuracy. Posters were made illustrating certain facts. Slides were shown, pictures collected, a museum visited, and costumes of the different periods were studied. Records were played, and sea chanteys were sung with much gusto. Models of log cabins were constructed. A study was made of the foods of the Indians and of white settlers. Poets and novelists of New England were studied.

The Middle Atlantic states were treated in the same way. Each bit of information led to more questions, and these in turn required more answers. Here, such tales as Rip Van Winkle and other Washington Irving stories were tied in with the Hudson River Valley and the Catskill Mountain area. Products and natural resources of the different areas were studied. It was found that the beginnings of the great coal and steel industries and the need for labor brought together people of different nationalities with their various tongues, customs, songs, and dances. Street-vendor songs of early Philadelphia and Baltimore were learned. Comparisons were made between the early settlers of Virginia, Maryland, Pennsylvania, and New England; and their influences upon the development of work, play, customs, literature, and music of each area were noted. Language differences were noted.

The Southeastern states brought a study of still different peoples. The Spanish of Florida, the French of Louisiana, Negroes and slavery, cotton, tobacco, and plantation life were introduced along with such characters as Daniel Boone. Children were fascinated by legendary heroes like John Henry, and they never tired of the ballads, spirituals, and songs of Stephen Foster. Folk stories of mountaineers and Negroes were collected and studied with reference to origins and similarities to the folk tales of other areas. Dialects were tried and dances learned. Present-day trends were noted: industrial changes, growth of cities, population adjustments, and changes in products.

Into the study of the Middle West came many characters, some real and some fictional: Johnny Appleseed and Mark Twain, to mention only two; and their contributions to our great American melting pot were noted. There were choral speaking, dramatization, map study, extensive reading and research. Spelling, art, and writing were all involved. Plains Indians were studied and the white man's mistreatment of them was noted. Cowboy dances and songs were learned. The long wagon trains and reasons for the westward movement were studied along with the growth of cities, population, and products. Contrasts of language with that of the South and New England were noted.

For a study of the Mountain and Western states, the class was divided into three parts representing the Oregon, California, and Santa Fe Trails. Questions were set up on a teacher-pupil basis, and each group studied a particular trail. The land, people, customs, history, products, songs, foods, etc., were investigated and then reported to the other groups. For instance, travelers on the California Trail reported on the Forty-niners, the Mormons, and such songs as "Clementine"; while the followers of the Santa Fe Trail showed pictures of Pueblo Indians and demonstrated some of the ceremonial dances. The Oregon Trail reporters told about Kit Carson, the Whitman family, and Buffalo Bill.

The study culminated in an operetta, the scene laid at a railroad station. A group of greeters entered singing "She'll Be Comin' Round the Mountain." Travelers arrived from many parts of the United States, exchanging news. There were songs and dances from the whole country: "Rip Van Winkle," "Down in the Coal Mine," "Cape Cod Chantey," "Old Stormalong," "Night Herding Songs," "Dixie," "The '49ers," and others. Such characters as Jesse James, Johnny Appleseed, and Rip Van Winkle were introduced as travelers. A narrator wrote his own script but improvised freely. A stationmaster called the stations as the imaginary trip progressed across the country. An original song for Paul Bunyan was written by the group, and a poem for Johnny Appleseed was given as choral speaking. Everyone helped with the simple stage setting and props. The children who were not actual characters on the stage were grouped around the piano as a chorus. The operetta ended with "This Is My Country," sung twice by the whole group.

Invitations were written to parents and to other rooms in the school. Posters were made advertising the operetta. A report was prepared for the school paper.

Arithmetic was involved in computing time, distances, population, costs, and dates, in meauring and construction work for the stage props, and in many other ways.

Had time permitted, science could have been strengthened by studying more of the industries and products of the areas, such as cars in Detroit, copper in Montana, oil in Texas, power production at great dam sites, irrigation, atomic energy in Nevada; and the study of weather, climate, soil erosion and fertility. The possibilities are endless, worthwhile, and thrilling.

In the study there was doubtless much which fifth graders could not fully appreciate, but the teacher felt that these children grew amazingly in learning how to search for information, sift facts from conjecture, weigh opinions, keep records, and make reports. Most important, perhaps, they had grown in an understanding of our nation and its people, and in understanding the influence of racial backgrounds upon our customs, industries, and speech. They learned that through our mixed heritage we are related to many peoples of the world; that working together requires understanding and acceptance; and that, as Americans, we must take an active, intelligent interest and do our part toward maintaining sound government and a stable social order.

Handling an integrated program

It must be apparent to the thoughtful reader of the preceding descriptions that an integrated program is a program of positive instruction, not a program of indifference and neglect. An integrated program does not offer an escape from the responsibility of definitely working to improve children's language ability. The teacher actually *teaches* language. Preparation and planning must be consistent and thorough. Because language work is not laid out in orderly blocks of time and treated separately, the teacher must constantly keep in mind all important aspects of language, and must recognize and take advantage of opportunities for providing specific training as they arise.

Instructional procedures developed in the preceding chapters apply as well to an integrated program as to a functional program. Situations arise for writing a letter, for conversation, for extending vocabulary, and for improving speech; and time out is taken, if advisable, to provide specific help on a particular phase of language work. Some teachers feel that to interrupt a social studies or a science lesson with How can we improve that report? How could we say it more clearly? or Let's think of some words that describe this color more accurately, is to steal time from science; and they feel guilty. Actually attention is not being diverted from science but is rather focused upon it, for by repeating a bit of information and expressing it more clearly and more exactly one is adding to understanding and retention.

In handling an integrated program the teacher needs a clear understanding of the important goals of language and of the course of the normal development of children. He must know what may be reasonably expected of children at the grade level and must recognize good work. It is helpful to keep a continuous inventory of individual and group needs as they arise in science and social studies. He may plan lessons or discussions in such a way as to provide practice in language work—letter writing, reporting, note taking, critical thinking, etc. The children are led to recognize their needs and to share in the responsibility of meeting them. There is continuous checking on language goals, and records of progress are noted on prepared checklists.

If a teacher is required to follow a rigid course of study, he may not be able to manage a fully integrated program. However, if alert, he can from time to time find opportunities to combine language with social studies, reading, science, and all other subjects. If a teacher has some freedom, imagination, and alertness, he will be able to quickly snatch at opportunities, often not clear-cut. Integration will take place regardless of what name is given to it. It is not so much a matter of experience as of enthusiasm, good judgment, courage, and above all an exploring spirit. Too many teachers are afraid to venture, lacking confidence in their judgment and ability. They lean too heavily on the printed word and want directions for every move. They feel they must have a syllabus, a course of study, or at least a workbook to guide them; and lacking such a crutch, they revert to their own school experience in which *their* teachers were probably following a book.

Within the limits of a basic framework or course of study, the teacher may maintain an open mind. He may set forth an initial aim as a sort of feeler, and may almost immediately discover leads going off in many directions. It is his responsibility to determine which of the many possibilities are most worthwhile and to skillfully lead the children to explore. To outline too definitely and to set up a detailed plan of study at the beginning may be as restricting as a workbook or syllabus, and the effect may be to destroy immediately his own freedom to explore.

References

ASHTON-WARNER, SYLVIA: *Teacher,* Simon and Schuster, Inc., New York, 1963.

BROENING, ANGELA M., AND OTHERS: *Conducting Experiences in English,* Appleton-Century-Crofts, Inc., New York, 1939, chap. 15.

BROWN, DOROTHY L., AND MARGUERITE BUTTERFIELD: *The Teaching of Language in the Primary Grades,* The Macmillan Company, New York, 1941, chaps. 9–10.

DAWSON, MILDRED A., M. ZOLLINGER, AND A. ELWELL: *Guiding Language Learning,* Harcourt, Brace & World, Inc., New York, 1963, pp. 48–50.

HATFIELD, W. W.: *An Experience Curriculum in English,* Appleton-Century-Crofts, Inc., New York, 1935, chap. 2.

HOLBROOK, DAVID: *English for the Rejected,* The University Press, Cambridge, England, 1964.

HUDSON, JESS S., AND OTHERS: *Language Arts in the Elementary School,* Twentieth Yearbook, National Education Association, Department of Elementary School Principals, Washington, 1941, chap. 7.

JARVIS, OSCAR T.: *The Transitional Elementary School and Its Curriculum,* W. C. Brown Company, Publishers, Dubuque, Iowa, 1966, chap. 9, pp. 275–325.

LAMB, POSE, AND OTHERS: *Guiding Children's Language Learning,* W. C. Brown Company, Publishers, Dubuque, Iowa, 1967.

MARSHALL, SYBIL: *An Experiment in Education,* The University Press, Cambridge, England, 1963.

NATIONAL COUNCIL OF TEACHERS OF ENGLISH: *The English Language Arts,*

Appleton-Century-Crofts, Inc., New York, 1952, pp. 179–186, 198–210.
———: *Language Arts for Today's Children,* Appleton-Century-Crofts, Inc., New York, 1954, pp. 297–301, 320–329.

SMITH, B. OTHANEL, AND OTHERS: *Language and Concepts in Education,* Rand McNally and Company, Chicago, Ill., 1961, chap. 8, pp. 112–126.

STRICKLAND, RUTH G.: *Guide for Teaching Language in Grades 1 and 2,* D. C. Heath and Company, Boston, 1962, chaps. 4 and 6.

WACHNER, CLARENCE: "Listening in an Integrated Language Arts Program," in J. C. MacCampbell and others: *Readings in the Language Arts in the Elementary School,* D. C. Heath and Company, Boston, 1964, pp. 141–148.

WOLFE, DON M.: *Language Arts and Life Patterns,* The Odyssey Press, Inc., New York, 1961, part 1.

INDEX

INDEX